LOCATING CAPITALISM

IN TIME AND SPACE

LOCATING CAPITALISM
IN TIME AND SPACE

Global Restructurings, Politics,
and Identity

EDITED BY DAVID NUGENT

STANFORD UNIVERSITY PRESS

Stanford, California   2002

Stanford University Press
Stanford, California
©2002 by the Board of Trustees of the
Leland Stanford Junior University
Printed in the United States of America

Library of Congress Cataloging-in-Publication Data

Nugent, David

   Locating capitalism in time and space : global restructurings, politics, and identity /
edited by David Nugent.
       p.   cm.
   Includes index.
      ISBN 0-8047-4230-8 (alk. paper) — ISBN 0-8047-4238-3 (pbk. : alk. paper)
   1. Capitalism—Cross-cultural studies.   2. Political culture—Cross-cultural
studies.   3. National characteristics—Cross-cultural studies.   I. Nugent, David.

HB501.L63   2002
330.12'2—dc21   2001049378

This book is printed on acid-free, archival-quality paper.

Original printing 2002

Last figure below indicates year of this printing:
11   10   09   08   07   06   05   04   03   02

Typeset at Stanford University Press in 10/13 Galliard

Contents

Preface

The last several decades have been witness to major restructurings—economic, political, and cultural—in the international arena. As many authors have noted, a general and marked acceleration in the "globalization" of material forces and cultural messages has been accompanied by equally strong countermovements in which "localisms" of multiple kinds have asserted themselves with great force.

This contradictory process of restructuring has turned a once familiar world upside down. In the metropolitan countries institutionalized and entrenched relations between labor and capital have come undone, resulting in the flight of capital, the devastation of once vital working communities, and a sweeping reorganization of communities of protest. Throughout the global arena attempts to "narrate the nation" have foundered, national communities and state structures have demonstrated an unprecedented degree of instability, and the entire "national question" has assumed an importance few could have imagined only a short time ago. Finally, a "politics of identity" has emerged in core and periphery alike as one of the key political and intellectual issues of the contemporary era, and long obscured links between power and knowledge have become transparent and widely contested.

The depth and scope of this process of restructuring has made it not only possible but also inevitable that anthropologists rethink many of their most basic assumptions, that they problematize issues that for decades had gone unexamined, and that they attempt to grapple with problems that are in many ways new or unique. Doing so has left the discipline profoundly unsettled. Existing standards of scholarship and methodologies of research have come under attack, key conceptual categories have been called into question, and truths once considered secure and firm have been subject to the most severe forms of scrutiny and even ridicule.

Seizing upon the unique opportunity afforded by the contemporary conjuncture of disciplinary crisis and redefinition, *Locating Capitalism in Time and Space* seeks to raise questions about two inter-related aspects of historical process and academic production. First, the volume seeks to contribute to ongoing debates concerning the degree to which the developments of recent decades represent the advent of a new historical era, a qualitative rupture with the past, the understanding of which requires its own unique conceptualizations and logics. In order to broach this question the volume assembles materials that place the present period of restructuring in the context of a broad history and geography of related restructurings.[1] Second, *Locating Capitalism* seeks to raise questions about the degree to which the *scholarship* of recent decades represents a qualitative break with that of the past. At issue here is how one understands the history of academic production—as a linear process of intellectual growth punctuated by major breakthroughs in understanding, or as a political process structured by the same sorts of inequalities and struggles that characterize the social worlds that are the object of anthropological analysis.

The original inspiration for this volume was two invited sessions organized for the 1995 annual meeting of the American Anthropological Association.[2] Both sessions carried the title "Locating Capitalism in Time and Space," with each panel exploring a different dimension of this general theme. The first session focused on "Empire, State, Region, Frontier," while the second concerned "Ethnicity, Race, Gender, Nation." As the conference sessions proceeded, it became clear that the papers spoke to each other in direct and powerful ways. A book based on the papers was the logical next step.[3]

[1] It should be emphasized that no attempt is made to reach definitive conclusions about this complex question.

[2] The organizers of these sessions were David Nugent and Anastasia Karakasidou.

[3] It has not been possible to include in the present volume all those who presented papers in the 1995 AAA sessions. The participants in the first panel, "Empire, State, Region, Frontier," were Myron Cohen, John Kreniske, William Roseberry, Cynthia Saltzman, Peter and Jane Schneider, and Gerald Sider. Michael Burawoy was to have been a participant as well, but unfortunately was not able to attend. To our good fortune, he has joined us in the volume. The discussant for this panel was Eric R. Wolf. The participants in the second panel, "Ethnicity, Race, Gender, Nation," were George Bond, Bela Feldman-Bianco, Anastasia Karakasidou, María Lagos, David Nugent, Aihwa Ong, and Ann Stoler. The discussant for the second panel was Richard Fox.

In addition to exploring the issues outlined above, the 1995 AAA sessions were intended to honor the eminent anthropologist Joan Vincent. Vincent has been a brilliant innovator and pioneer in the development of a processual anthropology that is at once attentive to the global arena while remaining sensitive to the particularities of time, space, and place. Vincent's work has had a profound effect on the scholarship of everyone who participated in the 1995 AAA sessions, and on all the contributors to the present book.

Shortly after the present work was accepted for publication, one of anthropology's most penetrating and creative minds, and one of the book's most distinguished contributors, was lost to us. In August of 2000 William Roseberry died, tragically, at the age of fifty. It is hard to imagine anyone whose life or scholarship exemplifies the critical and engaged spirit of the essays in this volume as much as does his. The void that has been left by Roseberry's passing cannot be filled. In addition to acknowledging the importance of the scholarship of Joan Vincent, we would like to dedicate this book to William Roseberry.

In the course of completing this book I have accumulated many debts, personal and professional. It is impossible to thank everyone who has helped make the volume possible, but certain people stand out. In addition to the late William Roseberry, Ida Susser, Christine Gailey, and Kofi Akwabi-Ameyaw played indispensable roles in helping organize the 1995 AAA conference sessions. Roseberry and Susser also offered invaluable advice and encouragement throughout the process of bringing the volume to fruition. Conversations with or written commentary from Catherine Besteman, Tom Biolsi, Zhang Hong, Constantine Hriskos, William Kelly, David Ludden, Chandana Mathur, Mary Beth Mills, William Roseberry, Parker Shipton, Ida Susser, and Joan Vincent proved unusually valuable for improving the argument in the book's Introduction. Stanford University Press's anonymous review process provided the same critical feedback for the volume as a whole. I would also like to express my appreciation to the book's contributors, who proved themselves to be what every editor hopes for—prompt, responsible, and cooperative. Finally, I owe a large debt to Muriel Bell, senior editor for Stanford University Press. May all authors be so fortunate as to have an editor as capable, reasonable, supportive, and understanding as she.

D.N.

Contributors

GEORGE CLEMENT BOND, a professor of anthropology, education, and applied anthropology at Teachers College, Columbia University, is the author of *The Politics of Change in a Zambian Community* (Chicago: University of Chicago Press, 1976) and coeditor of several volumes, including *African Christianity* (New York: Academic Press, 1979), *Social Construction of the Past* (London: Routledge, 1994), *AIDS in Africa and the Caribbean* (Boulder: Westview Press, 1997), *Contested Terrains and Constructed Categories* (Boulder: Westview Press, forthcoming), and *Witchcraft Dialogues* (Ohio University Press, forthcoming). He has also published articles on topics as diverse as education, kinship, politics, and religion.

MICHAEL BURAWOY teaches sociology at the University of California, Berkeley. He has conducted industrial ethnography in the United States, Southern Africa, and Hungary, and for the last decade he has been a participant observer of Russia's descent into capitalism. His most recent book is a collaborative work, entitled *Global Ethnography: Forces, Connections and Imagination in a Postmodern World* (Berkeley: University of California Press, 2000).

MARILYN COHEN is assistant professor of anthropology at Montclair State University in New Jersey. She has published widely on the Irish linen industry. She is the editor of *The Warp of Ulster's Past: Interdisciplinary Perspectives on the Irish Linen Industry, 1700–1920* (New York: St. Martin's Press, 1997), the coeditor of *Reclaiming Gender: Transgressive Identities in Modern Ireland* (New York: St. Martin's Press, 1999), and the author of *Linen Family and Community in Tullylish, County Down 1690–1914* (Dublin: Four Court's Press, 1997).

MYRON L. COHEN received his Ph.D. from Columbia University, where he is now professor of anthropology and also affiliated with the East Asian Institute. He has done fieldwork in southern Taiwan, and in the Hebei, Shanghai County, and Sichuan regions of China, and he has authored books and articles concerning his research in those areas. His current research interests include social and cultural change in China and Taiwan; Chinese family organization, religion, and economic culture; the historical anthropology of late imperial China; and the comparative study of marginalization categories ("peasant," "folk") in the context of modern evolving elite/mass dichotomies.

ANASTASIA KARAKASIDOU was born and raised in Greece. She received her doctorate in anthropology from Columbia University in 1992. She is presently an associate professor of anthropology at Wellesley College. Her book *Fields of Wheat, Hills of Blood: Passages to Nationhood in Greek Macedonia* (1870–1990) was published by Chicago University Press in 1997. In addition, she has published articles and presented papers on issues of nationhood, state, and ideology in Greek Macedonia. She is presently working on the biography of a turn-of-the-century Athenian-born national hero, Pavlos Melas.

MARÍA L. LAGOS is associate professor at Herbert H. Lehman College and the Graduate Center of the City University of New York. She has done extensive field and archival research on social transformations and cultural and political struggle. She is the author of *Autonomy and Power: The Dynamics of Class and Culture in Rural Bolivia* (Philadelphia: Pennsylvania University Press, 1994 [also published in Spanish in Bolivia by Plural Editores, 1997]).

DAVID NUGENT received his Ph.D. in anthropology from Columbia University, and is currently associate professor of anthropology at Colby College. He is the author of *Modernity at the Edge of Empire* (Stanford: Stanford University Press, 1997), and the coeditor (with Joan Vincent) of *A Companion to the Anthropology of Politics* (Blackwell Press, forthcoming). He has also published widely in journals on issues related to political and historical anthropology. He is currently working on a project involving the evolution of democracy and the public sphere in contemporary Peru.

AIHWA ONG is professor of anthropology and chair of Southeast Asian studies at the University of California, Berkeley. She is the leader of a "Globalization and Governmentality" initiative in her department. Her main works are *Flexible Citizenship* (Durham: Duke University Press, 1999); *Spirits of Resistance and Capitalist Discipline* (Albany: State University of New York Press, 1987); and the following edited volumes: *Ungrounded Empires* (London: Routledge, 1997); and *Bewitching Women, Pious Men* (Berkeley: University of California Press, 1995). Professor Ong is currently finishing a book on Asian immigrants and citizenship in California, and doing research on sovereignty and risk in globalizing Asian cities.

WILLIAM ROSEBERRY was one of the most creative and influential anthropologists of his generation. After spending more than twenty years in the Department of Anthropology at the New School for Social Research, in 1999 he moved to New York University, where he was professor of history and Latin American studies. He was the author or editor of five books and more than thirty-five articles, including *Coffee and Capitalism in the Venezuelan Andes* (Austin: University of Texas Press, 1983); *Anthropologies and Histories* (New Brunswick: Rutgers University Press, 1989); *Golden Ages, Dark Ages* (Berkeley: University of California Press, 1991); and *Coffee, Society and Power in Latin America* (Baltimore: Johns Hopkins University Press, 1995).

CYNTHIA SALTZMAN completed her doctoral work in anthropology at Columbia University. She has taught at Barnard College, Rutgers University at Camden, and Rosemont College. She has also been a visiting scholar at the Rutgers Institute for Research on Women, a postdoctoral fellow in Judaic studies at Yale University, and a visiting fellow at Yale's Institute for Social and Policy Studies. Her writing has focused on women and unions at Yale, and feminism and Judaism. She has also done applied work in institutional research.

IDA SUSSER, professor of anthropology at the Graduate School and University Center, City University of New York, and at Hunter College, has conducted ethnographic research in the United States, Puerto Rico, and southern Africa and has published extensively on urban transformations, gender, health, and social movements. Her ethnography, *Norman Street: Poverty and Politics in an Urban Neighborhood* (New York: Oxford University Press, 1982), documents daily struggles for survival and social protest among working-class people in New York City during its transition from a manufacturing center to an informational city. She has also coedited *AIDS in Africa and the Caribbean* with George Bond, John Kreniske, and Joan Vincent, and coauthored *Medical Anthropology in the*

World System (Westport, Conn.: Bergin and Garvey, 1997) with Hans Baer and Merrill Singer. As the founding president of the Society for Anthropology in North America, she recently coedited (with Thomas Patterson) *Cultural Diversity in the United States: A Critical Reader* (Malden, Mass.: Blackwell, 2001), sponsored by the American Anthropological Association.

LOCATING CAPITALISM

IN TIME AND SPACE

Introduction

The papers in this volume have been authored by scholars who came of age (intellectually) either during or after the "troubled" decade of the 1960s—a period when global political-economic developments and armed entanglements of the United States forced social scientists to come to terms with issues of power and inequality more directly than they had in the previous decade. Not only the discipline of anthropology but also the social sciences as a whole have been permanently transformed by the awarenesses that emerged as a result of that formative decade.

The 1960s are commonly regarded as an historical watershed, one in which the discipline finally came of age (or nearly did so) and began to move toward a more sophisticated and mature understanding of localities situated in global fields of culture and power. The implicit or explicit contrast is with the period before the 1960s, when anthropology is said to have been primitivizing, ignorant of historical process, and naive to the realities of power. In other words, the period before the 1960s is often considered to be a kind of prehistory to the mature understandings of today.[1]

The view of the historical development of the discipline implicit in this understanding of the 1960s is a familiar one. Indeed, both before and after the troubled decade, distinct cohorts of scholars have seen their own work as being as "revolutionary" as did that of the 1960s, have stressed the distinctiveness and originality of their concerns, have distanced themselves from the work of previous scholars.

Although significant (and not so significant) intellectual differences separate these cohorts of scholars, it is important to observe what they have in common. All conceive of the historical development of the discipline in like terms, as a largely linear process of growing intellectual Enlightenment, punctuated by major breakthroughs in understanding. Scholars argue vociferously as to when the breakthrough to Enlightenment took place, and what Enlightenment consists of, but the assumption that the discipline has had something like an intellectual history and a prehistory is widely shared.[2]

In other words, scholars throughout the discipline invoke the notion of *disjunction* to characterize the historical development of the field, and their own relation to past intellectual movements. Assertions of disjunction, it is widely recognized, have an important political function. They serve as mechanisms that simultaneously empower and delimit; they claim agency, creativity, and subjectivity for one's own reference group even as they disempower, objectify, and ultimately dismiss other groups.[3] In other words, assertions of disjunction, when applied to the history of the discipline, primitivize our anthropological forebears, exoticize (and trivialize) their concerns and understandings, and relegate them to an (intellectual) prehistory with little relevance, value, or connection to those of "us" who work in "the present."

In this opening chapter I seek to advance a different approach to understanding the historical development of the discipline, one that stresses the intimate relationship not between knowledge and enlightenment but between knowledge and power (Foucault 1980). In the process, I hope to establish a somewhat different genealogy for the work exemplified by the studies in this volume. I seek to locate the mature anthropology of the 1960s and after, with its concern with global forces of power, inequality, and culture, in an historical trajectory of similarly mature concerns. I have several goals in doing so. The first goal is largely descriptive. I hope to document a long history of concern with the very issues that are currently regarded as both recent and novel, to bring to light the existence of a mature period in the history of the social sciences that occurred during what is now regarded as our disciplinary infancy.

Documenting the existence of such a forgotten period in the history of the social sciences introduces my second goal in this opening chapter, for it immediately raises issues concerning the politics of memory. Much exciting work about memory and forgetting has been done of late, predominantly in contexts that are highly charged in political terms.[4] In these contexts issues such as who is allowed to engage in public remembrance, what is remembered in public discourse, and how the past is represented have obvious implications for the operation of hegemony and the encoding of various forms of inequality. In this opening chapter it is my explicit aim to focus questions about the politics of memory on the history of the social sciences. As with much of the recent literature on history as representation, my emphasis will be on the political processes that have allowed select dimensions of the past to be represented as "the past," while other dimensions of our history have been effaced from memory.[5]

As will become clear in the pages that follow, I seek to establish a somewhat deeper history for an anthropology of the global arena than is currently acknowledged in the discipline. Furthermore, I seek to identify the global conditions that generated this earlier concern with the global, much as the 1960s generated a more recent concern with forces of the same order. The genealogy I seek to inscribe is not exclusively concerned with anthropology per se, although anthropology figures prominently within it. Rather, just as the 1960s produced a more critical turn in the social sciences as a whole, I will show how the global conditions in the opening decades of this century (let us say, 1900 to 1940) produced on the part of social scientists a direct engagement with what was then the modern world order.[6] Indeed, it was the desire to understand the structure and probable tendencies of that emerging global order, and to ready those considered "unprepared" to participate in it, that led to the social sciences becoming institutionalized in their modern form at that time.

From today's vantage point, a close examination of the scholarship of the interwar period reveals it to have been remarkably sophisticated, global, and processual in nature. The following brief examples will provide a sense of the nature of the forgotten scholarship of that era. In the late 1920s and 1930s, Chinese scholars trained in the West were examining issues such as the impact of capitalist development on China (ISR 1933), and the extent and effects of industrialization on that country (Ho and Hsien 1929). Other Chinese scholars, also trained in the West, were analyzing the role of nineteenth-century British imperial expansion in bringing about the disintegration of the Chinese state, the role of plantation agriculture in the European colonies of Southeast Asia in drawing huge quantities of cheap labor out of southern China in the context of state breakdown, and the novel forms of political community that were emerging in the 1930s as communities of the Chinese diaspora in Southeast Asia sought formal political affiliation with China (Chen 1939). Western scholars working on China (Lattimore 1932) and Chinese scholars alike (Ho 1931; Chen 1931) were similarly preoccupied with issues of state hemorrhage and breakdown in the north of China—in particular, with the devastating impact of state disintegration on the rural populace of the north and the potential collision of three great empires (Russia, China, and Japan) in the volatile region of Manchuria, as massive numbers of displaced Chinese fled into this frontier region, the control of which was contested by Japan and Russia.

European expatriates raised in Africa, but trained in England, along with African scholars (Kenyatta 1962), were writing on related themes with regard to Africa. Just as Chinese scholars were examining the devastating impact of the European presence on Chinese populations, scholars like Richards (1939) and Wilson (1941) were analyzing the consequences of European colonialism and capitalist enterprise for indigenous groups in the mining region of what was then Northern Rhodesia. Just as their counterparts had been in China, these scholars were concerned with the role of colonialism in undermining indigenous economic and sociopolitical forms, with the forces that drew enormous quantities of African labor into industrial centers, and with the nature of relationships established between those in the home communities and in the industrial centers. Other scholars were examining similar questions in South Africa. Here, Hunter ([Hunter] Wilson 1936) focused on the distinctive pressures brought to bear on indigenous economic patterns, sociopolitical institutions, and religious practices in a settler colony where the expropriation of land and forced labor laws tended to convert the indigenous population into a class of dependent wage laborers. In addition to analyzing the forces that led to the breakdown of indigenous institutions, Hunter also discussed the emergence of racial consciousness, the growth of nationalism, and the formation of labor organizations and worker militancy.

In Mesoamerica indigenous scholars trained in the United States also addressed the question of the hemorrhaging of the state in the face of powerful pressures exerted by capitalist industry. In this case, however, the focus of analysis was the enormous number of Mexican nationals who resorted to migratory wage work in the face of extreme inequalities in land distribution, land scarcity, and an absence of work opportunities in Mexico—and in the process provided cheap labor for U.S. farms, ranches, and other enterprises (Gamio 1930). Western scholars working on Mesoamerica addressed similar concerns. Some (McBride 1923) analyzed the historical underpinnings of the Mexican land crisis that drove migrants across the border into U.S. capitalist enterprises. McBride focused in particular on the importance of the hacienda, the exacerbation of land inequality at the end of the nineteenth century during a period of rapid foreign capitalist investment, and the pivotal role of the land question in the 1910 Mexican Revolution. Other scholars (Tannenbaum 1929) provided in-depth analyses of the Mexican Revolution itself, focusing on the evolution of the land system and the role of capitalist industrialization at the close of the nineteenth century in provoking Mexico's great political upheaval.[7] Tannenbaum (1943) also sought to understand the movements of national and transnational identity that were sweeping through Latin America during this era.

In Europe scholars focused on the devastating consequences of the Great War, the role of the war in reconfiguring the political map of Europe, the emergence of new forms of political association (the Soviet Union and the Third Communist International [Toynbee 1928]), the growth of nationalism (MaCartney 1934), and the predicament of "stateless peoples" (King-Hall 1937: 43).

In other words, Western and non-Western scholars alike were involved in an historically based analysis of the role of North Atlantic capitalism and European colonialism in shaping regional and local arenas around the globe, in undermining indigenous economic and sociopolitical forms, in precipitating enormous population movements, and in stimulating novel cultural configurations and forms of political affiliation. This scholarship clearly had the potential to act as the basis of an alternative academic canon.[8] Work of this kind clearly deserves a place in the discipline's public understanding of itself. We now turn to a consideration of the forces that produced this earlier engagement with the dynamics of the global arena.

Infrastructures of Knowledge and Control

The emergence of a social science and an anthropology that was directly involved in the study of global forces of power, economy, and culture must be understood in the context of transformations in the organization of global capitalism in the decades after 1900. Particularly important in this regard was the growing dominance of the United States in world affairs, the expansion of the United States overseas to create a commercial empire of global scope (LaFeber 1963; Dobson 1978), and the gradually receding importance of the European powers (Hobsbawm 1994). Although this shift in the relative weight of the capitalist countries was underway at the turn of the century, it was accelerated by World War I, which left most countries in Europe devastated. Of all the major participants in the war, only the United States and Japan emerged in a stronger position than they had entered it (ibid.).

While the expanding United States was the most powerful political-economic and cultural "center of gravity" at that time, it was of course far from alone in the world. Competing centers of gravity located elsewhere, some with imperial intentions of their own (most notably Japan and Russia), created contested frontiers of capitalist modernity—especially along select inner-Asian frontiers of China, in China itself, and also in parts of insular Southeast Asia. Other centers of gravity had little in the way of imperial goals, but instead sought autonomy from Western domination, whether this domination was colonial in nature (as in Indonesia, India, and Africa), "neocolonial" (as in China and parts of Central Asia), or postcolonial (as in Latin America). These autonomy-seeking centers of gravity also presented serious challenges to the broad material and cultural project of the West. The globally oriented social science that took shape after the turn of the century emerged as the West's newly ascendant power sought greater knowledge about and ultimately control over social conditions, cultural patterns, and human subjects located along the contested margins of its expanding spheres of influence.

Prior to this internal reshuffling within the Western world, the European countries, as the dominant powers, had evolved complex bureaucratic infrastructures in their colonies that had codified detailed systems of knowledge about their subject populations, knowledge of a more-or-less "anthropological" nature. These infrastructures and their associated systems of knowledge, it has been shown, played an integral role in the implementation and reproduction of colonial rule (for example: Biolsi 1995; Cohn 1996; Dirks 1992; Pels 1997) by helping to constitute governable subjects within colonial domains (Foucault 1991).

After the turn of the century the United States shared with the European powers the need for detailed knowledge about the social groups and cultural patterns that were found along the contested frontiers of expanding U.S. control. In seeking to generate such knowledge, however, the United States was faced with an unprecedented set of problems. With a few notable exceptions (in particular, the Philippines, Hawaii, and parts of the Caribbean), in the process of establishing its growing empire the United States did not create formal political dependencies, the administration of which the United States then oversaw (LaFeber 1963). Because the United States did not erect bureaucratic, statelike structures that were empowered to administer territorially bounded colonies, the United States could not draw on existing (colonial) state-based infrastructures to generate the forms of knowledge and control needed to constitute governable subjects throughout its increasingly far-flung empire.

In the absence of existing bureaucratic infrastructures that could be mobilized to generate the requisite knowledge about the potentially "dangerous" peoples located along the contested frontiers of capitalist modernity, in the opening decades of the twentieth century a novel experiment occurred in the creation of such an infrastructure. The experiment was underwritten in part by the U.S. government, but predominantly by the great U.S. capitalist philanthropies, primarily Rockefeller and Carnegie.[9] Between them, the philanthropies invested enormous sums of money in the creation of a new infrastructure for the production and dissemination of social science knowledge.[10] In the process, they underwrote the vast majority of all social science research in the English-speaking world.[11]

The new infrastructure of training, research, publishing, and control that the philanthropies brought into being in many ways paralleled in its structure the emergent U.S. empire. The infrastructure was international and extraterritorial in scope and design, seeking to accommodate as it did spheres of U.S. influence that spanned the globe. The new infrastructure was also irreducible to (and incapable of being contained by) the bureaucracy of any particular state apparatus, although the philanthropies did not hesitate to draw on existing state institutions when it suited their purposes. As often as not, however, the philanthropies were compelled to create new institutions to achieve their novel goals, or to give a significantly changed direction to existing institutions.[12] Although the philanthropies were tied to a particular nation-state (the United States), during a period when nation-states were the main arbiters of cultural messages and capital flows, the social science infrastructure that the philanthropies helped to construct was largely independent of (though in no way in conflict with) national controls. In the long run, this infrastructure promoted a "flexible accumulation of knowledge" on a global scale, and in the process helped bring into being an international public sphere of social science knowledge.

The new infrastructure of knowledge and control that emerged in response to the exigencies of the era did not arrive on the scene full-blown. Nor was it the product of a carefully thought-out strategy or plan. Rather, it emerged on an ad hoc, piecemeal basis in the process of U.S. expansion, as the U.S. government and the great philanthropies struggled to understand and control conditions along particular contested frontiers.

Philanthropic activities abroad were a direct extension of these same activities at home, where the philanthropies directed their energies toward internal lines of fracture in the capitalist order. Problems of rapid industrialization, urbanization, immigration, and depression (in 1893) at the close of the nineteenth century had led to mounting pressures in the United States that seemed to threaten the country's social stability and system of democratic government (LaFeber 1963: 173, 198, 200). Social unrest had escalated in the context of growing urban poverty, ethnic conflict, and serious (and not uncommonly violent) clashes between organized labor and corporate capital (Berliner 1985: 12–13; Buck 1980: 54–55; LaFeber 1963: 173–75). Indeed, during the three years of 1893 to 1895 class conflict became so severe that the U.S. secretary of state referred to "symptoms of revolution" throughout the land (LaFeber 1963: 173).

These developments convinced an "enlightened elite" that the mechanisms that had formerly worked to ensure the stability of American society were no longer effective, and that new mechanisms were desperately needed in order to ensure social order (Berliner 1985: 13; Buck 1980: 59). The philanthropies saw themselves as aligned with expanded government in establishing new organizational structures that could promote social stability, the integration of the foreign-born into American life, and the general well-being of all. These organizations ranged widely in form and function, from a myriad of organizations designed to promote "social welfare" (for example, social work organizations, the YMCA and YWCA [Bulmer and Bulmer 1981]), to organizations promoting the control of gambling and prostitution, those promoting improved sanitation and hygiene, those encouraging government reform (less graft, more efficiency), and those empowered with surveillance functions (concerning prisons, reform schools, and so forth; Berliner 1985: 13). The philanthropies thus envisioned themselves as involved in a task of social control that consisted of helping the masses "adjust" to the rigors of industrial life and representative democracy.

Most of the problems that plagued the rapidly industrializing United States were believed by the philanthropies to be caused by the deteriorating physical conditions of U.S. cities, by what was perceived to be the lack of familiarity of the foreign-born population with democratic institutions, and by the resultant breakdown in social order. In order to counteract these developments, the philanthropies sought to instill in the minds and bodies of these "untutored" peoples the discipline and order needed to ensure social control. The philanthropies further sought to create or modify the institutions, public and private, needed to inculcate the new standards of discipline, and to train the personnel needed to oversee the process. The result was a sweeping program of social change and control.

Conditions abroad were thought to mirror those at home in many ways. Outside the United States it was abundantly clear that there were a great many "premodern" peoples and cultures that had been partially or wholly excluded from enjoying the advantages of modern life. Many, it was clearly recognized, had already been subject to the destabilizing forces of industrialization and commerce. Most were seen as weighted down by premodern social structures and value systems that made adjustment to the exigencies of modern, industrial life especially difficult. Virtually all were regarded as particularly burdened by living conditions not unlike those that afflicted the crowded and conflict-filled cities of the United States— poor hygiene and epidemic disease, on the one hand, and governmental structures incapable of addressing those crucial issues on the other. As the United States established its overseas empire after 1900, and thus brought increasingly large sections of the globe within its grasp, these regions were seen as needing precisely what was needed in the United States itself—the institutions and personnel necessary to instill in nonmodern societies the physical and mental discipline required of all subjects of the modern world.

This state of affairs was further complicated by other difficulties. Many of the non-Western peoples within the expanding U.S. spheres of influence were ignorant of or even hostile to the material and cultural project to which the philanthropies were so deeply committed. Indeed, some of these peoples professed ideals or practiced lifestyles that were nothing short of anathema to the values of capitalist modernity. The widespread existence of cultural configurations ignorant of or hostile to capitalist modernity was perceived to be a disturbing and potentially threatening state of affairs. In order to address this problem, the great philanthropies undertook "cultural work" on an enormous scale. In the broadest terms, the great philanthropies set as their long-term goal nothing less than the wholesale transformation of entire nonmodern modes of thought and forms of behavior. That is, the philanthropies sought to inculcate in peoples they viewed as non- or partially modern the virtues of Western rationality—the mental, physical, and behavioral discipline that the philanthropies regarded as the basis of a modern social order.

The philanthropies' efforts to modernize along these lines had several components. Educational institutions (broadly defined), however, played a prominent role in virtually all of the philanthropies' activities. From the turn of the century onward, the philanthropies contributed to a major expansion in and reorganization of higher education, both at home and abroad (Berliner 1985; Fosdick 1962; Geiger 1986). Philanthropic efforts initially focused on the *university* and the *laboratory* as the key sites for the transformations they sought.[13] Drawing on the model of the German research university, one important component of philanthropic efforts to reform higher education focused on promoting the development of research (rather than teaching) within a select group of elite universities. The research in question, however, was to be of a certain kind, and was to focus on specific issues. The philanthropies eschewed what they regarded as the "idle philosophical and historical speculation" that they believed dominated university intellectual life, speculation that was carried out at a great distance from the social world and its myriad problems. In place of such speculation the philanthropies sought to promote research that was empirically grounded, based on the "scientific method," and focused on the pressing social problems of the day.[14]

The philanthropies intended that universities reorganized along these lines, both at home and abroad, would act as shining and highly visible examples of the vast potential of Western rationality to make a positive contribution to social life. The philanthropies intended that these remade university centers would act as a kind of "cultural vanguard," that they would help establish (or strengthen) the legitimacy of Western rationality, empiricism, and problem solving. Once established, the philanthropies believed, these institutions would define new values and ideals that would radiate outward into society as a whole as more and more people recognized the value of and sought to emulate a Western cultural world view.

From the turn of the century onward the philanthropies invested many millions of dollars in the reform of higher education.[15] Within the United States, the University of Chicago was the showpiece of this effort, although Johns Hopkins, Clark, and the established Ivy League schools such as Harvard, Yale, Columbia, and Pennsylvania received considerable support as well (Berliner 1985; Bulmer and Bulmer 1981: 365, 372, 387). In the southern United States, the University of North Carolina was the focus of philanthropic efforts.[16] On the West Coast, the University of California and Stanford received the bulk of philanthropic largesse. In England the London School of Economics and Political Science received the lion's share of philanthropic funds (Bulmer and Bulmer 1981: 387). In France the philanthropies provided some support to the Institut d'Ethnologie and in Austria to the Institut fur Volkerkunde (Stocking 1985: 127), although other major research universities received support as well.[17] In China the philanthropies initially sought to build an entire new research university modeled on the University of Chicago (but settled for building the Peking Union Medical College and underwriting a public health program; see Buck 1980). Later, most philanthropic support to China went to the Department of Sociology at Yenching University and the Institute of Economics at Nankai University (Chiang 1986; Trescott 1997).

Prior to World War I, most philanthropic funds went into university general funds or focused on medical and public health-related research. Public health received such heavy emphasis because it was seen as having virtually unlimited potential to relieve the vast human suffering resulting from poor hygiene and epidemic disease, and thus to instill in nonmodern peoples essential disciplines of the body.[18] After the Great War the majority of philanthropic funds went to university-based social science centers of excellence in the United States, western Europe, and China (Bulmer and Bulmer 1981: 384). In these centers, philanthropic funds were used to free faculty from teaching responsibilities, to allow them to learn new research techniques, to carry out research projects, and to publish research results (Coben 1976: 226–27).

A second key component of the modernizing cultural work undertaken by the philanthropic/governmental nexus focused on efforts to form a new intellectual elite.[19] This elite was to be trained in the virtues of empirically grounded, practically oriented research within one of the philanthropies' remade institutions of higher learning. In order to make it possible to train a new elite along these lines, the philanthropies provided their remade institutions of higher learning with large sums of money specifically for the training of students.[20] The philanthropies made it possible for these institutions to offer scholarships to fund the entire graduate training of "promising" students. The philanthropies thus helped influence entire cohorts of graduate students, who were schooled in the scientific, empirically grounded, practically oriented concepts, methods, and techniques that the philanthropies believed would make a contribution to the pressing social problems of the day.

The decision to subsidize graduate education along these lines was to have significant and unanticipated consequences, for the philanthropies did more than simply expand the number of students who received graduate training. More important, the philanthropies made graduate school an option for social elements that had previously been unable or unlikely to attend. Furthermore, philanthropic sponsorship of graduate education came at a time when massive European immigration to the United States brought with it an infusion of critical social thought and political action (contributing to the very sort of social disturbances that led the philanthropies to intervene in the social arena in the first place). In a number of urban centers there was a growing sense of dis-ease with and criticism of the established state of affairs (Berliner 1985; Buck 1980; LaFeber 1963; Dobson 1978). As a result, social elements and issues found their way into the classroom that had formerly had little or no place there.

Many of the students whose graduate educations were funded in this manner were U.S. citizens, while a number of other students came from Europe. In addition, however, the philanthropies made a conscious decision to include a significant minority of students from outside the West. By bringing these latter students into their remade centers of higher learning, the philanthropies hoped to form an "indigenous intellectual elite" (see, for example, Berman 1983). They hoped that, once adequately trained, this indigenous elite would return to their homes to help school their countrymen in the virtues of a practical, empirically based, scientifically grounded approach to social problems.

The decision to train an indigenous elite in empirically grounded, practically oriented concepts, methods, and techniques was also to have significant and unintended consequences. This elite was to prove far less malleable than had been presumed. In many cases the philanthropies were only partially successful at best in "converting" these individuals to the reformist point of view implicit in their graduate training. Rather, as intellectuals from around the world journeyed to centers of higher learning in the United States and England they brought with them "indigenous" concerns—imperialism and state disintegration in China, colonialism and capitalist penetration in Africa and India, nationalism and revolutionary conflict in Mexico, and so forth. As foreign students with "indigenous" concerns passed through infrastructures of graduate training in the West they helped broaden the perspectives of their U.S. counterparts. They also learned more about and made common cause with the concerns of other foreign students (Dahrendorf 1995: 190). And when they returned home after their graduate training was complete, they not uncommonly occupied positions of authority and influence—as the philanthropies intended. As suggested by the trajectories of people like Jomo Kenyatta, Z. K. Matthews, Manuel Gamio—all of whom were trained under the conditions just described—and others, however, these individuals often used their positions of influence in ways that were far afield indeed from what the philanthropies had intended.

A third component of the cultural work undertaken by the great philanthropies consisted of subsidizing research into the nature of social conditions along the contested frontiers and the internal lines of fracture of capitalist modernity. Some of this research was carried out by university departments with funds provided directly by the philanthropies.[21] In terms of the quantity and quality of research and publishing sponsored, however, ultimately more significant were the new institutions created through philanthropic efforts, and the existing institutions whose activities the philanthropies considered worthy of support. These included such institutions as the Social Science Research Council (founded in 1923, and funded by Rockefeller philanthropy [RPH] as of 1924), the Institute of Pacific Relations (founded in 1925, and funded by RPH as of 1927), the Royal Institute of International Affairs (founded in 1919, and funded by RPH as of the early 1920s),[22] the International Institute of African Languages and Cultures (founded in 1926, and funded by RPH as of 1926), the American Geographic Society (founded in the early 1850s, and funded by RPH as of the early 1920s), and many others.

These institutions sponsored an enormous amount of research, virtually all of which was intended by the philanthropies to aid in the investigation, elucidation, and eventual amelioration of concrete social problems, at home and abroad, along the external frontiers and the internal lines of fracture of capitalist modernity. To take the most prominent example (the SSRC), raw dollar figures (not adjusted up for inflation) may help give some sense for the scale of research activities funded by the philanthropies. The Laura Spelman Rockefeller Memorial (LSRM)[23] provided the initial funding for the Social Science Research Council in December of 1924, with a grant of $425,000. The grant was provided for research fellowships, to cover the next five years (Fisher 1993: 31). The LSRM gave the SSRC an additional $2 million in 1927, of which the general research fund received $750,000 (ibid.: 67–68). In 1931, SSRC received an additional $575,000 from the Rockefeller Foundation (RF),[24] of which $225,000 was for general research projects over six years, $225,000 was for conferences and planning, and $100,000 was for grants-in-aid over four years (ibid.: 123). In 1932–33, the RF gave the SSRC $180,000 for postdoctoral fellowships over a two-year period, and continued support for that purpose throughout the 1930s (ibid.). In 1935, the SSRC began funding predoctoral research fellowships, and the General Education Board (another Rockefeller philanthropy) provided $100,000 for this purpose in each of three consecutive years—1935, 1936, and 1937 (ibid.: 161).

In some instances these institutions (especially SSRC) helped fund the university-based social science centers chosen by the philanthropies to remake social science research.[25] In other instances these institutions (SSRC, Institute of Pacific Relations, Royal Institute of International Affairs, and so forth) funded the research of individuals who had received training at one of the university-based social science centers funded by the philanthropies. What emerged as a result was an international network of mutually reinforcing institutions and processes in which research and publishing of a particular kind were underwritten for individuals with specific kinds of training (the training centers themselves having been funded by philanthropic largesse). In the process, the philanthropies established the material foundations for the subsequent development of an international discourse of social science debate—a kind of global public sphere of social science knowledge.

A fourth component of the cultural work underwritten by the philanthropies involved efforts at social engineering.[26] The ultimate goal of the research and publishing efforts sponsored by the great philanthropies was not knowledge per se, but rather "incorporation." Successful incorporation of peoples considered nonmodern often entailed the amelioration of social conditions that were seen as standing in the way of these people recognizing the superiority of, and adopting the values and behaviors of, modernity—social conditions that were therefore obstacles to the steady advance and long-term stability of U.S. influence. Accordingly, the philanthropies chose select problems or contexts that were considered especially significant (or problematic) and actively set out to mold social conditions in these contexts in the desired directions. Among the most important of these were: the widespread programs of public health and epidemic disease eradication instituted in many parts of the world (Buck 1980; Cueto 1994; Hewa and Hove 1977); the Tuskegee Program, which provided vocational education (as well as academic education for a tiny elite) for Blacks in the U.S. South (Berman 1980); the International Institute of African Languages and Cultures, which was originally an attempt to implement the Tuskegee Program in Africa (see below); and several more comprehensive attempts at social engineering in China (Hayford 1990; Trescott 1997).[27]

Part and parcel of the training offered within the network of institutions sponsored by the philanthropies was the inculcation of a particular view of social problems and their solutions. This view emphasized the observation, description, and amelioration of problematic conditions rather than the rapid and total reorganization or transformation of society as a whole. "Useful" knowledge was therefore knowledge that was grounded in the empirical observation and analysis of ongoing social conditions, and that offered some sense of direction about how to improve these conditions so as to ensure social stability.[28]

The philanthropies thus underwrote the production of knowledge that could be usefully applied to the amelioration of social conditions that were regarded as standing in the way of the advance of modernity, individuality, and consumption. They were interested in promoting forms of knowledge about the world that would help keep it safe, stable, and ordered.[29]

With this brief overview of the network of institutional processes underwritten by the philanthropies, we now turn to a more focused examination of (select) institutional networks that the philanthropies helped create, and the scholarship produced by those who passed through these institutional networks. As we will see, in many cases the individuals who were chosen by the philanthropies to direct the institutions in question, and those who received their training from these institutions, had concerns that were significantly at odds with the philanthropies themselves. Indeed, the willingness of the philanthropies to bring new social elements, foreign and domestic, into graduate training, combined with foundation policies of encouraging empirical research into ongoing social conditions in troubled contexts, was a potentially volatile mix. A number of the individuals brought into these networks seized upon the institutional space created through philanthropic largesse to produce scholarship of a remarkably sophisticated and critical nature.

The Political Geography of Philanthropic Intervention I: China

The philanthropic experiment in the creation of a new infrastructure for the production of knowledge and control deemed necessary for constituting governable subjects along the frontiers of capitalist modernity began just after the turn of the century. The activities of the philanthropies embraced a number of different geographic arenas, from southern and eastern Europe (Hewa and Hove 1997), to Africa (Berman 1980), to Latin America (Cueto 1994), the Philippines (Sullivan and Ileto 1997), Sri Lanka (Hewa and Hove 1997), and so forth. By far the bulk of philanthropic efforts, energies, and resources, however, were directed at China, a region that was both highly volatile and not under the direct political control of any European power.[30]

U.S. interest in and concern about China as a contested frontier of Western modernity was motivated by a number of factors. Primary among them, however, was the following. At the turn of the century the imperial designs of three of the world's most powerful expansionist states threatened to collide in China itself, along China's inner Asian frontiers and at its northern borders. As noted above, as a response to industrial crisis at home, circa 1900, the United States was involved in a concerted campaign to establish an overseas commercial empire (LaFeber 1963; Dobson 1978: 52–53). China, with its population of some four hundred million people, was regarded as absolutely fundamental to U.S. interests. This was especially so after the severe economic depression of 1893–97, which confronted the United States with the troubling prospect of having reached a stage in its industrial development where its capitalist engines regularly produced more than "the market" could possibly bear (Israel 1971; LaFeber 1963; McCormick 1967).

Although the potential market that was China was seen as offering a solution to the industrial dilemmas of the United States, at the turn of the century the future of U.S. interests in China seemed in doubt. This was due in large part to the disintegration of the Imperial Chinese state, and the political and cultural fallout that resulted from that disintegration. Symptomatic of the difficulties facing future U.S. interests in China was the Boxer Rebellion of 1900, with its blatantly anti-Western ideology, its defensive brand of Chinese nationalism, and its intention to purge China of Western influence. Although the Boxer Rebellion was eventually put down by the combined efforts of the Western powers, which organized a joint military expedition that lifted the siege of Beijing, the rebellion did a great deal to raise concerns in the United States about future developments in China. Missionary reports from China from just after the turn of the century, which expressed real alarm at what was characterized as "runaway Chinese nationalism," reinforced these concerns (Ninkovich 1984: 800; Spence 1990: 232–37). So too did the 1905 boycott on American goods that had been organized in China in protest over U.S. restrictions on Chinese immigration to the United States—at the precise moment when the China market was conceived of as a key long-term solution to the industrial woes of the United States (Buck 1980: 83; Israel 1971; McCormick 1967; Spence 1990: 238).

Further exacerbating U.S. concern over the future of China was the beginning of Japanese imperial expansion, which clearly manifested itself in 1894–1895 with Japan's victory over China in the Sino-Japanese War (Peattie 1984: 10). As a result of the settlement of the conflict, China ceded Taiwan to the Japanese, and was forced to recognize the complete independence of Korea—effectively making Korea a Japanese protectorate (Spence 1990: 223). In this way Japan demonstrated that it was a force to be reckoned with in the Far East (LaFeber 1963: 236, 308–9). Furthermore, just as Japan was expanding its influence in Korea and Manchuria, Russia was also seeking to establish a stronger presence along China's northern frontier regions—especially in Mongolia and Manchuria (Spence 1990: 231). This fact was especially troubling to the United States for two reasons. On the one hand, Manchuria was regarded as the most logical locale for future development by the United States (in part because the Manchurian textile industry was an important source of demand for cotton from the U.S. South; Israel 1971: 13–14). On the other hand, Russia had long been considered the chief rival of the United States in the Far East, and thus a stronger Russian presence in the key region of Manchuria was especially alarming (Israel 1971: 56).

Japan's subsequent defeat of Russia in the 1904–5 Russo-Japanese War gave the Japanese control over Korea and important ports in southern Manchuria, and completely transformed the international balance of power in the Far East. This in turn raised additional concerns in the United States about Japanese expansion not only into China but also into the Philippines, only recently brought under U.S. control (see Buck 1980; Israel 1971: 56; Peattie 1984: 17).[31] Further complicating these developments was a turn-of-the-century rush on the part of educated Chinese toward Japan to pursue university education. By 1905 it was estimated that as many as eight thousand Chinese students were receiving university education in Japan (Israel 1971: 44). This was interpreted in the United States as another sign of China's growing hostility toward Western tutelage (Ninkovich 1984: 800).

It was against this background that the U.S. government decided to take action.[32] In addition to military force (which ended the Boxer Rebellion), a central element in the strategy of the U.S. government to bring China within the U.S. orbit was "cultural" in nature. This element of the

U.S. strategy to counter Japanese and European influence in China focused on the uses to which were put the U.S. portion of the "Boxer Indemnity Fund," an amount of money that China paid to the United States for damages done to the latter's interests during the Boxer Rebellion of 1900. The cash settlement imposed on the Chinese by the United States was all out of proportion to the damages actually done to U.S. interests, a fact recognized by the U.S. secretary of state, John Hay, who negotiated the settlement (Hunt 1972: 541–42). Subsequent to the money's being paid, however, the U.S. "magnanimously" agreed to return a portion of the indemnity, but on the condition that the money thus returned was to be used exclusively to pay for the training of Chinese students in Western (predominantly U.S.) universities.[33] On this basis approximately twelve hundred Chinese students attended universities in the United States and England between 1908 and 1928 (Buck 1980: 47).

The Boxer indemnity scholarships were designed to serve several important and inter-related goals. One of the explicit aims of the scholarship program was to train the next generation of China's intellectual elite, whose Western educational backgrounds, it was hoped, would lead them to look to the United States for future leadership and intellectual connection. This training would also familiarize the Chinese with the new organizational structures that the philanthropies and the U.S. government were introducing in the United States in order to instill in the common man the mental and physical discipline necessary to adjust to the rigors of industrial life. The introduction into China of these institutions and standards of discipline, it was believed, and the existence of a Western-trained Chinese elite to oversee the process, would allow the Chinese to counteract the "downward tendencies of unregulated industrialism" that were widely regarded in the United States as responsible for the miserable state of China's masses (ibid.: 65, 76). Reforms of this kind were seen as indispensable in order to prevent further nationalist outbreaks like the Boxer Rebellion—a major preoccupation in the United States—to counteract Japanese and European ambitions throughout East Asia, and thus to promote political stability in the entire region (ibid.: 76–77). In the words of a well-known journalist writing at the turn of the century (quoted in Israel 1971: 44):

> If we desire the good will, the trade and an intellectual influence in China, there is no other way to get these things so directly as by welcoming and training the men who a few decades hence will exert a strong influence in governmental, educational, financial and industrial ways.

More than half of the Chinese students who received Boxer indemnity scholarships used their grants to study science, engineering, medicine, or agriculture.[34] A significant number, however, also chose to pursue one of the social science disciplines (Wang 1966: iii, 510–13). Of those students who pursued social science training, the vast majority attended particular university departments in the West that were especially highly regarded in China. For students of both economics and sociology (the latter generally embraced anthropology as well), for example, Columbia University was considered the most desirable until the early 1930s. Thereafter, for students of sociology the Department of Sociology and Anthropology at the University of Chicago gradually took over the first position from Columbia (Chiang 1986: 3). The London School of Economics and Political Science was another destination of a small but influential group of Chinese students in the 1930s.

One important consequence of this tendency on the part of groups of Chinese students to gravitate toward particular institutions was that graduate cohorts at several Western university departments became infused with, or at least consistently informed by, the concerns of Chinese students. As we will see presently, at times the concerns of these students had little in common with those of the policy makers who designed the Boxer scholarship program, or with the philanthropies that sought to remake social science research at the very universities to which these students gravitated. Indeed, although the vast majority of the Boxer indemnity scholarship students did indeed return to China when their education was complete, and not uncommonly occupied positions of responsibility, in many cases the future toward which they attempted to direct China, and their views on the factors responsible for the country's troubled past and present, were significantly different than the views of their Western sponsors.[35]

The career of Chinese sociologist Chen Ta (1892–1975) exemplifies many of the processes outlined above. Indeed, during his lifetime Chen Ta passed through much of the new social science infrastructure put in place by the philanthropic/governmental nexus. Although born the son of a Chinese peasant, Chen Ta was trained in the West at an elite institution that had been singled out by the philanthropies as one of their centers for empirically grounded, scientifically based, and practically oriented social science. As a result of his training he became a part of the intellectual elite of his country. He also received research funding from one of the institutes selected by the philanthropies to promote empirical, practical research, and published his research results under the auspices of this same institute. The scholarship that he (and others like him) produced thus reveals much about the actual uses to which was put the social science infrastructure brought into being by the philanthropies. His scholarship also documents the "mature" nature of (at least some) social science research before World War II.

The intellectually gifted son of a middle peasant family from a small village in Zhejiang Province (in southeast China, along the sea coast), Chen Ta was able to take advantage of the transformed conditions of early-twentieth-century China to accomplish things that would have been impossible in earlier times. After distinguishing himself academically in a small village school and later in the provincial capital of Hangzhou, Chen Ta went on to receive a scholarship through the Boxer Indemnity Fund to study in the United States. As were other Chinese sociology students at this time, Chen Ta was drawn to Columbia University, one of the elite schools that had been chosen by Rockefeller philanthropy (RPH) to re-make social science research. He received his M.A. in 1919 and his Ph.D. in 1923, both from Columbia.

Chen Ta returned to China immediately thereafter, where he assumed positions of considerable leadership and responsibility. In 1923 he accepted a sociology position at Qin Hua College, and when the college became a university in 1929 he became professor and chair of the Department of Sociology. During the 1920s Chen Ta was the editor of the social science journal published by his university.[36] As a graduate student Chen Ta had studied population and labor issues, and in China he helped organize the "Women's and Infants' Health Protection Association." Within this organization he established the "Birth Control Guidance Center" and promoted education about birth control and family planning. He was also head of the (Chinese) Institute of National Survey Research. From 1947 to 1949 he was vice president of the International Population Association, and was one of China's premier demographers (Yang and Quan 1981).

Chen Ta clearly became a part of China's intellectual elite as a result of his training in the West, which was in turn made possible by the turn-of-the-century effort of the U.S. government to establish an infrastructure to train the next generation of China's intellectual elite. It is therefore revealing to examine the way in which Chen Ta used his academic training—to examine the kind of scholarship he produced. Toward this end, we will review Chen Ta's major work in English, *Emigrant Communities in South China: A Study of Overseas Migration and Its Influence on Standards of Living and Social Change*, published by the Institute of Pacific Relations in 1939.[37] Chen Ta's main work in English will be the focus of discussion not because it was necessarily his most important or his best work, but rather because: (1) *Emigrant Communities* was the direct result of the new infrastructure of social science research produced by the philanthropic-governmental nexus; and (2) the fact that the work was available in English meant that it could have become part of an alternative academic canon, one that stressed such issues as European colonialism, international capitalism and labor migration, nation-state integrity, and other similarly "mature" concerns.

Emigrant Communities is based on fieldwork conducted in 1934–35; it was sponsored by the Institute of Pacific Relations—one of the institutes heavily sponsored by Rockefeller philanthropy.[38] The book is a study of the forces that resulted in the outmigration of large numbers of Chinese from villages located along China's southern and southeastern seacoast into the "Nan Yang"—the Philippines, Netherlands India, British Malaya and Borneo, Siam, French Indo-China, and Burma (ibid.: 5, note 4). *Emigrant Communities* was also intended as an analysis of the contemporary predicament of these emigrant communities.

Chen Ta notes as many as ten million Chinese in the Nan Yang, and at least twenty-two locales with a Chinese population of ten thousand or more (ibid.: 2). He argues that the presence of sizable and relatively prosperous communities of Chinese in the Nan Yang resulted in growing tensions between China and the "receiving" countries. The problems in question, he explains, revolved around issues of what we would today call national sovereignty. According to Chen Ta, cheap Chinese labor had been extensively used by European colonial enterprise in the Nan Yang for the expansion of cultivation on "rich virgin lands" (ibid.: 2), but this process had reached a point of "marginal productivity" (ibid.: 2). Furthermore, European colonial administrations began to draw on the indigenous populations of their colonies for agricultural production more fully than in the past. This, Chen Ta implies, created problems for the overseas Chinese, who began to be squeezed out of agriculture and other economic activities, but in the process of defending their positions were subjected to hostility from the indigenous populations of the colonies. These tensions were exacerbated, he explains, by the growing mechanization of agriculture, which reduced the demand for labor overall. Furthermore, what he refers to as "the over-production of commodities in relation to the effective demand the world over"—the global Depression of the 1930s—resulted in growing problems for all workers, and thus in growing tensions between Chinese and indigenous working groups (ibid.: 2).

These economic tensions, he goes on to explain, had political correlates. Just as did its imperial predecessor, the republican government of China claimed "jurisdiction over all persons of Chinese blood . . . who [do not] lose their citizenship . . . no matter for how many generations their ancestors have lived abroad" (p. 2). Because Chinese populations in the Nan Yang had been almost universally excluded from full citizenship in the regions into which they had migrated, and because the emigrant communities had maintained significant economic and social ties to mainland China, the question of who was to have sovereignty over these communities was of real significance (ibid.: 2–3).

In other words, Chen Ta sought to understand the contemporary predicament of overseas Chinese communities in the Nan Yang by placing them in the context of global, deterritorializing forces of power and inequality that include European colonial expansion, the dynamics of global capitalism, and the impact of these forces on relatively vulnerable populations.

Chen Ta then goes on to provide an historical analysis of the contemporary situation. While noting that emigration from southern China into the Nan Yang had a deep history, he nonetheless points to the mid–nineteenth century as the beginning of an historic watershed in the scale of emigration. At this time "a series of revolutionary changes" imposed upon China as a result of foreign (European) invasion ultimately led to the breakdown of the Chinese imperial state. On the one hand, the collapse of the imperial state meant that rural populations could no longer count on even the most minimal of protections or safeguards (ibid.: 1), and thus were increasingly prone to emigrate. On the other hand, armed invasion by foreigners, and the settlement of the wars provoked by these invasions, forced the Chinese government to open its borders to emigration on a hitherto totally unprecedented scale.

Chen Ta explains that since about the middle of the nineteenth century Europeans had imposed upon the Chinese a series of agreements that forced the Chinese government to allow its people to emigrate, especially to European colonies in Southeast Asia that were in desperate need of cheap labor. These impositions began with the Treaty of 1842, signed at the conclusion of the Opium War, and continued with other "conventions" in the decades that followed. The Chinese had a clear sense of what was happening, but their attempts to prevent it were to no avail. As one

Chinese official put it (ibid.: 55):

> To drive fish into other people's nets, or birds into other people's snares (says Mencius) is not a clever policy, but this is what we have been doing for England, Holland, and other countries. They get Chinese labor, and great towns spring up on their desert islands. Foreign countries thus use us as instruments for their own aggrandizement. We, the while, drive Chinese skill and the profits of it into their arms.

Having situated Chinese emigrant communities in this broader context, Chen Ta then seeks to assess the impact of these processes on China itself. Is it good, he asks, to have so many Chinese living abroad, enriching other countries (ibid.: 3)? What is the impact of such dramatic population loss on the economic, social, and political organization of the sending regions in China? Are Chinese living in the Nan Yang able to employ their ideas and social energies for the benefit of their own country, or are these expended or wasted in a foreign and hostile environment? (ibid.: 3).

As early as the 1880s the imperial government sent envoys into the Nan Yang in order to strengthen ties between China and its overseas nationals (ibid.: 55), resulting in struggles with European colonies regarding issues of sovereignty. Recognizing the importance of the emigrant communities, just after the turn of the century Sun Yat-sen granted them six senatorial seats in the Chinese government (ibid.: 56). In 1932 the Chinese national government set up an Overseas Affairs Commission to act as a liaison with the Nan Yang settlements (and with Chinese settlements around the world; ibid.: 57).

Chen Ta thus provides us with a sophisticated historical analysis, grounded in political economy, of the growth of the Chinese diaspora. His argument shows a clear awareness of the importance of capitalism, colonialism, imperial competition, and state collapse in precipitating population movement and labor exploitation on a massive scale. Furthermore, he discusses the forces that led to a novel form of political association—one in which the people who make up the "national" community do not live in a spatially contiguous territory.

The Political Geography of Philanthropic Intervention II: Africa

The emergence of "mature" scholarship on Africa in the 1930s was the result of two independent dimensions to philanthropic involvement in the social arena. These came together fortuitously to establish the material conditions in which anthropologists trained in empirical observation were able to spend extended periods of time living and working among Africans struggling to endure the rigors of colonialism and capitalism.

One of these two elements of philanthropic intervention was the founding of the International Institute for African Languages and Cultures (IIALC). Established in 1926, the institute initially grew out of efforts on the part of the British colonial administration in the early 1920s to arrive at a sound educational policy for Africans. Colonial administrators were determined to use education to teach Africans to be what they thought of as "good Africans." Administrators therefore favored an educational policy that taught Africans "useful skills" rather than "dangerous ideas" (that might lead to a desire for self-government). In short, African men were to be trained to be skilled farmers, while African women were to be taught the skills of being housewives and mothers. Neither were to be educated in ways that would cause competition with Europeans (Kuklick 1991: 205–7).

In pursuit of this policy of social control via education, colonial administrators looked elsewhere in the world for suitable models. They found a promising scheme in the educational policies designed for Black Americans in the U.S. South, in which philanthropies such as the Rockefeller Foundation, the Carnegie Foundation, and the Phelps-Stokes Fund had invested heavily with the same goal of social control. The philanthropies had sponsored an educational system in which Blacks were taught vocational skills and also taught to assume positions of leadership in their own communities (ibid.: 207).

It was this policy that British colonial administrators wanted to implement in Africa. In seeking to do so these administrators appealed to the above-mentioned philanthropies for financial support to underwrite a research institute to investigate the languages and cultures of the African peoples who were the intended target of the educational reform. The philanthropies responded favorably, and the IIALC was formed in 1926 (Brown 1973: 176; Kuklick 1991: 209). Although the institute initially received funding from a variety of sources, philanthropic and non, the Rockefeller and Carnegie philanthropies together contributed almost half the initial budget (Kuklick 1991: 210). The initial grant from RPH was one thousand pounds per year for five years (Goody 1995: 17).

The organizers of the IIALC felt strongly that anthropology would be indispensable to the success of their endeavor. This was especially so because the institute's initial focus on language was soon expanded to include a study of African social institutions, "with a view to their protection and use as instruments of education" (Stocking 1985: 123, quoting Smith 1934)—matters considered particularly pressing because "the rapid movement of capital into the African continent was seen as an important contributing cause of the continent's economic and social problems" (ibid.: 124; quoting Oldham). Indeed, many highly placed colonial officers believed that research into "the human factor" was the key to preventing the "impending racial conflicts" threatening Africa (ibid.: 123, quoting Bennet 1960).

Although the architects of the IIALC thus believed that anthropology could make a key contribution to their efforts at social control, it was clear to them that not just any kind of anthropology would suffice. The only form of anthropology that could suit their needs would have to be focused on practical, concrete problems rather than lofty theoretical matters. It was here that institute founders were able to link up with the second, above-mentioned philanthropic intervention into the social science sphere.

As explained earlier, from the turn of the century onward the philanthropies had invested enormous sums of money in higher education, seeking as they did so to promote research that was empirically grounded and practically oriented. To this end, the philanthropies selected universities and scholars that they believed had the most potential to contribute to this form of research, and provided these schools and scholars with the funds that would make it possible to develop the kind of research to which the philanthropies were committed.

One of the universities especially favored by philanthropic largesse was the London School of Economics and Political Science. Between 1924 and 1929 Rockefeller philanthropy (RPH) provided LSE with $1.25 million (Bulmer and Bulmer 1981: 395; RPH provided an additional $750,000 between 1929 and 1939; Goody 1995: 13). To develop international studies, $200,000 was awarded, as well as $500,000 for the general endowment and $20,000 per year to support the research of professors, readers, and lecturers (Bulmer and Bulmer 1981: 395).[39]

RPH chose LSE as one of its regional centers to promote social science excellence (ibid.: 384) in part because of LSE director William Beveridge's stated belief that the social sciences were too theoretical, and his commitment to making them more practical and empirical (Kuklick 1991: 212; Dahrendorf 1995). Rockefeller money effected a major shift in graduate training and faculty research at LSE. In part, this was because philanthropic funds were provided to particular members of the faculty. It was also because Rockefeller funds allowed the size of the graduate contingent to expand appreciably—ninefold from 1919 to 1937 (Bulmer and Bulmer 1981: 395).

One of the faculty members at LSE who was especially favored by RPH was Bronislaw Malinowski. Malinowski took up a position as an occasional lecturer at LSE in 1921 (Dahrendorf 1995: 144), but it was money provided by RPH that allowed him to assume the chair of Social Anthropology in 1927 (ibid.: 243). When the organizers of the IIALC began looking for an anthropologist whose work was empirically grounded and practically oriented, they turned to Malinowski and his functionalist anthropology (Kuklick 1991: 208). Between 1928 and 1930 Malinowski and influential members of the IIALC approached the Rockefeller Foundation with proposals soliciting large-scale funding to support research into the conditions of indigenous life in areas "into which Western capitalism is pressing" (ibid.: 210, quoting Malinowski memorandum to RF in 1926). Malinowski and his allies argued that research of this kind was essential in order "to protect the 'interests of the native population' in a period when world economic conditions foreshadowed 'rapidly increasing exploitation'" (Stocking 1985: 127, quoting Malinowski memorandum to RF in 1930). Ultimately, nothing less was at stake in Africa than "the possibility of race wars of considerable magnitude" (ibid.: 127). The RF was receptive to Malinowski's proposal, which stressed "the mutual unification of knowledge by practical interests and vice versa," especially in light of the fact that it focused on "problems of contact between black and white and the sociology of white settlement" (ibid.: 126, quoting Malinowski memo).

The Rockefeller Foundation accepted the proposal in 1930, providing a five-year grant of ten thousand pounds per year, to begin in 1931 (Goody 1995: 17; Stocking 1985: 127). The grant, which was administered through the IIALC, provided support for research grants and graduate student training. It is true that fellowships from the Rockefeller Foundation had supported graduate training at LSE under Malinowski as early as 1929 (Goody 1995: 15–16)—in keeping with the foundation's more general policy of bringing promising students into centers of social science excellence, training them in appropriate methods and concepts, and giving them the opportunity to conduct their own research (ibid.: 20, 27–28). Only a few grants of this kind, however, were available in 1929 and 1930. Once Malinowski and the IIALC had received their major grant in 1931, however, it became possible to expand both the number of promising students who came to LSE and also the amount of field research undertaken. Between

1931–32 and 1938–39, the IIALC provided seventeen graduate fellowships (for training at LSE), seventeen research grants (for field research), and published twenty-one volumes on Africa (Fisher 1986: 7).

The program of IIALC graduate fellowships underwritten by the RPH continued the foundation's policy of seeking to form an intellectual elite, whenever possible drawing on "indigenous intellectuals." A large percentage of the IIALC fellows who gathered at LSE to study under Malinowski were not from Britain. Among those who came from Africa were Jomo Kenyatta, N. A. Fadipe (Goody 1995: 27; see Fadipe 1970), and Z. K. Matthews (Goody 1995: 27; see Wilson 1981). European expatriates living in Africa were also among those who received IIALC fellowships. It is to the life and work of one of them that we now turn.[40]

Monica Hunter (1908–1982) was born in the small village of Lovedale in the eastern part of South Africa (she was later to become Monica Hunter Wilson). The daughter of missionary parents, she began her education at the Lovedale Mission School. Compared with other schools in South Africa, the Lovedale Mission School was quite unusual. It admitted black and white pupils alike.[41]

Hunter's nonsegregated upbringing was to have a direct effect on her long-term interests as she continued her education. In the late 1920s she went to Cambridge University to read history. Some sense of Hunter's interests, and of those of other South Africans of her generation, is revealed by the following comments, made by J. C. Smuts,[42] in the foreword to *Reaction to Conquest* (Wilson 1936: vii), Wilson's first book:

> I first met the writer of this work some years ago when as a young student she was on her way from South Africa to Cambridge to study social anthropology [sic]. I then warned her against a common failing of South Africans to be unduly preoccupied with the large political aspects of our native problems.

Hunter did indeed show herself to be concerned with precisely these issues. While at Cambridge she realized that virtually all of South African history was written from a white perspective, and that there was virtually no accurate information on black South African life. This realization led her away from the study of history and into anthropology.

Upon graduation from Cambridge in 1930, Hunter returned to the Eastern Cape to do fieldwork among the Pondo, a Bantu-speaking people in the Transkei. She received funding for this project from the IIALC, and with this support completed two years of work among the Pondo (ibid.: xii). This fieldwork was the basis for Hunter's first monograph, *Reaction to*

Conquest: Effects of Contact with Europeans on the Pondo of South Africa. The book was published by the IIALC, with the assistance of a grant from the Carnegie Corporation (through the Research Grant Board, Union of South Africa).

In keeping with the IIALC's focus on the impact of colonial capitalism on indigenous societies, Hunter examined living conditions in three of the four contexts representative of Pondo life as a whole: reserves, towns, and European farms (ibid.: 1). She had hoped to work in the fourth representative context, a mining compound, but found that the fact that she was a woman made this impossible (ibid.: 5).

Hunter begins her monograph with a discussion of the historical and political-economic production of the three "community types" that are the focus of her analysis. In so doing, she stresses the importance of European expansion, wars of conquest, the seizure of indigenous land, and also the activities of missionaries and traders. The combined impact of these forces, she explains, resulted in the establishment of reserves, "[b]locks of territory set aside for occupation by Natives only" (ibid.: 1, note 1). Conditions imposed by Europeans on the Pondo in these reserves, however, are such that indigenous patterns of life are impossible to maintain. Especially disruptive of pre-European practices are the following factors: land shortage (due to seizure of land by Europeans), the reduction in the powers of chiefs, the introduction of a new criminal code, European control of trade, and most important, the imposition of taxes by the Europeans (ibid.: 5).

As a combined result of these forces, Hunter explains, a large percentage of men and a significant number of women had to leave the reserves, either temporarily or permanently, in order to work for Europeans in towns, on farms, and in mines (ibid.: 5). It was particularly the growth of European towns after 1850, and the discovery of diamonds in 1870 and gold on the Rand in 1885, that resulted in an enormous increase in the demand for indigenous labor (ibid.: 3). Hunter recognizes the importance of these developments, and places them in a comparative context by distinguishing what we would today call "settler colonies" (ibid.: 551): "The history of the Union [of South Africa], the Rhodesias, and Kenya suggest that when territory is [attractive to] Europeans, or when minerals are discovered, complete control of economic contacts is impossible . . . land is alienated, and pressure brought to bear to secure labor for farm and mine."

Conditions for the indigenous population are such that there is a steady stream of laborers moving from reserves and farms to towns in search of work, and then back to the reserves (ibid.: 4). Relations between town and country are therefore of crucial importance in understanding the current state of affairs. Hunter also gives us a concrete sense for the scale of population movement, and for some of the factors that affect the scale. In 1927, she explains, more than half of all able-bodied men from the reserves were away at labor centers. The Depression of 1929, however, created a labor surplus, as a result of which native laborers were being turned away at the mines (ibid.: 4). Global forces are seen as impinging directly on indigenous life. "Pondo," she says, "are directly affected by affairs in England and Europe" (ibid.: 141).

After providing an insightful and detailed analysis of life in the reserves, as well as of the forces that are designed to drive Pondo out of the reserves in order to provide cheap labor for Europeans, Hunter turns to a discussion of town life. Here, the issues of over-riding importance concern a series of economic, social, political and legal restrictions that maintain Africans in a marginalized existence, providing low-cost wage labor for whites. Hunter shows that the social costs of this arrangement for Africans are very high. They are reflected in alarming rates of infant mortality (ibid.: 473), marital instability (ibid.: 485), and overall poverty (ibid.: 453). As Hunter puts it, "The creation of a population entirely dependent on wage earnings, and the partial breakdown of the [indigenous] system of mutual kinship obligations, results in distress and even starvation for the sick, the aged, and the unemployed" (ibid.: 449). Hunter concludes her discussion of African town life as follows (ibid.: 458):

> Here then is a Bantu community living under what approximate to western economic conditions. We have the familiar picture of a large number of people dependent entirely on their wage earnings, living in overcrowded unsanitary slums. I heard two Bantu men talking of the dangers of allowing women to enter industry and "take men's jobs," and the advantages of a war in which "all the unemployed would fight and be killed, and rich men would have to put their hands in their pockets." The situation differs from the European in the fact that of the total number of wage earners a proportion only are permanent workers . . . the standard of living is lower than in a white slum; and no provision is made for the sick, the aged, or the unemployed.

After a relatively brief section on the nature of life on European farms (Part III), Hunter concludes *Reaction to Conquest* with a discussion of how Bantu-speaking people like the Pondo have responded to their situation (in addition to interviews and observations, her analysis is based on an examination of Bantu newspapers, some of them communist [ibid.: 554, note 1]). In this regard, Hunter emphasizes nationalism, the growth of independent churches, union organization, and labor militancy.

Hunter notes that the discriminatory policies and attitudes of white society toward the Bantu have generated among the latter a powerful racial consciousness, and a rapidly growing sense of nationalism. Both are manifested in the Bantu press, where there are constant discussions of such matters as forced labor regulations, discrimination in taxation, education and the courts, the injustice of the pass system, and the fact that a great deal of Bantu land has been taken by whites (ibid.: 555–59). Bantu nationalism and racial consciousness are also manifested, Hunter argues, in the formation of churches formed and controlled by Bantu (ibid.: 562), and in the ties established between Bantu nationalists and blacks in the United States (in other words, a form of Pan-Africanism; ibid.: 562). Hunter also points to the formation in 1912 of the African National Congress (ibid.: 565–66), and the growing political instability following the emergence of the Bantu Trade Union in 1919 (ibid.: 566). By 1927 this union had 100,000 members, had made contacts with the Dutch and English union movements (ibid.: 567), and had organized a series of strikes (ibid.: 568–70). "No student of Bantu affairs," she says, "can doubt that the . . . disintegrating factors [discussed in the book] will eventually become submerged by the rising tide of Bantu nationalism" (ibid.: 573).

Hunter thus provides the reader with an analysis of the impact of colonial domination on an indigenous people of South Africa. Her work is informed by a clear understanding of the importance of European capitalist expansion, wars of conquest, the seizure of indigenous land, and the creation of a distinctive kind of indigenous wage-labor force along one of the key frontiers of the global economy.

After completing her fieldwork among the Pondo, Hunter returned to Cambridge, where she received her Ph.D. in anthropology in 1934. In 1935 she married Godfrey Wilson, who had read classics and philosophy at Oxford before developing an interest in anthropology through his friendship with Hunter (Brown 1973: 187).[43] Both received IIALC fellowships, and both trained with Malinowski at LSE before going to do fieldwork first in East Africa (among the Nyakyusa of what was then Tanganyika) and later in Central Africa (in Northern Rhodesia). Godfrey Wilson's work in Northern Rhodesia, in particular, *An Essay on the Economics of Detribalization in Northern Rhodesia* (Wilson 1941), is the next work from the interwar period to be discussed.

Wilson wrote his *Essay* while director of the "Rhodes-Livingstone In-stitute," which was established in the late 1930s on the initiative of Sir Hubert Winthrop Young, governor of the protectorate of Northern Rho-desia. Young believed that the institute would be of real help to him in his job as governor, in that it would assist in "the formulation of the correct economic and administrative policy for the mixed African and non-African community" of the protectorate. Stressing the institute's utilitarian role, Young stated that "relations between black and white in central and south-ern Africa were perhaps 'the greatest problem in the Empire today.'" He believed that "the institute 'will help me and my successors, and possibly other authorities, by providing expert advice upon the potential economic and political future of the two communities'" (Brown 1973: 178–79, quot-ing Young memoranda).

Although the proposed institute was opposed by important figures in the colonial office as well as industrialists working in Northern Rhodesia, Young eventually prevailed with the support of two important figures. One was Lord Lugard, the architect of indirect rule in British West Africa, author of *The Dual Mandate in British Tropical Africa* (1965 [1922]), and part of the inner circle of the IIALC (funded by RPH). The other figure who helped Young overcome the opposition to the proposed institute was Lord Hailey, author of the multivolume *African Survey* (Hailey 1939), a massive undertaking funded by a grant from Carnegie philanthropy and administered by the Royal Institute of International Affairs (one of the re-search institutes funded by both Rockefeller and Carnegie philanthropy).

The institute was subsidized by a combination of government and nongovernment sources (Brown 1973: 183, note 37). Among the latter were the major copper corporations working in Northern Rhodesia, which ap-pear to have viewed their contributions as a kind of "voluntary taxation" designed to maintain good relations with political authorities in London as well as with the governor (Young) of the territory in which they carried out their extremely profitable operations. (In the year ending September 30, 1937, the British South Africa Company earned 300,000 pounds in North-ern Rhodesia [ibid.: 185].)

The Rhodes-Livingstone Institute came into being at a time when the underlying climate of opinion favored the use of the brand of anthropology that Malinowski was advocating at LSE (with the support of RPH) to achieve practical ends (ibid.: 185). J. H. Oldham, one of the architects of, and a major force within, the IIALC, stressed the need for someone of high caliber to head the institute, and he recommended Godfrey Wilson for the

position. Both Lord Lugard and Hailey strongly supported this recom-
mendation, endorsing Wilson's credentials as a "functional" (that is, Mali-
nowskian) anthropologist (ibid.: 186). Wilson took up the appointment in
May of 1938 (ibid.: 187).

An Essay on the Economics of Detribalization in Northern Rhodesia (Wilson
1941) was Wilson's major work as director of the Rhodes-Livingstone Institute, and formed part of a broader research plan that embraced "the
evolving Northern Rhodesia social system" as a whole (Brown 1973: 189).
In specific terms, Wilson proposed (to the board of trustees of the Rhodes-
Livingstone Institute) investigation into three social contexts: (1) "the new
African society of . . . permanent and semi-permanent residents in urban
and industrial areas"; (2) "the group that alternates regularly between urban and rural areas"; and (3) rural African society (ibid.: 189, quoting 1938
Wilson memorandum). Wilson's *Essay on Detribalization* was the result of
his own investigations in urban/industrial areas.

One of the most striking features of the *Essay on Detribalization* is the
fact that from the opening of the book Wilson places the urban/industrial
community that is the focus of his analysis explicitly in the context of the
global, capitalist economy. Furthermore, he understands the distinctive
features of urban and rural Northern Rhodesia alike as being determined
to a significant degree by the dynamics of that global economic system. He
argues that "the territorial expansion of the economic system of Europe in
the nineteenth and twentieth centuries" (Wilson 1941: 17) led to a "disproportionate accumulation of capital" (ibid.: 17) in Europe and the
United States. At the same time "insufficient wealth was distributed in the
industrialized countries in the form of consumers' goods to exhaust the
products of the new industry" (ibid.: 17). As a result, he argues, "it was
only by continual expansion into new [regions] that the accumulating capital could continue to find profitable investment" (ibid.: 17). Among the
spatial frontiers into which this capital expanded was Northern Rhodesia.
Wilson argues that these new regions into which capital has expanded
served two crucial functions. They "were needed both as market for the
buying and selling of consumers' goods and also as sources of the raw materials of industry" (ibid.: 17). Nonetheless, "the capital ready for investment continued to pile up, [and] raw materials, . . . particularly metals to
make the machinery of future expansion, had a disproportionate significance" (ibid.: 17). And although the new regions into which capital investment flowed absorbed some of the excess production of industry,
"[t]he distribution of consumers' goods in the expanded economic field

[regions like Northern Rhodesia] was no more adequate to exhaust the products of industry than it had been in [Europe and the United States]. Wilson goes on:

> It is for this reason that the unevenness of the economic development of Northern Rhodesia consists, above all, in a disproportionate development of mining; agriculture, secondary industry, and the purchase of consumers' goods on the world market have lagged behind. So small a proportion of the goods which our present industrial plant can produce is distributed to consumers that, were it not that international warfare and preparations for it have temporarily replaced the lost [territorial] expansion and provided a market for otherwise unsaleable industrial products, industry would, under present conditions, be bankrupt all over the world. (ibid.: 17)

Wilson argues that the disproportion between capital accumulation and consumption helps to create class and race problems the world over. In Europe, it creates unemployment. In Northern Rhodesia, along with many other regions, it creates a migrant labor system (ibid.: 17–18).

The urban copper-mining center of Broken Hill is the focus of the analysis. Wilson explains: "The very existence of Broken Hill depends on its place in the world economy" (ibid.: 18). Mining began in 1906, a railway was constructed in that same year, and the urban center has grown up as labor has been drawn into Broken Hill in the context of industrial development. So intimately connected is Broken Hill with the world economy that its capital is bought and sold on the world market (most of it is held by English, South Africans, and Americans; ibid.: 18).

Wilson argues that the dynamics of capital accumulation are the most important forces in affecting life in and around Broken Hill. The African population of the region is seen exclusively as a source of cheap labor for industry, and not as producers or consumers of either food or consumers' goods. Nor are Africans seen as a potential source of skilled labor (ibid.: 27). The low level of wages has in turn resulted in the underdevelopment of secondary industry and agriculture, as Africans are unable to earn enough in wages to be able to pursue these alternative economic possibilities (ibid.: 27). Wilson argues that the "race problem" stems from this cause, from "the inevitable tension that must obtain in present conditions between a small group in skilled employment [who are white] and a large group [Africans] in unskilled employment, for the latter inevitably contains many potentially skilled workers" (ibid.: 28).

Wilson goes on to argue that the manner in which Africans have been integrated into the capitalist system—strictly as providers of cheap labor—

has had major consequences for life in rural areas, and for the general circulation of the population between town and country. The disproportion of young, able-bodied men who are drawn into wage work at Broken Hill drains the rural areas of crucial labor (a point developed at length in Richards 1939), and leaves the countryside "inhabited by a disproportionate number of old and infirm people, of women and children" (ibid.: 36). The fact that there is no effort to pay the mine workers a family wage (in order to maintain a low wage bill for capital [ibid.: 37]) means that women and other dependents are not able to follow men to the mines. This fact simultaneously prevents capital intensification in agricultural production (which would occur if there were sufficient demand to support it), and also undermines traditional farming techniques (because of the absence of most young men; ibid.: 37). Wilson also argues that the low wages, the poor conditions of work, and the oppressive nature of living and working conditions encourage laboring men to circulate constantly from one industrial center to another, and also between town and country. Indeed, the transient nature of the working population is one of Northern Rhodesia's most salient features (ibid.: 38).

Wilson thus argues that "[t]he economic problems of the rural areas . . . arise from the fact that they have been affected by a distant and incomplete industrial revolution, which has carried, for them, no agricultural revolution with it" (ibid.: 50).

Wilson thus stresses the dynamics of global capitalism, as manifested in a specific form in Northern Rhodesia, in seeking to understand economic and social life in the region. He clearly conceives of the working population as part of a worldwide proletariat. He characterizes them as

> members of a huge worldwide community . . . their lives . . . bound up at every point with the events of its history. . . . Their standard of living now depends on economic conditions in Europe, Asia and America, to which continents their labor has become essential. Their political development is largely decided in the Colonial Office and on the battlefields of Europe, while hundreds of their one-time separate tribes now share a single destiny. They have entered a heterogeneous world stratified into classes and divided into states, and so find themselves suddenly transformed into the peasants and unskilled workers of a nascent nation-state. (ibid.: 12)

The Political Geography of Philanthropic Intervention III: The United States in Latin America

As discussed previously, a major motivation for philanthropic intervention into society circa 1900 was the desire to establish mechanisms of social control that could effectively deal with the growing tensions in U.S. society resulting from rapid industrialization, immigration, and urbanization. The philanthropies targeted the institutions of higher education (among others) as an especially favorable sphere within which to instill in the untutored the mental discipline and the scientifically based, problem-oriented, rational world view deemed so essential to the rigors of modern urban life. In pursuit of this end, the philanthropies invested enormous sums of money in order to expand and transform higher education.

The life of historian Frank Tannenbaum (1893–1969) exemplifies both the social developments of this period that the philanthropies sought to control, and also the limits of their ability to do so. As did the individuals previously discussed, during his lifetime Tannenbaum passed directly through the new social science infrastructure erected by philanthropic largesse. The son of a European immigrant family that journeyed to the United States to escape poverty (Maier and Weatherhead 1974: 1), Tannenbaum nonetheless succeeded in finding a place at one of the elite institutions chosen by the philanthropies to remake social science research. His training at that school allowed him to rise directly into the intellectual elite of his country. From this vantage point he was able to secure research funding and publishing support over the long term from several of the key institutions selected by the philanthropies to promote the empirically grounded, practically oriented research to which the philanthropies were so committed. The scholarship that Tannenbaum produced thus tells us much about how members of an "indigenous elite" actually used the social science infrastructure created by the philanthropies. Tannenbaum's scholarship also further documents the "mature" nature of social science prior to World War II.

Tannenbaum was born in Austrian Galicia, and at the age of nine immigrated to the east coast of the United States with his family in order to escape the poverty of his homeland. As a teenager in New York City, Tannenbaum pursued a strategy not at all uncommon for immigrants during this era. He worked at odd jobs during the day and attended school at night when he could. Also like a number of marginally employed immigrants, Tannenbaum was drawn to the labor movement. This attraction affected the night school he chose to attend—the Ferrer School on Manhattan's Upper West Side, described by its president at the turn of the century as "the first institution devoted to the constructive side of anarchism." The Ferrer School was a gathering place for anarchist intellectuals, labor leaders, and other social activists, who discussed and debated how the world was and how it should be. Among Tannenbaum's teachers at the Ferrer School were Emma Goldman and Lincoln Steffans (ibid.: 3).

In the years following 1910 Tannenbaum joined the "Wobblies," the Industrial Workers of the World, and quickly became a labor leader. From this position he gained considerable notoriety in New York City by engaging in a new form of organized protest. The adolescent Tannenbaum took to leading hundreds of homeless and unemployed individuals in marches on the city's churches, where they demanded money for food and shelter.

Tannenbaum was arrested in 1914 as a result of his role in leading these marches, and he spent a year in jail. Parts of his trial testimony, however, were published in New York City–area newspapers, and caught the attention of Grace Childs, an elite woman who was deeply involved in the very kinds of social welfare institutions the philanthropies were promoting in order to help stabilize U.S. society.[44] On the basis of his trial testimony Childs invited Tannenbaum to visit her when he was released from prison in 1916. When he did so she was so impressed with him that she used her extensive contacts in the social welfare community to help secure a place for Tannenbaum at Columbia University's undergraduate college (after an interview with university officials he was accepted despite the fact that he had neither a high school education nor almost any formal schooling whatsoever). Tannenbaum went on to graduate from Columbia College with the highest of academic honors, obtained a Ph.D. in history from that same institution, and ultimately became not only professor of Latin American History but also an extremely influential force at Columbia (ibid.).

Tannenbaum clearly became a part of the intellectual elite as a result of his training at Columbia, which was in turn made possible because of a broader national context in which the philanthropies sought to contain the growing tensions of U.S. society by means of social and educational reform. Since Tannenbaum's life exemplifies the very social forces that the philanthropies sought to contain, it is revealing to examine the scholarship that he produced. Toward that end, we will examine *Some Latin American Research Problems. Memorandum for the Director of the Program in Interna-*

tional Relations of the Social Science Research Council (Tannenbaum 1933), released as a confidential, internal document for SSRC staff in 1933 but published almost verbatim the following year under the title *Whither Latin America? An Introduction to Its Economic and Social Problems* (Tannenbaum 1934). *Some Latin American Research Problems* will be the focus of discussion not because it was necessarily Tannenbaum's most important or best book, but rather because: (1) it was sponsored by the SSRC (and by the Brookings Institution),[45] the single most important research institute funded by the philanthropies in order to promote the forms of knowledge they regarded as so crucial to maintaining order; (2) the work was solicited by the SSRC with the goal of helping the SSRC identify research priorities in Latin America for those seeking SSRC funding; and (3) the publication of the volume in 1934 meant that it could have joined the books already discussed in forming an alternative academic canon.

Some Latin American Research Problems (SLARP) is intended as a broad overview not only of the singular characteristics of Latin America, but also of how Latin America is situated in relationship to the industrialized world. Tannenbaum is always careful to relate the particulars of different parts of the continent to the broader context of power and history in which these particulars are embedded. What emerges is an unusually sophisticated and thoroughly processual understanding of Latin America, one that loses sight neither of what is distinctive about the region nor the role of the broader world in helping to produce the region's distinctiveness.

The following passage from the preface does much to capture the conceptualization underlying the book:

> The relation of [Latin America] as a whole to the rest of the world is of exporter of raw materials and importer of manufactured products, of a borrower of capital from an investing world. It is an area where imperialism has expressed itself in all its forms, from direct annexation to subtle, indirect economic penetration. On this stage have been fought out large issues of national and international policy. . . . The peculiar position of the nations [of Latin America in] relationship [to] . . . the rest of the world [is] such as to make it a peculiarly fruitful field for the study of social and economic phenomena charged with international significance. It is important to observe how far-reaching are the effects of what seem purely local and national problems. A loan to valorize coffee in Brazil may affect the economic position of a dozen other nations, the development of banana plantations in the Caribbean by an American company may change the future racial composition of a region including a number of separate nations, the fiscal policy of a country like Chile may contribute to the development of artificial nitrate manufacturing in other

countries and, in turn, affect the American and European investments in Chile, raising broad problems of international policy. An American tariff on copper may affect the economic position of the leading Peruvian railroad which is owned by a British corporation and the attempt to control the price of rubber by Great Britain may lead to an attempt to develop enormous areas in the Amazon regions by American concerns. All of these examples are pointed out to illustrate that in the field of Latin American research it is difficult to draw a line between problems that have a purely internal and others a purely intercontinental significance. It is safe to assume that practically all important social and economic problems bear more or less directly on international relations.

Although there is much of interest in SLARP, the core of the argument concerns what today would be called the "dependent" position of Latin America with respect to the industrialized countries, and the reasons for the region's dependency. Indeed, Tannenbaum anticipated by several decades some of the more important arguments of the dependency school. In keeping with his earlier statement about the difficulty of distinguishing "internal" from "external" forces, Tannenbaum emphasizes the importance of a system of landholding (latifundia) imposed on the region from Europe at the Conquest, along with a series of post-Conquest institutions and exclusionary political processes (ibid.: 14, 16), that have marginalized the majority of the population, leaving them ill-disposed toward participation in broader national economic processes (ibid.: 14, 23–24). These same exclusionary forces, based on a highly stratified social structure, have also discouraged more recent waves of European immigration, preventing the emergence of a yeoman farmer stratum, as the European immigrant finds little in the way of opportunity in Latin America (ibid.: 14–15).

The marginalization of the majority, Tannenbaum argues, has significantly restricted the possibilities for internal economic development. As a result, Latin America's tiny economic elite remains committed to exporting one or two primary agricultural goods or raw materials in order to pay for the importation of expensive industrial and manufactured items from the industrialized countries (ibid.: 22, 43–44, 79, 84) that Latin American countries can ill afford. Tannenbaum identifies this disbalance between the limited revenues derived from exporting a small number of agricultural goods and raw materials and the high costs of imported, manufactured goods as one of the key problems facing Latin America (ibid.: 43–44, 79).

Such a situation, Tannenbaum suggests, has left Latin America heavily dependent on the financial resources of the industrialized countries in order to carry out the limited amount of industrial investment and national development that has taken place. Tannenbaum points in particular to the region's increasing dependence on foreign loans, the growing difficulties for Latin American countries that have stemmed from efforts to pay interest on these loans with the limited revenues derived from monocrop exports, and the persistent government deficits that have resulted (ibid.: 32–33).

Tannenbaum deepens this analysis with a discussion of industry itself, particularly those branches of industry best positioned to accumulate capital that could be used to further industrial development and the growth of national economies in Latin America (ibid.: 24–25). He notes that virtually all industry of this kind is in foreign (U.S. and European) hands. That includes railroads,[46] oil development, mining, telegraph, telephone, radio, and airplane communications. It includes as well public utilities and a very large proportion of the manufacturing sector. Even a considerable portion of the agricultural goods that enter the international market is produced by foreign-owned enterprise (ibid.: 24). In addition to mining, agriculture, transportation, communication, and manufacturing, wholesale and retail merchandising (import and export firms) are also largely in foreign hands (ibid.: 24–25).

These are important considerations, Tannenbaum notes, because the profits from these multiple spheres of economic activity are exported out of Latin America and into the industrialized world ("repatriated," in modern parlance). "It is only insofar as the industrialists, manufacturers and agriculturalists become nationalized that they contribute to the development of a native middle class" (ibid.: 25). Because capital investment in most key economic sectors of Latin America is foreign, however, and because profits from these sectors are exported from the region, the industries in question have few positive effects on the regions in which the foreign capital is invested (in modern parlance, the industries in question are "enclave" in nature).

In this work Tannenbaum presents us with an unusually sophisticated analysis of the predicament of Latin America. He shows that the current situation of the region can only be understood against an historical background of European conquest that bequeathed to Latin America class structures and political institutions that: (1) have marginalized the majority of Latin America's population; and (2) have played a key role in placing Latin America in a dependent position with respect to the industrialized world. Colonialism, class, imperialism, and capitalism all figure prominently in this account of the interconnectedness of regional and global processes. Tannenbaum provides the reader with a way of understanding the specificity of Latin America in the context of global forces of power and inequality.

The works reviewed above, along with many others from the same period that address similar themes, clearly represent an attempt on the part of the scholars of the era to understand the global structure and the regional manifestations of what was then the modern world order. Indeed, the new infrastructure of social science knowledge that emerged during this period—that established the material conditions in which these scholarly studies could be conducted—was designed by its sponsors (the great philanthropies) with this precise goal in mind.

The world order that social scientists of the interwar period sought to comprehend was one in which the forces of colonialism, capitalism, and imperialism were in the process of transforming sociocultural practices and political-economic relationships around the world. Indeed, scholars seeking to make sense of these developments were confronted by such phenomena as the breakdown of indigenous polities, the massive displacement and movement of populations (often across state boundaries), proletarianization, economic dependency, the growth of extraterritorial forms of political community, the emergence of "stateless persons," and the rise of nationalisms of various kinds.

As we have seen, the social scientists of the interwar period who sought to understand these processes brought to their analyses a truly global perspective. Their analyses consistently showed that events in what appeared to be the most distant of frontier regions were intimately interconnected with, and impossible to understand without a consideration of, forces of power emanating from more "core" arenas. Today, it is startling to discover such direct concern with forces that conventional histories of the social sciences depict as having entered into scholarly consideration only beginning in the 1960s.

The scholarship contained in the present volume represents a more recent attempt to locate capitalism in time and space. As one would expect, this work differs from the earlier scholarship in a number of important ways. On the one hand, the works in the present volume have emerged in response to a different moment in the long process of capitalist restructuring—the end of Fordism, and the beginnings of flexible accumulation (Harvey 1989).

In addition, this more recent scholarship has emerged out of institutional and funding structures distinct from those of the 1920s and 1930s. Particularly important in this regard has been the state-sponsored normalization of university education (initially via the G.I. Bill) and the institutionalization of social science research that took place after World War II (as part of the Fordist pact; ibid.).

Furthermore, the work in the present volume has emerged out of a national and international context of a significantly different order than that of the interwar period. Beginning in the 1960s, the Black Power and Civil Rights movements, the feminist movement, the Vietnam War, and the movement of protest surrounding the war combined to precipitate a period of real questioning in the United States. Since that time developments such as the fall of the Soviet Union, the end of the Cold War, the crisis in the international system of nation-states, and ongoing problems of racial, gender, and class-based inequality have all deepened the process of questioning that began several decades past. These developments have led to extensive critical analysis of the role of nation-states and powerful economic interests in national and world affairs, and of the public responsibilities of academics in relation to the activities of economically and politically powerful groups.

Despite differences, however, there are some striking similarities between these two periods that have both produced concerted efforts to locate capitalism in time and space. These similarities, it can be argued, are a function of several inter-related factors. First, although the processes of capitalist restructuring that began in the late 1960s are significantly different from those of the opening decades of the century, it is nonetheless true that both of these periods have been times of crisis. Both, that is, correspond to eras during which there have been major reorderings in global political and economic relations. Thus, although the "object of analysis" may have changed between the two periods, it is nonetheless true that in both periods the object itself has been in a state of flux and reconstitution.

Second, although the social science infrastructure brought into being by the great philanthropies in the interwar period has changed a great deal in intervening decades, it is nonetheless true that the funding structures of both periods have something in common. Both periods have opened graduate education in the West to social groups, domestic and foreign, that otherwise would have been very unlikely to have received graduate training in the social sciences. Institutional structures specific to each period have thus made it possible for new concerns to be brought into the classroom and into the field.

Finally, although the national and international context in which the social science of the 1960s and afterward has developed differs profoundly from that of the 1920s and 1930s, these two eras nonetheless share an important feature. Much as Western and non-Western scholars who have helped reconfigure social science beginning in the 1960s have been responding to the chaotic conditions of their era, the scholars of the interwar period discussed in this chapter (many of whom were non-Western) were responding to crisis conditions in non-Western parts of the world—whether these were state collapse and civil war in China, the devastating impact of colonial capitalism in Africa, or poverty and political upheaval in Latin America.[47]

Despite these similarities it is nonetheless true that the "object of analysis," funding structures, analysts' social backgrounds, and broader context have all changed since the interwar period. This being the case, it is instructive to compare the scholarship of the two eras in order to assess what has remained broadly similar and what has changed. Such an assessment will place "Whiggish" intellectual histories of the social sciences, with their narratives of progress through rupture, in a critical light.

William Roseberry begins this volume with a challenge to the Euro-centered, world-systems models of capitalist development based on a fixed spatial hierarchy of core, semiperiphery, and periphery. Arguing that capitalism is an inherently unstable set of relationships that generates ongoing restructurings as part of its very nature, Roseberry examines the continually changing spatial hierarchies, redefinitions of global and local spaces, and historical continuities and discontinuities that have characterized the capitalist order since its inception, and will continue to do so in the future. What emerges from this analysis is a sophisticated, nuanced understanding of capitalism as an emergent field of relationships, contingent in time and through space, and not exclusively focused on Europe and the United States. Roseberry's contribution both draws on and adds to other work done in a similar vein that attempts to historicize and contextualize the social relations of capitalism (Harvey 1989; Jameson 1981; Mandel 1975; Pred and Watts 1992; Gunder-Frank 1998).

A number of the studies in the present volume provide detailed analyses that situate and contextualize the social relations of capitalism in precisely the terms called for by Roseberry and others. Myron Cohen's contribution is one of these. Cohen is especially suggestive in pointing to the existence of what some authors refer to as capitalisms (see Ong, this volume) rather than a single, overarching capitalism rooted permanently and exclusively in the North Atlantic. Cohen does this by providing a richly detailed analysis of the process of commoditization in late imperial China at the end of the nineteenth century. While his analysis focuses on the commoditization of land, and land-related rights, he makes it clear that commoditization extended into many spheres of life. Especially startling about his analysis is what it reveals about the highly developed and sophisticated nature of markets in one of the two "fictitious commodities" upon which capitalism is based (Polanyi 1944). Indeed, Cohen demonstrates a level of economic complexity and institutional development that alerts us to alternative possible histories and trajectories of capitalist organization (a point made forcefully for East Asia of late by Gunder-Frank [1998]). Cohen's article thus adds weight to the growing corpus of scholarly work that questions "Western exceptionalism," that seeks to deorientalize our understanding of global power relations (Mallon 1995: 1–20).

Marilyn Cohen's contribution, a fine-grained historical analysis of the destabilizing effects of capitalist restructuring in nineteenth-century Ireland, brings us within the purview of North Atlantic capitalism. Rather than the commoditization of land being the focus of her analysis, it is the commoditization of labor that she addresses. Focusing on County Down, Cohen uses the Great Irish Famine of midcentury as a key event that both reveals and magnifies broader transformations in regional society that were a consequence of restructurings in the linen industry. Cohen does this by comparing the fate of petty commodity producers and proletarianized households in the famine, and in the process reveals how gender, class, and uneven capitalist development intersected in ways that were to have devastating consequences for the region. Petty commodity-producing households weakened in previous decades by an expanded putting-out system found themselves especially hard pressed to reproduce themselves in the famine. While these households were extensively impoverished as a result, it was particularly women and children who were the most vulnerable. Many responded by seeking the relative security of urban wage employment. Major population displacement and class formation occurred, Cohen shows, as the famine accentuated the growing fault lines of regional society.

David Nugent's article explores the consequences of restructuring along a different frontier: the Chachapoyas region of Peru in the early twentieth century. Nugent's point of departure is the flood of new laboring people, social doctrines, political ideologies, and investment capital that poured into Peru as a result of the late-nineteenth-century crisis in North Atlantic capitalism. Nugent focuses on the ways in which these influences helped precipitate a nationalist movement in an outlying section of the national territory, among subaltern groups seeking to end their marginalization at the hands of an aristocratic elite. Subaltern groups in Chachapoyas coalesced into a unified political movement that successfully challenged aristocratic control. Unity was established by rejecting the derogatory racial categories that divided the subaltern, subsuming formerly separate (and antagonistic) racial groups within a single nonracial category (*el pueblo*) derived from the egalitarian discourse of the nation-state, and openly embracing the institutions and values of the nation-state. Only with el pueblo's victory over the elite, Nugent shows, was the central government able to consolidate control over this region.

Anastasia Karakasidou examines the consequences of restructuring along what might be called an "internal line of fracture" of the capitalist order. In the process, she provides a penetrating analysis of the dynamics of state and nationhood in a setting radically different from that discussed by Nugent. Karakasidou's contribution focuses on the mechanisms and rituals of national integration in (Macedonian) northwestern Greece during this century, and on state efforts to form a national consciousness among the region's inhabitants. Karakasidou pays particular attention to the broader geopolitical context in which these nationalizing efforts have taken place. Her point of departure is the late-nineteenth-century disintegration of the ethnically diverse Ottoman Empire, which exercised control over this section of Macedonia (until 1913). The focus of her analysis is the subsequent struggles of a series of nation-states—Bulgaria, Germany, the Yugoslav Socialist Republic of Macedonia, and Greece—to replace this diversity with the cultural and linguistic homogeneity characteristic of the modern nation-state. Karakasidou documents the slow, violent, and painful process by which the Greek nation-state eventually prevailed over its competitors, and (partially) succeeded in nationalizing the populace. She also shows the crucial role played in this process by the state apparatus—both as a mechanism of coercion and as an agent of hegemony.

María Lagos also makes the dynamics of state and nationhood the focus of her analysis, but in Bolivia in the second half of the twentieth century and with a more explicit focus on gender. The broader context of her analysis is the Bolivian Revolution of 1952, and postrevolutionary changes in the organization of the state and society. Lagos is especially concerned with the ways that post-1952 state policies reinforced pre-existing socio-economic structures and cultural understandings regarding the gendered nature of labor and politics. The consequences of this conjuncture, she shows, were twofold. The public sphere was defined as the realm of "real" politics, and as controlled by men, while the private sphere was defined as essentially nonpolitical and as being the domain of women. Lagos is particularly astute at showing how this sociopolitical construction of household and community has set the parameters within which men and women engage in political struggle, with the state and with each other. Indeed, Lagos shows that laboring women's ambivalence about their husbands' political involvements stems from women's awareness that men's political activities, necessary though they may be, reproduce women's subordinate position in work and politics. Lagos closes her paper with a revealing discussion of women who have begun to challenge this structure, and of the limits to and contradictions inherent in their attempt to do so.

George Bond also concentrates on the relationship between the state, capitalist expansion, and changing gender hierarchies. Bond analyzes these topics in the social field encompassing Muyombe, capital of the Oyombe chiefdom in northern Zambia, in the postindependence era. Bond is especially interested in the manner in which processes of hegemony operate so as to reproduce an agnatic-based social hierarchy of male authority that is accepted by the very categories of individuals its subjugates. Bond is particularly astute in showing how the hegemonic ideology of gender inequality is far more than an issue of ideas or discourse. Rather, it is built into the structure of everyday life, such that it is impossible to become a socialized Yombe individual without having lived this hierarchical construction. Bond also identifies the forces that have begun to transform this hegemonic structure. In 1972 the Zambian government began to promote the production and marketing of hybrid maize, a development that ended up favoring female-headed households that were on the margins of the agnatic system. As women became successful commercial farmers they became autonomous of their male kin and increasingly able to regulate their own affairs. Bond shows how these have been the very women who have begun to challenge male prerogatives over women in multiple spheres of life, and thus to transform the hegemonic structure of male domination.

Cynthia Saltzman's fascinating contribution analyzes the relations among capitalist transformation, shifting gender hierarchies, and organized political activity. Saltzman does this by examining a massive strike among predominantly female clerical workers at Yale University in 1984.

The strike, she argues, can be understood only in relation to general shifts in the political economy of the United States: the end of Fordism, the rising importance of service and clerical employment, and the growing feminization of the workforce. Saltzman is especially interested in how unity of consciousness and action was forged among a working population with major internal divisions. She is particularly astute at showing how union leadership's decision to frame the strike rhetorically as an issue of "comparable worth" appealed to multiple constituencies. Comparable worth, Saltzman argues, raised general issues of justice, equality, and discrimination that resonated with diverse groups. In addition to local clerical workers, these included male blue-collar workers, national union leaders, prominent feminist organizations, prominent politicians, and the national media. Saltzman documents how a "culture of activism" formed in this context as comparable worth helped generate a "transformational politics" that built coalitions among groups, blurred boundaries of gender and identity, and brought together diverse constituencies.

Ida Susser also provides us with a penetrating analysis of the impact of capitalist transformation on the lives of working people, and on their capacity for organized resistance. Susser focuses her analysis on the deterioration of the lives of New York City's poor since the mid-1970s. The broader context she invokes includes the end of Fordism, and the remaking of the NYC economy as a center of corporate finance, investment, and real estate. The particular focus of her analysis, however, is the effect of this restructuring on community life. Susser traces the process by which stable, working-class neighborhoods that remained intact until 1975 were thereafter unable to reproduce themselves in the face of industrial flight (and loss of jobs) and a drastic reduction in city services. She shows how the remaking of the city economy encouraged landlords to neglect and even destroy their buildings in working-class neighborhoods in order to clear the way for higher-paying tenants. As working people were driven out of their jobs, homes, and neighborhoods, they were forced out of stable and spatially localized forms of community. They were forced to adopt deterritorialized forms of support and association as they moved frequently among neighborhoods where violent crime, the drug trade, and high levels of neighborhood neglect left residents alienated and withdrawn from their surroundings. Not only are New York City's poor losing the battle for food, rent, and community, she explains, but also the capacity for organized protest.

Michael Burawoy offers a fascinating analysis of the failure of Western efforts to transform the former Soviet Union from a state socialist to a market-based capitalist economy. Building on the work of Polanyi (1944), Burawoy attributes this failure to the absence of institutional structures that were key to the rise of market society in nineteenth-century England. Paramount among these was a strong sovereign state able to regulate the national economy so as to ensure business confidence and a stable national currency. Equally important was the state's ability to draw on the ample resources provided by an expanding industrial sector to tame the market and provide safeguards to a mobilized working class. Russia in the 1990s, Burawoy shows, could not present more of a contrast with nineteenth-century England. In postsocialist Russia, a weak state was unable to impose effective national economic controls or stabilize the currency (resulting in extensive efforts on the part of the general population to circumvent both). The state was also confronted with a shrinking industrial sector and dwindling revenues, and thus was in no position to provide safeguards to a working class threatened by the dangers of the self-regulating market. In short, conditions in Russia meant that neither the elite nor the workers could turn to the state for protection from the sudden and radical market reforms imposed by the West. Russia's response to market peril was "involution"—a generalized and pervasive retreat from the market. The Russian economy withdrew into noncapitalist forms of production and nonmarket forms of exchange. Russian society turned inward, abandoning socialist institutions and reconstituting itself as a disarticulated aggregation of social networks deployed around the strategic manipulation of resources. The Russian state lost considerable control to the regions, whose assertions of autonomy helped precipitate a structure of parcialized sovereignty rather than centralized control. Burawoy's analysis has important implications for other states undergoing the shock therapy of neoliberal reform.

Aihwa Ong offers an incisive analysis of the restructuring of capitalist social relations in Southeast/East Asia during the post-Fordist era, and of a concomitant restructuring of the public sphere and subaltern political consciousness. She argues that in the late 1970s this region saw the rise of new transnational classes of capitalists, technocrats, and professionals, whose flexible accumulation strategies brought them astonishing wealth and made them the new economic elite in Asia. Ong is particularly interested in the transnational commercial and political discourses that have emerged to explain (and exalt) the success of these entrepreneurs. She is especially astute at deconstructing the moral messages regarding family, gender, ethnicity, race, and nationality embedded within these mass media representations, and the ways that these messages shape political consciousness. Ong makes very creative use of the notion of "family romance" to show how commercial and political representations of the "invented Confucian family" provide a moral template for appropriate behavior in multiple arenas of life: between men and men, ethnic Chinese and indigenous groups, the state and its citizens, and men and women. By coordinating the moral economy of the family with that of the firm, the state, and the transnational business arena, mobile capitalism has generated powerful myths about Chinese cultural exceptionalism. These myths resonate deeply in subaltern consciousness, and play a powerful role in setting the terms within which the subaltern imagine their life possibilities.

We live in an era during which theories of material and cultural disjunction are unusually widespread and persuasive.[48] The scholarship contained in this volume, when seen in relation to the work of the interwar period, should perhaps give us pause as we reflect on what is unprecedented and what is not about our own era. One notable feature of formulations that stress the novelty of contemporary scholarship is that these formulations often compare this scholarship with past works that became part of the academic canon. In other words, these comparisons draw on what might be called "official histories" of the social sciences.[49] As the forgotten work from the interwar period discussed earlier in this chapter shows, however, official histories and academic canons conceal as much as they reveal (see Vincent 1990).

A final comparison should help bring this out. The year 1940 saw the publication of *African Political Systems* (Fortes and Evans-Pritchard 1940), a volume that has been extremely influential in political anthropology. Indeed, this book was to define the academic canon in political anthropology for decades to come. It is revealing that just one year later, in 1941, Godfrey Wilson's *Essay on Detribalization* (Wilson 1941) appeared, and furthermore that all the scholarship reviewed above in this chapter had appeared in the decade prior to the publication of Wilson's work. In other words, by the time of *African Political Systems*, ample scholarship had been produced that could have acted as the basis of an alternative academic canon.[50] This alternative canon would have looked a great deal like the canon that did emerge, if fleetingly, in the 1960s. Had this possibility come to pass, we would today have a very different understanding of who we are, where we have been, and where we are going.

Notes

1. This view is implicit or explicit in much of the radical literature of the late 1960s and early 1970s, and is exemplified by the response to Talal Asad's influential volume, *Anthropology and the Colonial Encounter* (Asad 1973).

2. One is reminded here of James Clifford's fascinating discussion (1986) of successive generations of anthropologists lamenting what each generation understands to be the recent passing away of pristine society (see also Diamond 1974; Williams 1973). When discussing the history of their discipline, however, successive generations of anthropologists have been more prone to see backwardness and ignorance than harmony and holism, and to celebrate rather than lament.

3. The argument in and especially the response to *Black Athena* (Bernal 1987) exemplify this process.

4. The literature is vast, but notable examples include the special issue of the *American Ethnologist* on "Imagining Identities: Nation, Culture, and the Past" (vol. 19, no. 4, 1992); Anderson (1983); Handler and Gable (1997); Hobsbawm and Ranger (1983); Price (1983); and Rappaport (1990).

5. Although it is beyond the scope of the present work, two forces seem overwhelmingly responsible for the fact that this earlier period of maturity in the history of the discipline remains obscure. The first relates to national politics, in particular the impact of the political repression of the 1950s on the limits of public discourse—on what was and was not utterable in the social sciences (this is an important but understudied topic; however, see Price 1998; Wallerstein 1997). The second relates to disciplinary politics, and concerns the widespread tendency to tell the history of the field from the point of view of the victors, the "great men" and their "great books" (Goody 1995; Stocking 1995). In light of how widely discredited this approach is to the study of social contexts other than our own, it is revealing that histories of anthropology based on such an approach are assumed to be authoritative.

6. For reasons that will become clear as the argument proceeds, at times it will be necessary to stray somewhat from these precise dates.

7. McBride (1936) provided a similar analysis of the socioeconomic and political structure of Chile.

8. Joan Vincent's magisterial work, *Anthropology and Politics* (1990), provides extensive documentation of the existence of a subterranean tradition of similarly forgotten work in anthropology since the 1870s. The present work is heavily indebted to Vincent's pioneering analysis.

9. Other philanthropic foundations were involved as well, among them the Brookings Institution, the John Simon Guggenheim Memorial Foundation, the Phelps-Stokes Fund, the Julius Rosenwald Fund, and the Russell Sage Foundation.

10. "Social science" should be understood in quite broad terms. Officers of the Rockefeller Foundation, for example, considered biology to belong to the social sciences (Bulmer and Bulmer 1981). This blurring of what we would consider conventional boundaries between different branches of knowledge, and the effort to

reclassify them, was undoubtedly related to the foundation's vision of public health as part of a package of interventions, most of which were more properly social in nature, that would help instill in nonmodern people the mental and behavioral discipline necessary to participate in the modern world. Symptomatic of this orientation was the following: Rockefeller philanthropy actively encouraged interdisciplinary work in virtually all the social science endeavors it sponsored, and consciously sought to break down disciplinary boundaries (Fisher 1993: 59).

11. This was especially true for the period between the two world wars.

12. This is not to say that the philanthropies had a conflictual relationship with the nation-states in which they operated. To the contrary. The goals of the philanthropies and the nation-states in which they worked were often (but not always) quite similar.

13. From the end of the Civil War onward there was a gradual shift in higher education in the United States away from the predominance of the small college, with its focus on a fixed classical curriculum and rote memorization. Increasingly, university education at a core group of more research-oriented institutions was based instead on "cognitive rationality," on "knowing through the exercise of reason." Between 1890 and 1900 "cognitive rationality" emerged as the dominant value in a core group of elite universities (Geiger 1986: 9). The shift was a function of many factors acting in combination. Prominent among them was the establishment of the system of land grant colleges in 1862, the growing desire to make higher education more practical, and the advances in science and scientific investigation as developed especially in the context of the German research university (ibid.: 9–10). These were the broader processes into which the philanthropies tapped.

14. Funds from the philanthropies freed up faculty from heavy teaching responsibilities, and provided them with the money they needed to pursue research.

15. The General Education Board, a Rockefeller-financed philanthropy, contributed approximately $60 million to the endowments of a select group of universities in the opening decades of the century (Coben 1976: 231). The philanthropic sponsorship of higher education did not occur in a vacuum. Just as research universities grew in size during this period, and in the number of students who attended them, so did the fund-raising abilities of these institutions. In addition to the philanthropies, two other sources of additional funds were important: (1) individual (wealthy) public donors; and (2) alumni of the institutions in question (Geiger 1986: 43–45).

16. Rockefeller Philanthropy (in the specific form of the Laura Spelman Rockefeller Memorial) contributed heavily to the Institute for Research in Social Science at the University of North Carolina, as part of the philanthropy's program of creating and strengthening regional social science centers of excellence (Bulmer and Bulmer 1981: 390–92).

17. The latter institutions were funded by the General Education Board and the International Education Board, both Rockefeller-funded philanthropies (Coben 1976: 231).

18. Frederick T. Gates, John D. Rockefeller Sr.'s most trusted advisor on the

philanthropic use of Rockefeller funds, played a key role in orienting philanthropy in the direction of public health. Gates was the person who convinced Rockefeller of the potential of this field to alleviate human suffering (Buck 1980: 243, note 6).

19. As with the growth of the research university itself, philanthropic sponsorship of graduate education took place in the context of a general increase in the number of students attending the country's leading research universities (Geiger 1986: 12–13). From the 1890s onward, more and more families from society's middle ranks had sufficient income to be able to spare the labor of their young adult sons. The increasingly career-oriented nature of university education made it an avenue of (modest) social mobility for these families (ibid.: 13–14).

20. Examples include the fellowships offered to Chinese students by the Rockefeller Foundation's China Medical Program, which allowed Chinese students to study medicine in the West; the RF grants to the London School of Economics and Political Science, which funded students to engage in graduate study at LSE; the International Institute of African Languages and Cultures fellowships, also provided by the Rockefeller Foundation, which also provided funds for graduate study (in anthropology) at LSE; the RF Humanities Division grants of the 1930s; the SSRC graduate fellowships; and the Southern Fellowship program of the SSRC. Between them, these programs provided funds that made it possible for literally hundreds of students, domestic and foreign, to receive graduate training at one of the select universities chosen by the philanthropies to remake the social sciences (see, for example, Cueto 1994: xi; SSRC 1934: 82–84).

21. The anthropology program at the London School of Economics and Political Science and the University of Chicago's departments of sociology and anthropology were among the schools especially favored by Rockefeller philanthropy.

22. Prior to receiving its royal charter, the RIIA was known as the British Institute of International Affairs, under which name it was founded in 1919. In addition to receiving funding from Rockefeller philanthropy, the RIIA also received financial assistance from Carnegie philanthropy (King-Hall 1937).

23. The LSRM, a Rockefeller-funded philanthropy, was the most important source of funds for social science research during the 1920s (see Bulmer and Bulmer 1981; Fisher 1983, 1993).

24. By this time the LSRM had been absorbed into the Rockefeller Foundation.

25. SSRC did so primarily by creating committees that replicated SSRC's own organizational structure within the elite universities chosen to remake the social sciences. These university committees were interdisciplinary, being made up of representatives from each of the major social science disciplines. The committees dispersed research funds (provided by SSRC) to particular departments, discussed research priorities, etc. (Fisher 1993).

26. In one sense, of course, all of the philanthropies' cultural work should be understood as an effort at social engineering.

27. Most of these programs were funded either by Rockefeller philanthropy, by Carnegie philanthropy, or by a combination of the two. The Julius Rosenwald Fund and the Phelps-Stokes Fund were involved in funding education programs for blacks in the U.S. south.

28. For a fascinating discussion of the subsequent normalization of fieldwork, and "the field," into anthropology, see Gupta and Ferguson (1997).

29. There is striking continuity between the cultural work undertaken by the great philanthropies and the work of nineteenth-century missionaries (see, for example, Hewa and Hove 1997). Indeed, one might think of the social science work sponsored by the philanthropies as a secularized form of missionary activity, one that proselytized the virtues of modernity rather than Christianity (see Coben 1976: 236; Hewa and Hove 1997: 6). In this regard, it is revealing that the man who was more responsible than any other for convincing J. D. Rockefeller Sr. (a devout Baptist and generous contributor to missionary activities) to establish a philanthropic foundation was Frederick T. Gates. Gates was himself an ordained Baptist minister (Berliner 1985: 26), who was head of the American Baptist Education Society when he joined the Rockefeller staff in 1892. He remained Rockefeller's most trusted advisor in decisions regarding the uses to be made of philanthropic funds.

30. Although none of the Western European powers had colonized China, most were seeking to deepen their involvement in the decaying empire as much as possible at this time.

31. Revealingly, the Japanese-Russian peace treaty was negotiated in Portsmouth, New Hampshire, under the watchful eye of Theodore Roosevelt (Myers and Peattie 1984).

32. The Rockefeller Foundation also took action at this point. The RF's original plan was to build a research university in China modeled on the University of Chicago. This plan was eventually discarded, and instead the foundation built the Peking Union Medical College and launched a program of public health in China. The RF was to spend $45 million on its Peking Union Medical College (Buck 1980: 47). Foundation officials appear to have conceived of the program as an ideal combination of what China needed most—the ability to train personnel in scientific methods that could address real, practical problems, and the institutional structures to instill in the Chinese modern disciplines of mind and body (ibid.).

33. The Chinese had other ideas about how to best use the returned indemnity funds. Recognizing their weak position vis-à-vis Russia and Japan in Manchuria, the Chinese sought to use the funds to strengthen their presence along this contested section of their northern border (Hunt 1972).

34. It was originally stipulated that 80 percent of the Boxer scholarships were to go to students in scientific and technical fields (Buck 1980: 75).

35. For a fascinating discussion of the development of Chinese anthropology and its relation to Western expansion, see Hriskos (n.d.).

36. See ibid., chapter 5, for an overview of the issues discussed in this journal.

37. The Institute of Pacific Relations (IPR) commissioned and helped fund Chen Ta's work as part of a broader, comparative study of migration, population movements, and standards of living throughout the Pacific region.

38. From 1927 to 1930 the Institute of Pacific Relations received the bulk of its funding from the Laura Spelman Rockefeller Memorial and the Social Science Research Council (Condliffe 1930: 666–68), both Rockefeller-funded organizations.

After 1930 the Rockefeller Foundation was the main source of financial support for the Institute of Pacific Relations.

39. Until 1929 these funds were provided by the Laura Spelman Rockefeller Memorial. Thereafter, moneys were made available by the Rockefeller Foundation.

40. Of the three Africans who studied with Malinowski at LSE, only Kenyatta (1938) produced a book-length work during the time period considered in this chapter (prior to World War II), although Matthews published articles on indirect rule (1937), race relations in South Africa (1938), and native policy in South Africa (1932). A significantly shortened version of Fadipe's dissertation was eventually published in 1970 (see Fadipe 1970), while Matthews published his *Social Relations in a Common South African Society* in 1961 (Matthews 1961). Kenyatta (1938) is the subject of a work in progress.

41. Information on the life of Monica Hunter Wilson, in this and the following paragraphs, is based on West (1988).

42. In 1933, J. C. Smuts was leader of the South Africa Party. Together with J. B. M. Hertzog of the National Party, Smuts and his party formed a Coalition Government that played a key role in moving South Africa toward an increasingly racially stratified and segregated society. Smuts was prime minister of South Africa before, during, and immediately after World War II.

43. Godfrey Wilson (1908–44) was the son of the prominent Shakespearean scholar John Dover Wilson (Brown 1973: 187; West 1988: 382).

44. Grace Childs was heavily involved in social work in the Charity Organization Society. Her husband was a prominent national figure in municipal government reform (Maier and Weatherhead 1974: 11). Both social work and municipal government reform were major preoccupations of the philanthropies.

45. The Brookings Institution was formed in 1927 out of an amalgamation of formerly independent organizations: the National Bureau of Economic Research, the Institute of Economics, and the Institute of Government Research. All of these organizations were funded by the Carnegie Corporation (Bulmer and Bulmer 1981: 351). The Brookings Institution also received a major grant from RPH in 1928 (ibid.: 387)

46. Tannenbaum recognizes that a number of railroads in Latin America are government owned, but explains that they have generally been built with foreign loans, and that the revenues are used to repay these loans.

47. Much the same could be said about conditions in Europe and the United States. In Europe, the national rivalries that culminated in World War I, and the unresolved nature of these tensions after the Great War, were particularly important (Hobsbawm 1994). In the United States, the instability precipitated by the massive processes of urbanization, industrialization, immigration, and depression at the end of the nineteenth century were the key factors. In Europe and the United States alike, of course, the crash of 1929, and the Great Depression that followed, created widespread instability.

48. There is, of course, much about the current era that is unprecedented. For

attempts to conceptualize what is novel about the present, see Appadurai (1996); Gupta and Ferguson (1992, 1997); Harvey (1989); Jameson (1981); Ong (1999); Pred and Watts (1992); Vincent (n.d.). For an overview of scholarship that focuses on political developments of the contemporary era, see Nugent and Vincent (n.d.).

49. For a brilliant analysis of the ways in which academic politics have unfolded so as to produce an official history of the discipline during recent decades, see Roseberry (1996).

50. I am indebted to Tom Biolsi for drawing my attention to the significance of the coincidence in publication dates of Fortes and Evans-Pritchard (1940) and Wilson (1941).

References

American Ethnologist. 1992. "Imagining Identities: Nation, Culture, and the Past." *American Ethnologist* (Special Issue) 19(4).

Anderson, Benedict. 1983. *Imagined Communities*. London: Verso.

Appadurai, Arjun. 1996. *Modernity at Large: Cultural Dimensions of Globalization*. Minneapolis: University of Minnesota Press.

Asad, Talal, ed. 1973. *Anthropology and the Colonial Encounter*. Atlantic Heights, NJ: Humanitarian Press.

Bennett, G. 1960. "From Paramountcy to Partnership: J. H. Oldham and Africa." *Africa* 32: 356–60.

Berliner, Howard S. 1985. *A System of Scientific Medicine: Philanthropic Foundations in the Flexner Era*. New York: Tartstock.

Berman, Edward H. 1980. "Educational Colonialism in Africa: The Role of American Foundations, 1910–1945." In Robert F. Arnove, ed., *Philanthropy and Cultural Imperialism: The Foundations at Home and Abroad*, 179–201. Boston: G. K. Hall.

———. 1983. *The Idea of Philanthropy: The Influence of the Carnegie, Ford, and Rockefeller Foundations on American Foreign Policy*. Albany: State University of New York Press.

Bernal, Martin. 1987. *Black Athena. The Afroasiatic Roots of Classical Civilization*. New Brunswick, NJ: Rutgers University Press.

Biolsi, Thomas. 1995. "The Birth of the Reservation: Making the Modern Individual among the Lakota." *American Ethnologist* 22: 28–53.

Brown, Richard. 1973. "Anthropology and Colonial Rule: The Case of Godfrey Wilson and the Rhodes-Livingstone Institute, Northern Rhodesia." In Talal Asad, ed., *Anthropology and the Colonial Encounter*, 173–197. Atlantic Heights, NJ: Humanitarian Press.

Buck, Peter. 1980. *American Science and Modern China, 1876–1936*. Cambridge: Cambridge University Press.

Bulmer, Martin, and Jean Bulmer. 1981. "Philanthropy and Social Science in the 1920s: Beardsley Ruml and the Laura Spelman Rockefeller Memorial, 1922–29." *Minerva* 19(3): 347–407.

Chen, Hansheng. 1931. *Notes on Migration of Nan Min to the Northeast*. Published under the auspices of the China Council of the Institute of Pacific Relations. Shanghai: Comacrib Press.

Chen, Ta. 1939. *Emigrant Communities in South China: A Study of Overseas Migration and Its Influence on Standards of Living and Social Change*. New York: Institute of Pacific Relations.

Chiang, Yung-chen. 1986. "Social Engineering and the Social Sciences in China, 1898–1949." Ph.D. diss., Committee on History and East Asian Languages, Harvard University, Cambridge, MA.

Clifford, James. 1986. "On Ethnographic Allegory." In James Clifford and George E. Marcus, eds., *Writing Culture*, 98–121. Berkeley: University of California Press.

Coben, Stanley. 1976. "Foundation Officials and Fellowships: Innovation in the Patronage of Science." *Minerva* 14: 225–240.

Cohn, Bernard S. 1996. *Colonialism and Its Forms of Knowledge: The British in India*. Princeton: Princeton University Press.

Condliffe, J. D. 1928. *Problems of the Pacific, 1927*. Chicago: University of Chicago Press.

———. 1930. *Problems of the Pacific, 1929*. Chicago: University of Chicago Press.

Cueto, Marcos, ed. 1994. *Missionaries of Science: The Rockefeller Foundation and Latin America*. Bloomington: Indiana University Press.

Dahrendorf, Ralf. 1995. *LSE: A History of the London School of Economics and Political Science, 1895–1995*. Oxford: Oxford University Press.

Diamond, Stanley. 1974. *In Search of the Primitive: A Critique of Civilization*. New Brunswick: E. P. Dutton.

Dirks, Nicholas B. 1992. "From Little King to Landlord: Colonial Discourse and Colonial Rule." In Nicholas B. Dirks, ed., *Colonialism and Culture*, 175–208. Ann Arbor: University of Michigan Press.

Dobson, John M. 1978. *America's Ascent: The United States Becomes a Great Power, 1880–1914*. Dekalb: Northern Illinois University Press.

Fadipe, N. A. 1970. *The Sociology of the Yoruba*. Edited by Francis Ulu Okedijii and Oladejo O. Kediji. Ibedan: Ibadau University Press (revision of the author's dissertation, University of London, 1939).

Fisher, Donald. 1983. "The Role of Philanthropic Foundations in the Reproduction and Production of Hegemony: Rockefeller Foundations and the Social Sciences." *Sociology* 17(2): 206–33.

———. 1986. "The Scientific Appeal of Functionalism: Rockefeller Philanthropy and the Rise of Social Anthropology." *Anthropology Today* 2(1): 5–8.

———. 1993. *Fundamental Development of the Social Sciences: Rockefeller Philanthropy and the United States Social Science Research Council*. Ann Arbor: University of Michigan Press.

Fortes, Meyer, and E. E. Evans-Pritchard, eds. 1940. *African Political Systems*. London: Oxford University Press.

Fosdick, Raymond D. 1962. *Adventure in Giving: The Story of the General Education Board*. New York: Harper and Row.

Foucault, Michel. 1980. *Power/Knowledge*. Edited by Colin Gordon. New York: Pantheon.

————. 1991. "Governmentality." In G. Burchell, C. Gordon, and P. Miller, eds., *The Foucault Effect: Studies in Governmentality*, 165–172. Chicago: University of Chicago Press.

Gamio, Manuel. 1930. *Mexican Immigration to the United States: A Study of Human Migration and Adjustment*. Chicago: University of Chicago Press.

Geiger, Roger L. 1986. *To Advance Knowledge: The Growth of American Research Universities, 1900–1940*. New York: Oxford University Press.

Goody, Jack. 1995. *The Expansive Moment: Anthropology in Britain and Africa, 1918–1970*. Cambridge: Cambridge University Press.

Gunder-Frank, Andre. 1998. *ReOrient: Global Economy in the Asian Age*. Berkeley: University of California Press.

Gupta, Akhil, and James Ferguson. 1992. "Beyond 'Culture': Space, Identity and the Politics of Difference." *Cultural Anthropology* 7(1): 6–23.

————. 1997. *Anthropological Locations: Boundaries and Grounds of a Field Science*. Berkeley: University of California Press.

Hailey, William Malcolm. 1939. *An African Survey: A Study of Problems Arising in Africa South of the Sahara*. Published under the auspices of the Royal Institute of International Affairs. London: Oxford University Press.

Handler, Richard, and Eric Gable. 1997. *The New History in an Old Museum: Creating the Past of Colonial Williamsburg*. Durham: University of North Carolina Press.

Harvey, David. 1989. *The Condition of Postmodernity*. Oxford: Basil Blackwell.

Hayford, Charles W. 1990. *To the People: James Yen and Village China*. New York: Columbia University Press.

Hewa, Soma, and Philo Hove, eds. 1997. "Introduction." In Soma Hewa and Philo Hove, eds., *Philanthropy and Cultural Context: Western Philanthropy in South, East, and Southeast Asia in the Twentieth Century*, 3–17. Lanham, MD: University Press of America.

Ho, Franklin. 1931. *Population Movement to the North Eastern Frontier in China*. China Institute of Pacific Relations. Shanghai: Comacrib Press.

Ho, Franklin, and Hsien Ding Fong. 1929. *Extent and Effects of Industrialization in China*. Industry Series no. 1. Tientsin, China: Nan Kai University Committee on Social and Economic Research.

Hobsbawm, Eric. 1994. *The Age of Extremes: A History of the World, 1914–1991*. New York: Vintage Books.

Hobsbawm, Eric, and Terence Ranger, eds. 1983. *The Invention of Tradition*. Cambridge: Cambridge University Press.

Hriskos, Constantine. n.d. *Insight and Innovation: The Birth of a Critical Social Science in Republican China*. Ms. Files of the Author.

Hunt, Michael H. 1972. "The American Remission of the Boxer Indemnity: A Reappraisal." *Journal of Asian Studies* 31: 539–60.

ISR (Institute of Social Research). 1933. *The Institute of Social Research: A Summary of Its Work, 1926–1932*. Peiping, China: Institute of Social Research.

Israel, Jerry. 1971. *Progressivism and the Open Door: America and China, 1905–1921.* Pittsburgh: University of Pittsburgh Press.

Jameson, Frederic. 1981. "Postmodernism, or the Cultural Logic of Late Capitalism." *New Left Review* 46: 53–92.

Kenyatta, Jomo. 1938. *Facing Mount Kenya.* London: Secker and Warburg.

King-Hall, Stephen. 1937. *Chatham House: A Brief Account of the Origins, Purposes, and Methods of the Royal Institute of International Affairs.* London: Oxford University Press.

Kuklick, Henrika. 1991. *The Savage Within: The Social History of British Anthropology, 1885–1945.* Cambridge: Cambridge University Press.

LaFeber, Walter. 1963. *The New Empire: An Interpretation of American Expansion, 1860–1898.* Ithaca: Cornell University Press.

Lattimore, Owen. 1932. *Manchuria: Cradle of Conflict.* New York: Macmillan.

Lugard, Frederick John Dealty. 1965 [1922]. *The Dual Mandate in British Tropical Africa.* London: F. Cass.

MaCartney, Carlile Aylmer. 1934. *National States and National Minorities.* Issued under the Auspices of the Royal Institute of International Affairs. London: Oxford University Press.

Maier, Joseph, and Richard W. Weatherhead. 1974. *Frank Tannenbaum: A Biographical Essay.* New York: University Seminars, Columbia University.

Mallon, Florencia. 1995. *Peasant and Nation: The Making of Postcolonial Mexico and Peru.* Berkeley: University of California Press.

Mandel, Ernest. 1975. *Late Capitalism.* London: New Left Books.

Matthews, Zacheria Keodireloug. 1932. "The Native Policy of the Union 1910–1932." *Round Table:* 365–72.

———. 1937. "An African View of Indirect Rule." *African Affairs: Journal of the Royal African Society* 36: 433–37.

———. 1938. "The Future of Race Relations in South Africa." *Race Relations Journal* (Johannesburg) 8(2).

———. 1961. *Social Relations in a Common South African Society.* Johannesburg: Anglo American Corp. of South Africa.

McBride, George McCutchen. 1923. *The Land System of Mexico.* American Geographic Society Research Series no. 12. New York: American Geographic Society.

———. 1936. *Chile: Land and Society.* Port Washington, NY: Kennikat Press.

McCormick, Thomas J. 1967. *China Market: America's Quest for Informal Empire, 1893–1901.* Chicago: Quadrangle Books.

Myers, Ramon H., and Mark R. Peattie. 1984. *The Japanese Colonial Empire, 1895–1945.* Princeton: Princeton University Press.

Ninkovich, Frank. 1984. "The Rockefeller Foundation, China, and Social Change." *Journal of American History* 70(4): 799–820.

Nugent, David, and Joan Vincent, eds. (Forthcoming.) *A Companion to the Anthropology of Politics.* Oxford: Blackwell.

Ong, Aihwa. 1999. *Flexible Citizenship: The Cultural Logics of Transnationality.* Durham, NC: Duke University Press.

Peattie, Mark R. 1984. "Introduction." In Myers and Peattie 1984, 3–58.

Pels, Peter. 1997. "The Anthropology of Colonialism: Culture, History, and the Emergence of Western Governmentality." *Annual Review of Anthropology* 26: 163–83.

Polanyi, Karl. 1944. *The Great Transformation*. Boston: Beacon.

Pred, Allan, and Michael John Watts. 1992. *Reworking Modernity: Capitalisms and Symbolic Discontent*. New Brunswick, NJ: Rutgers University Press.

Price, David. 1998. "Cold War Anthropology: Collaborators and Victims of the National Security State." *Identities* 4(3–4): 389–430.

Price, Richard. 1983. *First Time: The Historical Vision of an Afro-American People*. Baltimore: Johns Hopkins University Press.

Rappaport, Joanne. 1990. *The Politics of Memory: Native Historical Interpretation in the Colombian Andes*. Cambridge: Cambridge University Press.

Richards, Audrey L. 1939. *Land, Labor, and Diet in Northern Rhodesia: An Economic Study of the Bemba Tribe*. London: Published for the International Institute of African Languages and Cultures by the Oxford University Press.

Roseberry, William. 1996. "The Unbearable Lightness of Anthropology." *Radical History Review* 65: 2–25.

Smith, E. W. 1934. "The Story of the Institute: The First Seven Years." *Africa* 7: 1–27.

Social Science Research Council. 1934. *The Social Science Research Council: Decennial Report, 1923–1933*. New York: Social Science Research Council.

Spence, Jonathan D. 1990. *The Search for Modern China*. New York: W. W. Norton.

Stocking, George W. Jr. 1985. "Philanthropoids and Vanishing Cultures: Rockefeller Funding and the End of the Museum Era in Anglo-American Anthropology." In George W. Stocking Jr., ed., *Objects and Others: Essays on Museums and Material Culture*, 112–45. Madison: University of Wisconsin Press.

———. 1995. *After Tyler: British Social Anthropology, 1888–1951*. Madison: University of Wisconsin Press.

Sullivan, Rodney J., and Reynaldo C. Ileto. 1997. "Americanism and the Politics of Health in the Philippines, 1902–1913." In Soma Hewa and Philo Hove, eds., *Philanthropy and Cultural Context: Western Philanthropy in South, East, and Southeast Asia in the Twentieth Century*, 36–64. Lanham, MD: University Press of America.

Tannenbaum, Frank. 1929. *The Mexican Agrarian Revolution*. New York: Brookings Institution.

———. 1933. *Some Latin American Research Problems: Memorandum for the Director of the Program in International Relations of the Social Science Research Council*. Confidential [Washington, D.C.?].

———. 1934. *Whither Latin America? An Introduction to Its Economic and Social Problems*. New York: Thomas Y. Crowell.

————. 1943. "Agrarismo, Indianismo, y Nacionalismo." *Hispanic American Historical Review* 23(3): 394–423.

Thomas, John. 1974. *The Institute of Pacific Relations: Asian Scholars and American Politics*. Seattle: University Washington Press.

Toynbee, Arnold J. 1927. *Survey of International Affairs, 1920–1923*. Published under the auspices of the Royal Institute of International Affairs. Oxford: Oxford University Press.

————. 1928. *Survey of International Affairs, 1924*. Published under the auspices of the Royal Institute of International Affairs. Oxford: Oxford University Press.

————. 1933. *Survey of International Affairs, 1993*. Published under the auspices of the Royal Institute of International Affairs. Oxford: Oxford University Press.

Trescott, Paul B. 1997. "American Philanthropy and the Development of Academic Economics in China before 1949." In Hewa and Hove 1997, 159–75.

Vincent, Joan. 1990. *Anthropology and Politics: Visions, Traditions, and Trends*. Tucson: University of Arizona Press.

————. Forthcoming. "Introduction." In Joan Vincent, ed., *The Anthropology of Politics: Ethnography, Theory and Critique*. Oxford: Blackwell.

Wallerstein, Immanuel. 1997. "The Unintended Consequences of Cold War Area Studies." In Noam Chomsky et al., eds., *The Cold War and the University*, 195–231. New York: New Press.

Wang, Y. C. 1966. *Chinese Intellectuals and the West, 1872–1949*. Chapel Hill: University of North Carolina Press.

West, Martin E. 1988. "Monica Hunter Wilson." In U. Gacs et al., eds. *Women Anthropologists: A Biographical Dictionary*. New York: Greenwood Press.

Williams, Raymond. 1973. *The Country and the City*. New York: Oxford University Press.

Wilson, Godfrey. 1941. *An Essay on the Economics of Detribalization in Northern Rhodesia*. Livingstone, Northern Rhodesia: Rhodes-Livingstone Institute.

Wilson, Monica Hunter. 1936. *Reaction to Conquest: Effects of Contact with Europeans on the Pondo of South Africa*. London: Published for the International Institute of African Languages and Cultures by the Oxford University Press.

————. 1981. *Freedom for My People: The Autobiography of Z. K. Matthews, Southern Africa, 1901 to 1968*. London: R. Collings.

Yang, Fang, and Queu Weitian. 1981. "Sociologist Chen Ta." *Chinese Sociology and Anthropology* 13(3): 59–74.

Understanding Capitalism—
Historically, Structurally, Spatially

An ethnographic sensibility that is attentive to the relationship between "the global" and "the local" needs to address two related problems: (1) an historical analysis that attempts to understand the development of capitalism in time and space; and (2) an ethnographic conceptualization that attempts to delineate appropriate "local" constellations for analysis at particular moments and structural configurations of a historicized capitalism. This essay concentrates on the first problem and briefly considers work that has attempted to understand capitalism historically, structurally, and spatially.

My aim here is to explore three literatures that allow us to pose more specific historical and structural problems with regard to accumulation processes: (1) the literature on "long waves" of capitalist development, originated by Kondratieff (1979 [1926]) and developed by a number of authors, including Gordon (1980), Mandel (1978), Wallerstein (1974, 1980, 1989), and Wolf (1982); (2) the literature of the "regulation" school in France on "regimes of accumulation" (Aglietta 1979; Boyer 1990; Lipietz 1987), and of a group of radical political economists in the United States on "social structures of accumulation" (Bowles, Gordon, and Weisskopf 1983, 1986, 1990; Gordon 1980; Gordon, Edwards, and Reich 1982); and (3) the work of geographers like David Harvey (1982, 1989) and Michael Watts (1992) on the construction of space. These literatures, separately or in combination, can not be mechanically appropriated and applied to ethnographic analysis. For one thing, most deal with accumulation processes, or aspects of those processes, derived from analysis of the centers of capital accumulation. I discuss them here because I think they allow us to approach a less static and essentialized, and a more historical and structured, understanding of capitalism; and because they make possible the posing of more specific problems concerning the relation of particular processes of capital accumulation with the constitution of particular social fields.

The specific applications of most of the literature I am discussing have been economic, but this neither makes them irrelevant for cultural analysis nor makes cultural analysis irrelevant for the understanding of long waves or social structures of accumulation. In my view, the authors I consider here are creating a framework that makes possible new linkages of political, economic, and cultural questions, that pose new, specific questions for ethnographic and cultural analysis and that lead to debates that may be more interesting and substantive than the ones that emerge from broad oppositions between capitalism and noncapitalism. The agendas of the economists and geographers may not be anthropological, but this does not mean that their work cannot be used as we pursue our own agendas.

Capitalism first needs to be understood historically, as a dynamic economic and social system that has been structured and shaped differently at particular moments in its development. This dynamism can be seen at various levels. From the beginning of the industrial revolution in late-eighteenth-century England, the most dynamic industries at particular moments have created particular types of firm, particular sources of supply for raw material and machinery, particular configurations of workplace and community. As the most dynamic industrial centers and activities have changed, so have the types of firm, sources of supply, and configurations of workplace and community. With shifts in centers and activities, particular regions have been caught up in circuits of commodity circulation or capital investment, only to become marginal or peripheral at another moment as other regions or other commodities become central. Thus the capitalist world has been structured in specific ways at particular times, and as part of periodic restructurings, there has also been a periodic making and remaking of space, on global, regional, local, and personal scales.

At any particular moment or period, the structural and spatial organization constitutes a hierarchy, with one or a few powerful centers and a range of peripheries, which may be differently defined depending on whether we are referring to sources of labor, of raw material, of food, of machinery and tools, to market for finished products, or to the political organizations and communities (states, empires, and so forth) in, through, and across which the hierarchies are instituted. A central task in any attempt to understand capitalism historically, structurally, and spatially is to outline and analyze specific hierarchies and relations of core and periphery.

This does *not* mean, however, that the world-systems model as originally outlined by Wallerstein in the 1970s is adequate for the analysis of such hierarchies. The most important problems with the early formulation are well known: (a) the spatial hierarchy of core, semiperiphery, and periphery, once established, was relatively static. Particular regions or states might move from core to semiperiphery or vice versa, but the hierarchy itself was stable across centuries; (b) dynamics within the system as a whole, or within particular sections or regions of the system, were understood in terms of the functional requirements of the system, and the structured hierarchy of core, semiperiphery, and periphery. The first dimension tended, especially among those who mechanically applied the early formulations, to static and unhistorical conceptions of capitalism. Given such an approach, one can understand Marcus and Fisher's remarkable claim (1986) that capitalism could be treated as a backdrop or context, a known system of structures and relationships, "there so to speak to be invoked," against which all of the more creative actions of human subjects could be arrayed. The second dimension was straightforwardly functionalist.

In contrast, the historical and structural model I am suggesting is one that sees dramatically shifting relations and hierarchies of core and periphery at particular moments in capitalist history. For example, the dominance of textiles during the first industrial revolution in late-eighteenth- and early-nineteenth-century England involved a particular mapping of sources of supply and of labor, as well as of markets. The dominance of railroads and steel from the mid–nineteenth century involved a quite different mapping of sources and markets. In each case, we can discern emerging core and peripheral areas with little difficulty. But the structure and dynamics of capitalism as a global system were significantly different during each period. Moreover, the dynamics in any sector or region within the system could not be understood solely in terms of core/periphery relations, despite the fact that the placement of a sector or region within emerging spatial hierarchies is an essential part of our understanding of such dynamics. Instead, the placement of accumulation processes within specific spaces involves particular sets of relationships and struggles—at both the emerging "core" and the emerging "periphery": the proliferation of cottages of outworkers on the outskirts of villages and towns in northern England; the development of mines and mills, and the making of particular working classes with particular community traditions and values; the spread of cotton plantations across the U.S. South and the specific relations between planters, slaves, and yeoman; and so on.

In each case, a specific set of economic and social relations is created within an already existing set of economic, social, and political relations and cultural understandings. While the new relations are part of wider processes of capital accumulation, they are introduced in local spaces with earlier relations, which may be "noncapitalist" or may represent the sedimentation of earlier periods of capital accumulation. In either case, they will carry their own configurations of factory and field or town, community and kin, class and ethnic or racial relation, church and chapel, and polity and politics in, through, and against which the new relations will be implanted, will do their transformative work, or encounter insurmountable obstacles and resistances.

While I have referred to the creation of new relations and accumulation processes and their implantation in settings characterized by earlier relations and accumulation processes, it needs to be remembered that in each case the *agents* of implantation are human—a merchant or group of merchants; a corporation, plantation, or consortium; a state marketing board, a village of smallholders or knitters; a loose assemblage of former slaves who have become "squatters," moving back and forth between plantation lands and bush; and so on. The institutions, powers, agencies, resources, and resistances will always necessarily be locally configured (again, at both "core" and "peripheral" locations), and this is why any attempt to understand such dynamics solely or primarily in terms of the "system" or the relationship of "periphery" to "core" will always fail.

Thus, ethnography, understood here as the attempt to understand a local configuration of relationships and understandings, powers and resistances, is necessary to any understanding of the making of the modern world. Because local relations are also embedded within accumulation processes of wider scope, however, the definition of significant local actors, relations, and understandings must make those wider processes and relations *internal* to their conception of the local. For such understandings, a flexible concept of the social field—one that stresses context, that traces networks, and that defines its central terms and units (including the "local" and the "global") as relations rather than essences—is necessary.

In order to include central features and relations of wider accumulation processes within one's conception of a social field, it is not necessary to write a history or political economy of those wider processes. In order to analyze the consequences of a copper mine for the reconfiguration of social and cultural relations in a region of, say, Panama or Papua New Guinea (Gjording 1991; Polier 1996), it is not necessary to write a detailed history of world capitalism, or of copper mining, or of long-term price series or of the lending policies of the World Bank. Because certain aspects of each of these figure crucially within the local social field and constitute central dimensions of the field of power, however, the attempt to make them internal to one's conception of the social field requires that these dimensions of wider accumulation processes be engaged and understood analytically. Thus, a major task of any ethnographic project that attempts to make "external" powers and forces "internal" to the social field involves the attempt to place the local in *specific* relation to *specific* accumulation processes.

I turn now to literatures on temporal, structural, and spatial dimensions of capitalism for suggestive guides to more particular analyses.

Long Waves of Capitalist Development

There are a wide range of temporalities and ways of organizing time in the long history of capitalism and the much longer history of a global economy that preceded it. One of the most easily available and widely used, both by Marxists and non-Marxists, is an evolutionary or epochal conception of capitalism that distinguishes it as a phase or stage in economic and social history. Whether defined (in the Wallersteinian sense) as a global system based on exchange for profit or (in the Marxian sense) as a mode of production based on free wage labor, "capitalism" can be fit within a broad historical canvas and distinguished from other ("earlier," "later") modes of economic and social organization. Given the characteristics used as defining features, one can then suggest certain regular, even constant, features of the epoch. From both Weberian and Marxian perspectives, this kind of analysis has critical insights, and despite the current disfavor into which "master-narratives" have fallen, these epochal perspectives and analyses remain *necessary* for any critical understanding of the modern world.

At the same time, the *epochal* development of capitalism has always emerged in *historical* times and places, and an evolutionary temporality alone is insufficient for understanding most of the specific relationships and processes associated with capitalist modernity.

At the level of the organization of work, for example, the factory, once thought to be the organizational form par excellence of capitalism, turns out to have been one of a range of forms of organizing work through capitalist social relations. A history organized around the factory form, necessary for any specific understanding of capitalist relations, would look rather different in, say, England, France, Italy, the United States, Mexico, or Brazil.

At the level of specific commodities in a world of commodities, one discerns quite different temporalities when organizing an analysis in terms of the production, exchange, and consumption of sugar, coffee, cotton, cloth, gold, steel, automobiles, or petroleum. Each has involved its own specific periods and patterns of growth and decline; each has engendered a distinct hierarchical organization of national and global spaces.

At the level of economic fluctuations, which Marx saw as central to the process of capitalist organization, reorganization, and accumulation, one can easily discern a series of cycles of boom and bust, some quite global in scope, others restricted to particular states and regions, or to particular commodities or groups of commodities. These cycles impose a complex set of temporalities upon particular social fields.

To these need to be added the individual times and cycles of firms; the turnover time for particular commodities at particular levels of technification at particular points, business cycles; and so on. At a spatial level, particular regions and states receive and organize these distinct forms of organization, commodities, and cycles in locally specific ways with particular temporalities along the lines and for the reasons suggested above.

It is in terms of this complex of epochal and historical temporalities that I wish to consider the theory of "long waves" of capitalist development as suggested by the Russian economist N. D. Kondratieff in the 1920s. It represents yet another way of organizing capitalist time, one that complements and needs to be placed in the context of other ways of organizing capitalist time, such as those suggested above. In a provocative analysis, Kondratieff (1979 [1926]) suggested that in addition to short term (three- to five-year) economic cycles of boom and bust or growth and recession, capitalist history has also been characterized by "long waves" of growth and decline, encompassing periods of approximately fifty years. During each, there is an early period of relatively rapid growth and capital accumulation, lasting roughly twenty-five years, followed by another period of about twenty-five years characterized by lower rates of growth and increasingly severe crises. Kondratieff identified three such waves beginning in the late eighteenth century: one from the 1780s to about 1850; a second from about 1850 to the mid-1890s; and a third, which he saw as having entered a period of decline at the time he was writing (1926), that began in the mid-1890s.

Moreover, each of the waves could be divided into growth (or "accelerated accumulation") and decline (or "gradually decelerating accumulation" [Mandel 1978: 121]) phases, so that the first wave had a growth phase from the 1780s to 1810–17, and a decline phase from 1810–17 to 1844–51; the second wave had a growth phase from 1844–51 to the 1870s, and a decline phase from the 1870s to the 1890s; and the third wave had a growth phase from the 1890s to 1914–20, and a decline that Kondratieff thought had begun in the 1914–20 period.

Kondratieff supported his argument with economic statistics on wages, prices, interest rates, trade, and production of selected items. He also attempted to anticipate and respond to potential criticisms from other economists about the role of technological change, the opening up of new lands, the timing of wars and revolutions, and the like. Though he attempted to de-emphasize the importance of these social, political, and historical phenomena as determining economic fluctuations, their potential relation to the long waves is of exceeding interest.

Ernest Mandel (ibid.: 108–46), writing at the beginning of the decline phase of yet another long wave (from 1940), appropriated Kondratieff's analysis, extended it into the 1970s (by extending the decline phase of the third wave through the Great Depression of the 1930s and postulating a fourth wave beginning in 1940 and covering the postwar boom until the onset of probable long-term decline in 1966), and tied each of the waves to particular technological complexes and innovations. Thus the growth phase of the first long wave was based on the "handicraft-made or machine-made steam engine"; the growth phase of the second by "the machine-made steam engine"; the growth phase of the third by "the generalized application of electric and combustion engines"; and the growth phase of the fourth by "the generalized control of machines by means of electronic apparatuses" and nuclear energy (ibid.: 120–21).

On the face of it, this periodization is both schematic and mechanical, and several analyses that do little more than place particular phenomena within a long wave or an "A" (expansion) or "B" (decline) phase of such waves fully realize the model's mechanistic potential. For this particular organization of capitalist time to be useful, it needs to be placed in the context of other temporalities. One such contextual direction, for example, would take us back to the epochal analysis of capitalism, and Kondratieff's starting point in the late eighteenth century is implicitly based on such an analysis. Here we might place the long waves of capitalist development within a wider temporal context of the emergence of a global economy dominated by Europe. In *Europe and the People without History*, for example, Wolf (1982) found Kondratieff's analysis of long waves helpful for his understanding and analysis of capitalism proper, but he situated capitalism proper within a longer history of European mercantile expansion, which was in turn situated within an even longer history of "global" exchange in which Europe had played a peripheral role.

Moving toward some of the other ways of organizing capitalist temporality, we find a much more complex relationship to long waves. At the level of commodities, for example, because the boom period of particular commodities may be intimately linked with a specific wave, the fit between the temporality of that commodity and a part of the history of long waves will be quite close. For other commodities, the fit is problematic, but the history of expansion and of economic cycles can be placed within the waves in interesting ways. In no case, however, is there a neat correspondence between the various types and levels of temporality, nor can one level or type be reduced to another. Kondratieff's long waves remain one among many ways of organizing and understanding capitalist history.

It is an especially interesting one, however, because it moves significantly beyond the epochal understanding of capitalism while maintaining a vision of capitalism as a global, structured, dynamic set of relations and powers. While one would not want to simply and mechanically relate particular phenomena to a position within one of Kondratieff's phases or waves, the postulation of long waves allows us to pose more specific relational questions.

Kondratieff's model is also interesting because it has served as the starting point for a series of attempts by economists and social scientists to suggest new ways of thinking about the social, political, and spatial structuring of capitalist life, and it is to such attempts that I now turn.

Regimes and Social Structures of Accumulation

Just as one may discern a variety of capitalist temporalities, it is also important to recognize a range of capitalist structures. There is, first, the structure of a global economy, understood in terms of a hierarchy of core and periphery, of capitalist and noncapitalist sectors, of capital, commodity, and labor markets, of regulatory mechanisms and agencies, banks and financial organizations, tariff barriers and immigration restrictions. There is the structure of particular state economies, also in terms of core and peripheral sectors, capital, commodity, and labor markets, state policies and regulations, investment programs, labor laws, and so on. One also has to consider the structure of regions and cities along similar lines, as well as the structure of firms and of families. Any one of these dimensions is also structured in specific and complex ways.

As with temporality, we can see these various structural levels and dimensions as related but semiautonomous. I am interested in pursuing here two groups of structural analyses that (a) recognize the semiautonomy but suggest the formation of a reasonably coherent structural or institutional complex that organizes accumulation in particular states for specific periods of time, and (b) link their notions of institutional complexes to the analysis of long waves.

During the 1970s, two separate groups of economists in France and the United States entered into critical dialogue with Marxian analyses of capitalist accumulation in an attempt to understand the long prosperity of post–World War II capitalism and the increasingly discernible crisis that postwar capitalism confronted. On the one hand, Marx's analysis of the dynamics and contradictions of capital accumulation provided necessary guides to any analysis of capitalist accumulation and the generation of crises. On the other, understanding of an emerging crisis and of potential routes beyond it required an examination of the *specific* characteristics and contradictions of particular processes of capital accumulation and collapse. In their attempt to grasp the specificity of postwar capitalism and its emerging crisis in the 1970s, they continued to base themselves in (Marxian and other) analyses of economic relations and processes, but they also began to examine a series of institutional questions and relationships — the social, political, and cultural relations and institutions in and through which processes of capitalist accumulation occur.

Both groups began to see and say that capitalist accumulation processes are instituted and organized through particular social and political structures and that these social and political structures have not been uniform or constant throughout the entire period of capitalist history. Instead, they suggested, one can discern certain social and political structures of accumulation that are characteristic of particular periods of capitalist history. It was but a small step to link this notion with the model of long waves and claim that each wave has been characterized by a particular social and political structure of accumulation.

Because the theory of long waves is at basis a theory of crises, these theorists went on to suggest that the crises were linked to the formation and collapse of specific structures through which accumulation is organized and instituted. If, then, a particular social structure of accumulation organizes the economy during a particular long wave, making possible the high rates of growth during an "A" phase, the onset of lower rates during a "B" phase signals not simply a series of economic imbalances but a crisis in the social and political structures that have organized accumulation for a number of decades. During the "B" (decline) phase, new structural forms and institutions begin to emerge, forms that resolve some of the problems or contradictions that had emerged during the previous wave. The new structures and institutions make possible a new mode of organizing accumulation processes, which then dominates or characterizes the "A" (ascent) phase of a new long wave and structures or regulates accumulation for a long, relatively stable period. The onset of a long period of declining rates of growth and profit (the "B" phase) signals a crisis for a particular model of accumulation but also for the social, political, and cultural forms through which it was instituted.

Despite important theoretical and conceptual disagreements and differences within each group, each is small and distinctive enough to constitute something of a "school," the French identified as the "regulation school" (Aglietta 1979; Boyer 1990; Lipietz 1987; for critiques see Amsden 1990; Brenner and Glick 1991; Gordon 1988) and the Americans identified with the concept of Social Structures of Accumulation (SSA, for short) (Bowles, Gordon, and Weisskopf 1983, 1986, 1990; Gordon 1980; Gordon, Edwards, and Reich 1982).

Both formulations offer promise for the analysis of historically specific capitalisms in time and space. That is, on one hand, we can specify particular structural or institutional configurations tied, historically, to long waves of capitalist development—configurations that characterized and *organized* accumulation during a given period. On the other hand, within any wave, we might examine a series of state-specific regimes or social structures of accumulation, which share certain basic features with other state-specific regimes within an international economy during a period of capitalist history, but which will also have quite distinctive features based, in part, on the features postulated in the theories themselves (specific configuration of class relations and struggle, of markets, credit, and capital, a particular organization of space, and so on). In practice, however, only part of this promise has been realized, as both the regulationists and the theorists of social structures of accumulation have paid more attention to differentiation over time. Though both groups have paid attention to (particularly U.S.) labor history, their most important efforts at economic analysis have concentrated on the post–World War II economic boom and the crisis that ensued in the 1970s.

Here we find the regulationists' postulation and analysis of "Fordism" as the regime of accumulation that organized the postwar boom, or the "A" phase of the most recent long wave, and of "flexible accumulation" as an emerging regime of accumulation in response to Fordism's crisis. These terms and concepts have become quite familiar to anthropologists, thanks especially to David Harvey's important use and extension of them in *The Condition of Postmodernity* (1989). Harvey's analysis, in particular, is quite suggestive, and I have found certain features of it helpful (Roseberry 1996).

Some skeptical observations are necessary, however. First, it is worth noting that Gordon and his associates avoided the model of Fordism, despite the fact that they concentrated almost exclusively on the purported home of Fordism, the United States. They opted instead for an analysis of the "postwar corporate system," composed of a complex of "flying buttresses" having to do with particular structures of domination including U.S. hegemony of the international economy, a management/labor pact that produced a quiescent labor force, and the state management of domestic conflicts (Bowles, Gordon, and Weisskopf 1983: ch. 4). Though some of these elements figure in the definition of Fordism (especially the management/labor pact), and all entered into crisis in the late 1960s and 1970s, flexible accumulation is a response to only part of the structural complex (or only one or two of the buttresses), and Gordon was skeptical about the concept of "flexible accumulation" to characterize a new social structure of accumulation (1988).

Even if we could agree on a label and model to characterize the postwar accumulation regime, however, it would then need to be fit into an analysis that paid attention to differentiation among states and across space. Neither "Fordism" nor "flexible accumulation" can be used as a kind of mantra that can be repeated while we pretend that we have done all the necessary political economic analysis. As models, "Fordism," "flexible accumulation," and "the postwar corporate system" are at best starting points, suggestions of structural complexes that organize a series of economic and political processes which, in turn, might undercut the structural complexes themselves.

Both groups of theorists have devoted their energies to exploring the economic implications of their models, which is understandable given their disciplinary affiliations and loyalties. To an extent, they have also treated aspects of the formation of social and political structural complexes as unproblematic; in practice, they become long-wave-specific institutional complexes through which a particular period of accumulation is organized. For social scientists and historians who take the formation of such complexes as a central problem, and who are interested in the formation and interaction of different complexes in space, however, the two groups of economists have suggested a framework that opens up a whole range of interesting questions. These include:

1. the extension of the analysis of social structures of accumulation beyond the analysis of the post–World War II economy toward an examination of structures and institutions that organized accumulation during previous long waves;
2. the extension of the analysis of such structures during the post–World War II period to states and regions beyond the United States and Western Europe (for which labels like "Fordist" and "flexible" will be inappropriate); and
3. the move toward more political, sociological, and cultural analyses of social structures of accumulation, including the conflict-laden, problematic, and contingent processes of their formation and institution, their contradictory effects in unevenly developing spaces, and the conflict-laden periods and processes of crisis and dissolution.

Each of these extensions is necessary if we are to avoid the dangers of mechanical and functionalist application and abuse to which structural analysis is subject. The response to such potential abuse is not to replace an abstract notion of "structure" with an equally abstract notion of "agency," but to make our understandings of structure as historically and politically specific as possible and to treat the formation and dissolution of structures as contradictory, conflict-laden, and contingent processes. The theorists of social structures of accumulation have suggested a framework that creates historical and political specificity; the examination of their processes of formation and dissolution requires anthropological and historical analysis. Such analysis requires that the structures be placed in social space, a problem to which I now turn.

Capitalist Spaces

In recent years, social scientists have been discovering the importance of space and "spatiality," and in the rush to "theorize" this discovery, they have said many foolish things. My aim here is to follow Harvey in his linkage of spatial organization with both the history of long waves and the emergence of structural complexes that characterize such waves. It needs to be noted, first, that just as capitalism produces different temporalities and structurings, it also produces different *spatialities*. First, there is the construction of global space in the making of a world economy differentiated sectorally and hierarchically, partially captured by notions of a "world-system." Second, there is the emergence of state or national economies, each with a social structure of accumulation that is connected with other social structures of accumulation in other states in a global economy and that therefore shares certain features with other social structures of accumulation, but that also represents a historically specific—and therefore unique—configuration of forces, relations, and institutions. Third, part of a state-specific social structure of accumulation is a particular organization of space, an organized hierarchy of regions, cities and towns, states and districts, urban and rural, core and periphery, industrial and agricultural, plantation and peasant, Latino and indigenous zones and sectors, representing a concentration of local history and capitalist reorganization. Fourth, within any particular "locality" (region, city, town, village) is an organized hierarchy, again of core and periphery, laden and mestizo, plantation and peasant, industry and neighborhood, silk-stocking district and slum, and so on.

Cross-cutting these spaces, and making impossible any conception of them as nesting boxes or levels of integration, there are spaces of movement—the daily space defined by individuals at home, work, school, neighborhood, shop, church, and so forth; the more complex and dispersed spaces defined by households, which may move across each of the levels indicated above; the spaces defined by a particular commodity, such as cotton, coffee, or sugar, including sources of supply, sites of processing, lines of shipment, sites of bulking, distribution, and consumption; the spaces of particular corporations, along lines at once similar to and different from those of commodities; the spaces of finance capital; and so on. Taking any of these cross-cutting spaces, we might well conclude that we are witnessing a form of "deterritorialization," but I think it is more useful to engage in a complex mapping of local, regional, ethnic, national, and global spaces in relation to an equally complex mapping of cross-cutting spaces and flows.

In constructing such maps, two considerations need to guide us. First, there is no singular structuring principle that makes each of the spaces a variation on a basic theme, or that makes possible a two-dimensional map distinguished by different colors for particular (national, regional, local) spaces. Each of the ways of marking space is semiautonomous because it engages other social, political, and cultural ways of constructing spaces. Take the spaces created by a particular commodity, for instance. If we consider coffee and examine the range of spaces suggested above (zones of supply, sites of processing, lines of shipment, and so forth), each involves a power-laden interaction between the forces and relations associated with the formation of, say, a zone of supply, and pre-existing, contemporaneous, potentially competing "spaces," or forces and relations associated with the making of other products, or of ethnic formations, or regional political blocs, and so on. For any of the levels or flows we might select, we find similar forms of insertion or interaction, making for a multiplicity of structuring or spatializing principles.

Nonetheless, despite semiautonomy and in the midst of multiplicity, we can discern structure. Here I wish to consider the importance of the two instituting principles already discussed in this essay—the long waves of capital accumulation, and the configuration of social structures of accumulation. For both, David Harvey's work (for example, 1982, 1989) has been enormously influential and helpful. Let us begin with long waves, and the possibility of designating each wave (*in part*, of course) in terms of particular technological-material configurations (textiles and cotton in the first wave, railroads and steel in the second, and so forth). For each, maps of increasing complexity can be drawn that designate sources of supply, lines of shipment, sites of fabrication, and so on. Consider, for example, the map Eric Wolf offers of centers of manufacture and zones of supply for cotton textiles in the industrial revolution in *Europe* (1982: 279). It immediately suggests a more interesting way of conceptualizing a global economy than a simple division into "core" and "peripheral" zones. It represents, of course, a first approximation of spatial divisions for a single long wave. For any of the zones indicated on the map, we want to ask questions about the structuring and restructuring of regional and local spaces in both the zones of supply and the centers of manufacture. As we ask such questions, we engage the prior, contemporaneous, and competing forces and relations alluded to above. But a consideration of the way in which a particular long wave of capital accumulation involved a new spatial organization of the global economy allows us to pose these questions in a more interesting, serious way. Should we map the world of railroads and steel during the second long wave, it would look rather different, and more complex. It would have to be laid over the map of the previous long wave, and the local spaces indicated would include some that were "filled in" on the map of the earlier long wave as well as spaces that were previously "blank." In each case, the kinds of insertions and interactions involve processes that are structured by a particular moment in capital accumulation, *and* by a specific local configuration of forces and relations, *some* of which may be the results of an earlier interaction during a previous long wave.

To consider specific spatial processes during long waves of capital accumulation, it is useful to return to the concept of social structures of accumulation. One of the central claims both in the work of Gordon and his colleagues and of Harvey concerns the importance of spatial organization and reorganization in the constitution of particular regimes or social structures of accumulation. In one sense, of course, the very concept of a social structure of accumulation draws our attention to space in that we are considering the accumulation of capital in particular states. If "Fordism" is to have any meaning, it needs to be applied to specific capital/labor pacts, and specific state structures, legal instruments, and regulating mechanisms in particular countries. One of the weaknesses of the literature on "flexible accumulation" thus far is that it does not necessarily draw our attention to specific social structures of accumulation. Indeed, the basic thrust of much of this literature is that states matter much less, that transnational flows are so important that the economy is now, for the first time, truly global. While it is true that states matter less in that the social structures of accumulation associated with Fordism have been undermined, this does not mean that states do not matter at all. Flexible accumulation, as a concept, works in contrast to Fordism, but much analytical work remains to be done on the constitution of new spatially configured social structures of accumulation, or new structures of domination, which may follow regional (or "ethnic" or "national") lines. The fact that they may not follow the boundaries of old states makes the analytical task more difficult and interesting.

But the importance of particular states is not the only way in which "space" matters in social structures of accumulation. Equally important is the fact that the very constitution of a social structure of accumulation involves spatial organization—the emergence of core and peripheral zones within states and regions, the making of cities, towns, and hinterlands, the centralization of certain production processes in regions, the concentration of finance and services in cities, the building of roads and railroads, the construction of ports and transportation nodes, or of factories, warehouses, distribution facilities, and so on. Harvey (1982) considers this fixing of capital in space the making of a "social infrastructure." The point to be made here is that one of the characteristics of a given social structure of accumulation (which, it needs to be remembered, organizes accumulation during a particular long wave) is a specific spatial organization of such social infrastructure—an organization that has a certain stability over time. But one of the things that happens over time is that the spatially organized social infrastructure (plants, roads, railroads, ports, cities) wears out, and this becomes *one* element in the onset of crisis, or of a "B" phase of a long wave. *One* resolution of crisis can be what Harvey calls the "spatial fix," understood globally as the expansion of capital to new regions, or within states as the move to new regions, within regions and cities as the destruction and reconstruction of social infrastructure. Such spatial fixes always involve spatial reorganization—the move from central city to suburban mall, from the northeastern United States to the southwestern rim, from New York to Los Angeles—and this reorganization in turn can become part of the relatively stable social infrastructure of a new social structure of accumulation.

The construction, maintenance, abandonment, destruction, and reconstruction of social infrastructure, seen as an integral part of the making of long-wave specific social structures of accumulation, provides a mechanism through which various spatialities become intertwined—even as they retain a *semi*autonomy. Michael Watts has expressed this intimate interconnection as follows:

> Within the confines of a unified world market and a concomitant international division of labor, there are both national and local capitalisms, a spatial sensitivity that takes us back to Trotsky's ideas of combined and uneven development. The global reach of capitalism has transplanted capitalist relations onto foreign soils, whose different social structures produce different class configurations and different institutional forms of capital and labor.
>
> To assert the local is in no sense to deny the *global* character of capitalism (both take place simultaneously, of course) or to obviate the need to theorize the abstract properties (for example, the crisis-proneness) of capitalism. Our (spatial) point is simply that how things develop depends in part on *where* they develop, on what has been historically sedimented there, on the social and spatial structures that are already in place there. . . . A sensitivity to space, and to time, reveals that there are a multiplicity of capitalisms contained within the brittle edges of capitalist laws of motion and within the inner contradictions of the capital-labor relations. [Watts 1992: 11; see also Soja 1989]

Conclusion

Let us return to the ethnographic problem with which this essay began: the combination of an ethnographic sensibility and project with a knowledge of wider configurations, structures, and relations of power. The kinds of historical, structural, and spatial relations and processes adduced here demand a detailed mapping of *specific* powers and structures in particular ethnographic situations. Dualisms of various sorts (noncapitalism/capitalism, periphery/core, local/global, culture/history, territorial/deterritorialized, space/time) are thoroughly inadequate for such a task. Similarly inadequate are simple labels that allow us to assign an ethnographic situation to a particular epoch or structure (feudalism, capitalism, long wave I-A or III-B, Fordism, flexible accumulation, and so forth) that seems to provide political economic context or "background." Dualisms and contextual labels cut off analysis at the point at which it should begin—the mapping of the powers and relations associated with particular moments of capitalist development, specific social structures of accumulation, and reconfigurations of social space into the social field that characterizes the ethnographic situation.

Among the oppositions that we need to move beyond is one between time and space (compare Soja 1989). I have tried to suggest here the necessity of analyses of structure for an adequate understanding of capitalism in time and space. In examining these three literatures, I have tried to show their necessary relation: an organization of capitalist time in terms of long waves serves as a framework for the analysis of social structures of accumulation specific to particular long waves, but an adequate understanding of such structures requires that they be placed in unevenly developing social spaces, and that the organization of space be seen as an integral part of the institution of a particular structure of accumulation. The relationship of these literatures to ethnography is, then, dual. On the one hand, they are necessary for situating the ethnographic setting within wider fields of power, for placing the "global" *within* the "local." On the other hand, the literatures need to be given an ethnographic reading and extension. That is, ethnographic analysis is necessary for an adequate understanding of the formation of specific structures of accumulation within time and space.

References Cited

Aglietta, Michel. 1979. *A Theory of Capitalist Regulation: The U.S. Experience*. London: NLB.

Amsden, Alice. 1990. "Third World Industrialization: 'Global Fordism' or a New Model?" *New Left Review* 182: 5–32.

Bowles, Samuel, David M. Gordon, and Thomas E. Weisskopf. 1983. *Beyond the Waste Land: A Democratic Alternative to Economic Decline*. New York: Anchor Press/Doubleday.

———. 1986. "Power and Profits: The Social Structure of Accumulation and the Profitability of the Postwar U.S. Economy." *Review of Radical Political Economics* 18, no. 1/2: 132–67.

———. 1990. *After the Waste Land: A Democratic Economics for the Year 2000*. Armonk, N.Y.: M. E. Sharpe.

Boyer, Robert. 1990. *The Regulation School: A Critical Introduction*. New York: Columbia University Press.

Brenner, Robert, and Mark Glick. 1991. "The Regulation Approach: Theory and History." *New Left Review* 188: 45–120.

Gjording, Chris N. 1991. *Conditions Not of Their Choosing: The Guaymi Indians and Mining Multinationals in Panama.* Washington, D.C.: Smithsonian Institution Press.

Gordon, David M. 1980. "Stages of Accumulation and Long Economic Cycles." In Terence Hopkins and Immanuel Wallerstein, eds., *Processes of the World-System*, 9–45. Beverly Hills, Calif.: Sage.

———. 1988. "The Global Economy: New Edifice or Crumbling Foundations?" *New Left Review* 168: 24–65.

Gordon, David M., Richard Edwards, and Michael Reich. 1982. *Segmented Work, Divided Workers: The Historical Transformation of Labor in the United States*. New York: Cambridge University Press.

Harvey, David. 1982. *The Limits to Capital*. Chicago: University of Chicago Press.

———. 1989. *The Condition of Postmodernity*. Oxford: Blackwell Publishers.

Kondratieff, N. D. 1979 [1926]. "The Long Waves in Economic Life." *Review* 2, no. 4: 519–62.

Lipietz, Alain. 1987. *Mirages and Miracles: The Crisis in Global Fordism*. London: Verso.

Mandel, Ernest. 1978. *Late Capitalism*. London: NLB.

Marcus, George, and Michael Fisher. 1986. *Anthropology as Cultural Critique*. Chicago: University of Chicago Press.

Polier, Nicole. 1996. "Of Mines and Min: Modernity and Its Malcontents in Papua New Guinea." *Ethnology* 35, no. 1: 1–16.

Roseberry, William. 1996. "The Rise of Yuppie Coffees and the Reimagination of Class in the United States." *American Anthropologist* 98, no. 4: 762–75.

Soja, Edward. 1989. *Postmodern Geographies: The Reassertion of Space in Critical Social Theory*. London: Verso.

Wallerstein, Immanuel. 1974. *The Modern World-System: Capitalist Agriculture and the Origins of the European World-Economy in the Sixteenth Century*. New York: Academic Press.

————. 1980. *The Modern World-System II: Mercantilism and the Consolidation of the European World-Economy, 1600–1750*. New York: Academic Press.

————. 1989. *The Modern World-System III: The Second Era of Great Expansion of the Capitalist World-Economy, 1730–1840s*. San Diego: Academic Press.

Watts, Michael John. 1992. "Capitalisms, Crises, and Cultures I: Notes Toward a Totality of Fragments." In Allan Pred and Michael John Watts, *Reworking Modernity: Capitalisms and Symbolic Discontent*, 1–19. New Brunswick, N.J.: Rutgers University Press.

Wolf, Eric R. 1982. *Europe and the People without History*. Berkeley: University of California Press.

MYRON L. COHEN

Commodity Creation in Late Imperial China

Corporations, Shares, and Contracts in
One Rural Community

China's late imperial period has been characterized by William Rowe as one of "intensified commercialization, monetization, and urbanization" (Rowe 1992: 1, n1). Commodification should be added as being of growing importance during this time, because while "commercialization" refers to the extent that the economy has gone beyond family self-sufficiency in the production and distribution of food and other necessary or desired goods, "commodification" relates more to economic culture itself. In the anthropological literature concern with what is termed commodification is expressed largely with reference to the introduction or expansion of the use of money, or to the movement from exchange to marketing arrangements in the circulation of valued goods or the employment of labor, with the stated or unstated assumption being that such developments have an alienating, disruptive or exploitive impact on labor and production arrangements.[1] Ironically, this view of commodification actually privileges the West, confirms its continuing global dominance, and represents non-Western cultures as hapless victims whose own—implicitly weaker—economies and cultures cannot but be totally reconfigured by the impact of such outside forces. This perspective denies the societies and cultures being impacted upon any independent agency except that of resistance and response to the crushing economic, social, political, and ideological forces exerted upon them by the all-powerful West, forces variously characterized as capitalism, the "virus," colonialism, modernization, or various combinations thereof. This view, to mix different traditions of jargon, takes the underdog's independent agency to be a dependent variable. Such a Western-oriented view of commodification may to varying degrees be applicable in certain regional settings but nevertheless is badly in need of the comparative perspectives that could be provided by China and other East Asian societies; such views would incorporate, among other things, local, historically specific sources of modernity, especially as regards economic development. But for my present purposes I want only to take the small step of broadening the idea of commodification to include the cultural invention of things that can be bought and sold, such as particular rights to land, or shares in corporations, and I want to show how during China's late imperial period such invention went on at a high pitch.[2]

In this paper I use data pertaining to what is now Meinong Township, an administrative subdivision of Gaoxiong [Kaohsiung] County, in southern Taiwan. These data derive from a larger project involving analysis of materials concerning culture and society in the Meinong region before the Japanese occupation, when, like the rest of Taiwan, it still was part of the old Chinese empire under the Manchu Qing dynasty, the last of China's imperial lines. The Qing ruled mainland China from 1644 to 1912, but in Taiwan they gained control in 1683 and were ousted by Japan in 1895. In Meinong, settlement by Hakka-speaking Han Chinese did not begin until 1736. During Qing the region was known as Minong—the Japanese changed the name to Meinong in 1920—and since my concern is with the pre-Japanese period it seems appropriate to use the older term. When Minong came under Japanese control its almost entirely Hakka-speaking population, which I estimate to have been about ten thousand, was composed of either the descendants of Han Chinese who had emigrated from the China mainland or, in a very few cases, of immigrants themselves. In any event, economic culture in Minong was representative of that generally characteristic of the Han Chinese during late imperial times. In that culture commodification loomed large indeed, such that the creation of marketable commodities vastly outstripped the creation or definition of the products or other physical things, such as land, which this commodification involved. Land and the commodities associated with it will be my focus here, both because land was an obviously key resource in a primarily agrarian setting, and also because it is to land that the data at my disposal concerning late imperial period commodification or, indeed, hypercommodification, primarily relate. One major data source is the cadastral survey carried out by the Japanese in 1902. Having overcome armed resistance and obtained Minong's surrender in November 1895, the Japanese had been in control of the area for a little over six years. Yet the cadastral data do accurately depict the land-linked commodification of pre-Japanese times, for the purpose of the survey was precisely to set the stage for the imposition of Japanese land taxes and new ownership regulations. In other words, the survey was carried out so that the Japanese could start making changes in land relationships which, subsequent to the survey, they indeed did.

Both the survey and various documents dating from the pre-Japanese Qing period that I was able to copy, such as contracts and account books, show that land-linked commodities well known in late imperial China were represented in Minong.[3] With respect to a particular plot of land, the three most important commodities were "redeemable sale" or *dian* rights, "small rent" or *xiaozu* rights, and "large rent" or *dazu* rights. Redeemable sale involved payment giving the purchaser rights to land use until such time that the money was returned, with use-rights then likewise returned. A "small rent" owner was obligated to make usually annual or biannual payments to the "large rent" holder, with the latter generally responsible for the land tax. With respect to all of these rights and, indeed, most commodities of any sort, families—as represented by their almost invariably male family heads—and not individuals were the units of ownership. Shareholding corporations could also own such rights, but under such circumstances the shares themselves would be family-owned or, in some cases, owned by other corporations, as shall be shown. Later in this paper we will also come across a few cases where women owned commodities and property as individuals,[4] and so-called public entities such as village temples might own property on a nonshareholding basis, but it is clear enough that the vast majority of all assets were family-owned. In terms of land-rights, the simplest situation would be where a family had full ownership rights to a particular plot that they also cultivated themselves, with no differentiation of "small rent" and "large rent" rights and without pledge of land through redeemable sale. At the other extreme, a plot of land might have a tenant, and different owners of small rent, large rent, and redeemable sale rights, such that rights of one kind or another to this land would be distributed among four parties. In fact, both extremes and a variety of intermediate arrangements were all well represented in Minong, precisely because each kind of right was a marketable commodity.

These rights, which could be held with respect to farmland or land used for other purposes (such as house sites), said nothing regarding who actually worked the land or lived in the house: tenancy was common, with rent received by holders of redeemable sale rights or small rent rights as the case might be. Unfortunately, tenancy information was not entered into the survey forms, although from the survey it can be inferred that tenants constituted a considerable proportion of Minong's population. The 1902 cadastral survey classified all land into the nine categories of wet rice, dry field, building site, grave site, temple site, miscellaneous, mountain, pond, and undeveloped or waste land. In economic terms the most important was wet rice land, followed by dry field. The 3,128 plots of wet rice land, having a total area of 1,733 *jia* (a Taiwan land unit equivalent to 0.97 hectare, and thus a hectare for all intents and purposes), amount to 43 percent of all 7,243 plots and 39 percent of Minong's total area of 4,379 jia. Dry field, with 2,345 plots covering 1,983 jia, amounted to 32 percent of all plots and 45 percent of all land. The 1,545 plots listed as building sites had a total area of 189 jia, or less than 0.5 percent of all land, but accounted for 21 percent of all plots, as might be expected of residential land in an area where farming was dominant in the economy. Land in the other categories amounted to a little more than 10 percent of all land and need not be dealt with here.

People or other entities (such as associations or the state itself) were listed in the survey by name and with respect to the right they controlled: proprietor (*yezhu*), large rent owner (dazu), and owner of redeemable or dian rights (*dianzhu*); if a particular plot had a large rent owner, then the proprietor would be the small rent owner as far as local property relations were concerned. For each of these three rights yet other persons might be listed as managers;[5] this was always the case if an association rather than a person were listed as owner of a particular right. By manipulating the Japanese cadastral survey so as first to eliminate all associations and other entities that were not people, and then the duplication of names as among persons listed as landowners, as having dian or redeemable purchase rights, as holders of larger rent rights, or as "managers" with respect to any of these rights, there yielded a total of 2,600 persons, or 2,387 persons after discounting nonresidents of the area. These were those having registered rights to land in Minong, although, as noted, in almost all cases they in fact were family heads, with the family as a corporation being the unit of ownership.

Unsurprising but nevertheless notable is the near-total absence of women from the data sets, there being only 18 out of all 2,600 persons recorded, with 4 of these women not resident in Minong. Fourteen of the 18 women are listed as managers of land owned by men outright or through redeemable purchase; one of these women is also listed as owner of a plot, while the remaining 3 women are listed as owners. A male manager is registered for the land listed under the name of one of these latter women. Among the other 2 women owners, as well as those listed as managers, presumably were widows whose sons, if any, were too young to be taken as family heads. But since available data from the household registers shows that one or two of these women were owners whose husbands were alive at the time of the cadastral survey, there is also suggested the possibility that some land or rights thereto were held by women as their personal property, although the holdings so indicated were so few as also to suggest that more may have been registered in the names of their husbands. But the dominance of men was in any event overwhelming, thus confirming the male-headed corporate family as the key actor in the context of late imperial commodification.

Of the 2,387 owners of rights, 629, or 26 percent, were listed as having rights to building sites only, with such rights usually based upon their established residence as agnates in local compounds. Even though it is possible that some among these people owned or had rights to land outside of the area covered by the available cadastral data, I take them largely to represent a landless population within which tenants were dominant. Some may have been short- or long-term field workers or engaged in one form or another of nonagricultural work. Others who were farmers were both shareholder members of and tenants in Minong's many corporate associations, given that these owned or held through redeemable sale about one-third of all Minong wet rice land. However, others among the landless clearly were tenants on holdings of the larger private Minong landlords, it being understood that a tenant might have more than one landlord and might also in some cases also own land. Nevertheless, the 629 persons shown to own only building sites clearly indicate the presence of a rather large proportion of landless residents, fitting the circumstances of land ownership concentration as between the associations and a minority of private family landowners. For example, the four largest private (that is, family) landowners owned or had purchased redeemable rights to 113 jia of wet rice and 99 jia of dry field, accounting for more than 15 percent of all wet rice land and about 5 percent of dry field; for the top fifty private landowners, or a little more than 2 percent of all persons represented, such control was over 346 jia of wet rice land, or more than 47 percent, and 421 jia of dry field, or about 21 percent. Thus while there was no extreme concentration of landlordism in the hands of one or two families, land rights were indeed concentrated at the higher reaches of the index as far as private family ownership was concerned; this, when combined with association ownership, accounted for most that was available.

However, these various rights hardly exhaust the inventory of land-related commodities available in Qing dynasty Minong. As already noted, there were also shareholding corporations. Most of these latter were dedicated either to an ancestor—genealogically close in some cases, in others quite remote—of a group of agnates or to a particular deity or cultural hero, such as the goddess Mazu or even to figures such as Confucius. On the basis of Qing period account books and the Japanese cadastral records, I estimate at this stage of research that minimally there were more than 110 ancestral corporations and more than 70 other shareholding corporations in Minong; assuming an average of 20 shares per corporation, 180 corporations would provide a total of 3,600 shares, again a minimal estimate—this with respect to a population of about ten thousand, and, obviously, a much smaller number of the family units in which most share ownership was vested.[6] Share-ownership was widely distributed among local families, with many, especially the wealthier ones, having shares in several corporations. Likewise, I was told that a strategy of poorer farmers who could not afford to purchase land was to purchase shares giving them rights of cultivation as tenants. Membership in a corporation gave privileged access to corporate assets, as in the form of loans or first rights to rent corporate land, while some corporations also provided shareholders with annual dividends. Shares were commodities: the ancestral corporations restricted sales to other agnates, but owners could sell shares of other corporations to anyone in the community, or to a different corporation. Because the survey separately recorded land data from the six administrative villages into which the Japanese divided Minong, different corporations in different villages might have the same name (such as the very common earth god corporations), such that the survey data do not facilitate an accurate count. Nevertheless, the religious or other charter of a corporation usually can be identified from its name and on the basis of other information at my disposal.[7]

The survey does tell us about the relative representation of corporations with respect to the ownership of the various rights discussed so far. As already noted, wet rice and dry field taken together account for almost all farmland, with rights to the far more productive wet rice obviously being far more expensive. So as to simplify the discussion, I deal with all corporations as in one category: corporations owned "small rent" rights or full rights to 972 plots of wet rice or 25 percent of the total, amounting to 510 jia, or 29 percent, of all wet rice land; furthermore they owned redeemable sale rights to another 98 plots of wet rice having an area of 39 jia, thus giving them access to rental income from about 32 percent of all Minong wet rice land. At the same time, these corporations were making payments to the owners of "large rent" rights held with respect to 321 plots of their wet rice land, amounting to 174 jia, or 34 percent, of the total. The corporations owned "small rent" rights or full rights to only 184 out of 2,345 dry field plots, amounting to 152 jia, or 8 percent, of the total area of 1983 jia; they owned redeemable sale rights to another 41 plots totaling 44 jia, or a mere 2 percent, of all dry field land. That the corporations had rental income from only about 10 percent of dry field as opposed to almost one-third of all wet rice land was similar to the proportional distribution of ownership by land type among richer private landlords, as noted above, and reflects an investment strategy geared to assuring returns that were greater and also steady rather than dependent on fluctuating rainfall.

It is of some interest that the cadastral records show each of two earth god associations as having purchased redeemable sale rights to land owned by two different ancestral associations, one purchase involving three plots, and the other one. With respect to the three plots of wet rice land owned by one of these associations, "large rent" rights were held by yet another party such that rights of one sort or another were held by two corporations, the owner of "large rent" rights, and by whoever might actually be doing the farming. In a 1915 entry in the account book of yet another ancestral association, this corporation's assets—obtained well before the Japanese occupation—are recorded as including, in addition to land, shares in two Qingming or grave associations, these themselves being a variety of ancestral association; two shares in the Guansheng or God of the Military Association; one share in the Old Earth God Association (Laobogong hui); one share in the Quandou Village Lantern Association; one share in the Old Association of the God of Literature or civil bureaucracy; one share in the Lantern Festival Association; one share in the Association for Cemeteries for the Unworshiped Dead; one share in the Yongxing Bridge Association; one share in the Confucius Association; and one share in a local burial society. Although these different cases of corporations owning each other's shares hardly loom as dominant in the overall distribution of share ownership, they do illustrate how a corporation was a well-defined actor or entity with respect to property and other commodity transactions. Indeed, they were so recognized by the Qing imperial state, as during the islandwide cadastral survey begun in 1885 (ten years before the Japanese conquest) by the then–Chinese governor Liu Mingquan and, later, by the Japanese in their own cadastral survey.[8]

An association's shareholders generally met once a year, usually at the home of one shareholder who served as corporation manager, often under an arrangement whereby management was assigned among shareholders on a rotation basis. With all expenses paid out of corporation funds, key events at such a meeting included worship of the corporation's charter deity or ancestor, a banquet, a report by the manager on corporation finances during the previous year, and entry of this report into the corporation's account book, of which two copies were usually kept, with two shareholders other than the manager making identical entries in each.[9] An account book was a rather thick printed volume something like a notebook and was commonly purchased and used by all sorts of enterprises and businesses. In such a book there was first written an introductory statement expressing the corporation's ideals and religious-ritual raison d'être, often followed by the texts to be recited during the ritual proceedings that took place during the annual shareholders meeting. The next few pages of the account book have the names of all founding shareholders; transfers of share ownership are indicated under the name of the particular share involved. In some account books there is also itemization of land and ritual objects (such as tablets) possessed by the association, with land holdings sometimes described according to the historical sequence of purchases, including each plot's date of acquisition. The rest of the book is devoted to the annual entries, each taking up two or three pages, such that by the time a new account book had to be used the old one might contain a record of several decades of corporation finances. When a new account book was required, the introductory and religious texts and the list of original shareholders was copied in, so that in every account book a statement of the lofty religious and social ideals held to represent corporate aspirations prefaced the subsequent businesslike entries concerning membership changes and finances. This combination of texts mirrored the combination of ritual and business that characterized the annual meeting of the corporation. The distribution of corporate dividends may be illustrated by the following entry for December 17, 1886, from the account book of the Ritual Estate of the Five Manifestations (Wuxian Sidian):[10]

> Guangxu reign period 12th year, 11th month, 22nd day. Accounting session of the Ritual Estate of the Five Manifestations.
> Received: winter rent-grain from Zeng Xiuna, 55.000 piculs
> Paid out: large rent on our fields, 13.640 piculs
>   watchmen's grain on our fields 1.364 piculs

Total paid out: grain in the amount of 15.004 piculs
After payments, sum remaining 40.000 piculs [exact amount should be 39.996]
Paid out: for 14 [association] shares, [dividends] each at 2.5 piculs [for a total of 35 piculs]
Balance: 5 piculs equal to 3.6 dollars
Today's banquet: 3.00 dollars
Writing materials 0.20 [dollar]
After disbursements left with 0.40 [dollar]
Made into 14 shares equally divided for 0.029 dollar per share [these have total value of exactly 0.406 dollar].[11]

Throughout the Qing period new corporations were being formed, while those already present might be purchasing additional land. It is also probably the case that some corporations were also dissolved; although I have no direct evidence for this from Minong, Qing-period corporation dissolution contracts signed by all shareholders are known from other parts of Taiwan (see Appendix A). A corporation was formed when several people agreed to contribute money for the purchase of shares having a specified value, with the accumulated sum then used to acquire land. Obviously, such corporations could not be formed if land rights were not available as a freely marketable commodity, and if there were no place in local economic culture for the creation of the shares that became yet other commodities. For an ordinary farmer (that is, for him in his capacity as family head), among possible advantages of association membership through purchase of shares was availability of loans from the association, or access to additional land for a sum far less than that required for purchase of "small rent" or full land rights. In some cases, I was told, a farmer too poor to purchase land might opt to acquire association shares as an affordable alternative. He would have to pay rent, to be sure, but he, like other shareholders, might also receive dividends. Also of no little significance was the opportunity provided for rather intimate social interaction with wealthier elite shareholders during the annual meetings. For the latter, shareholding was a relatively inexpensive form of investment; their families tended to own far more shares in more corporations than did ordinary people, such that shareholding among the wealthy can be seen as but one dimension of their accumulation of diversified investment portfolios. Shares could be sold outright or transferred to another party through redeemable sale. That this was frequent enough can be seen from the many transfers noted in the association account books, although these data await investigation. There is other evidence for the sale of shares, and elsewhere

(Cohen 1993: 19, 22–23) I have shown through an analysis of two family division contracts how during the Qing dynasty a Minong man who was one of three brothers and a nephew involved in an 1863 family division received 4 out of the 21 shares in 10 or 11 religious and ancestral corporations that the family then owned, while upon the division of his own family in 1898, the 13.5 shares that were then distributed among three brothers reflected the purchase of at least 9.5 new shares and the sale of at least 2 of the original 4 during the intervening twenty-five-year period. Of course, shares bought and then sold after 1863 but before 1898 would not be noted in either contract. As with the sale of land rights and other valuable commodities, share ownership transfers were on the basis of written contracts; although I have found none from Minong they were indeed written there, and examples of such contracts from other parts of Taiwan have survived (see Appendix B).

The overwhelming bulk of land-linked commodities were owned within the Minong community; with certain important exceptions to be noted below, the few outside parties involved were mainly from elsewhere in the larger south Taiwan Hakka settlement zone that was organized in the form of the Six Units (Liudui) militia confederation and in many ways constituted a higher-level territorial community, with Minong forming its northernmost extension and comprising most of the confederation's Right Unit (Youdui) (Cohen 1993; Pasternak 1972, 1983). That the creation and marketing of such land-related commodities, and many others, occurred almost entirely within the Minong community context is attested to, for example, by the rarity of so-called "red" contracts (*hongqi*)—those registered with the county government office (*yamen*)—from among the many Minong Qing period contracts I have been able to copy or refer to.[12] Such localization hardly reflects a situation whereby commodification is disruptive of local solidarities or somehow is subversive with respect to local society assumed to comprise a "moral economy."[13] There were indeed pronounced differences in wealth in Minong, and the area had its share of often violent internal conflict, while at the same time conflicts between the Minong Hakka and neighboring Hokkien-speaking Han Chinese or non-Han native communities were frequent and severe, but none of this is relevant to commodification as such, especially if this is assumed to be a socially and morally disruptive force in its own right. Such an assumption would be dead wrong in the context of late imperial Chinese economic culture, for precisely the opposite was true: in the marked absence of significant intervention by the state or by other outside forces with respect to the enforcement of most contractually defined economic links, it was community solidarity and the highly strategic significance of social ties within the Minong community that provided the environment within which commodification could flourish. Minong, like elsewhere in late imperial China, was a community whose high degree of commodification was powerfully supported by an equally high propensity to resort to written contracts with respect to transactions where things of value were involved, as I have noted. These overwhelmingly "white" contracts (*baiqi*),[14] or contracts not registered with the local county magistrate's office, were supported precisely by social relationships, using the time-honored Chinese device of involving a third-party middleman and other cosignatories, such that violation of a contract's stipulations would place into jeopardy a very large network of social ties of the kind vital to survival. This is not to say that the state was irrelevant. Certainly, aggrieved parties could sue in the magistrate's court and bring forward both red and white contracts as evidence. Although negative evidence is hardly conclusive, I have no record of anyone in Minong going to court during Qing, but in any event such actions were quite rare in relation to the number of contracts entered into in any particular region, so that ultimate recourse to the state was powerfully subordinate to reliance on social ties in the protection of contractual agreements.[15]

Kinship ties were among the most critical, but their importance did not take the form of a domination of relationships such that within the marketing domain the family's managerial autonomy—as represented by the family head—was compromised. In this context family members need to be clearly distinguished from kin outside the family. In Minong it was generally but not invariably the woman who moved from her natal family to her husband's, leading of course to the creation of kin ties between the two families, if there had been none previously.[16] Likewise, upon family division married brothers underwent a massive change of status from being siblings within a unified family to being kin, each heading his own family. Kin beyond the family were reduced to being ordinary actors in the commodity market, including that for human labor, at the same time that they were key participants in the family's long-term ritual, cooperative, and gift-exchange relationships. Rather than there being conflict between the world of commodified relationships on the one hand, and that of enduring social ties on the other, there was mutual support precisely on the basis of clear differentiation. For example, in Minong, as in much of China, there was the distinction between "labor exchange" and "help" relationships.

The first, a simple contractual undertaking, could involve kin, neighbors, or anyone else deemed reliable, and was a common procedure especially during the busiest farm periods, such as planting or harvest. This labor swapping was supposed to involve equal contributions by all parties. If one party were to contribute less family labor than the others they would have to hire workers to supply labor for the families to whom labor was due. Help relationships were quite different, although they might involve the very same kin, among others: cooperation such as in house construction or repair and a variety of other tasks allowing for flexibility in timing during the agricultural slack season was not precisely measured, such that in terms of help relationships there were cooperative ties sustained over many years. Social ties, as among kin, neighbors, or local community members, framed feasting and gift-exchange, as in the banquets provided those attending and bringing cash gifts to weddings, funerals, and other family-sponsored events. Social ties might be strained or severed if a family expected on the basis of social links to be invited (always in the name of the family head) and was not, or if invited, it did not attend (in the person of the family head or his representative). The weakening or destruction of social ties would have obvious negative consequences with respect to a family's ability to negotiate the world of contracts and commodity transactions.[17]

The contracts that were major instruments in both the creation and the transfer of commodities thus confronted kinship and other long-term supportive social relations in two major ways. In the first, close kin and sometimes other persons of local prominence were asked to serve as signatories to the contract. The middleman's participation as a signatory was crucial in any contract involving a transaction between two parties, for he would have pre-existing social ties of one sort or another with each and serve as guarantor; he often was instrumental in putting a deal such as a land transfer together and for this would be awarded a commission. In most cases another signatory was the amanuensis or scribe, who might be paid for his services but frequently enough was also kin to one of the contracting parties. In most contracts one or more witnesses also signed on, and these people were indeed tightly linked socially to the contract's executor, most often by kinship connections. Usually, only the seller, and not the recipient of the commodity, would be signatory to contracts involving sales of one kind or another, such as sale or redeemable sale of land, housing, or other items, or transactions in people, such as the adoption or sale of children (young daughters, but in some cases sons). The party receiving the commodity would also get the contract, which served as evidence that the property belonged to the family whose head had negotiated the purchase. The involvement of kin as signatories represented a positive use of kinship sentiments in that they could be recruited on the basis of generalized kinship obligations.

But, turning to the second major confrontation between contract and kinship, it was precisely these sentiments of kinship that had to be controlled in the negative sense of insulating commodity transactions from their potentially disturbing consequences. In part this was also achieved by having kin sign as witnesses. Since, as noted, the party selling or otherwise transferring the commodity was the contract's key signatory, it would be that party's kin who would acknowledge the transfer by signing on. In other words, they would indicate their acceptance of whatever the transfer meant in terms of something of value being removed from their kinship domain, in this context comprising, among other things, various secondary claims, such as the inheritance rights of close agnates to property in the absence of male successors in the family. But the kinship circle from within which claims might be generated could hardly be totally covered by the recruitment of agnates and affines as signatories; "marked" kin, identified as noted above as through labor swapping or by reciprocal invitations to wedding and funeral banquets, could comprise a large group indeed, one that could scarcely be mobilized for the signing of every contract. And there was no way to prevent yet others from asserting kinship or some other kind of social connection so as to make a claim. While only the closest agnates would have inheritance rights to property where the family owning it had died out in the absence of male offspring, larger circles of kin might join in regretting the sale of a family's land or other assets to which they might otherwise have indirect access, as through the adoption of agnates or affines into that family. Therefore it is common to encounter in contracts rather standardized statements to the effect that especially agnatic kin are to keep away and mind their own business, and that the transaction is totally between the two parties and no one else.

Examples of such statements can be seen in the following contract for the sale of a plot of land in Niupu, a small village in the larger Minong community:

> The executor of this contract for the irrevocable sale of a parcel of land, Chen Jiayong of Niupu Village, obtained through succession from his paternal grandfather a plot of river bank land that grandfather had developed. Using local place names, the property is above [that is, to the east of] Niupu Village, on the southern edge of the river. Its boundaries extend eastward to the irrigation

canal, westward to the plot belonging to Qiu Tinghai, southward to the bank of the river, northward to the edge of the seller's [clearly a mistake, should be buyer's] field. The boundaries in all four directions have been inspected and clearly demarcated in the presence of the middleman. Now, because of family financial difficulties, the contractor desires to sell this land. After having first thoroughly inquired among his close kin of the same patrilineal branch, and with none able to make the purchase, he has availed himself of the introduction of a middleman, through which Liu Baozhi of Minong Lower Village has come forward to purchase this property. On this day, in the presence of the middleman, the three parties [buyer, seller, and middleman] have agreed on the basis of market value to the plot's sale at the price of nine large dollars.[18] In the presence of the middleman, contract and cash are exchanged on the same day in full without any short-changing and without such fraudulent practices as the discounted sale of property with debt obligations or the multiple pledging of property to different parties. This plot of land was handed down to the seller by his own paternal grandfather, who developed it and established it as property. It has no connections with any of his uncles [generationally senior agnates] of other patrilineal descent branches. After sale the land is to be given over immediately and in person [by the previous owner] to the buyer, for him to manage and cultivate as his property. The seller's close agnatic kin of the same branch are not to dare dispute the sale, obstruct it, or make any trouble. As soon as the sale is done, the seller is to see to it that any complications are ended forever. Hereafter, the seller shall not dare to speak of redeeming the property or requesting gift-money [from the buyer]. This contract is entered into voluntarily by both parties, without any constraints. Because we fear that an oral agreement will be unreliable, we have drawn up this contract for the irrevocable sale of a parcel of land, and it is transferred [to the buyer] as certification.

On this day it is clearly noted that in the presence of the middleman there was received payment of nine dollars as per this contract. Noted.

Mediator/middleman: Lin Chuanshan
Witness and amanuensis: Matrilateral cousin, Song Qinchuan
Tongzhi reign period, 5th year, 3rd month, 6th day [April 20, 1866].
Executor of contract for the irrevocable sale of a parcel of land: Chen Jiayong.

This is a relatively simple contractual transaction involving transfer of a less expensive plot of land. Nevertheless it is of interest because it establishes that the parcel of land is a commodity unto itself in that there are no attached commodified rights in the form of "large rent," "small rent," pledges, or the like. As an "easy" contract it has as signatories only the buyer, the middleman, and one witness who also is the necessary scribe. It concerns land created as property by the seller's grandfather, who developed it in the context of the ongoing settlement of the Minong region, with property creation, and therefore commodity creation, being a consequence of such development, in the absence of prior claims by other parties [at least as far as the Han Chinese were concerned]. The contract is for an "unconditional sale" in that the seller waives all future claims. That the seller "thoroughly inquired among his close agnatic kin of the same branch" before proceeding to arrange sale to a nonrelative is a standard "boilerplate" phrase commonly encountered in contracts concerning sales, as well as in others. Among such close agnates would be those with secondary inheritance rights to this property, effective only in the event that the owning family were unable to produce its own male successors through birth or adoption, or by skipping a generation and producing such a successor through uxorilocal marriage. Nevertheless, the first rights of refusal held by close agnates with respect to purchases and other transactions should not be taken as evidence that kinship sentiments and obligations formed a moral encumbrance interfering with the play of market forces in the circulation of commodities. On the contrary, the rights of refusal held by close agnates simply give them prior opportunity to make the purchase, but at no advantage with respect to price or other conditions. Thus these "first rights" represented precisely the adjustment of even such kinship ties to the leveled playing field of a commodified environment. That the phrase is so frequently encountered suggests that these agnates far more often than not were unable or unwilling to purchase, a circumstance hardly surprising given that within any region the effective market encompassed a population far greater than the number of people eligible to exercise first rights on the basis of close kinship ties.

The following contract is introduced to show how property indeed obtained through secondary inheritance is nevertheless sold as a commodity, with the seller confronting and denying all potential claims of his close agnates:

> The executor of this contract for the absolute sale of a house and house site is Liu Awen. In the past, paternal grandfather's brother Qingjie had handed down a three-room tiled house with earth foundation. Using local place names it is situated in Zhongtan Village, to the south facing north; to the east this plot extends to the base of the common wall shared with the house of Liu Deng'er; to the west it extends to the base of the common wall shared with the room of my own central-room house [that is, the house at the base of the compound with common room and ancestral hall]; to the south it extends to the bamboo fence at the edge of the well; to the north it extends to the eaves of Liu Deng'er's old house. The boundaries in all four directions have been inspected and clearly demarcated in the presence of the middleman. Now because of financial difficulties, and after having thoroughly inquired among my paternal

uncles, each and every one of whom is unable to undertake purchase, I have relied on a middleman for an introduction to [honorific] elder brother Zhong Xigou who has come forward to buy. On the same day through the middleman the three parties have agreed to a market price of 38 silver dollars exactly and on that day money and contract have been straightforwardly exchanged, with no cheating or short-changing during the proceedings. From the time of purchase this property is transferred to the buyer for him to control as his residence; the paternal uncles, nephews, and brothers of the seller are not to raise objections or cause disturbances. This house site is a property originally bequeathed by [my father's] junior paternal uncle [father's father's younger brother] Qingjie and has no connection with my brothers or paternal uncles and nephews; the seller bears all responsibility. This contract is entered into voluntarily by both parties, without any constraints. Fearing that verbal agreement leaves no evidence, I have executed one copy of this contract for the absolute sale of house and house site, which is given over [to the buyer] as certification.

On this day it is clearly noted that received in accordance with the specifications of this contract is the sum of 38 dollars. So noted.

It is also clearly noted that the flat surface in front of the main gate is an area of traffic and cannot be obstructed. So noted.

Also clearly noted is that the well water is drunk in common by the houses on both sides of the well. Clearly noted.

Also clearly noted is that after the sale of this house it cannot ever be expanded. So noted.

Middleman: Chen Lianfa
Witnesses: paternal uncle Liu Huilin
    older brother [father's brother's son] Liu Aming
[Contract written with] my own pen
Witness: Liu Asheng
Tongzhi 10th year, 6th month, [blank] day [between July 18 and August 15, 1871]; Executor of contract for the absolute sale of a house and house site, Liu Awen.

Qingjie, "paternal grandfather's brother," died without offspring, bringing to an end his agnatic line. As to the executor himself, Liu Awen, he has as witnesses Liu Hiulin, who is Liu Awen's father's youngest brother, and Liu Aming, the oldest son of yet another father's brother, already deceased at that time. Because the three other brothers of Liu Awen's father all died without offspring, Liu Awen and these two witnesses account for all surviving descent lines focusing on Awen's paternal grandfather. In other words, with these two witnesses signing on, agreement for the sale has been obtained from those close agnates who might have shared secondary rights of succession with respect to both Liu Qingjie and Liu Awen. Once again, although initially involved in a dense network of agnatic ties, the house and its building site are transformed by contract into a commodity, albeit one whose use is conditioned by additional contractual clauses. Under more complicated circumstances, the number of witnesses will be larger, in light of the fact noted above, that social relationships are the framework for the protection of contractual integrity. Such circumstances can be seen in the following contract for the five-year pledge of land in return for a redeemable cash payment:

Li Changhua'er, the executor of this contract of pledge, now owns as his portion through family division land obtained from his late paternal grandfather consisting of two wet rice plots, one the old site [purchased earlier] and one the newer site. Their position in terms of local place-names is at the entrance to the Tanshui Stream outside of Jianshanliao Village. Their boundaries extend eastward to the wet rice plot of the Wen Family Ancestral Estate, westward to Xingxiu's wet rice plot, southward to the wet rice plots of Li Fan'er and the Lin family, and northward to the foot of the mountain. These four boundaries have been clearly identified through personal investigation by the three parties, including the middleman. The land carries with it a native large rent of **four piculs of unhusked grain** [bold text overstamped with seal reading "SEAL OF WULUO NATIVE SETTLEMENT LARGE RENT OWNER PAN WENYA"]. At present, because of financial difficulties, I am willing to pledge through redeemable sale the fields to others. I first thoroughly inquired among my close agnatic kin of the same branch and they all were unable to take the land in pledge. Through the introduction of a middleman, Lin Changshu has come forward to contract for these fields in pledge. In the presence of the middleman, the three parties have agreed on the basis of market value to pledge the land in return for two hundred dollars. Contract and cash are straightforwardly exchanged on the same day, without things like shortchanging and without such fraudulent practices as the multiple pledging of property. These fields truly are mine, obtained as property by succession to my paternal grandfather's land through [family] division. In the event that there is lack of clarity concerning previous ownership of this land, or arrears in large rent payments, none of these matters have anything to do with the party taking on the land as pledge. The party pledging out the land bears full responsibility for such things. Starting from the day the land is pledged out, the fields are to be turned over to the party contracting this land on pledge, for him to manage and collect rent as his own enterprise. The period of pledge starts from the winter of the guisi cyclical year [1833] and extends to the winter of the wuxu cyclical year [1838]. After five years, upon return of the purchase price the land can be redeemed. This transaction is undertaken completely voluntarily by the two parties, without any compulsion. Today because we desire evidence we have written out this contract for the pledge of land, and it is transferred [to the party obtaining the land] as certification.

On this day it is clearly noted that there was received payment of two hundred foreign dollars as per this contract of pledge; this sum was indeed received.

It is also clearly noted that these fields are irrigated by spring water from the Shuidi Spring; the flow of water must be from higher to lower levels.

It is also clearly noted that the middleman's signature fee of four dollars [his commission] will be repaid in full on the day that the fields are redeemed [the party pledging the land out now pays; he is reimbursed by the party taking the land when it is redeemed]

Middleman: Wen Fengchang
Witnesses: affine, Gu Guangchun
      fathers elder brother's wife, Li née Liu
      father's elder brother, Yanlang
      father's elder brother, Qilang
      elder brother with adjacent field, Xingxiu
      elder brother, Xingzhu
      younger brother, Duanbo
      with adjacent field, Lin Zaiguan
Amanuensis: older brother, Huaxing
OWNER OF LARGE RENT RIGHTS:
[SEAL] SEAL OF WULUO NATIVE SETTLEMENT LARGE RENT OWNER PAN WENYA [same seal as above].
Daoguang reign period, 13th year, being the guisi cyclical year, 10th month, 26th day [December 7, 1833]
Executor of contract for the pledge of wet rice land: Li Changhua'er.

As in this contract, five-year periods were common for land pledges, that is, for redeemable sales of land. The large number of people signing on serves to protect Li Changhua'er in several ways. Since most are brothers or father's brothers or, in one case, the widow of father's brother,[19] they are in the category of close agnates of the same branch with first rights to purchase and share a strong interest in this land. As close agnates they also have residual inheritance rights to the land in the event that Li Changhua'er should leave behind no male descendent through birth or adoption. Their signing the contract indicates that they accept this loss of land to an outside party, for they were quite aware that the loss might be permanent if the seller were unable to come up with redemption money.[20] Finally, because these were the very agnates involved in the family division that gave this land to Li Changhua'er, their signatures confirm their agreement that this land does now belong to him (that is, to the family of which he is head and representative). The older brother and the other man identified as owners of "adjacent fields" sign on as such because their land shares with the plot being transferred the irrigation setup mentioned in the contract;

they acknowledge that in this transfer of land there is a transfer of responsibility with respect to the coordination of irrigation arrangements. The large-scale involvement of kin serves precisely to commodify this plot of land, for the final result is a straightforward commodity transaction between two parties.

This contract also bears the seal of the holder of "large rent" rights, in this instance the representative of a collective owner, the native settlement of Wuluo, but more usually, as far as Minong was concerned, private Han Chinese owners based in nearby towns such as Tainan or Aligang (present-day Ligang, in Pingdong County). Given that they were due rental payments from the holders of "small rent" rights, it is not surprising that the latter actively sought their endorsement of land transfers; it was obviously in the interest of someone selling "small rent" rights that the "large rent" owner be informed that "large rent" payments were now due from another party. Likewise, it was in the interest of the "large rent" owner to keep track of those from whom payments were due. The "large rent" rights differed from the rest of the commodities discussed so far in that while they could be purchased throughout the Qing period, their creation was conditioned by circumstances particular to the years of Taiwan's colonization by the Han Chinese, during the late seventeenth and early eighteenth centuries. As has been well described in the literature, during this early period entrepreneurs who had obtained government land-grant patents and had taken up obligations to pay land taxes in some cases developed the land themselves and then let it out to ordinary tenants who would farm it. In other cases, however, those obtaining the land grants recruited settlers to undertake the land reclamation on their own, and in consideration of their investment of capital and labor these settlers received the permanent use rights known as "small rent," on condition that they pay a stipulated "large rent." A variant of this process, as illustrated by the above contract, involved some of the non-Han native peoples of Taiwan, who likewise made available to Han settlers such rights with respect to land that the Qing government had recognized as belonging to the native communities (Shepherd 1993: 8–9). With "small rent" and "large rent" rights established, both were marketable commodities, but their creation appears largely to have ended together with the era of colonization.

The circumstances behind the creation of "large rent" rights explain why, as far as Minong was concerned, most were owned by outside families or corporate groups, while those owned by Minong residents or corporations appear to have been purchased at one time or another from these outside parties. Another kind of property where outside ownership loomed large was associated with the development of irrigation systems. Some canals were privately developed and owned; these canals themselves were commodities, in that they could be sold, and they also represented investments whose return was in the form of water use fees paid by those farmers whose fields benefited from the irrigation. Unlike the land grants of the era of early colonization by Han Chinese, the development and expansion of irrigation systems in Minong continued throughout the Qing period. From the point of view of the farmers it was the water that formed the commodity, yet another element in an already highly commodified environment, and certainly one no less "natural" than any of the others, as attested to by the fact that water fee obligations, like those pertaining to "large rent," could be noted in contracts of land sale or pledge. Although they were well known in Minong, I was unable to locate any surviving examples of such contracts, so for purposes of illustration I use a contract from the Fangliao region, to the south of Minong and east of the larger Hakka zone:

> Yang Jilao is the executor of this contract of irrevocable transfer through sale. I and my partners Huang Xishi and Liu Duansheng jointly purchased two [adjacent] plots of wet rice land whose location in terms of local place names is by the northern dike of Dexing Village in Fangliao. The eastern, western, southern, and northern boundaries of this parcel, as well as the large rent fees and water fees are clearly shown in the earlier [attached] contracts. Today, because I need money for other endeavors, I wish to sell what I ought to have as my share, as based upon division into three shares. I first thoroughly inquired among my close agnatic kin of the same branch and they were unwilling to take up my offer. Through the introduction of a middleman, Liu Duansheng has come forward to purchase my share. On this day, the three parties including the middleman have agreed on the basis of market value to a price of exactly one hundred and forty five dollars. On this day through the middleman the money has been received in full, and the land has been transferred forthwith to the Liu family for them to manage as one [with their earlier share]. It is guaranteed that this land was purchased at the time by Yang Jilao and his partners and that this sale does not involve such matters as lack of clarity concerning previous ownership. In the event that there is lack of clarity or other irregularities, Yang Jilao bears full responsibility and these matters will be of no concern to the party purchasing the land. This transaction is undertaken completely voluntarily by the two parties, and neither intends to renege on it. Fearing that verbal agreement leaves no evidence I have executed one copy of this contract for irrevocable transfer through sale, attached to which are two earlier contracts, for a total of three documents which are given over [to the buyer] for him to hold as certification.

On this day there was definitely received payment of one hundred and forty five dollars as per this contract, this again being confirmation of payment in full.

Present as Village Manager [i.e., village head] and as amanuensis: Wu Er
Middlemen/witnesses: Huang Guangxing, Huang Tiansong
Qianlong, 57th year, 5th month, [blank] day [between June 19 and July 18, 1792].
Executor of contract for irrevocable transfer through sale: Yang Jilao.[21]

In addition to showing how water fee obligations, like those pertaining to large rent payments, were recognized as being attached obligations in the context of the sale of small rent rights, this contract also illustrates the connection between full formalization of a contract on the one hand, and full commodification on the other. Yang Jilao is selling his one-third share to one of the other two original partners, yet this presumably "in house" deal is given full contractual treatment, so to speak, including insertion of the standard clause concerning fulfillment of the obligation to give close agnates first rights of refusal, and participation of outside parties. First, the contract creates Yang's share as a commodity; then, through this contract the sale is brought fully into the public domain of commodified transactions as defined precisely by the kinship and other long-term social relationships that the contract must both acknowledge and resist.

Such relationships would have less immediate relevance for commodities such as irrigation systems or "large rent" rights, given that the usual circumstance was ownership by parties external to local communities. Thus the collection of large rent and water-use fees could hardly be supported by kinship and other ties within a socially intimate community framework. Under such particular circumstances the state might be requested to step in, as illustrated by the following proclamation by the Fengshan county magistrate, whose jurisdiction included the Minong area, and within it the villages of Zhongtan and Jingualiao.

Li, serving as Expectant Appointee for the Directly Administered Department, transferred to Fengshan County as Acting Magistrate, by imperial command praised and encouraged for his work, issues the following decree. Whereas on the 8th day of the 3rd month of this year [April 13, 1894], Tao née Zhang, the wife of the late Brigade Commander-General, Provincial Military Commander Tao, petitioned through her family representative Tao Maoqi, who reported to me in her name stating:

"My late husband Tao Maosen formerly served as Brigade-General of Xi'an Prefecture, Yan'an Prefecture, Suide Department and Yulin Prefecture in Shaanxi Province [in north China]. Coming to Taiwan to offer his services, he was appointed as the Forward Coastal Defense Army Commander concurrently responsible for pacification and land reclamation. Therefore, in areas of Fengshan County bordering the mountains he built irrigation canals and brought lands under cultivation; he also raised capital and built irrigation canals in Yanpu, Litoubiao, and Zhongtan, as well as a tile-roofed house in Jingualiao. All these canals irrigated lands of local people, which have become lands of happiness. Annual irrigation fees are paid by the people using the canals so as to provide in compensation a very modest profit. If there is need to repair the canals, the people who use them will assist with their labor. My late husband Maosen reported this clearly to the higher provincial authorities and undertook all proper procedures, as is on record. Unexpectedly my husband died after achieving those successes, resulting in my family being reduced to poverty here, and we have wished to return to our home region for a long time. But we have had no way to raise funds for traveling expenses. So I have sold the irrigation canals at each site, connected through Yanpu, as well as the tile-roof house in their entirety to the Tan Family Agricultural Bureau (Tan wusetang). I received from them 800 dollars; I need this sum so as to escort my husband's coffin back to his native region for burial. I request that an edict be issued in order to let those people using water from the canals to irrigate their fields know that they should pay annually all of the irrigation fees and the management fees to the Tan Family Agricultural Bureau. Henceforth the canals and the house will have no connection with our Tao family."

Upon receipt [of this communication] I have found that these irrigation canals and the tile-roofed house were built by Brigade Commander-General Tao with his own funds, as is on file. Now that the properties have been sold and his coffin escorted home, all irrigation canals and the house are to be managed by the Tan Family Agricultural Bureau. It is therefore necessary to issue this proclamation:

It is proclaimed that we expect all farmers to know that if the irrigation canals in Yanpu, Liutoubiao, and Zhongtan water their fields they must pay fees to the Tan Family Agricultural Bureau. If later this bureau rents the canals to other people, the farmers should also pay the fees accordingly, and must not fall into arrears so as to accumulate their own capital. If there are abuses such as being behind in fee payments or doing damage to the canals, as soon as these have been reported, without fail the offenders will be arrested and punished with no leniency. This will invigorate irrigation and secure respect for the proper payment of fees. The tile-roof house in Jingualiao also belongs to the Tan Family Agricultural Bureau and is under their management; it is their permanent property.

Each of these commands is to be tremblingly obeyed. Do not disobey! Special proclamation!

Guangxu, 20th year, 3rd month, 15th day [April 20, 1894].

Magistrate Li's proclamation is an effort to put the weight of the Chinese state behind the Tao family's sale of irrigation systems to the Tan

Family Agricultural Bureau. Tan himself, who fully controlled his "agricultural bureau," had been brought from mainland China to Taiwan by Magistrate Li, for whom he had served in Fengshan County as a private secretary in charge of taxation and irrigation matters. Tan, who was not a native Hakka-speaker, married a woman from Zhongtan, a major village in the Minong area, and moved there from the Fengshan county seat.[22] The proclamation refers to a house in Jingualiao, a smaller village in Minong; this building served as headquarters for the entire irrigation enterprise. It also mentions irrigation systems in Yanpu and Liutoubiao, as well as in Zhongtan, with the first two being outside the Minong region, populated by Hokkien-speaking Han Chinese, and quite beyond the confines of the larger Hakka settlement zone. Thus what was indeed a contractual undertaking between Tao's widow and Tan's bureau could hardly be supported by a dense network of local ties. Least significant in this case was the fact that the two parties to the contract did not share local community roots, for both were indeed participants in a broader network of bureaucratic connections. It was more important that the distribution of these irrigation systems straddled several communities, with the obligations of individual farmers to pay water fees likewise appearing to have no support in terms of local social ties, but simply comprising the asset that had changed hands. In other words, the sale of the irrigation systems represented commodification at a level extending well beyond the local community. Commodification at such higher scales, as in the form of wide-ranging commercial ties that could cover large areas of the Qing empire, not to speak of Taiwan, involved contracts that could be supported by the ramified social ties of "functional" communities such as merchant guilds, and by the structure of the contracts themselves, as these might require, for example, that the two or more parties involved fulfill their obligations at exactly the same time (Brockman 1980). By reporting the transaction to Magistrate Li, Tao's widow did satisfy the requirements of her contractual undertaking in yet another way: given that the irrigation systems formed an asset only to the extent that they yielded income in the form of farmer's water fees, hers was an appeal to the state to ensure that these payments continued.

State support of commodification was consistent with commodification's entrenched social support at the local level, as confirmed, among other ways, by pervasive reliance on written contracts. These contracts made an impression on the Japanese, for shortly after assuming control over Taiwan in 1895, the new colonial administrators began to survey local practices, an early result of which was a report presented by Okamatsu Santaro, who remarked as follows:

> Where the power of the government is weak the people cannot hope for any
> security of property and when their rights are not protected by the courts, it is
> natural that they should devise some means of self-protection. In Formosa
> [Taiwan] the custom of drawing up deeds [that is, contracts] for every kind of
> legal act was established. From the acquisition, loss or transfer of property
> rights to a hundred other matters relating to personal affairs, even to marriage,
> adoption, succession, etc., special ints[r]uments were in constant use. Such doc-
> uments are possessed by the people throughout the island and a careful examina-
> tion of them affords the best material for investigating Formosan usages. Upon
> such documents the present report is largely based. (Okamatsu 1902: 18)

It is not surprising that Okamatsu would seek to place the Japanese
conquest within a progressive context by linking the propensity of the
Taiwanese to engage in contractual transactions to the weakness, that is to
the backwardness, of the Qing imperial regime. Of course, contract as a
symptom for backwardness flew in the face of many then-current theories
of progress, summarized in Maine's famous statement that "the movement
of progressive societies has hitherto been a movement *from Status to Contract*" (italics in original; Maine 1861: 141). But if this be progress, certainly
it would have to have been denied by the Japanese conquerors of Taiwan,
who could hardly have been expected to characterize their new colonial
domination as being anything other than a boon to the local inhabitants.
Okamatsu was not concerned as such with the larger issue of interpenetra-
tion of contracts and commodification—that is, with economic culture as a
whole. In mainland China it was with respect to this economic culture—as
characteristic of the mainland as of Taiwan—that a new and decidedly
negative perspective would soon emerge. Under the impact precisely of
later versions of Euro-American theories of progress, with Marxism-
Leninism prominently included, China's new postimperial intellectual and
political elites engaged in a different interpretation of their own past, one
fed by strong nationalist impulses, to be sure, but importantly focused not
only on the political weakness of the old Manchu regime but also on what
they took to be the cultural weaknesses of the Chinese people in general.[23]

There were certainly exceptions, but the dominant new elite view was
that the Chinese people were superstitious and backward, especially the
vast rural majority, characterized since the early twentieth century as
"peasants," or *nongmin*, using a loan-word from Japanese, given that in the
spoken Chinese of the time there were terms referring to occupationally
defined "farmers" but not to the culturally defined "peasant" that was now

an object of new-elite scrutiny, if not contempt.[24] In the context of the reformulation of late imperial China's economy as "feudal," popular religion
became "feudal superstition," and the "peasants" the principal upholders
of all that was culturally backward about China. There was no room in this
perspective for the entrepreneurial, managerially competent, commodity-
and contract-engaged rural inhabitants, such that the twentieth century
can be held to be an era of full-scale denial by China's modern nationalist
elites of their own country's independent roots of economic modernity. At
the very same time that these elites—including otherwise bitter enemies
from the Nationalist and Communist camps—were collaborating in a re-
writing of Chinese tradition that fitted "peasants" into a framework of
backwardness, and that defined the popular religion of the Chinese people
as "superstition," some European and other foreign observers were re-
marking on rural culture and society with a sympathy made ironic by its
contrast with the hostility of China's own elites. Surely it was this ongoing
denigration of China's own past that prompted R. H. Tawney, in his famous survey of China's economy, to remark as follows:

> [China] is not afflicted by the complicated iniquities of feudal land law; mano-
> rial estates worked by corvees, if they ever existed, have left few traces. . . .
> [L]andlord and tenant are parties to a business contract, not members of dif-
> ferent classes based on privilege and subordination. Hence, though questions
> of land tenure are in some regions acute, their character and setting are not
> those of Europe. (1932: 63)

In other cases foreigners might comment with hostility on what they perceived to be the economic and business sophistication of the Chinese in
China's foreign-dominated "treaty ports," or of ordinary migrants from
some of the poorest regions of rural China to southeast Asia and elsewhere,
such immigrants being precisely the kinds of people China's elite would
take to epitomize peasant backwardness.[25]

   With the Communist victory in 1949, the image of traditional Chinese
backwardness, earlier already dominant, became unchallenged and to this
day is widely but certainly not universally accepted in elite political and intellectual circles, there being no readily apparent distinction in this respect
as among the current government's supporters, its opponents, or those
who are neutral. Hence the almost bizarre contrasts between discussions
of Chinese "economic sophistication" taking place outside of China (for
example, Freedman 1979) and purported descriptions of Chinese "peasants" generated within China, of which the following, in the October 1992

issue of the prestigious *Politics and Law Tribune* is quite typical:

> As our rural society operated for thousands of years on a narrow, single-track natural economy, Chinese peasants have evolved enormous psychological momentum suited to it, so that a commodity economy is to them a novel idea to which they would like to adopt but do not know how. As sudden reform changes have put all old customs and new strange and conflicting ideas into a process of exchange and collision, they have naturally created a temporary imbalance in our peasant mentality. (Wei 1992: 33)

Observers of economic development during recent decades in Taiwan, Hong Kong, and indeed in mainland China, might find such a characterization of the "mentality" of China's so-called peasants—and its supposed historical background—to be of little help in understanding the cultural sources of economic change in these regions. What might appear equally perplexing is the linking of "peasant" economic backwardness to "feudal superstitions," for what are held to be the latter have emerged from hiding with the greatest of vigor precisely where recent economic dynamism has been most pronounced. As an article entitled "Severely Combat Feudal Superstitions Leading to the Commission of Crimes," in the February 1994 issue of *Outlook*, another important journal, put it: "According to the analysis of parties concerned, the resurgence of feudal superstitions in the 1990's started in the economically developed southeastern coastal regions" (Li 1994: 46).

Other than by linking popular religious beliefs to crime, the ongoing critique of "feudal superstition" seems unable to explain the strong association of popular religion with economic progress. However, we have seen the connection between religion and economic culture to be historically rooted. In Minong during Qing, the definition of the many shareholding corporations largely in religious terms hardly detracted from their economic significance in the context of wide-scale commodification, but rather provided further evidence that the instruments of commodification, as much as those of religion, were deeply entrenched elements of Minong's culture, and more generally of that of late imperial China as a whole. Such religious definition was but one aspect of the role of religion as providing a vocabulary for the expression of the overall arrangement of society. As elsewhere in China, religion highlighted the Minong community's organization, its history, and indeed its connections to the totality of Chinese society. Religion also reflected the community's conflicts with its neighbors. It was through religion that social arrangements received constant emphasis during the ceremonial year, when at different times various features of the social landscape were given ceremonial and ritual expression. Thus those currently so hostile to the popular religion they call "feudal superstition" might appear to be unaware of how it was generally the case in late imperial China, as in Minong, that just as one honored the gods and the ancestors through the creation of commodities, one honored commodities through the gods and the ancestors.

Appendix A: Share Sale Contract, Hsinchu (Xinzhu) Area, North Taiwan

Contract for the sale of ancestral association shares. We, Lin Changtong and his [four] brothers have received an allocation [of property] as bequeathed to us by our father, who in the past together with his agnatic uncles and nephews contributed funds for the establishment of the Dayi Gong Ancestral Estate with 52.5 shares. We, [Lin] Changtong and his brothers, obtained four shares, with the land, cash [value] and names [of the shareholders] specified in the [association] account book. Today, because we are in need of funds, we are willing to sell our four ancestral association shares, including all property and income they entail. With [agnatically close] members of our [agnatic] branch unwilling to purchase [the shares] as offered through a middleman, we now through a middleman sell them to our junior agnates [literally, agnatic nephews] Shenduo and his brothers who have come forward to purchase [them]. On this day, with the agreement of the three parties [sellers, purchasers, and middleman], and on the basis of their market value of 100 large dollars, the shares have been received in person [by the purchasers] in full settlement. [As recorded in the account book] the names of the owners of the four shares received by [Lin Chang]tong [and his brothers] today have been changed in conformity to this contract and [the shares] have been given to [Lin Shen]duo [and his brothers] as their permanent holdings. It is guaranteed that this property had belonged to [Lin Chang]tong and his brothers, that their branch agnates had no involvement with this [property], and that there has been no sale or redeemable sale [of this property] to other parties, or the like. If in the future such circumstances should arise [involving claims of other parties to the property], these will be forcefully dealt with by [Lin Chang]tong and his brothers and will be of no concern to the purchasers. This [contract] is entered into willingly by both parties and neither will renege on it. Today, desiring proof [of this transaction], we have drawn up one copy of this contract for the sale of ancestral association shares and it shall be kept as evidence.

Today it is affirmed that the sum of 100 large dollars has been received in full [by the sellers].

Middleman: branch younger brother [Lin] Changtang

Witnesses: branch older brother [Lin] Changling
    [Lin] Changse
    [Lin Chang]man
    [Lin Chang]dou
Sellers of ancestral association shares Lin Changtong
    [Lin Chang]zuo
    [Lin Chang]zu
Daoguang 2nd year 10th month [between October 14 and November 12, 1822]
[Original Chinese text provided by Professor Chuang Ying-chang, Institute of
    Ethnology, Academia Sinica, Nankang, Taipei, Taiwan. My translation.]

Appendix B: Contract for division of ancestral corporation, also North Taiwan

We, the parties to this contract for the division of management, being Qing-meng, Qingqing, Shengfu, Shengkui, Shengshan, Shengchao, Qijian, and Qi-hui, have inherited the Gonghuangong estate for ancestor worship which our ancestors established in the past in central Taiwan with contributions for the accumulation of a capital fund. The estate's share capital is divided into eight large portions, with each portion distributed equally into ten shares; there is an annual sacrifice on the 22nd day of the 11th [lunar] month to the ancestors on their death anniversary, and [after the expenses for the sacrifice] there remain additional funds [with respect to income from the estate] for interest [pay-ments, to be distributed to shareholders]. Now because the descendants are numerous, it is difficult [for all of us] to be rewarded together [with feasting and interest distribution]; we members of this ancestral association have delib-erated and have expressed willingness to individually sacrifice on the [ances-tor's] death day. Therefore we have asked that our lineage elders be present and determine through the drawing of lots the distribution of the land and funds of the sacrificial estate of the Eleventh Ancestor as well as the assets of the es-tates(s) dedicated to earlier ancestors. On the death dates of our ancestors, each one of us individually will at the appointed time offer sacrifices. As to the equal distribution of the rental payments for the military lands [originally set aside for cultivation by local garrisons but later leased out by them], each household to which this responsibility rotates will make the payment in accor-dance with the amount due and shall not shirk its responsibility. As of the ini-tiation of this division of management, with management of [the ancestral as-sociation's assets] based upon [the drawing of] lots, there does not remain [as association property] the slightest amount of land or money; each person will manage his own affairs, and from now on the descendants shall not squabble over trifles. Now, wishing to have proof [of this agreement], we have specially made three copies of this contract for the division of management; each [party] will keep one copy, which shall always serve as evidence.
    [Four clauses omitted]

Daoguang, 29th year, eighth month [between November 17 and October 15, 1849]
[Signatories omitted]
[Original Chinese text in Chuang 1985: 216]

Notes

1. For some recent discussions along these lines, see Appadurai 1986; Parry and Bloch 1989.

2. For more on commodification in the Chinese context, see Cohen 1994a.

3. Most documentary sources concerning Minong during the Qing era, including the land survey data as well as copies of contracts, account books, and genealogies, were obtained in 1971–72, as was some additional information from historically well-informed residents, all in the context of fieldwork carried out jointly with Professor Burton Pasternak (see Pasternak 1983). Several additional contracts and other documents were acquired later, some as recently as during the summer of 1999, and yet a few more were discovered through examination of published collections. Unless otherwise noted, all Qing-period documentary materials introduced or translated in this paper are drawn from photocopies; the original documents are held by private families in Meinong Township who kindly gave us permission to copy and use them.

4. See Cohen 1976 for discussion of women's property.

5. The cadastral survey did depart from Qing categories of land ownership and other rights through its requirement that for every plot of land owned by a corporation a "manager" be identified; likewise, in the absence of documented family succession, as through a family division agreement, ownership might still be listed in the name of a deceased party, with his son, widow, or another party cultivating the land listed as "manager." As far as corporations were concerned, every "manager" was indeed a shareholder, but in some cases he was also the renter on that particular plot of corporate land, while in others he was at the time of the survey the designated manager of the corporation as a whole; but even this position might be held on a rotation basis. My ongoing analysis of these records simply takes the "manager" designation as a signal indicating need to determine the underlying relationship.

6. As noted, the cadastral survey lists 2,387 persons resident in Minong as owners of land rights of one kind or another. This figure must closely approximate the total number of family units, given that in the vast majority of cases each person listed in the cadastral survey is a family head. However, while a very few of those listed were women owning rights to land as their private property, some of the men listed were in fact deceased, and some completely landless families might not have appeared even as sharing ownership in residential compounds. Precise figures as to family numbers and composition must await completion of presently ongoing analysis of the Japanese-period household registers, first compiled about four years after the cadastral survey. In the registers, the number given as the household address is the same as the plot number for residential land given in the cadastral sur-

vey. The two bodies of data are thus totally compatible and in fact cross-index each other. When the job is done we should know exactly who was where in Minong just prior to the arrival of the Japanese.

7. Such other information includes genealogies giving names of ancestors that match names listed as owners, thereby showing them to be ancestral corporations. Most important is the identification of corporation charters by informants during fieldwork in Meinong Township at different times between 1964 and 2000.

8. Both the Liu Mingquan and the Japanese surveys simply listed by name an association as owner, when appropriate. Liu Mingquan's surveyors issued a *zhang-dan,* or "certificate of measurement," for each plot of land, and I have copies of association zhangdan with the association listed as owner. Liu's survey was implemented in Minung in 1891.

9. An annual or periodic meeting including worship, banquet, and managers' report was the common arrangement among many different kinds of associations during Qing. For urban occupational associations ("guilds"), for example, see Morse 1909. Such a widespread pattern, over large areas of China and firmly entrenched in city and countryside alike, represents yet another example of the many rural-urban cultural continuities in culture and society during late imperial times, continuities later ignored, denied, or forgotten with the postimperial construction by China's own intellectual and political elites of that country's "traditional backwardness."

10. For more on this god, see Cedzich 1995.

11. The picul (*dan* in Chinese) is equivalent in weight to about 133 pounds. Prior to the 1895 Japanese occupation, money in Taiwan for larger purchases usually was largely in the form of Mexican, Spanish, or Japanese silver dollars, reflecting in Taiwan, as elsewhere in the Chinese empire, the centuries-long importation of foreign silver and silver coinage in consequence of the trade advantage enjoyed by China over the Western mercantile-imperialist powers; the trade balance turned to China's disadvantage only with the expansion of opium imports during the first half of the nineteenth century. In contracts from Minong and elsewhere in Taiwan these imported silver dollars were commonly referred to as "dollars" (*yuan*), "large dollars" (*da yuan*), or "foreign silver" (*foyin*). The value of foreign dollars was calculated, at least in the southern part of Taiwan, on the basis of weight, at 68 Chinese ounces or "taels" (*liang*) for 100 dollars. Smaller purchases would use Chinese state-minted copper "cash," usually at the rate of between 1,000 to 1,300 cash per dollar. See Clark 1896: 76–77, 127–28, 136–37.

12. I have a total of forty-five Minong contracts, of which fourteen concern the outright sale of land or house sites. Only one of the latter is a red contract; two more red contracts are referred to in other contracts as attached documents. The other thirty-one contracts relate to pledge sale, family division, loans, or transactions in people, such as uxorilocal marriage contracts or contracts for the sale-adoption of children.

13. See Scott 1976.

14. The distinction between "red" and "white" contracts concerns contracts related to transfers of rights pertaining to land, including house sites. It does not ap-

ply to contracts in other domains, such as involving adoption or marriage, and such contracts are not dealt with in this paper.

15. As one of his duties, a Qing-period county magistrate had to hold court and serve as judge periodically during the week. On the magistrate's court, see Allee 1994.

16. Only a minority of marriages were uxorilocal, where there was the possibility that the man who married into his wife's home had no family, or had come from one so poor as to yield little significant payoff in the form of important affinal ties. Likewise "little daughter-in-law marriages," also often associated with much weaker links between affines, were rare compared with other areas of Taiwan. For more on this, see Pasternak 1983.

17. See Cohen 1970, 1981, for more on the interconnections between social and contractual relationships.

18. "Large dollars" are foreign dollars; see note 11.

19. For this contract I have rendered as "Li née Liu" the woman's signature *Li Liu shi*, which literally might be translated as "the woman Liu, now of the Li family." Her signature follows the format generally used for the few female contract signatories and in many other contexts where women are named. But unlike men, in most cases they are named without being given personal names, a circumstance considered in some detail by Watson 1986.

20. In an 1840 contract, not included in this paper, Li Changhua'er for receipt of additional funds does indeed give up all rights to the land.

21. Original contract published in RTKC 1910–11, vol. 1, section 3: 428–29.

22. Information concerning Tan was provided me by his grandson, who also gave me access to an original copy of Magistrate Li's proclamation, which he kindly allowed me to transcribe.

23. Cohen 1994a gives background and details of this development.

24. For more on the invention and promulgation of the Chinese peasant, see Cohen 1994b.

25. See Cohen 1992 for details.

References

Allee, Mark A. 1994. *Law and Local Society in Late Imperial China: Northern Taiwan in the Nineteenth Century*. Stanford: Stanford University Press.

Appadurai, Arjun, ed. 1986. *The Social Life of Things: Commodities in Cultural Perspective*. Cambridge: Cambridge University Press.

Brockman, Rosser H. 1980. "Commercial Contract Law in Late Nineteenth-Century Taiwan." In Jerome Alan Cohen, R. Randle Edwards, and Fu-mei Chang Chen, eds., *Essays on China's Legal Tradition*, 76–136. Princeton: Princeton University Press.

Cedzich, Ursula-Angelika. 1995. "The Cult of the Wu-T'ung/Wu-Hsien in History and Fiction: The Religious Roots of *Journey to the South*." In David Johnson, ed., *Ritual and Scripture in Chinese Popular Religion*, 137–218. Berkeley: Chinese Popular Culture Project.

Chuang, Ying-chang. 1985. "The Formation and Characteristics of Taiwanese Lineage Organization." In Chiao Chien, ed., *Proceedings of the Conference on Modernization and Chinese Culture*, 207–20. Hong Kong: Chinese University of Hong Kong.

Clark, John D. 1896. *Formosa*. Shanghai: Shanghai Mercury.

Cohen, Myron L. 1970. "Introduction." In *Village Life in China*, by Arthur H. Smith [original 1899], ix–xxvi. Boston: Little, Brown, and Co.

———. 1976. *House United, House Divided: The Chinese Family in Taiwan*. New York: Columbia University Press.

———. 1981. "Kinship and Cooperation in a Chinese Setting: Labor Exchange in Mei-Nung, Taiwan." In *Proceedings of the International Conference on Sinology, Section on Folklore and Culture*, 129–46. Taipei: Academia Sinica.

———. 1992. "Family Management and Family Division in Contemporary Rural China." *China Quarterly* 130: 357–78.

———. 1993. "Shared Beliefs: Corporations, Community and Religion among the South Taiwan Hakka during Ch'ing." *Late Imperial China* 14, no. 1: 1–33.

———. 1994a. "Being Chinese: The Peripheralization of Traditional Identity." In Tu Wei-ming, ed., *The Living Tree: The Changing Meaning of Being Chinese Today*, 88–108. Stanford: Stanford University Press.

———. 1994b. "Cultural and Political Inventions in Modern China: The Case of the Chinese 'Peasant.'" In Tu Wei-ming, ed., *China in Transformation*, 151–70. Cambridge: Harvard University Press.

Freedman, Mayurice. 1979 [1959]. "The Handling of Money: A Note on the Background to the Economic Sophistication of Overseas Chinese." In G. William Skinner, ed., *The Study of Chinese Society: Essays by Maurice Freedman*, 22–26. Stanford: Stanford University Press.

Li Guodong. 1994. "Severely Combat Feudal Superstitions Leading to the Commission of Crimes" (Excerpted in JPRS-CAR-94-025, April 19, 1994, pp. 58–59). *Liaowang (Outlook)* 6: 45–46.

Maine, Henry Sumner. 1861. *Ancient Law: Its Connection with the Early History of Society and Its Relation to Modern Ideas*. London: J. Murray.

Morse, Hosea Ballou. 1909. *The Gilds of China, with an Account of the Gild Merchant or Co-Hang of Canton*. London: Longmans, Green and Co.

Okamatsu Santaro. 1902. *Provisional Report on Investigations of Laws and Customs in the Island of Formosa*. Compiled by order of the governor-general of Formosa. Kobe: Kobe Herald.

Parry, Jonathan, and Maurice Bloch, eds. 1989. *Money and the Morality of Exchange*. Cambridge: Cambridge University Press.

Pasternak, Burton. 1972. *Kinship and Community in Two Chinese Villages*. Stanford: Stanford University Press.

———. 1983. *Guests in the Dragon: Social Demography of a Chinese District, 1895–1946*. New York: Columbia University Press.

Rowe, William T. 1992. "Women and the Family in Mid-Qing Social Thought: The Case of Chen Hongmou." *Late Imperial China* 13, no. 2: 1–41.

RTKC, comp. 1910–11. *Dai Ichi-Bu Chosa Dai 3-Kai Hokokusho Taiwan Shihō Fu-*

roku Sankōsho. Compiled by Rinji Taiwan Kyūkan Chōsakai (First Investigation, Third Report, Private Law of Taiwan, Supplementary Reference Materials, Compiled by Temporary Commission for the Survey of Traditional Customs in Taiwan). Tokyo: Rinji Taiwan Kyūkan Chōsakai. 3 vols. in 7 sections.

Scott, James C. 1976. *The Moral Economy of the Peasant: Rebellion and Subsistence in Southeast Asia*. New Haven: Yale University Press.

Shepherd, John Robert. 1993. *Statecraft and Political Economy on the Taiwan Frontier, 1600–1800*. Stanford: Stanford University Press.

Tawney, Richard Henry. 1932. *Land and Labour in China*. London: George Allen and Unwin.

Watson, Rubie S. 1986. "The Named and the Nameless: Gender and Person in Chinese Society." *American Ethnologist* 13, no. 4: 619–31.

Wei Pingxiong. 1992. "An Analysis of China's Current Rural Crime Problem." (Excerpted in JPRS-CAR-92-004, January 25, 1993, pp. 50–56). *Zhengfa Luntan (Politics and Law Tribune)* 47: 29–36.

Toward an Historical Ethnography of the Great Irish Famine

The Parish of Tullylish, County Down, 1841–1851

Over the past two decades anthropologists working in Ireland have moved away from holistic community studies toward more contextualized historical approaches. This movement requires a balance between the compelling significance of place and explicitly drawn connections between a locale and the larger world historical processes in which they are embedded. Attempts to locate capitalism in time and place using Irish case studies are of interest because analysis of uneven capitalist development must consider the nature of dependent colonial ties to the English state and the nature of local power relations, especially class and gender.

This chapter traces connections between the uneven development of the capitalist linen industry, which was central to the economy of the north during the nineteenth century, and the impact of the Great Famine (Almquist 1977; Vincent 1992, 1996). It focuses on the parish of Tullylish, part of the industrializing Bann Valley in County Down in the Province of Ulster (Kinealy 1991: 26–31; Kinealy and Parkhill 1997; MacAtasney 1997). Tullylish provides an ideal context for making such connections because divergent subregional patterns of linen development emerged by the mid–eighteenth century and continued throughout the nineteenth (Cohen 1997; Hudson 1986: 3). Along the industrializing midsection of the parish on the banks of the River Bann, numerous centralized bleaching and finishing mills were established by the late eighteenth century. After 1825 several local manufacturers, bleachers, and merchants met the challenges posed by British technological innovations in wet spinning linen yarn by investing in mills and factories themselves, ensuring the transition to mill-based spinning based on the exploitation of a growing proletariat.

In the northern townlands of the parish, on the other hand, handloom weaving by domestic petty commodity producers continued into the early twentieth century.[1] Because landlords in Ulster had profited from leasing small, high-priced plots to weavers since the late eighteenth century (Kauf-system), farms in northern Tullylish were smaller and therefore less viable than the national average through the 1860s (Crawford 1993: 3–4). Once the putting-out system (Verlagsystem) became generalized after 1825, the earnings of these households fell, their independence was undermined, and they had to struggle in order to reproduce themselves in increasingly difficult circumstances.[2] These different rhythms of capitalist development, I argue, are crucial to explaining the different trajectories of the Famine in the parish.

Amartya Sen's work (1981) on "exchange entitlements" provides a useful framework for understanding how these distinct subregional patterns structured the impact of the Famine. Sen defines exchange entitlements as the set of all commodities that a person can acquire in exchange for what he owns. Exchange entitlements are affected by numerous factors, including the terms of employment, what is produced with one's labor power, the cost of purchasing resources, the value of the products sold, taxes to be paid, and benefits from the state. Exchange entitlements thus differ depending on the economic prospects available in any given setting, and on a person's position within a field of economic relations (ibid.: 1–6). Sen argues that, in order to understand either the transformation of food shortage into famine, or the nature and severity of that famine, it is necessary to analyze in detail the nature of exchange entitlements. Although Sen does not develop the point, one might add that gender constructions play a crucial role in structuring exchange entitlements. Indeed, in the case to be discussed, gender is a particularly salient social relation in mediating the connections between natural disaster, sickness and death, internal migration, and centralized industry—in large part because of the gender-based division of labor in both industrial factories and petty commodity producing households.

Background to the Famine: Irish Political and Economic Dependency

Exchange entitlements in nineteenth-century Ireland had been structured in major ways by Ireland's centuries-long status as a colony of England. A lack of economic diversity, a dependence on exports and foreign capital investment, and vulnerability to the boom/bust cycles of capitalism all characterized the Irish economy in the nineteenth century (Franke and Chasin 1980: 85–88).

The Irish linen industry, linked as it was to the process of empire-building and English mercantilism, was subject to most of these forces (Ogilvie 1996: 23–37). The flourishing Irish woolen industry was suppressed by the English state in 1699 in response to pressures from English woolen interests. In its place, the state sought to promote the production of Irish linen and provisions (that is, barreled and saltbeef, butter, tallow, sheep, pork, wool). The competitive advantages of duty-free access to English and colonial markets after 1696 made it possible for imports from Ireland to drive foreign linen out of the English market. However, the substitution of linen for wool was not an exchange of like industries with equal economic potential, but rather one that ensured Ireland's dependence on the English economy. Irish linen exports were particularly vulnerable to changes in English commercial policies and overseas market demand.

The nineteenth century was the critical period for securing and consolidating capitalist social relations in Ireland, as elsewhere in the United Kingdom. The nature of exchange entitlements in Ireland was complicated by the fact that the nineteenth century was also the period when the hegemony of the "ethical state" emerged in England—a state that operated through the processes of bureaucratic institutional differentiation and administrative intrusion into social life (Lloyd and Thomas 1998). While these processes had considerable influence on English society, their impact was much greater in its colony Ireland. For example, a state system of poor relief was introduced into Ireland in 1838 after prolonged debate on the nature of poverty in the country, its connection with overpopulation, and the most effective means to alleviate poverty. The administration of the Poor Law, with its emphasis on local responsibility through local taxation, was regarded as the ideal mechanism to organize relief to the poor. The Irish system was supervised by a full-time Board of Poor Law Commissioners in London who administered the English system. They, in turn, appointed a number of full-time assistant commissioners, each responsible for a number of Poor Law Unions in adjoining counties. Unions were made up of various electoral divisions, each consisting of a number of townlands, where tax rates were established and taxes collected. In accordance with the state's goal of making the Poor Rate as local a tax as possible, electoral divisions were made the unit area of taxation, within which taxes were levied on property owners in relation to the value of their holdings. Each union had a workhouse (centrally situated near a market town) and a Board of Guardians—men elected by the tax-paying individuals of the union as well as its ex officio locals (who were predominantly successful local businessmen, landlords, or large farmers). In Tullylish, the subregional economic distinctions outlined above were reflected in the division of the parish between two administrative Poor Law Unions—Banbridge, with a population in 1841 of 87,323, and Lurgan, with a population of 71,128 (referred to hereafter as Tullylish/Banbridge and Tullylish/Lurgan) (see [P.R.O.N.I.], BG.6/A/1, April 8, 1839–July 25, 1842; BG.22/A/1, February 22, 1839–January 18, 1842).[3] Irish workhouses opened their doors in 1845, just in time for the Famine, a disaster they were not prepared to handle (O'Neill 1958: 15; Kinealy 1995: 107; Kinealy 1994: 23).

From Food Shortage to Famine: The Demographic Impact in Tullylish

Ireland suffered a severe food shortage during the Famine because an infestation of the fungus *Phythophthora Infestans*, which resulted in the loss of the potato crop, the principal food source for the majority of the population (O'Grada 1989, 1999). The failure of the potato crop was partial in Ireland in 1845, general in 1846, and absolute in 1847. In Ulster, the south and west fared worst because of high population pressure, subdivision of holdings, increasing reliance on the potato, and narrowing economic opportunities in agriculture and rural industry. Intermediate levels of mortality were felt in counties Tyrone and parts of Armagh. The northeast (counties Antrim, Down, and northeast Armagh), with its stronger more diversified economic base and diet, more advanced communications and food retailing system, was generally the least affected (Kennedy 1985: 28–29). In County Down (where both Tullylish/Banbridge and Tullylish/Lurgan were located), on the eve of the Famine in 1845, 86,753 acres of land were under potatoes. In that same year, 46 to 50 percent of this potato crop was affected with blight. Between 1845 and 1848 the acreage devoted to potatoes decreased by 50 percent (O'Grada 1999: 21; Daly 1986: 54). In both subregions of Tullylish, food shortages commenced in 1846, when reports from the Banbridge and Lurgan boards of guardians indicate that the potato crop had failed in their areas. In Tullylish/Banbridge, one-sixth of the district was planted with potatoes in 1844, one-fifth in 1845, and one-eighth in 1846 (the decrease being due to the high price and scarcity of seed). In Tullylish/Lurgan, one-eighth was planted in potatoes in 1844, one-seventh in 1845, and one-tenth in 1846 (when turnips and oats were sown to replace potatoes; [P.R.O.I.], 1A/50/86).

Sen (1981: 1) argues that the investigation of starvation in a region should begin with an analysis of the relationship of persons to the commodity food. In Tullylish on the eve of the Famine (1841), this relationship was structured by an unusually high population density, extreme fragmentation of landholdings, widespread reliance on the potato as the basic food crop, and an economy in which petty commodity producers and proletarians alike had few viable options for how to earn a livelihood. As elsewhere in Ireland, the impact of the famine in Tullylish depended on social class, since exchange entitlements were largely a function of access to land and labor power. Laborers, cottiers, and cottier/weavers, who had inadequate landholdings (in the range of one to five acres), were the group most affected by the failure of the potato crop (Kennedy 1985: 29). These smallholders, so prevalent in pre-Famine Ulster, declined from 44.9 percent of the population in 1841 to 15.5 percent in 1851. Weavers who had a more substantial subsistence base (five to fifteen acres), on the other hand, and who relied less exclusively on the potato, suffered much less of a decline (from 36.6 percent of the total to 33.6 percent; see MacDonagh 1976: 357–446).[4]

In order to understand the demographic impact of the Famine in more detail, it is instructive to compare population shifts in Tullylish/Banbridge and Tullylish/Lurgan, and to relate these shifts to subregional differences in economic organization and exchange entitlements. Table 1 summarizes the population trends for Tullylish as a whole and for the Poor Law Unions separately. It can be seen that while growth slowed in the parish of Tullylish as a whole (due to death and migration), the parish gained 740 inhabitants between 1841 and 1851.[5] Of these 740 people, 61.6 percent were female, reflecting the growing work opportunities for females in the mills located along the River Bann. Indeed, what population gain there was in Tullylish all occurred in the industrializing Tullylish/Banbridge subregion (where there was an increase of 887 individuals, 62 percent of whom were female).

The skyrocketing population of the factory town Gilford between 1841 and 1851 (from 643 to 2,814) accounts for most of the population increase in Tullylish/Banbridge. Many people moved to Gilford to take advantage of employment opportunities in the newly opened spinning mill of Dunbar McMaster & Company. Although females predominated in the local mi-

TABLE I

Demographic Change in Tullylish, 1821–61

Union	1821	1831	1841	1851	1861
Tullylish Total	9259	10501	12660	13400	12908
Males	4532	5161	6143	6427	6168
Females	4727	5340	6517	6973	6740
Inhabited Houses	1687	1850	2142	2181	2378
Persons per House	5.5	5.7	5.9	6.1	5.4
Tullylish/Banbridge	—	—	7049	7936	7594
Males	—	—	3388	3721	3563
Females	3661	4211	4031		
Inhabited Houses	—	—	1232	1287	1446
Persons per House	—	—	5.7	6.2	—
Tullylish/Lurgan	—	—	5217	5116	4969
Males	—	—	2563	2531	2433
Females	—	—	2654	2582	2536
Inhabited Houses	—	—	897	914	981
Persons per House	—	—	5.8	5.6	—

SOURCES: *Census of Ireland, 1821–1861, Co. Down, P.R.O.N.I.; Abstract of the Population of Ireland, vol. 14 (1822); Return of the Several Counties in Ireland as Enumerated in 1831, vol. 39 (1833).*

gration stream to Gilford, the relative proportions of males (43.6 percent) to females (56.3 percent) suggest that both sexes were moving to the town in search of waged work, and in large numbers. The linen industry was notorious for its dependence on the cheap labor of children (Cohen 1992), and Dunbar McMaster & Company was no exception. Enrollments at the new Gilford Mill National Schools, built by the company, soared from 189 in 1846 to 410 in 1847 to 701 in 1848.[6] The Gilford Mill National Day Schools were the only schools in the parish that catered to the needs of half-timers—children who divided their time between school and work under the Factory Acts. The soaring enrollments at the schools suggest that child labor was of major importance for parents and linen capitalists alike.

Aside from Gilford and its surrounding hinterland, of the other fourteen townlands in Tullylish/Banbridge, only those that were the sites of linen mills experienced population growth during the Famine.[7] All townlands in the agricultural south of the parish, on the other hand, lost population. The attendance at Lisnafiffy National School, for example, dropped from 132 in 1846 to 67 in 1847, prompting the landlord to repossess the schoolhouse.

Demographic trends in Tullylish/Lurgan, on the other hand, are in marked contrast to those of the industrializing sections of Tullylish/Banbridge, but had much in common with the latter's rural sections. Tullylish/Lurgan reached its population peak in 1841 (prior to the Famine), and during the Famine lost 101 individuals. The vast majority of these people (71.3 percent) were female. Indeed, every townland in Tullylish/Lurgan except one lost women at this time.[8] Shifting the focus to children in Tullylish/Lurban, all three schools in this union—Ballynagarrick, Ballylough, and Clare—show fewer children in 1849 than in 1846, suggesting death, illness, and parental demand for their children's labor.[9]

A consideration of the gendered division of labor and the exchange entitlements characteristic of Irish proto-industrial households sheds light on why so many young women migrated from Tullylish/Lurgan to Tullylish/Banbridge during the mid–nineteenth century. Throughout the eighteenth and nineteenth centuries, the townlands included in Tullylish/Lurgan were densely populated with domestic handloom weavers who typically leased small plots of land for high rents (Kaufsystem). These small plots of land allowed proto-industrial households to partially reproduce themselves, but also made it possible to pay household members wages lower than those needed by urban proletarians. Prior to mill-based spinning in 1825, the division of labor in these proto-industrial households was organized by age and sex, with women and children spinning and winding yarn, while men and older male children wove cloth. This gendered division of labor relaxed after the generalization of the putting-out system in the early decades of the nineteenth century, when handloom weavers' wages fell. Many women and girls turned to weaving to help make up for the decline in household income.

Despite these changes in the organization of production at the household level, however, inheritance rules remained essentially unchanged, with land and looms passing through the male line. The result was a gendered pattern of migration, since male weavers were ensured of more secure entitlements concerning land and tools. Female labor was more "expendable," particularly in the context of expanding employment opportunities for young women and girls in nearby yarn-spinning mills. Thus, more young females were proletarianized as the putting-out system depressed the wages of handloom weavers and potato blight weakened the ability of proto-industrial households to partially reproduce themselves.

The Famine and Strengthening Economic Structures: Tullylish/Banbridge

Proletarians can be exposed to famine when their exchange entitlements are threatened, whether because of a drop in wages, an unexpected rise in food prices, a drop in demand or value of the commodities produced, or changes in company or state benefits (Sen 1981: 3). In 1847 a temporary depression in the linen industry occurred, resulting in a short-term but significant increase in the number of people requiring relief in the parish of Tullylish. Most of these people were domestic handloom weavers from the nonindustrial sections of the union, who were very prevalent in the population. Proletarianized households living along the industrializing River Bann in Tullylish, on the other hand, appear to have been insulated from starvation (O'Grada 1999: 140). Still, despite the expansion of industrial employment opportunities in the linen industry along the River Bann, the Famine did not bypass Banbridge Union. Strengthening industrial economic structures, however, shortened its duration and lessened its destructive consequences.

The archival records that indicate most directly the extent of suffering in Tullylish/Banbridge are the actual workhouse records for Banbridge Union. The data reveal that, as elsewhere in Ireland, the effects of the Famine were most severe in "Black '47" and 1848. In Banbridge Union, the Famine itself was largely over by the summer of 1849. By 1849, both new admissions and deaths in the workhouse had dropped dramatically, even though the average number in the workhouse was still high both in absolute terms and relative to its eight-hundred-person capacity.

The importance of wage work in providing a cushion against the loss of exchange entitlements is revealed by the following. The level of suffering in Banbridge Union was not great enough for all of its electoral divisions to be included under the Temporary Relief of Destitute Persons (Ireland) Act of 1847. This Act (known as the Soup Kitchen Act) was designed to provide additional relief beyond what was available in workhouses to especially destitute individuals, who would be provided with food in exchange for work, or at times, for free.[10] In Ireland as a whole, 1,677 of the total 2,049 electoral divisions (81.8 percent) were under the act. In Banbridge Union, however, 13 of the 23 electoral divisions (56.5 percent) were under the act, not including the electoral division of Tullylish, where wages, on the whole, ensured access to exchange entitlements.[11]

The bureaucratic dimension of the "ethical state" in structuring exchange entitlements in the context of the Famine is clearly revealed by the activities of the Board of Guardians, who were responsible for managing the affairs of the workhouse and administering poor relief. In the worst years of the Famine the workhouse filled quickly. When it was full, guardians provided other forms of relief. They commonly admitted additional people, provided free meals in the workhouse, gave destitute individuals food to take home, and admitted parts of rather than whole families. To extend the provision of workhouse relief, guardians were empowered to erect temporary sheds and "galleries" in all parts of the workhouse where additional accommodation could be afforded. Since outdoor relief was prohibited by the Poor Law, guardians faced with unrelenting demand for workhouse relief often provided relief in "ways categorically prohibited by the legislature" (Kinealy 1995: 111).

Between 1847 and 1849, Banbridge Workhouse policies reflected both the structural dominance of the linen industry in the region's economy and an ideological perspective on poverty that stigmatized the poor for receiving state assistance. Since hard work was linked with morality, respectability, and gendered class identity, all paupers were seen to require a steady diet of hard work. Poor Law commissioners in London also believed that hard work would make life in the workhouse sufficiently unattractive to discourage "unnecessary" demands. The Banbridge guardians concurred, consistently maintaining that if "prevented from carrying on active and unremitting industry in the House we will be wholly unable to keep the establishment from being crowded with a lazy, idle and demoralized population" ([P.R.O.N.I.], BG.6/A/10, March 2, 1850). Workhouse inmates were made to perform a variety of regionally specific manufacturing tasks (including spinning flax, winding yarn, weaving cloth, and sewing calico), which lessened the burden of the poor on the rate-payers and eased the strain on workhouse resources. If inmates refused to work, as did Sarah Macken and Isabella Mathews, they were discharged. When inmates could not be put to work in the workhouse itself, they might be apprenticed to those in weaving or other trades.[12]

These strategies by the Banbridge guardians to keep inmates at productive work reflected laissez-faire doctrines dictating that workhouses in Ireland be self-supporting establishments rather than drains on the local ratepayers (Robins 1980: 68, 240–41; [P.R.O.N.I.], BG.22/A/2B, 3, February 1842–March 1845). The master of the workhouse was required to provide sufficient work for which no wages were paid. Items manufactured by workhouse paupers could be used only within the workhouse, and not sold for profit. Poor Law Commissioners would not interfere with the free market system or undermine the livelihood of independent laborers (Kinealy 1994: 199; O'Neill 1958: 20).

Gender Mediations in the Alleviation of Distress

Although middle-class Victorian conceptions of gender linked breadwinning to masculinity and domesticity to femininity, both poor men and women were expected to work hard, albeit in gender specific ways. Victorian cultural conceptions of respectable masculinity categorically excluded able-bodied male paupers, as well as many Irish peasants whose poverty was seen to result from laziness and excessive fecundity. Vincent (1990: 8; Hatton 1993) has argued that the imposition of the Poor Law, and the way that it structured exchange entitlements, reflected these gendered conceptions. In the context of the Famine, in which large numbers of men and women alike lacked the means to provide for themselves, the Poor Law accorded greater recognition to the hardship of men. Victorian cultural perceptions of "natural" feminine weakness, dependency, and maternity, on the other hand, tended to make Poor Law guardians blind to the symbolic space pertaining to women's specific suffering. For example, according to the provisions of the Poor Law, women were not to be included among those who could receive relief in exchange for laboring at public works. Because providing relief to women who were not working represented a strain on workhouse resources, however, and because guardians were anxious to avoid undue expenditure, gender distinctions relating to what forms of work were appropriate for women were often suspended. For the same reasons, moral dilemmas over the separation of employed mothers from their children were at times ignored. For example, Poor Law commissioners ordered the master at Banbridge Workhouse to "employ the able-bodied women in any way he may deem proper," including the arduous and despised task of breaking stones. Although the commissioners at first were doubtful whether grinding corn at the corn mill was suitable work for women, the Banbridge guardians ultimately were "unanimously of the opinion that the employing of able-bodied women in the grinding of corn for their own use is not a severe or labourious employment nor likely to be injurious to their health."

Economic exigency could thus lead commissioners and workhouse masters to suspend their concerns about the frailty of women, and to insist that they provide even the most onerous of labor services. When debating to whom they could legitimately provide relief, however, guardians' decisions continued to reflect Victorian conceptions about gender. For example, after the provision of outdoor relief was granted in January 1848, the Banbridge guardians continued to deliberate over the duration of relief to able-bodied widows with children, and whether women with husbands who had emigrated were legally entitled to outdoor relief. Women who were deserted temporarily or permanently were not, despite their hardship, considered equivalent to widows with two or more children and were denied outdoor relief ([P.R.O.N.I.], BG.6/A/8, July 1848–February 1849: 257, 276). Even soldiers were not held legally responsible for the maintenance of their wives ([P.R.O.N.I.], BG.22/A/6, May 1, 1847–March 27, 1848). The combined effect of these policies was the pauperization of women and children.

Given the prevalence of women in the Banbridge Union and Workhouse, providing them even minimal relief strained guardians' resources. As a result, guardians periodically encouraged women to emigrate. Early in 1848, for example, the master of Banbridge Workhouse suggested that the guardians try to reduce the number of young unemployed women by invoking the 18th Section of the 1847 Poor Law Amendment Act.[13] He was subsequently ordered to make a list of all girls in the workhouse who were willing to emigrate and to write the guardians of each electoral division asking whether they would consent to a tax increase for that purpose. The active encouragement of emigration to Canada and Australia from the Banbridge Workhouse continued from 1848 until 1850 ([P.R.O.N.I.], BG.6/A/10, May 1849–October 1850: 733).

Even as guardians and masters sought to reduce the pressure on relief resources by encouraging women to emigrate, however, migration into Tullylish/Banbridge from rural areas continued unabated (see Table 1). When we keep in mind the fact that wage labor provided a cushion against the Famine, it is easy to understand why migration into the linen-based settlements along the Bann continued, pushing population figures upward until they reached their peak in 1861.

The Famine and Weakening Economic Structures: Tullylish/Lurgan

Patterns of landholding and petty commodity linen production in rural Tullylish/Lurgan differed widely from those of the industrial sections of Tullylish/Banbridge. The decreasing viability of independent petty commodity production in Tullylish/Lurgan in the decades leading up to the Famine, and the distinctive nature of exchange entitlements among petty commodity producers, meant that the impact of the Famine in this subregion was much more severe than in Tullylish/Banbridge. On the small farms of Tullylish/Lurgan, which were so important to linen-producing households' ability to reproduce themselves, potato blight significantly reduced the quantity of food produced, thus reducing the exchange entitlements of petty commodity producers and cottier weavers. There were a great many of these small farms. Landholdings of one acre or less accounted for more than one-third of all holdings in the union. Weavers' wages fell during the depression in the linen industry, and their earnings were further reduced by the generalization of the putting-out system. When combined with potato blight, reduced earnings meant that weavers were forced to purchase more food at just the time that they had less money with which to do so. Making their situation more difficult was the fact that there was rapid inflation in the price of food. In Lurgan Union, potatoes increased in price (per hundredweight) from 1s 11d in April 1845 to 2s 3d in March 1846 (MacAtasney 1997b: 38–39). Domestic weavers, who earned little and farmed tiny plots of land, were especially vulnerable to blight and high food prices—much more so than were proletarians, who were insulated by steady employment, tenement housing, and employer-provided medical care (as provided by the owners of Dunbar McMaster & Company in Gilford, for example).

Famine-related distress in Lurgan Union was comparable to that of rural Ireland in general. Concern over the state of the potato crop was voiced early in November 1845, when guardians noted that the quantity of potatoes was under average and a considerable amount injured by blight. By April of 1846 the effects of blight, epidemic disease and cultural disruption, signified by deserted women and children, were pressing heavily upon the workhouse. Guardians were actively looking into substitutes for potatoes, such as Indian cornmeal, with which to feed the growing number of inmates. Guardians were also seeking ways to expand the capacity of the workhouse, especially in the nursery and female apartments. Between 1844 and 1846 potatoes became so scarce that they were dropped from workhouse diets and were replaced by white bread. The number of inmates with fever also increased sharply, generating anxiety over crowded conditions in the fever hospital ([P.R.O.N.I.], BG.22/A/4, April 12, 1845–March 28, 1846: 40,58,306,365; BG.22/CJ/1, 1846).

The workhouse at Lurgan was severely overcrowded during the Famine, and the prevalence of epidemic disease and death were widespread and notorious. Additional space was needed in the Portadown Hospital and in the distillery, and a temporary workhouse was built along with temporary fever sheds to relieve overcrowding in the permanent fever hospital ([P.R.O.N.I.] BG.22). The minutes of the Lurgan Board of Guardians during the Famine reveal the extent of mortality in the workhouse and region caused by epidemic disease. By January 1847, the number of deaths in the workhouse was so high that the Poor Law Commissioners wrote from London to express their concern and regret. During the week of January 16, 1847, fifty-five inmates died, thirty-five of whom were under the age of fifteen. In that month, the number of deaths rose from eighteen to sixty-eight. Medical officer Dr. Bell's explanation points to a combination of economic and cultural causes—the high cost of provisions, the "great dislike of going to the workhouse among the lower classes," and the desire to be buried in a coffin by many who could not otherwise afford this expense. He maintained that many who arrived at the workhouse were already dead, close to death, or died within twenty-four hours of being admitted ([P.R.O.N.I., BG.22/A/5, April 1846–April 1847: 426). Sanitary conditions in the workhouse were so poor and knowledge about the spread of epidemic disease so limited that those fever patients admitted who were not already close to death died soon after.

Consequently, the number of corpses in the Lurgan Workhouse on a weekly basis was extremely high during the peak Famine years, contributing to chaotic and unsanitary conditions. The chaplain, who visited the sick and dying routinely, reported on March 18, 1847, that "James Vaughan died about 12 o'clock last night and his remains were in the male infirm ward this afternoon at 4:00. . . . [H]is corpse was allowed to remain sixteen hours after his death in the ward, before it was removed to the dead house" ([P.R.O.N.I.], BG.22/FO/2, August 31, 1846–March 4, 1848). He continued:

The medical officer states that from the great increase of inmates, being four times the ordinary number and from the crowded state of the house, it has been impossible to provide dry beds in many instances in cases of those wetted by weakly ill children and by persons in a sickly state. This sleeping upon damp beds also increased fever and bowel complaints, which have in many instances proved fatal. ([P.R.O.N.I.], BG.22/A/5, April 1846–April 1847: 426)

Although the guardians ordered a large supply of new beds and a proper drying house, in the interim they considered it their "duty to have a consultation with two or more of the most eminent physicians which this part of Ireland can supply" to learn about the causes and treatment of the prevalent epidemic and "to show the earnest desire of the Board to leave no means untried to meet this dreadful situation" ([P.R.O.N.I.], BG.22/A/5, April 1846–May 1847: 456). Dysentery continued to increase nevertheless, along with measles and smallpox among children recovering from dysentery—a situation that prompted the medical officer to request immediate fundamental remedies, including warmer clothing and a more nutritious diet to counter extreme debilitation caused by inadequate food and sanitation ([P.R.O.N.I.], BG.22/A/6, May 1, 1847–March 27, 1848: 37). In 1849, "the proper discharge of the onerous duties" prevented Dr. Bell's successor, William Ross MacLaughlin, from submitting annual reports and from attending to "those prolific external sources of disease," such as filthy yards, deficient drainage, proper ventilation, and surface water at the workhouse ([P.R.O.N.I.], BG.22/CJ/1, September 29, 1849).

A comparison of workhouse records for both unions relating to monthly admissions, residents, and deaths shows that the Famine crisis began to affect the people in Lurgan Union slightly earlier than in Banbridge, and it continued longer. Banbridge Union began to cope with the Famine by December of 1846, when the workhouse was over capacity by eighty-one persons. Better records for Lurgan Union reveal that the number of monthly admissions began to increase dramatically between February and March of 1846 and reached crisis proportions by December of that year (when a full workhouse reported fifty-eight deaths). The early months of "Black 47" were a time of severe distress in both unions, when workhouse resources and staff were pressed far beyond capacity and capability. Large numbers of people were admitted to both workhouses during this time, and many of those who were admitted died, the majority of infectious disease.

Constabulary reports suggest that, as legal means of obtaining food became less reliable, some people resorted to larceny in order to provide for themselves. For example, on January 13, 1847:

> between the hours of one and two o'clock this morning a boat lying at a place called Madden's Bridge about half a mile from Gilford Castle, with flour in transit for Newry, the property of a miller in Tandragee was attacked by men to the number of five and twenty or thirty most of whom were armed with flint locks and nearly half of the freight that is to say 80 bags of flour was carried off.

After searching the area, the officer found high-quality flour in many of the surrounding houses and concluded that it was the same flour stolen from the boat. However, since the bags were well hidden, he could not prove his allegations. About five or six weeks later, a similar attack was made on a cargo of Indian meal at Madden's Bridge and another theft of flour near Portadown ([N.A.D.], Outrage Papers, 1845–50; Hanagan 1994: 809–10).

Even though Lurgan Union had taken measures to increase the number of people it could accommodate (from 800 up to 1,812 in October 1848), 634 more people died in Lurgan Workhouse and its fever hospital than in Banbridge. In Banbridge Workhouse, 18.7 percent of those admitted died, with an average of 41.5 deaths per month. The death rate in the Lurgan Workhouse, on the other hand, was 30 percent of total admissions, with an average of 94.3 deaths per month—a figure more than twice that of Banbridge. Both workhouses had to resort to turning desperate people away to reduce the resident population and to cope with those currently sick and dying.

The crisis in Lurgan Workhouse abated somewhat in 1848, when the death rate dropped to 23 percent of admissions and the average number of deaths per month fell to a rate nearly equal to Banbridge's (30 for Banbridge, 31.3 for Lurgan). Although the linen industry revived in 1848, however, Lurgan Workhouse still admitted 1,637 more people in 1848 than did Banbridge Workhouse, and large numbers of people were still being admitted to the workhouse in 1851. Available data suggest that intense Famine-related distress in Lurgan Union and Workhouse did not end until 1852.

Indoor Relief Registers for Lurgan Union Workhouse permit more fine-grained analysis of inmates from the densely populated electoral division of Tullylish/Lurgan. Between 1845 and 1848, the proportion of inmates from the five Tullylish/Lurgan townlands was low, 12–13 percent of the total admissions. Table 2 shows the resident townlands for inmates from Tullylish/Lurgan. It is significant that very few residents from Ballymacanallon, a townland flanking industrializing Gilford/Dunbarton, en-

TABLE 2

Residence and Sex Characteristics of Famine Inmates
from Tullylish in Lurgan Workhouse, 1845–48

Townland	1845	1846	1847	1848
Ballymacanallon	5.2%	0%	1.0%	2.4%
Bleary	15.5	57.0	51.2	24.6
Clare	51.0	16.6	15.0	45.1
Ballynagarrick	12.1	5.2	10.0	18.0
Ballydougan	17.2	21.2	22.6	29.9
Males	45.8	39.4	51.0	47.0
Females	54.2	60.6	49.0	53.0
TOTALS	59	208	349	217

SOURCE: *P.R.O.N.I., BG.22/G/1–2 Lurgan Workhouse Indoor Relief Register.*

tered the Lurgan Workhouse. Many displaced persons from this townland entered the expanding workforce of Dunbar McMaster & Company. Despite the predominance of handloom weavers and winders in Tullylish/Lurgan, the proportion of inmates with these occupations was relatively low, 29 percent in 1846, 24 percent in 1847, and 32 percent in 1848. This suggests that despite dislocation in the linen industry in 1847, wages earned by members of fine linen weaving households were high enough to insulate the majority, especially when supplemented by the wages earned by those members migrating locally in search of employment in mills. Those at the bottom—landless laborers, and cottier weavers with less than five acres who earned low wages—constituted the majority of inmates with these occupations. Finally, an examination of sex composition reveals that with the exception of 1847, the proportion of women inmates was consistently greater than that of men, probably because of the elimination of hand spinning and desertion by husbands.

Another source of demographic data is the half-yearly abstracts of accounts for the various electoral divisions in Lurgan Union between 1845 and 1851 ([P.R.O.N.I.], BG.22/CJ/1). These data also confirm the heavier toll taken on women and children during the Famine, with children consistently composing about half of those who received relief. More adult females were relieved than males since women, whose principal occupations in this region were winders, weavers, and sewers, earned lower wages than skilled male weavers. Because widows with children, deserted women, and women with illegitimate children were particularly vulnerable to impoverishment, they figure prominently in statistics on the workhouse population.

The poor rate in Tullylish/Lurgan was 50d. per pound of land value, with 20d. allocated for outdoor relief and 30d. for indoor or workhouse expenses. The Poor Law commissioners were determined to ensure "vigorous collection" of these rates despite growing resistance. In July of 1847, however, the Lurgan Board of Guardians responded that it was senseless for rate collectors to press hard upon impoverished rate payers:

> [T]he Board begs leave to lay before them the real state of this part of the country. There are in this Union a great portion of rate payers or rather occupiers liable to rates whose sole dependence for the support of their families at this moment is a loom and nearly the entire amount of their furniture a bed, often of a most wretched description with only one or two cooking utensils. On these the collector may lay his hands in default of payment, but what must follow? Struggling industry will be driven forth upon the world, the addition of an entire family made to the pauper's list and a few shillings collected at the eventual cost of many pounds. ([P.R.O.N.I.], BG.22/A/6, May 1, 1847–March 27, 1848: 98)

The economic base of much of Lurgan Union was handloom weaving of fine linen cloth such as cambric, damask, and diaper, organized by the putting-out system. Some weavers were highly skilled and earned wages that were sufficient to ensure independence and the retention of their land. Still, in the context of declining independence during the nineteenth century, this group's prosperity was not increasing, and under Famine conditions the extra rates and high food prices bore heavily on weavers' exchange entitlements. Even before full demands for relief were made in 1846, the Lurgan guardians were in debt. By October 1847, reports of local resistance to the collection of poor rates began ([N.A.D.], Outrage Papers, 1845–50). Examination of the half-yearly abstract of accounts for Tullylish/Lurgan between 1842 and 1851 reveals that the rate struck for the Electoral Division of Tullylish was a persistent problem. Despite rising expenditures between 1846 and 1849, in 1846–47 only a pittance was collected and the union remained bankrupt ([P.R.O.N.I.], BG.22/CJ/1).

One consequence of debt and the persistence of labor-intensive handloom weaving of fine linen was that the Lurgan guardians were not as eager to promote or finance the emigration of the numerous resident female paupers. Inmate labor in Lurgan Workhouse was from its inception oriented toward filling the labor supply needs of the domestic linen industry

([P.R.O.N.I.], BG.22/A/7, April 1848–March 1849). Neither winding yarn nor weaving were as yet mechanized. Although Inspector Senior visited the workhouse in March of 1848 and selected a number of young women for emigration, the guardians wanted neither to pay the cost of three pounds per head nor lose the contribution to be made by their labor. Prospects for employment temporarily brightened for those handloom weavers who managed to survive. Indeed, a combination of declining supply and persistent demand for handloom weavers' labor caused wages to rise.[14] By 1848 the Lurgan Board of Guardians recognized the emerging labor supply problem and sought to remedy it by providing cheap child labor for apprenticeships instead of promoting emigration. Although the commissioners stated that there was no provision in the Poor Law Act enabling guardians to take such actions, girls continued to be taken out as winders and servants ([P.R.O.N.I.], BG.22/A/8, April 5, 1849–February 28, 1850).

Conclusion

This chapter has applied locality-based historical ethnography to trace the connections between the uneven development of the capitalist linen industry and the impact of the Great Irish Famine. The focus of the paper has been on the specific nature of exchange entitlements in the industrializing sections of Tullylish/Banbridge versus the petty-commodity producing regions of Tullylish/Lurgan. Such a focus has made it possible to identify the famine's historical verities at the regional level and the forces that were responsible for the plight of the suffering. When we "refine the categories of the suffering" by focusing on entitlement relations, women, children, and petty commodity producers emerge as those most vulnerable to pauperization and proletarianization (Vincent 1990: 16). The famine's uneven impact in the parish was linked to occupational differences among workers in the local linen industry and to Victorian cultural constructions of gender that structured power relations at all levels of society.

In closing, we may note two additional consequences of the Famine for processes of class formation in subsequent decades. First, the Famine dealt a fatal blow to a proto-industrial system already weakened after 1825 by the generalization of the putting-out system. Although the decline in the number of handloom weavers in Tullylish/Lurgan after the Famine temporarily decelerated the proletarianization of surviving weavers, rising variable capital costs (that is, wages) created a powerful impetus to mechanize linen weaving, a process that began in the 1860s and penetrated fine linen weaving by the end of the century (Cohen 1997b).

Second, the dislocation of population during the famine in Tullylish parish permanently solved the labor supply problem for capitalists along the River Bann in Tullylish/Banbridge. As occurred in Belfast and other industrializing towns in Ireland, many distressed people, particularly young single women, migrated to Gilford/Dunbarton and other factory hamlets along the Bann in search of employment opportunities, creating unbalanced sex compositions, housing shortages, and social and sanitation problems. Employment in the linen mills offered survival and limited security in the form of entitlements to wages, housing, and sometimes medical care. Thus, many domestic weavers migrated to townlands along the Bann or, more commonly, sent their daughters. The soaring population of the Bann between 1841 and 1851 made possible unusually high rates of capital accumulation, and defined a new set of material constraints for those Famine survivors who now swelled the ranks of the working-class (Cohen 1992, 1993, 1997b).

Notes

1. The townland was the traditional Irish land measure. It was conceived by the Irish as a measure of land suitable to graze a certain number of cattle; hence the better the land, the smaller the townland. During the Plantation in the early seventeenth century, the English conceived it as a unit of land containing a minimum number of acres of profitable land. It also served as the unit for landlords in leasing land.

2. In other words, although petty commodity producers retained a modicum of independence, the terms and conditions of domestic handloom weavers' work were increasingly set by the capitalist mode of production (Kriedte 1981: 138).

3. Banbridge Union included the thirteen townlands of Tullyrain, Tullylish, Moyallon, Loughans, Mullabrack, Drumiller, Lenederg, Drummaran, Knocknagore, Drumhorc, Lisnafiffy, Coose, and Drumnascampf. Lurgan Union included Ballydugan, Ballymacanallon, Ballynagarrick, Bleary, Clare, and Ballylough.

4. These were the more prosperous fine linen weavers concentrated near Lurgan in northeast Armagh, in northwest Down, and in northeast Antrim whose higher wages and possession of small plots of land allowed them to cling to independence.

5. The population of Tullylish reached its nineteenth-century peak in 1851, and remained high through 1861.

6. The Gilford Mill National Schools absorbed children drawn from the older Gilford No. 1 school and surrounding townlands. *Thirteenth Report of the Commis-*

sioners of National Education (Ireland) for the year 1846, vol. 17 (1847); *Fourteenth Report of the Commissioners of National Education (Ireland) for the year 1847*, vol. 29, (1847–48); *Fifteenth Report of the Commissioners of National Education (Ireland) for the year 1848*, vol. 23 (1849); and *Sixteenth Report of the Commissioners of National Education (Ireland) for the year 1849*, vol. 25, (1850).

7. The townlands were Coose, Drumnascamph, and Lenaderg, which had modest population increases during the Famine. These townlands, which also flanked the River Bann, were the sites of long established mills, such as Milltown Bleachgreen at Lenaderg. This townland absorbed twenty-two persons, with another forty moving to neighboring Drumnascamph.

8. This included two townlands with modest population gains: Ballydugan gained 44 men and lost 21 women; Ballymacanallon, a townland flanking Gilford, lost 25 women but gained 10 men. Finally, Clare lost the most population during the Famine: 125 women and 90 men. Bleary gained 88 men and women.

9. Child labor was used either on farms or for ancillary tasks associated with fine linen weaving, both of which disrupted schooling. The Factory Acts did not yet regulate children's labor in handloom weaving households classified as workshops. *Thirteenth Report of the Commissioners of National Education (Ireland) for the year 1846*, vol. 17 (1847); *Fourteenth Report of the Commissioners of National Education (Ireland) for the year 1847*, vol. 29, (1847–48); *Fifteenth Report of the Commissioners of National Education (Ireland) for the year 1848*, vol. 23 (1849); and *Sixteenth Report of the Commissioners of National Education (Ireland) for the year 1849*, vol. 25, (1850).

10. Grants were given by the Poor Law commissioners to help subsidize local public works or to distribute rations either free of charge or at the cost of 2½ d. per ration, during the period May 24 to August 15, to those destitute who were unable to gain admission to the workhouse.

11. *First Report of the Relief Commissioners Together with Treasury Minute of March 10, 1847*, vol. 17 (1847); *and Fifth, Sixth and Seventh Report of the Relief Commissioners Constituted Under the Act 10 Vict. c.7. and Correspondence Connected Therewith, vol. 29* (1847–48).

12. In April 1848, handbills were "issued by the Board offering to Apprentice out 50 boys and 50 girls, inmates of the workhouse, to weaving and other trades for such period as may be agreed on not less than 3 years" to lessen the burden on the ratepayers ([P.R.O.N.I.], BG.6/A/9, December 1848–October 1849). The practice of using the labor of pauper children to extend domestic production of linen yarn and cloth extended back at least until the mid–eighteenth century. A local source of apprentices for local weavers or linen manufacturers in Banbridge Union was pauper children from the Lurgan Workhouse. In contrast to England, there was no statutory provision to allow Irish boards of guardians to apprentice children, limiting their ability to intervene in behalf of a child. Although securing positions for girls was far more difficult than for boys elsewhere in Ireland, in northeast Ulster the opposite circumstance prevailed. Because of the prevalence of domestic weaving in Lurgan Union, many girl paupers were discharged from the workhouse to be taught winding bobbins, sometimes weaving, and to spin linen yarn on spinning

wheels. Pauper boys were also occasionally taught winding and frequently taught weaving.

13. This act increased the powers of guardians to assist poor persons, notably smallholders who occupied land valued at under five pounds, to give up their land to their landlord and emigrate. Two-thirds of the cost was to be paid by the landlords, with the remaining third to be paid by the guardians who raised the poor rates in the electoral division in which the person was situated.

14. Indicative of the changing conditions of supply and demand for handloom weavers' labor was the following: in 1846, domestic linen weavers constituted 26 percent of the resident population of Lurgan Workhouse. By 1847, their proportion had fallen to 12 percent.

References

PRIMARY SOURCES

Public Record Office of Ireland
[1A/50/86]: Constabulary Reports.

National Archive, Dublin
Outrage Papers, 1845–50.

Public Record Office of Northern Ireland
[D.1252/20/8]: Dickson Estate, Wages Book. 1849.
[D.1252/20/10]: Dickson Estate, Day Book of Costs of the Gilford Estate. 1849–1901.
[BG.6]: Banbridge Workhouse Statistics during the Great Famine.
[BG.6/A/1]: Minute Book, Banbridge Board of Guardians. April 8, 1839, to July 25, 1842.
[BG.6/A/6–10]: Extracts from the Minutes of the Board of Guardians of Banbridge Poor Law Union. November 1846 to October 1850.
[BG.22]: Lurgan Workhouse Statistics during the Great Famine.
[BG.22/A/1–8]: Minute Books, Lurgan Board of Guardians. February 22, 1839, to February 28, 1850.
[BG.22/CJ/1]: Half-Yearly Abstracts of Accounts, Lurgan Board of Guardians. 1841–51.
[BG.22/FO/2]: Chaplain's Book, Lurgan Board of Guardians. August 31, 1846, to March 4, 1848.

British Government Documents
H.C. First Report of the Relief Commissions together with Treasury Minute of March 10, 1847, vol. xvii (1847).
H.C. Fifth, Sixth and Seventh Report of the Relief Commissions Constituted un-

der the Act of 10 Vict.c.7 and Correspondence Connected Therewith, vol. xxix (1847–48).

H.C. Thirteenth Report of the Commissioners of National Education (Ireland) for the Year 1846, vol. xxvii (1847).

H.C. Fourteenth Report of the Commissioners of National Education (Ireland) for the Year 1847, vol. xxix (1847–48).

H.C. Fifteenth Report of the Commissioners of National Education (Ireland) for the Year 1848, vol. xxiii (1849).

H.C. Sixteenth Report of the Commissioners of National Education (Ireland) for the Year 1849, vol. xxv (1850).

SECONDARY SOURCES

Almquist, Eric. 1977. "Mayo and Beyond: Land, Domestic Industry and Rural Transformation in the Irish West 1750–1900," Ph.D. diss., Boston University.

Campbell, Michael P. 1984. *A History of Tullylish*. Lurgan: Ronan Press.

Cohen, Marilyn. 1992. "Paternalism and Poverty: Contradictions in the Schooling of Working-Class Children in Tullylish, County Down, 1825–1914." *History of Education* 21, no. 3: 291–306.

———. 1993. "Urbanisation and the Milieux of Factory Life: Gilford/Dunbarton, 1825–1914." In Chris Curtin, Hastings Donnan, and Thomas M. Wilson, eds., *Irish Urban Cultures*, 227–42. Belfast: Institute of Irish Studies Press.

———. 1997a. "Rural Paths of Capitalist Development: Class Formation, Paternalism and Gender in County Down's Linen Industry." In Lindsay Proudfoot, ed., *Down: History and Society*, 567–97. Dublin: Geography Publications.

———. 1997b. *Linen, Family and Community in Tullylish, County Down, 1690–1914*. Dublin: Four Courts Press.

Crawford, William H. 1993. "A Handloom Weaving Community in County Down." *Ulster Folklife* 39: 3–4.

Daly, Mary E. 1986. *The Great Famine in Ireland*. Dundalk: Dundalgan Press.

———. 1995. "The Operations of Famine Relief, 1845–47." In Cathal Poirteir, ed., *The Great Irish Famine*. Dublin: Mercier Press.

Franke, Richard W., and Barbara H. Chasin. 1980. *Seeds of Famine: Ecological Destruction and the Development Dilemma in the West African Sahel*. Montclair, N.J.: Allheld, Osmun and Co.

Frogatt, Peter. 1989. "The Response of the Medical Profession to the Great Famine." In E. Margaret Crawford, ed., *Famine: The Irish Experience 900–1900*. Edinburgh: John Donald Publishers.

Gallogly, Fr. Dan. 1997. "The Famine in County Cavan." In Christine Kinealy and Trevor Parkhill, eds., *The Famine in Ulster*, 59–75. Belfast: Ulster Historical Foundation.

Geary, Laurence M. 1995. "Famine, Fever and the Bloody Flux." In Cathal Poirteir, ed., *The Great Irish Famine*, 74–85. Dublin: Mercier Press.

Grant, Jim. 1997. "The Famine in County Tyrone." In Christine Kinealy and Trevor Parkhill, eds., *The Famine in Ulster*, 197–222. Belfast: Ulster Historical Foundation.

Hannigan, Ken. 1994. "Wicklow before and after the Famine." In Ken Hannigan and William Nolan, eds., *Wicklow: History and Society*. Dublin: Geography Publications.

Hatton, Helen. 1993. *The Largest Amount of Good: Quaker Relief in Ireland 1654–1921*. Montreal: McGill-Queen's University Press.

Hudson, Pat. 1986. "The Regional Perspective." In Pat Hudson, ed., *Regions and Industries*, 5–38. Cambridge: Cambridge University Press.

Kennedy, Liam. 1985. "The Rural Economy, 1820–1914." In Liam Kennedy and Philip Ollerenshaw, eds., *An Economic History of Ulster, 1820–1939*, 1–61. Manchester: Manchester University Press.

Kinealy, Christine. 1991. "The Lisburn Workhouse during the Famine." *Lisburn Historical Society Journal* 8: 26–31.

———. 1994. *This Great Calamity: The Irish Famine 1845–52*. Dublin: Gill and Macmillan.

———. 1995. "The Role of the Poor Law during the Famine." In Cathal Poirteir, ed., *The Great Irish Famine*. 104–22. Dublin: Mercier Press.

Kinealy, Christine, and Trevor Parkhill, eds. 1997. *The Famine in Ulster*. Belfast: Ulster Historical Foundation.

Kriedte, Peter. 1981. "Proto-industrialization between Industrialization and De-industrialization." In Peter Kriedte, Hans Medick, and Jurgen Schlumbolm, eds., *Industrialization before Industrialization*. Cambridge: Cambridge University Press.

Lloyd, David, and Paul Thomas. 1998. *Culture and the State*. London: Routledge.

MacAtasney, Gerard. 1997a. *"This Dreadful Visitation": The Famine in Lurgan/Portadown*. Belfast: Beyond the Pale Publications.

———. 1997b. "The Famine in County Armagh." In Christine Kinealy and Trevor Parkhill, eds., *The Famine in Ulster*, 35–57. Belfast: Ulster Historical Foundation.

MacDonagh, Oliver. 1976. "The Irish Famine Emigration to the United States." *Perspectives in American History* 10: 357–446.

O'Brien, Seamus. 1999. *Famine and Community in Mullingar Poor Law Union, 1845–1849*. Dublin: Irish Academic Press.

O'Grada, Cormac. 1989. *The Great Irish Famine*. London: Macmillan.

———. 1999. *Black '47 and Beyond: The Great Irish Famine in History, Economy and Memory*. Princeton: Princeton University Press.

O'Neill, Thomas P. 1958. "The Irish Workhouses during the Great Famine." *Christus Rex* 12: 15–25.

Ogilvie, Sheilagh. 1996. "Social Institutions and Proto-Industrialization." In Sheilagh C. Ogilvie and Markus Cerman, eds., *European Proto-Industrialization*, 23–37. Cambridge: Cambridge University Press.

Robins, Joseph. 1980. *The Lost Children: A Study of Charity Children in Ireland 1700–1900*. Dublin: Institute of Public Administration.

Sen, Amartya. 1981. *Poverty and Famines: An Essay on Entitlement and Deprivation*. Oxford: Oxford University Press.

Silverman, Marilyn, and P. H. Gulliver. 1997. "Historical Verities and Verifiable

History: Locality-Based Ethnography and the Great Famine in Southeast Ireland." *Europaea* 3, no. 2: 141–70.

Vincent, Joan. 1990. "Culture, History and Place." Paper presented at the annual meeting of the American Anthropological Association, New Orleans.

———. 1992. "A Political Orchestration of the Irish Famine: County Fermanagh, May 1847." In Marilyn Silverman and Philip H. Gulliver, eds., *Historical Anthropology through Irish Case Studies*, 75–98. New York: Columbia University Press.

———. 1996. "Linen in the Irish Northwest: Unfinished Business, or Lived Experience in the 1830s." In Marilyn Cohen, ed., *The Warp of Ulster's Past: Interdisciplinary Perspectives on the Irish Linen Industry, 1700–1920*, 139–57. New York: St. Martin's Press.

———. In press. *Seeds of Revolution: The Culture and Politics of the Great Irish Famine in the Irish Northwest*. New York: St. Martin's Press.

DAVID NUGENT

Erasing Race to Make the Nation

The Rise of "the People" in the
Northern Peruvian Andes

In this paper I analyze the complex set of economic, political, and cultural processes that resulted in the modern Peruvian nation-state attaining a concrete presence in the Chachapoyas region of the northern sierra. Rather than approach this problem from the perspective of the centers of power, however, I examine how subaltern groups in this peripheral section of the national space regarded modernity and nation-state. This "view from the margins" presents a challenge to current "state-centered" understandings of how states and national cultures are formed (Nugent 1994). Unlike what is described in the literature, in the Chachapoyas region subaltern groups openly embraced modernity and actively sought out participation in the national community. Indeed, so passionately did the subaltern feel about joining the nation that in 1930 they risked their lives in an armed uprising that overthrew the local elite, and thereafter played the key role in establishing the institutions and values of the nation-state. In other words, the emergence of the modern nation-state in the Chachapoyas region was contingent upon the *active collaboration* of the subaltern in the project of state-building and nation-making.

In order to explain how and why this came about, I first analyze conditions within the Chachapoyas region prior to 1930. I then discuss changes in global, national, and local arenas that took place in the 1920s that combined to effect a rupture in the local social order, culminating in a subaltern revolt that ushered the modern nation-state into being within Chachapoyas.[1]

A Plea for Justice

On August 1, 1924, a leading member of the Oyarce family—one of the oldest and most prestigious in the Chachapoyas region—sent the following appeal to the departmental prefect:

> [F]or more than five years I have suffered the mortal hatred of my neighbor Sra. Laura Castañeda . . . , who, assisted by her sons Hector and Eloy . . . make continuous attempts . . . on my life and that of my family. . . . On May 17, 1921, I was treacherously attacked by Hector . . . and others, all of whom were armed, and was seriously wounded. . . . On June 17 of the past year, in [a] public thoroughfare . . . and in the presence of Sra. Laura Castañeda . . . Eloy attempted to shoot my nephew . . . who, miraculously, was able to escape this attack. . . . [Eloy] and ten other men have [also] had the cowardice to make an armed attempt on the life of my young son Estanrófilo, who is only a boy. . . . Not only our lives but also my family's economic affairs are subject to the furor of th[is family] and their followers who, armed with Winchester carbines and Mauser rifles, continually lay waste to my properties, killing and carrying off my livestock. . . . [Because of] the danger to my life and to the lives of those dear to me, I write to demand to be provided with the individual rights [*garantías*] that the Constitution grants to all its citizens. . . . I can scarcely believe that at a time when our national culture has reached such an advanced state, scenes occur that belong more properly to the medieval epoch, for nothing else can explain the attitude of my . . . enemies, who have set themselves up as the arbiters of a life I do not owe them, as the arbiters of my economic affairs and of my individual labor. [APA 1924, Decreto No. 142]

When placed in context, this account expresses the central contradiction of state-society relations in the "pre-modern" period (before 1930). From Sr. Oyarce's appeal, one would suppose that regional society in Chachapoyas was organized along the familiar lines of liberal democracies—in which citizens enjoy individual rights and protections, the rule of law obtains equally for all, and private property is sacrosanct. Indeed, not only does Sr. Oyarce write as if these very notions carry moral weight with the government apparatus, but the justice of his entire position assumes that the values and institutions of the modern nation-state are the reigning social realities of the time. That is, he is an ordinary citizen who attempts to live out a normal life of peace and prosperity according to the "advanced" precepts of "modern," national culture. His barbaric neighbors, on the other hand, cling to archaic and outmoded forms of behavior, arrogating to themselves the "feudal" privilege of being the arbiters of his fate.

As a result, Sr. Oyarce has been forced to endure what no citizen should have to—perpetual insecurity of person, property, and family.

It turns out, however, that this account misconstrued regional affairs in a fundamental but nonetheless revealing way. Sr. Oyarce's representation of what was normal and what was aberrant in the Chachapoyas region actually *reversed* the existing state of affairs. Rather than liberal democracy and popular sovereignty being the organizing principles of the social order, the precepts of aristocratic sovereignty (Foucault 1980) governed the organization of everyday life. It was specifically *racial* divisions (Indio, mestizo, blanco) that acted as the matrix that granted privilege, power, wealth and standing to the privileged few but denied these to the vast majority.[2] So distant were actual social conditions from the egalitarian principles invoked by Sr. Oyarce that the hierarchies and inequalities of the aristocratic order were acted out and celebrated on a daily basis in virtually all walks of life. In other words, regional society was organized in such a way as to celebrate what Sr. Oyarce claimed to deplore, and to deplore what he pretended to celebrate.

To invoke Enlightenment principles of equality and justice in a social context in which privilege was continuously naturalized, legitimated, and publicly displayed would seem either disingenuous or absurd. And yet Sr. Oyarce's decision to represent the normal as aberrant and the aberrant as normal was far from unique. Virtually all discourse directed to members of the government apparatus, whether from Indio, mestizo, or blanco, was similarly constructed. That is, regardless of their place in the aristocratic order, all those who sent communiqués to government representatives wrote as if the order in which they lived did not exist. Instead, they wrote as if a nonexistent state of equality and democracy was the norm, and actual social conditions (based on hierarchy, privilege, and gratuitous violence) were the exception. Furthermore, everyone adopted this discursive strategy despite the fact that everyone—including the government representatives receiving these communiqués—knew the opposite to be the case.

In no sense, then, did those employing the *language* of equality and citizenship at this time even remotely resemble a true community of individual citizens, equal in the eyes of the law. Nor did they make any attempt to become such a community. To the contrary. Although the precepts of popular sovereignty represented the sole terms in which legitimate and illegitimate actions, laudable and reprehensible intentions could be *repre-*

sented—and while these same principles formed the basis of all political ritual and discourse—the precepts of popular rule bore no relation whatsoever to everyday life.

Within just years of Sr. Oyarce sending his plea to the prefect, however,
the uses put to notions of individual rights, constitutional guarantees, the
sanctity of private labor, and the equality of all citizens changed profoundly. By the late 1920s these notions had begun to mobilize people to
action. Indian and mestizo groups that had long been denigrated within
the cultural logic of aristocratic sovereignty temporarily set aside their differences, and coalesced into a broad-based political movement intent on
challenging aristocratic privilege. Referring to themselves as *el pueblo* (the
people), at a moment of crisis in the national political order these subaltern
groups rose up against and overthrew the elite in an armed uprising.
Thereafter, "the people" did their utmost to form a new kind of public culture in Chachapoyas, one that made a reality of the principles of equality
and democracy that had long been voiced in political ritual and discourse.
By the early 1930s the aristocratic order was undone, a "democratization"
of local life was well under way, and the institutions and cultural values of
the modern nation-state attained an autonomous presence in the region for
the first time.

This transformation of politics and discourse, which "freed the people
to make the nation," is the focus of the present paper. Specifically, I focus
on two inter-related themes. First, I examine the juxtaposition within the
Chachapoyas region of the two contrasting modes of political sovereignty
to which Sr. Oyarce alludes in his plea to the prefect—aristocratic and
popular. That is, I analyze the ways in which notions of "individual rights
and guarantees" were integrated into a regional, social context in which
neither individuality nor equality (in the contemporary, Western sense)
existed. Second, I trace out the ways in which these same notions of individual rights, in the context of radical social and political transformation,
became the basis for articulating a new cultural order—one that subverted
the existing terms of cultural legitimacy.[3] A final section of the paper draws
out the implications of the Chachapoyas case in comparative terms.

Political Conflicts and Discursive Contradictions: Chachapoyas, 1885–1930

The emergence of Peru as an independent nation-state in 1824 was the culmination of several years of anticolonial struggle with absolutist Spain—a process that affiliated the new Peruvian polity directly with the liberal democracies of western Europe and the United States. Indeed, Peru as a nation was founded on the very Enlightenment principles that figured so prominently in the charters of France and the United States—democracy, citizenship, private property, and individual rights and protections. Despite this fact, however, political realities internal to the country were such that these "rights" remained elusive for the vast majority of the population even one hundred years later. While such precepts were uniformly invoked in all political ritual and discourse, many parts of the country were organized according to principles diametrically opposed to these precepts of "popular" sovereignty. Among these regions was Chachapoyas.

The population of the Chachapoyas region was divided into a series of racial categories that did much to prescribe the life possibilities of the individuals who were born into them.[4] A small handful of families that claimed descent from Spanish forebears made up the ruling, white elite. These families prided themselves on the racial purity of their families, and went to great lengths to ensure that neither their blood lines nor their family names were tainted by admixture with the "commoners." Indeed, these elite families saw it as their exclusive right to control regional affairs without interference from the *runa* and *cholos* that made up the bulk of the population.[5] So distinct were the social and political worlds of these racial groups that they had little contact with one another. Members of the elite in particular avoided contact with their "inferiors" whenever possible. In those instances where interaction was unavoidable, it was always highly structured and ritualized, and in such a way as to require public deference and subservience from the subaltern.

Although unified on the basis of race, the landed class was deeply divided according to politics. All members of the elite saw themselves as an aristocratic nobility that was entitled to occupy positions of power and influence by right of birth. Neither the central government nor other members of the elite could legitimately deny them what they regarded as their birthright. Those who attempted to interfere with this natural right did so at their peril, for the elite did not hesitate to use violence in the defense of prerogatives they considered legitimately theirs and theirs alone. In this regard consider the following anecdote, related to me by an elderly member of the Echaiz family, one of the region's elite, aristocratic families:[6]

> In August of 1930 [President] Leguía finally fell from power [in a military coup]. We received word from an ally in Lima by telegram, who told us to take the Prefecture immediately. My grandfather [José María Echaiz], father [Eleodoro Echaiz], and uncles quickly assembled a very large group of followers and attacked the Prefecture. The Prefect at that time was Sr. Távara, an ally of the Rubio [Linch family], who along with his secretary and the Military Assistant of the Prefecture quickly fled once the fighting began, so we had no difficulty in taking control. . . . My family had suffered for many years at the hands of the Rubio [the eleven-year period of the rule of President Leguía and his local clients, the Rubio Linch], and my grandfather and father were very anxious to avenge themselves for all the outrages they had been forced to tolerate. After they took the Prefecture, they attacked the house of Miguel Rubio [Linch], hoping to catch him and make an example of him . . . but he and [his brother] Arturo escaped to [their hacienda] *Boca Negra* [located just outside Chachapoyas]. Later, fearing my family, the Rubios left Amazonas. . . . With my father [Eleodoro Echaiz] in control of the Prefecture, we sent a telegram to Lima [to the Ministry of Government] informing them of what had happened. The reply came quickly—a new Prefect had been appointed, and would soon be traveling to Chachapoyas. When my father received this telegram he became *very* angry, and immediately sent back his own reply; *"I rule in Amazonas!"* The new Prefect never arrived.

There was a sense in which elite men regarded themselves as having no true peers, and certainly no masters. Rather, each believed he had the right to use power in defense of prerogatives that were legitimately his because of the elite station in life which he enjoyed by right of birth. No one—not even the state—had the right to interfere with these privileges. Because of peculiarities of the Peruvian political order, however, it was inevitable that each faction of the elite continually interfered with the ability of other factions to exercise positions of power. During this period Peru was an internally fragmented polity (Burga and Flores Galindo 1979: 88–94; Caravedo 1979; Cotler 1978: 119–84; Gorman 1979). The era as a whole was characterized by numerous coup attempts, frequent outbreaks of civil war, and constant turnover in the central government apparatus.[7] Unable to control its national territory directly, the central regime chose select elite groups in each region to act in its name. In the process, the remainder of the elite was denied access to political power (Gorman 1979; Miller 1982, 1987). The result was endemic conflict as elite-led factions, each of which recruited an extensive clientele from among the region's peasant and mestizo families, struggled among themselves to control the local apparatus of state. These factions were called *castas*, and were referred to by the name of the elite family that led them. Despite the rigidity of the racial order, then, in terms of political conflict vertical ties between families of different classes were more important than horizontal, class-based divisions.

In the Chachapoyas region, this intra-elite competition to control political office (in particular, the positions of prefect, subprefect, police chief, judge, senator, and deputy) was especially intense. Because the region was unusually isolated from external markets, landed families could not rely on the sale of products grown on their estates to provide them with the wealth so necessary to live according to their aristocratic self-conceptions (Nugent 1988). Rather, only by controlling political office could elite families gain access to the tribute-taking mechanisms that were the main source of affluence and power.[8] If an elite family wished to live according to its own aristocratic self-image it was therefore obliged to gain control over political office.

The fact that agrarian pursuits were not a viable source of wealth thus meant that competition among elite-led factions to control the local apparatus of state was exceptionally fierce. Once in control of local government, the ruling elite faction used its broad powers of appointment to name elite allies and nonelite clients to positions in the judiciary, police, and government bureaucracy throughout the entire department. Such a position of strength allowed the ruling faction to safeguard its own position, and to harass members of opposing factions in a systematic manner—to remove them from public office, prosecute them for supposed crimes, seize their goods, and do harm to their person and property in whatever way possible.

The ruling casta persecuted its rivals so viciously because opposing factions refused to accept the position of the ruling faction as legitimate, and thus sought constantly to depose the ruling faction through violent means. Only by engaging in consistent and coordinated persecution of opposing factions could the ruling faction fragment this hostile opposition sufficiently to preclude united action on the part of its enemies. The following incident, in which appointees of the ruling casta (an officer and a foot soldier in the Guardia Civil, or national police) broke into the home of a member of a rival casta, and robbed, raped, and attempted to kill the under-aged girl they encountered in the process, exemplifies the ways that the ruling casta used its control over the means of force to marginalize the opposition. It also reveals the kinds of abuses to which members of opposing castas were continually subject at the hands of those who controlled departmental affairs:[9]

> *Sr. Judge of the First Instance.* November 21. In compliance with my duty, I write to inform you that at 9:00 P.M. yesterday Don Esteban Santillan [a client of the Pizarro-Rubio casta] appeared before me on behalf of his under-aged niece, Roza [sic] Gamarra, both residents of this town [Chachapoyas], accusing Don Genaro Reyes Alvares [a foot soldier in the Guardia Civil] and Don Ramon Hurtado [a high-ranking officer in the Guardia Civil] . . . of having broken into the house of the aforementioned minor, of having robbed her, of having raped her, and of having attempted to kill her, acts . . . committed at 4:00 P.M. in the home of Gamarra. Political authorities being charged with the preservation of order and of public morality, immediately upon receiving the denunciation I had the aforementioned Reyes Alvares apprehended, and this morning had Hurtado [apprehended], both of whom are now in detention in the barracks of the Guardia Civil. . . . From the investigation . . . that I have conducted, I have discovered that Don Santos Vigil knows something of what occurred, as he assisted Srta. Gamarra when, fleeing from her attackers, she managed to escape by the roof of her house.

Foot soldier Reyes Alvares received a slight reprimand for his involvement in the crime, while officer Hurtado received no punishment whatsoever.[10]

As the above suggests, the rise of one elite faction inevitably meant persecution and emiseration for the others, and thus each faction fought viciously to protect itself. As a result, struggles among the various factions were continuous and violent in nature.

Members of *all* social classes and *all* elite-led factions thus suffered continual insecurity of person and property—for no one faction was able to retain control of the regional political apparatus for any sustained period of time (typically, about five to ten years). Rather, as each new faction rose to power it went in pursuit of those who had formerly been its persecutors, using its control over the police and the judiciary to do harm to its enemies in whatever way it could.

By virtue of the fact that it occupied the region's most important political positions (prefect, subprefect, police chief, judge, senator, deputy) the ruling faction was also the official representative of the independent republic of Peru within the department of Amazonas. As noted above, Peru was a republic founded on liberal, Enlightenment principles of individual rights and protections, the sanctity of person and property, and equality under the law. Indeed, these principles of popular sovereignty were the sole terms in which political life as a whole could be discursively represented. As a result, although committed to making constant attacks upon the life and property of the opposition in order to maintain its position of dominance, in all political ritual and discourse the ruling faction was equally compelled to present itself as the sole and true defender of state-endorsed principles of *popular* sovereignty. In these rhetorical and ritual spaces the ruling elite elaborated a mythical social order that was the antithesis of factional politics and aristocratic hierarchy. In place of the violence, insecurity, and privilege that characterized everyday life, in the realms of ritual and discourse the ruling elite asserted the existence of a "peaceable kingdom." In this alternative world the ability to rule was not contingent upon ongoing demonstrations of force. Instead, governance was depicted as consensual and orderly, and individuals were portrayed as universally enjoying the protections of life, liberty, and property granted them by the constitution.[11] In ritual and discourse, unity and harmony prevailed, and distinctions of race, gender, and class ceased to exist. In place of such distinctions the ruling faction asserted the existence of a mass of identical "citizens," each indistinguishable from the next, all of whom were united behind the cause of promoting "progress" and "advancement."

The particular elite faction that controlled the apparatus of state was thus forced to offer public accounts of its deeds by invoking notions of equality, individual rights and protections, progress, and the "common good" that were in direct contradiction with its own actions—and which also provided a critical commentary on the cultural and material logic of aristocratic privilege itself. Aristocratic "sovereignty" could not be celebrated, or even acknowledged, in formal political spheres. Popular sovereignty had to be celebrated, on an ongoing basis, despite the fact that it had virtually no relation to any existing social reality. Indeed, there is a conspicuous silence about the very *existence* of the aristocratic order in all political ritual and discourse.

Capitalist Crisis and the Emergence of Popular Rule

This casta-based political-economic structure dissolved in the context of the massive changes in economy and polity experienced throughout Peru beginning in the late nineteenth century—changes that were intimately tied to global transformations in the organization of capitalism. At this time the crisis in and reorganization of North Atlantic capitalism resulted in a flood of new laboring people, social doctrines, religious dogmas, political ideologies, and investment capital pouring into Peru at an unprecedented rate—changes that stimulated two inter-related processes: one of state reorganization and expansion, and another of widespread economic dislocation and transformation.

As a result of state expansion, the central government began to assert itself in what had been the affairs of regional elites throughout the nation. It did so via two main mechanisms. First, the central government sought to weaken regional elites' hold over local resources, territory, and people by absorbing into its own expanded bureaucracy as many elite powers and privileges as possible. In this way the state undermined the positions of these elites as mediators, who controlled the flow of local resources from region to center, and dominated the subaltern classes within their spheres of influence. Second, the central government began a more concerted effort to form a unified political, economic, and cultural community of national scope. The government did so via massive investments in road construction and transport (which resulted in the formation of a more integrated, national economy), and by expanding and integrating central control over media, communication, and education (Burga and Flores Galindo 1979). In this way the government attempted to dissolve regional boundaries and identifications and replace them with a national community and consciousness, one based on individual rights and protections, the sanctity of person and property, and equality under the law (Nugent 1997).

At the same time that the central government was attempting to consolidate its hold on the territory of the nation via these two mechanisms, however, it was confronted with conditions that were increasingly chaotic and transformative. Within Lima the early decades of the twentieth century saw the emergence of strong working-class and student protest movements (Sulmont 1975; Burga and Flores Galindo 1979). In 1919 the two joined forces, and the populist movement that emerged as a result presented a fundamental challenge to Peru's traditional elite.

Outside of Lima, conditions were also changing rapidly. Movements of national and international capital over which the state had no control disrupted extant patterns of production and exchange all around the country, creating new regional economic configurations, transforming existing configurations, and undermining formerly viable relations among regional arenas.[12]

The result of these unstable and rapidly changing conditions was a degree of violence and individual insecurity that was unusual even by the standards of the time. Much of the difficulty focused on regional elites, who were anxious to retain their traditional powers and privileges, and to claim whatever they could in the way of new prerogatives. Because the central government had only a minimal presence in most parts of the countryside, these elites were left to fight among themselves, and with the subaltern, in deciding how the emerging set of economic possibilities would be institutionalized. Symptomatic of the chaotic conditions that prevailed during this period was the fact that in the 1920s and 1930s, both before and after the world economic crisis of 1929, large-scale movements of secession or revolt broke out all across the country.[13] And for a brief period in 1931 there were two and according to some sources three different men in different parts of Peru, all of whom simultaneously claimed to be the president.

In other words, just as the central government sought to form a more cohesive national community based on a discourse of popular sovereignty, it was faced with increasingly violent and unstable conditions that violated these very principles. The response to these conditions varied according to region and social group. In many parts of Peru, elites who lost in the intra-elite struggles to control the new economic opportunities of the era responded by organizing armed resistance to the central government and its local clients (those members of the elite who prevailed in these struggles). The latter in turn called upon the central government to provide the resources necessary to contain these threats. The overall result, however, was a pattern of escalating violence and personal insecurity for nonelite groups. In regions like Chachapoyas, these nonelite groups responded by embracing the principles offered by the central government as providing the only legitimate basis of the national community—individual rights and protections, the sanctity of person and property, and equality before the law.

Massive dislocations in culture and economy experienced throughout Peru during this period thus provided the context in which new forms of regional and national community came to mutually construct one another in Chachapoyas. Two political movements emerged in Chachapoyas as a result of the combination of forces outlined above, predominantly among urban middle-class elements. Both were intent on "democratizing" the aristocratic social order. The first movement, which began to solidify in the mid-1920s, eventually became the Partido Laboral Independiente Amazonense (the Independent Labor Party of Amazonas). The second movement, which made its appearance in 1929, was the local manifestation of a national political party, the Alianza Popular Revolucionaria Americana (APRA; the Popular American Revolutionary Alliance). These movements attracted much of the local population—who were drawn to the appeal made by the movements for regional unity, moral behavior, and national integration.[14]

Beginning in the latter half of 1929 the cemetery of Chachapoyas began to be the site of new nocturnal happenings. Fifteen to twenty adolescents began to meet on the hallowed ground in secret, on Sundays, at midnight. These youth were the vanguard of a new political party, the APRA,[15] that was persecuted by the central government. The young Apristas were deeply committed to remolding regional society in a new form—one in which the individual would be freed from relations of servitude with the more powerful, in which equality, democracy, and justice would obtain for all.

The party members had to take great care in order to arrive at the cemetery undetected by the gendarmes, appointees of the ruling casta who patrolled the town armed with rifles, constantly on watch for "suspicious nocturnal activities." Each Aprista had to leave his or her home at a separate time, and then pass along the quiet streets of Chachapoyas without being seen, as far as the town's eastern perimeter. Once beyond the town there was a wooded ravine that offered concealment, and that led southward toward the cemetery. Several times the gendarmes spotted the young people as they attempted to reach the ravine, and gave chase while shooting their rifles. Although no one was killed or wounded, the fleeing Apristas were forced to seek refuge in the forested area that lay beyond the ravine in order to escape. This meant a cold and hungry night in the woods, as no one would compromise the party by attempting to return home before daybreak, when they could leave the woods without attracting attention.[16]

The young Apristas met, in reverence, at the grave site of Victor Pizarro Rubio—ironically at one time the favorite son of the town's ruling Pizarro-Rubio casta. Victor was the son of Pablo M. Pizarro Farje and Rosa Rubio Linch, one of three couples who made up the core of the Pizarro-Rubio casta. The Pizarro-Rubio casta was unusually well connected to the country's centers of power. Victor's father was the *compadre* of Peru's president/dictator, Augusto Leguía, the latter having played a key role in bringing the Pizarro-Rubio casta to power within the region, and in helping the casta remain in power thereafter. Because of the very close ties between the Pizarros and President Leguía, Victor's father had arranged for Victor to be awarded a scholarship to attend the Naval Academy in the nation's capital. Thereafter, Victor was further honored with an additional scholarship to continue his military studies at a Naval Institute in France.

The Pizarros hoped that Victor would return to Peru after finishing his military training and would occupy an important post in the armed forces or the government—a position from which he could give great assistance to his family and casta. Victor, however, turned out to be a major disappointment to his family. Not only did he fail to take up such a role, but he betrayed virtually everything his family, class, and casta stood for by becoming a communist. Indeed, Pizarro played a key role in leading the fight against the entire casta order in Chachapoyas.

Victor Pizarro went to Lima in the years following 1910 and was transformed. As noted above, the Lima of the 1910s and 1920s was in the throes of profound economic, social, and political change. Confronted by startling new ideologies—social, religious, and political—young Pizarro was intensely drawn to communism. When he was sent to France—supposedly to continue his military studies—he "deserted," and instead went to the Soviet Union, where he lived for several years. In 1921, in the aftermath of the Third World Congress of the Communist International, he returned to Latin America, going to Uruguay, where he became involved in organizing efforts for the Communist Party. Several years later he moved on to Peru, with the same goal in mind.

Although Pizarro was deeply committed to the cause, his activities as a communist organizer came to an abrupt end in 1927 as the result of a bad beating he received at the hands of the Lima police during an anticommunist raid. Severe damage to his kidneys resulted from the police attack, and shortly thereafter Pizarro learned that he had only a short time to live. At that point he decided to return home to Chachapoyas, to live out his remaining days in his native land.

When he returned to Chachapoyas, however, Pizarro found that his elite family refused to take him in. As a result, he was reduced to living in a small shack owned by a muleteer located on the outskirts of town, an outcast from the entire casta order. For the relatively brief period that he remained alive, Pizarro gave lectures on Marxism several times a week to whoever cared to listen. His audience generally consisted of a small group of adolescents from the families of urban artisans, muleteers, petty shopkeepers, and *cantina* owners—people whose life possibilities had been severely circumscribed by the powerful casta families, and who were drawn to Pizarro's message of social critique and egalitarian change.

Pizarro's lectures on communism were brought to an abrupt end when he died shortly after his return to Chachapoyas. While the youth who risked their lives to gather at his grave site had been profoundly influenced by what he had told them, communism failed to captivate them. Nor did it

draw significant numbers of the local population. Instead, the young listeners (along with much of the local population) were drawn to the
APRA—a political party of a more regional, Latin American nature.[17]

The founding members of the APRA chose the gravesite of Victor Pizarro on which to commit themselves to one another and to the cause.
Thereafter, the graveside meetings were used to discuss and settle matters
of the utmost secrecy and importance to the party—matters that could not
be broached in any other setting, that is, where those not completely loyal
to the cause might be listening.

An early decision made by the original members of the APRA was to
open a local branch of the Universidad Popular Gonzalez Prada, or Popular University, in Chachapoyas. Originally established in Lima in 1921 by
the APRA's founder (Victor Raúl Haya de la Torre) as part of his effort to
forge links between the student movement and Lima's new but rapidly
growing working class (Klaiber 1975; Stein 1980: 129–57), the Universidad
Popular suffered growing repression by the government of Augusto
Leguía after the exile of Haya de la Torre in 1923, culminating in the arrest
of most of its important leaders in 1927 (Stein 1980: 143, 146). When word
began to circulate in 1929 that Haya de la Torre would return to Peru,
however, the Universidad Popular began to resurface—a development that
was spurred on by the fall of Leguía in August of 1930. It was in relationship to these changes that a university branch was established in Chachapoyas.[18]

Party members in Chachapoyas developed the Universidad Popular
along two different fronts, formal and informal. Formal teaching was offered at a prearranged meeting place in each of the town's four neighborhoods. The meeting places had to be moved within their respective neighborhoods on an intermittent basis, in order to avoid detection by the police. These formal gatherings provided an opportunity for a carefully
screened group of people to discuss issues of interest to the party and to the
townspeople (see below).[19]

The party's founders also instituted the Universidad Popular—which
was more commonly referred to as the Universidad del Pueblo, or the People's University—on an informal basis. As one of the original party members put it, the Universidad del Pueblo was to be held everywhere—in the
street, in people's homes, in chance meetings along trails in the countryside, in casual discussions in bars. The Universidad del Pueblo was to be
immediately "called in session" in any situation where it was possible to
talk about the region's problems. In these more informal settings the name

of neither the party nor the university was to be mentioned, for great caution had to be exercised in order to avoid informers. But the party and its beliefs could be promoted in these settings nonetheless. One of the early Aprista organizers described this aspect of the Universidad del Pueblo in the following terms:[20]

> We began the Universidad del Pueblo by talking with people in ordinary conversations, never mentioning the APRA, but talking about social problems, about poverty, about the lack of any connection between those who have something and those who have nothing:
>
> [speaker takes on the role of anyone who might speak to him casually while at a public market]: "Ay, I cannot afford to eat—rice is too expensive; I cannot afford to buy the things I need."
>
> [speaker takes on role of himself responding]: "I haven't bought rice today either. There is no rice to be found. How are we ever going to get rice if there is no road to Bagua, where all our rice comes from?" How will we ever be able to afford the things we need if there is no road to the coast?
>
> [speaker addresses anthropologist]: and from there we began to talk about these kinds of problems, and we organized among ourselves in the villages to bring people together so that we could build good roads. . . . We began in this way, person-to-person, and we never let the darkness or the rain or the sun or *any* obstacle interfere with our astonishing determination; but in politics you have to astonish people if you want to convince them that you are sincere. You have to astonish them in the field of demonstration and in the field of action if you want them to change the things that have shamed them in the past. You have to convince them that you can be trusted, that you are a true friend.

According to the founding members of the APRA, all of their organizing efforts were "educational" in nature. All, that is, fell under the rubric of informal gatherings of the Universidad del Pueblo. The conception of education held by the original Apristas, and the role of the Universidad del Pueblo in relation to the existing power structure, went far beyond education as understood in any conventional sense. As will become clear in the pages below, the Apristas conceived of education as a broad-ranging project of cultural transformation that had the primarily political objective of undoing the existing, highly stratified social order, and of forming rational, autonomous, principled subjects out of the region's men.[21] This view of the function of education and the Universidad del Pueblo informed virtually all the "subjects" covered by the teachers of the university—from lessons on the history and geography of Peru to literacy training to general condemnations of the existing power structure.

Teachers in the Universidad del Pueblo devoted most of their educational efforts to presenting a scathing critique of those who ruled the region. They focused their attack on the cultural logic of the elite order. This cultural logic was regarded as so important because it was invoked by members of the elite in order to naturalize and legitimate their exalted position in local society. In other words, elite exactions of wealth and services from local producers, and elite insistence that the local population at all times show the proper forms of deferential behavior, could only be justified according to the cultural claims of aristocratic sovereignty.

In fashioning their critique of casta control, the Apristas drew upon two distinct notions of legitimate cultural order—one oriented toward the future (the modern nation-state) and the other toward the past (the Inca empire). Teachers in the Universidad del Pueblo combined these two sources in novel and creative ways, and in the process were able to forge a new cultural identity that acted as a powerful force in unifying the two groups that made up the region's laboring poor. These were the marginalized, middle sectors of the towns, and the Indian peasants of the countryside.

These two sources of legitimate cultural order reflected efforts on the part of the Apristas to reach different constituencies. In attempting to appeal to the marginalized middle sectors of the towns, the Apristas emphasized notions deriving from the egalitarian discourse of the nation-state. They emphasized the great things that would be possible once the aristocratic order was done away with, equality and justice were achieved, and success came to be a function of individual merit rather than inherited social position. Notions of popular sovereignty were thus used in order to project a golden future for the region and its inhabitants. In an effort to appeal to the rural peasantry, on the other hand, party members drew upon images of a golden age in the past, during the reign of the Inca, when "the people" had been united against their enemies. This was a period when harmony had obtained, when the people had achieved truly remarkable things—until the *Imperio Inca* had been destroyed by the marauding Spanish Conquistadors.

The Apristas thus drew upon promises of a modern future still to be won and upon images of a golden past tragically lost in order to turn the conventional cultural assertions of the elite upside down. Interviews with surviving Apristas reveal the ways in which teachers in the Universidad del Pueblo developed a critique of the region's aristocratic families, and forged a new cultural identity for the region's laboring poor—mestizo and Indian alike:[22]

We were forced to meet in secret . . . and so we were constantly on the lookout for [informal] opportunities to talk to others [about the ideas of the party]. Family celebrations were good for this:

[speaker takes on the role of someone else talking to him]: "Today is the birthday of the daughter of my compadre, let's have some coffee to celebrate . . ."

[speaker addresses anthropologist]: and from that point we began, we began to talk about what a family was, and what kinds of things families shared, all the while attacking the potentate, who refused to share *anything*, and from there we were able to get into everything—why we must all be united and why we have to defend our own situation.

[speaker takes on the role of himself talking to others at the family gathering]: "All of us make up a single community, a single family. We served as the basis for the Incanato [the period of rule of the Inca empire], did we not? The Incanato built the great Inca Highway. The Incanato built huge fortresses. We could do so then because we were united. You were neither cholo nor white nor ugly; we were all united, and we want to continue being united; and none of this [speaker takes on the role of a member of the elite speaking about himself]: 'My ancestors came from Spain; we are all white; we speak properly, and dress properly.' NO SEÑOR! I AM YOUR EQUAL! WE ARE ALL EQUAL!"

Anthropologist: So you criticized the powerful?

Speaker: That was our primary goal.

Anthropologist: How did you do it?

Speaker: We would say to them [people at family gatherings like the one described above], that it was essential for the people [*el pueblo*] to learn to defend themselves. As an example, we explained that, by building fortresses the Inca had defended themselves from attack by their enemies, and so we needed to understand that *our* enemies were those who had money, those who exploited us. . . . [We] explained that those who have always taken advantage of the people have been the upper class, the castas, the priests, and the *tinterillos*, who pretend to know a great deal but who know nothing . . . :

[speaker takes on the role of himself addressing others at a family gathering]: "Why do they treat us like cholos, like Indios, like runa?"

Notions of equality and justice derived from the discourse of the modern nation-state and the principles of popular sovereignty were thus grafted onto a narrative of the accomplishments of the Inca empire— evidence of which was clearly visible throughout the region in the form of huge and impressive ruins. The people were as one during the reign of the Inca, the Apristas asserted, and thus great things had been possible. Neither race, nor ancestry, nor language nor culture had been used to denigrate some and to celebrate others. When the Inca were supreme the people were equal among themselves, said the APRA, and were united against their enemies. And so they must be once more.

The Apristas' construction of a united Inca past was, of course, wholly fictitious. The Inca empire actually suffered from extreme factionalism, largely because the many "ethnic kingdoms" that fell to Inca expansion continued to resist imperial rule (Larson 1988; Spalding 1984). The pre-Columbian stone fortresses and towns that dotted the Chachapoyas landscape were symptomatic of the divided state of the Inca empire. These huge ruins were not even built by the Inca, but by a rival ethnic kingdom—the Sachapuyan—one of the many victims of Inca imperial expansion. The Sachapuyans fought fiercely to retain their independence from the Inca, were conquered by the Inca with great difficulty toward the middle of the fifteenth century, and thereafter continued to resist Inca domination (Aguilar Briceño 1963: 107–8; Collantes Pizarro 1969: 6–8). So hated were the Inca by the Sachapuyans that they eventually helped the Spanish defeat the Inca, rather than vice versa (Aguilar Briceño 1963: 109–11; Zubiate Zabarburú 1979).

The imposing ruins that the Apristas pointed to as a symbol of the unity and strength of the Inca thus represented precisely the *opposite*—the internally divided and factionalized state of a weak empire. The struggles and divisions of the past, however, were made to disappear in the context of the exigencies of the present; a unified Imperio Inca was created out of the prehistoric past to stand as an example of what one possible future for the region might look like. Remote past and imminent future thus became mirror images of one another—and helped mutually construct one another—as the Apristas sought to remake history.

The Aprista critique focused on the stratified *racial* hierarchy of the aristocratic order, on the unequal distribution of wealth and power associated with this hierarchy, and on the servile and dependent relations that these inequalities encouraged between Indios and mestizos, on the one hand, and the elite on the other. For it was this racially inscribed system of organization, argued the Apristas, that prevented el pueblo from unifying among themselves. It was this system that stood in the way of el pueblo becoming strong once more, of being able to do great things—as they had in the past.

The Apristas attempted what might be called a strategy of "subversion from within" in challenging this hegemonic order. Rather than deny the existence of the racial categories per se, the teachers of the Universidad del Pueblo refashioned the categories in such a way as to transform them from mechanisms of oppression into mechanisms of liberation. The Aprista critique thus preserved the category of blanco (white)—but equated it with "monied, immoral, oppressor" rather than with "aristocratic, Spanish-descended member of the nobility." The Apristas also collapsed cholo, Indio, and runa into a single category, el pueblo—but equated it with "poor, mistreated descendent of a great civilization/true representative of the modern nation" rather than with "uncouth, semirational savage." The "oppressors" thus remained within the racial classification of the aristocratic order, and were associated with social division, hierarchy, and privilege. This made it possible to depict them as premodern, nonegalitarian, and therefore antinational. By stressing these themes the Apristas sought to justify their assertion that the elite belonged at the bottom rather than the top of the social order. The "victims," on the other hand, were freed from the aristocratic racial hierarchy, and were united under a single category derived from the egalitarian, inclusive discourse of the modern nation-state and popular sovereignty. This new category stressed the strength, unity, and equality of the group, therefore qualifying them as pre-eminently national.[23]

In their attempt to reconfigure the aristocratic racial hierarchy, the Apristas invoked a national form of authority and a national system of social classification. In so doing, they were able to draw on a category and a concept—el pueblo—with which all social groups were already intimately familiar, because they had long heard it voiced in public political ritual and in political discourse. Furthermore, the Apristas' assertion that el pueblo was a noble, even sacred entity whose interests and needs took precedence over all private interests was likewise anything but foreign to local society. Ruling casta families had been saying precisely this in political ritual and discourse for decades (although their actions made a public mockery of popular rule). The Apristas were thus able to lay claim to a category publicly declared moral and legitimate by the state and the casta families alike. And they used the fact that the casta families had consistently betrayed the principles of popular sovereignty to delegitimate the elite, and to mobilize the local population in the name of "the people" and "the nation."[24]

The Apristas sought to forge relations of a more horizontal, "class" character, both at regional and national levels, to replace the vertical ties upon which casta organization was based. That is, they attempted to construct not only an inner, moral frontier between themselves and the casta families, but also a boundary of national proportions. This latter frontier was between the aristocratic order and the larger Peruvian nation. It was the elite families, argued the Apristas, that were responsible for the region's and the nation's ills. The Apristas wanted to bring an end to the outrages to which everyone was subject at the hands of the region's casta families, so that the people and the nation could again be strong.

As the teachers elaborated their critique of the casta order they were able to seize upon experiences of abuse and humiliation with which all their listeners could identify—the insecurities of person and property that were ongoing realities for virtually everyone:[25]

> We would remind them of the abuses that had been forced upon them by the casta families—about the girls who had been raped, the money that had been stolen, and the humiliation that they had all endured:
>
> [speaker begins to explain to the anthropologist]: in those days the elite families all chose servants from among the *colono* [peon] families on their haciendas, to cook and clean their great homes [of the elite], and to look after their children. Even boys in their teens had maids to look after them, to clean up for them, and also to bathe them! It was very common for boys of the elite to force themselves on their maids while they were being bathed. The poor girls could do nothing to defend themselves. When they became pregnant the child was baptized, but not with the name of the father—for the casta families were determined to preserve the purity of their family names. So the child was given the name of the Prefect or the Subprefect, and the girl was sent back to her family on the hacienda to raise the child.
>
> We also spoke about the problem of justice. I would say to them [people at family gatherings; people engaged in casual conversations], "What can you do when they [the rich] steal your livestock and get away with it because they have money? What can you do when they use their money to buy justice when you protest [about the theft] to the judge, and you lose your court case after you have spent all your own money?"
>
> We also reminded them about the way that they were not allowed to enter the homes of the rich by the front door nor to wait in the drawing room [*salon*] nor to sit on the furniture:
>
> [speaker addresses the anthropologist]: We were forced to enter by the side door, and to wait [outside] where there was a dirt floor and to remain standing while we waited. You couldn't enter [the drawing room] because they said you were a cholo, a runa.
>
> [speaker takes on the role of a member of the elite speaking in a deprecatory manner to a cholo or a runa]: "You are going to soil the chair if you sit in it!"
>
> [speaker addresses the anthropologist]: and the chair was nothing but a wooden plank!
>
> We also spoke about how the people had been abused in all the wars and battles that had been started by the castas. It was el pueblo, the Indios, who had been forced to fight in the wars, to die in the battles, while the blancos gave the orders, but always from a position of safety.

According to the teachers of the Universidad del Pueblo, there was nothing that the casta families had been unwilling to do in order to satisfy their desire for wealth. They had violated the sexual honor of el pueblo's women, had stolen the livestock of its men, had extorted the little money that el pueblo was able to save, and had forced the sons of el pueblo into battles to be killed and maimed. Beyond even these crimes, however, the casta families also humiliated and denigrated el pueblo on a daily basis by treating its members as inferior, as less than fully human.

The claim made by the casta families that they were a hereditary elite descended from noble Spanish forebears—and thus were entitled to rule over their social inferiors—also came under attack by the Apristas. The Apristas argued that the Conquistadors had been anything but a noble stratum of cultured elite, but rather had been brutal and rapacious. Indeed, the Spaniards had engaged in the most barbarous forms of behavior imaginable over a course of centuries in their search for wealth. They had first destroyed the great Inca empire, and thereafter had turned brother against brother. The heritage they had left Peru was the source of her *problems*, claimed the Apristas, and not her greatness.

In contrast to all of the abuses of the aristocratic order, the APRA proposed a society based on equality, justice, and the mutual respect of one person for another:[26]

> The APRA was for *equality*. And straight away [after critiquing the abuses of the elite] we would talk about the famous storming of the Bastille in France on the 14th of July and about the call for Human Rights. . . . We would tell them about how the Bastille fell, about how the people seized the Bastille, and we would explain that we must be just as united against the landowners.
>
> For example, concerning the 28th of July—Independence Day—we asked for *whom* is this Independence Day? We spoke of what it means to be independent, to not have to be beholden to anyone, so that no one can dominate us, so that no one can command us.

The Apristas thus sought to place Chachapoyas within an historical imaginary wholly different from the history of noble lineage claimed by the region's aristocratic elite. The Apristas invited members of el pueblo to imagine themselves as centrally involved in a process whose importance went far beyond the parochial claims to nobility of the backward, local elite. People who had long been denied social value of any kind were asked to think of themselves as important actors involved in the progressive unfolding of democratic and egalitarian ideals on a world-historical scale. The glorious history of this movement stretched back at least as far as revolutionary France in the West. It also encompassed ideals already uttered (in political ritual and discourse) but as yet to be made real in the recent history of Peru. El pueblo could become a part of this history—could become a part of their *own* history—if they so chose.

A strong and unified (but invented) Inca past was thus integrated with contemporary movements of democracy and equality to construct an alternative origin myth for el pueblo. Remote Inca past and modern present were interconnected, the Apristas asserted, because both shared the same democratic and egalitarian ideals. According to this alternative history the Spanish Conquest and the entire colonial period represented a Dark Age— a tragic, but ultimately temporary interruption of a more fundamental history involving the progressive realization of principles of justice and equality. According to this new historical vision, neither the Spanish nor their heritage truly belonged in Peru. Both were utterly foreign to what was essentially *of* the region and the nation. Therefore, both had to be exorcised from local affairs.

There was much that el pueblo would have to do, according to the Apristas, in order to purge local life of its Spanish heritage. Those who made up el pueblo would have to be prepared to confront those who oppressed them if they were to rid themselves of the pernicious influences of the casta families and become strong once more. In order to convey this dimension of the APRA's vision to the region's laboring poor, teachers in the Universidad del Pueblo drew upon images of a strong Inca past:[27]

> [speaker takes on the role of himself addressing people informally]: "Why do you submit to this humiliation of, *Taitito, buenos días, buenas tardes* [that is, addressing members of the elite with terms of deference and respect]? It is enough to say, *Buenos días,* and nothing more, with your forehead held high [and not looking down at the ground, as cholos and runa were expected to do when addressing members of the elite]. The Inca always looked upward at the sun—the Indio, the most humble creature of all, always looked at the sun. It was for this reason that they built their fortresses on the tops of the mountains, so that from there they could gaze up at the sun; with their heads held high and toward the sky. Why do you do otherwise?. . . . You are the equal of that man [a member of the elite]. You are all *closer* to God than he, for it is he who steals what belongs to you. On the other hand you are a humble man, a humble creature, so why this humiliation?"

In appealing to el pueblo to resist the abuses of the powerful, the Apristas also invoked the principles of popular sovereignty—specifically, notions of equality and justice:

> [speaker takes on the role of himself addressing people informally]: "Whenever the governor says to you, 'You must pay me, if not with money then with a

chicken, a guinea pig, with a few eggs,' you must tell him, 'No, no, if you want my things you must pay for them.' If you do otherwise, it is a form of adulation. Never show adulation to anyone!"

Regardless of whether they referred to a proud Inca past or a modern future, however, teachers in the Universidad del Pueblo told their students that they must stand up to injustice, so that the great and the humble would be treated in the same way:

> [speaker takes on the role of himself addressing people informally]: "You must fight if you want justice, justice means everyone being on the same level, not on different levels; so that what is possible for the humble is the same as what is possible for the great."

The Apristas did more, however, than just encourage el pueblo to stand up for its rights. Teachers in the Universidad del Pueblo also explained concrete strategies to "the people" that would help them to resist the demands of the region's *políticos*—those in Chachapoyas as well as in the rural districts. The APRA's strategy of resistance stressed above all else the strength that came from unity:[28]

> The peasants, el pueblo, had very little power at that time. So we always tried to find ways to help them overcome this problem. In addition to those who ruled from the capital of the department [Chachapoyas] there was always the local boss in the village—the compadre of those in the capital:
> [speaker takes on the role of a local boss in a village addressing a villager]: "You, go to Chachapoyas to deliver this message to the Subprefect."
> [speaker assumes the role of himself addressing villagers]: "And you go? Does he come to your house to visit you, and ask you to go as a favor? Does he offer to pay you? You must be paid, and you must be free to refuse him. . . . And you must help one another resist. If [the governor] has a revolver and he threatens you, return with ten or twenty people together. In front of everyone, refuse him. Make it a communal cause. Together, you will overcome the ambition of this one person, the person whose ambition is *don dinero*."

Continually stressed was the idea that unity was the most effective way of resisting the abuses of local political bosses.[29] As the passage above continues, we find the teacher of the Universidad del Pueblo recommending this strategy as a way of resisting a different kind of abuse by a local boss:

> [speaker continues in the role of himself addressing villagers]: "If the governor tries to arrest you and take you prisoner for refusing his order, you must all unite, and twenty or thirty of you together should go to the governor and tell him, 'We are going to take you prisoner and we are going to burn down your house.' And you must burn down the house of the governor. But you can only

do these things in common, when you are united. But each one alone and afraid, as you are now, never. We have to be united like our ancestors [the Inca] were in order to do tremendous things like this. Close by to us here are the great ruins, the *huacos* built by our ancestors. We must be united, as they were, in order to do great things like they did."

There was one other element in the Apristas' plan for unifying the local population, one that recognized the need for change at the level of the individual. In the eyes of the Apristas, the problems with the regional social order extended beyond "structural" issues involving the unequal distribution of wealth and power. El pueblo would also have to undergo profound personal transformations if they were to liberate themselves from the influences of the casta order. In other words, in addition to having had their lives limited in material terms, the Apristas believed that most Indios and mestizos (particularly the former) were similarly underdeveloped in psychological/developmental terms. Teachers in the Universidad del Pueblo viewed the majority of "the people" as having accepted the cultural claims of the elite, as having come to believe in the reality of racial difference, in the elite's superiority and their own inferiority. Suffering as they did from a low self-image, and being in awe of the elite, without changes of a more personal nature they could never be counted on to defy or confront their oppressors, or to contribute to remaking the social order in egalitarian form.

The Apristas sought to correct this situation by transforming the region's servile subaltern masses into disciplined, proud, and autonomous subjects, each of whom would be capable of resisting oppression and speaking out against inequality. In order to accomplish this goal of transformation, the Apristas believed that a major transformation in the *consciousness* of the subaltern was needed. That is, it would be necessary to instill in the minds of the masses the independence of thought and the respect for justice upon which resistance was necessarily based. The most effective way to reach into the minds of the populace, believed the Apristas, was by instituting schooling and a program in literacy training. The rationale behind this dimension of the APRA's vision is revealed by the teachers of the Universidad del Pueblo:[30]

All of these problems [of inequality, oppression, and servility] resulted from the ignorance of the people, and the lack of schools, where people learn to form their personalities and learn to defend their interests, to refuse to be humiliated. . . . [We] explained to el pueblo that the reason that [the elite] wanted us to remain ignorant was so that they could exploit us, so that we were not able to protest against this or that abuse. . . . [The elite] didn't want anyone to build new schools because they knew that schools produce leaders, and that when there is leadership then domination comes to an end automatically.

It was for this reason that we called our school La Universidad del Pueblo (the University of the People)—there we taught reading and writing. We brought with us loose pieces of paper and notebooks and we gave them to the students, and we told them that . . . in this notebook we would learn to write from "A" to "M":

[speaker takes on the role of himself as a teacher in the Universidad del Pueblo, instructing a student]: "Now you repeat [what I have written]: now in the other part [of the notebook] the other letters. Now let's do your name. The most important thing of all is for you to learn to write your name, because your name is *you*."

[speaker addresses anthropologist]: And from there we would begin to talk about what it means to be a person, dragging the conscience of the student along behind.

[speaker returns to his role of teacher, addressing a student—a peasant in the countryside]: "Well then, your name is Luis—write that."

[speaker takes on the role of his own student, excitedly responding to his teacher's request]: "I know how to write now; I wrote my name on the wall [of his house]."

[speaker addresses anthropologist]: And we would see his name, written on the wall of his house with a piece of charcoal from the fire. "Luis," or in that men always had two names, "José Luis." "José Luis Chasquirol." This is how he learned to write his name. . . . All of this was to form the personalities of these people.

The Apristas thus conceived of their mission as going beyond protesting against abuse, beyond organizing the local population to resist the casta families. If local society were to be rid of all residual influences of the casta order, it would be necessary to carry out a "cultural revolution" of sorts, one that would form rational, autonomous subjects out of the local population. It would be necessary to free people from all feelings of inferiority and servility, so that they would not be in awe of the elite and their noble pretensions. The Apristas sought to form men who knew their own worth as individuals, who knew that they were the equals of any member of the elite. Men such as these would be most capable of resisting their oppressors, would be able to fight for justice, would be able to stand up for their rights.

Secret cells of the APRA had been formed in virtually every district of all three provinces of Amazonas by early 1930—fifteen in Chachapoyas, sixteen in Luya, and six in Bongará. These cells had anywhere from one to eight members (see below). All district-level members were actively involved in promoting the Universidad del Pueblo, and in increasing the ranks of the party.[31] The following internal communiqué (dated February 8, 1930) is from a graduate of the Chachapoyas Universidad del Pueblo who went on to become the secretary general of the party for the province of Bongará. He writes to his former teacher in the Chachapoyas Universidad del Pueblo, who was also the departmental secretary general of the APRA (this secretariat was located in Chachapoyas). The letter conveys something of the party's organizational efforts, and its internal chain of command. It also shows the relationship between the activities of provincial and departmental party representatives, on the one hand, and the party's national headquarters in Lima on the other.[32]

After listing the names of the party members in each of the province's six district-level cells, the provincial secretary general for Bongará reports the following:[33]

> As always, I continue moving forward, recruiting more adepts. . . . As soon as possible, I will make up a complete list of all party personnel, as well as of all comrades and sympathizers, and I will send it to you.
>
> I have received a circular from the Secretariat of Organization in Lima, in which I have been ordered to establish the U.P.G.P. [the Universidad Popular Gonzalez Prada] in Jumbilla [capital of Bongará province], as well as branches [of the university] in all of the districts . . .
>
> Until now I have received no communication from [the secretary general of] Luya [province], nor any APRA leaflets or newspapers from him . . .
>
> The Secretariat of Organization in Lima informs me that I have been sent the instructions necessary to start the University previously referred to. These instructions have yet to arrive.
>
> Your student and comrade . . .

The social backgrounds of the clandestine members of the APRA mentioned in the document reveal much about the kinds of people who were drawn into the vanguard of this movement of social transformation. Virtually all came from social backgrounds that would qualify them as cholos in the eyes of the elite. That is, they occupied a kind of intermediate racial/occupational stratum between the white, landed elite of Chachapoyas and the Indian peasants of the countryside. While many owned plots of land in the countryside, none were peasants. Rather, they made up a rural "middle class" that as a whole was involved in a variety of economic activities—predominantly agriculture, petty trade, work as public employees, artisanry, and transport activities. Interestingly, they were literate as well—all had attended elementary school in Chachapoyas, and many had finished high school in Chachapoyas. In other words, they were precisely the kinds of people to whom a critique of the casta order and a call for justice and democracy were most likely to appeal.[34]

It is difficult to gauge the precise number of people who became involved in the APRA, and when they became so involved. It is clear, however, that Aprismo was an exceptionally widespread, unusually influential social movement from its earliest days. One indication of the popularity of the APRA can be gleaned from the party's involvement in the presidential election of 1931—when it was (temporarily) not against the law to belong to the party. The Departmental Committee of the APRA for Amazonas claimed that 3,200 Apristas had voted in the election (*La Tribuna,* November 2, 1931, p. 3). When it is kept in mind that illiterate peasants and women were still denied the franchise at this time, and that the entire population of Chachapoyas was only about 5,000, this figure clearly represents a social movement of major proportions.[35]

A more important measure of the APRA's influence, however, comes from the party's role in transforming regional affairs. In August of 1930, at a moment of crisis in the national political order, the Apristas joined forces with other middle-class elements in Chachapoyas, and together el pueblo overthrew the landed elite in an armed uprising.[36] Once they had defeated their adversaries, el pueblo went on to dominate the very positions of economic, social, and political prominence from which they had been excluded in the past. From this vantage point they were able to take important steps to establish a new kind of public culture in Chachapoyas—one based on the principles of popular sovereignty, and the participation of a much broader spectrum of the local population.[37]

The APRA had a clear and distinct vision of a transformed social order, and the role of the forces of modernity in effecting these changes. The movement saw the department of Amazonas as a remote backwater where archaic forms of behavior and association lingered that had long since disappeared from the rest of the civilized world. The movement also identified what was variously referred to as the "feudal," or -"medieval," or "colonial" political structure as the most important obstacle to bringing the region into the modern world. The APRA also believed in the importance of bringing to an end the region's physical remoteness—by integrating it directly into national networks of communication, transportation, and education. And finally, movement participants agreed that effecting these changes depended critically on the ability to remake the region's laboring poor—to mold them into rational, autonomous, independent subjects who would carry within them the ideals of popular sovereignty.

In addition to lifting the weight of material oppression from the backs of el pueblo, the APRA thus sought to free people from the feelings of cultural inferiority from which they suffered within the hegemonic racial hierarchy of the casta order. This latter goal entailed constructing a new cultural identity for the laboring poor of Amazonas. It depended on locating them within an historical trajectory that was both independent of and more powerful than the historical vision of classical nobility claimed by the region's aristocratic families. Such an alternative trajectory had to subsume the origin myth of the elite. It had to show that the racial hierarchy that authorized elite privilege was anything but a fixed point of origin that could be invoked as representing something essential about people in society. An alternative historical imaginary for the poor had to show that there was nothing *natural* or inevitable about the cultural assertions of the elite.

The new vision of history and human nature authored by the APRA showed precisely this. It succeeded in subsuming the historical vision of the elite because it revealed classical nobility, and its associated hierarchy of races, to be wholly *artificial*. That is, the Apristas showed that the putatively permanent and fixed world of the elite was in reality a temporary and retrograde interruption of an historical and social process of sweeping proportions—the progressive realization through time and space of democracy, equality, and universal justice. This more fundamental social and historical process was well underway (among the Inca) before the Spanish arrived to temporarily derail it. It was a process whose influence expanded in scope thereafter to engulf most of the globe (outside of Amazonas). The Apristas sought to apprise the laboring poor of this alternative history, to make them aware of the privileged position they occupied within this process of global transformation. They sought to do so by means of "education"—conceived of as a broad project of transformation in culture, consciousness, and politics.

It was in this sense that the local population looked outside the boundaries of Amazonas, toward the nation and beyond, for the region's salvation. It was in this sense that subaltern groups reached out to the state as their true friend and potential benefactor: for the central government, as the national representative of this global-historical process, was the most logical ally to help the laboring poor rid themselves of the aristocratic elite. Indeed, all the government would have to do in order to bring this about would be to honor the principles of democracy, equality under the law, and individual rights and protections upon which it was founded as an independent state—principles whose legitimacy it had given voice to in political ritual and discourse for decades.

Chachapoyas in Comparative Perspective

The movement of democratization that swept through Chachapoyas in the 1920s and ultimately led to the overthrow of the landed elite exhibits several features worthy of comment. First, contrary to what is described in much of the literature on state-building and nation-making, modern, national culture did not come to Chachapoyas in the form of an externally imposed set of cultural forms whose arbitrariness had to be naturalized by the institutions of the state. Rather, those involved in the movement embraced modern notions of time, space, and personhood without having been coerced or coopted, prior to the establishment of state institutions and their normalizing gaze. Indeed, the entire mobilization of the middle sectors occurred in the context of a broad cultural movement that opposed tradition to modernity—that branded the former as a backward, oppressive structure based on artificial and imposed distinctions that were used to justify brutality and greed. Modernity and nationhood were embraced as powerful moral forces of emancipation—forces that would liberate the region from its oppressors and would allow the true potential of the people at last to be realized.

In other words, in challenging the aristocratic order the movement of democratization openly embraced "things modern" and "things national." In addition to doing away with exclusionary racial divisions, to reconfiguring history, and to reconceptualizing space, this challenge also included the acceptance of modern notions of discipline, order, hygiene, and morality. These "personal" characteristics were seen as the antithesis of the violent and abusive behavior of the decadent, aristocratic elite. In short, as an outgrowth of the movements of democratization, time and space were nationalized and individuality was modernized. All of this occurred, however, *prior* to the arrival of state institutions that could impose their normalizing gaze on the local population.

Second, the new cultural identity and alternative moral universe authored from within the movement of democratization appeared to movement participants as anything but imposed, external, or arbitrary. Rather, this alternative cultural order was to a significant degree created by the people themselves, and emerged in the form of a *recognition* on their part of the region's most basic, essential, and enduring characteristics. Indeed, these features were regarded as being timeless and eternal. They could be seen reflected in phenomena as diverse as the ancient architecture of the Inca and the personal proclivities of el pueblo. They were perceived to be integral to the region and its people.

National culture thus first emerged from *within* local society as something natural, eternal, and true—and as sufficiently meaningful and motivating to the subaltern that, in order to make it a reality, they risked their lives in order to overthrow the elite in an armed confrontation. Thereafter, the formerly marginalized middle sectors took it upon themselves to actualize a new form of public culture based on popular sovereignty. It was only at this point that the modern nation-state began to take on a real presence in the Chachapoyas region—and that the state was able even to begin to implement the individualizing, homogenizing, naturalizing institutional practices discussed at length in the literature on making national cultures.

The process by which the nation-state took on a tangible presence in the Chachapoyas region thus *inverts* the scenario described in much of the literature on the formation of modern nation-states. It is to the reasons for this inversion that we now turn.

Much of the recent literature on states and national cultures has emerged out of the study of nineteenth- and twentieth-century western European nation-states and their colonies. Little of this literature, on the other hand, has focused on the study of Latin America.[38] This contrast, I believe, is key to understanding the problem at hand.

European nation-states of the nineteenth and early twentieth centuries differed in fundamental ways from Peru and Chachapoyas. In Europe, the rise of capitalism meant that during the nineteenth century centralized bureaucratic states hundreds of years in the making came under the control of bourgeois classes deeply committed to modernity, nationhood, and popular sovereignty. The bourgeoisie employed the regulatory capacities of the state apparatus to monitor the gradual incorporation into the political community of those subaltern groups that adopted "proper" and "respectable" (bourgeois) attitudes and forms of behavior. The result was to mold subjectivity in "modern" directions, to produce a national citizenry and more pliable labor force, to naturalize differences of race and gender, and to *exclude* from the political community those who exhibited a "nature" that deviated from the culture of the bourgeoisie.

These developments in the metropole had significant repercussions throughout the empire. The rise of the nation-state, citizenship, and the centrality of Enlightenment thought in defining legitimate political association in western Europe created unique tensions in the colonies. For the coercive and exclusionary relationships of the colonies were in blatant contradiction with the universalistic and voluntaristic discourses of the metropole. In the colonies, exclusionary practices were more rigid than within the metropole and were organized more explicitly on the basis of *race*— because the "indigenous races" exhibited so little in the way of "civilized" human nature. Furthermore, the threat to rule and respectability represented by the blurring of boundaries between colonized and colonizers (via social relationships and sexual liaisons) led to elaborate attempts to regulate sexual and family life, to police racial divides, and even to prohibit sexual unions. Indeed, the sexual morality and virtue of the colonized (and the colonizers!) often became matters of "public" concern.

Peru and Chachapoyas could not represent more of a contrast. Chachapoyas was not colonized by a centralized, European nation-state during the nineteenth and early twentieth centuries, and the Peruvian state had very limited capacity to implement its central decisions, or to monitor the activities of its populace. Most analysts argue that no centralized state existed in Peru whatsoever during this period.

Not only was the Peruvian state poorly developed, but no self-consciously modern bourgeois class committed to popular sovereignty controlled the state. Rather, a "pseudo-state" remained in the hands of shifting groups of regional elites who were strongly wedded to notions of *aristocratic* sovereignty. As a result, popular sovereignty did not become harnessed to a strong state as a means of molding a national citizenry and managing discontent among working classes—as it did in western Europe. Nor was modernity used as a rationale for the exclusion of "inferior races"—as it was in the colonies.

To the contrary, in Chachapoyas popular sovereignty was used as an explicitly antielite ideology—one seized upon by marginal sectors to confront aristocratic privilege. It tended toward *inclusion* of marginal categories rather than exclusion. In the hands of the subaltern, popular sovereignty was used to reconfigure racial boundaries from below. The subaltern did away with several derogatory racial categories completely (cholo, Indio, runa) by aggregating them into a single, nonracial category derived from the discourse of popular sovereignty—el pueblo. Because el pueblo was constituted by erasing/collapsing the boundaries between formerly distinct racial categories, there was no interest in policing racial divides, or in prohibiting sexual liaisons. Only the racial category of the oppressors—blanco—became the object of hostility. By exorcising blanco from the local scene, el pueblo did away with superordinate and subordinate racial categories altogether, defined itself in explicitly nonracial, national terms, and thus eliminated race as a means of social classification.

In direct contrast with the behavior of European bourgeois classes, in Chachapoyas the aristocratic elite played no positive role in the implementation of popular sovereignty. To the contrary, they were completely opposed to it. El pueblo's embrace of modernity and popular sovereignty must be understood in this light. El pueblo did indeed adopt modern notions of time, space, and personhood, discipline, order, and hygiene—but voluntarily, as a way of differentiating themselves from this aristocracy in moral and ethical terms.

In other words, subaltern groups could realistically seize upon both modernity and a strong state as liberating forces. Modernity condemned traditional privilege and provided the subaltern with the vision of an alternative moral/ethical universe. And a strong state promised to safeguard and defend this alternative social order. The interest of the subaltern in implementing the institutions, values, practices, and so forth of modernity after they had seized control of state institutions must be understood in the same terms. Thus, modernity and nation-state were regarded as powerful forces of liberation that were spontaneously adopted from below rather than imposed from above.

Notes

I would like to thank Catherine Besteman, Thomas Biolsi, and Christine Bowditch for their insightful comments on an earlier version of this paper. The research upon which this article is based was generously funded by the Henry L. and Grace Doherty Charitable Foundation, Sigma Xi, the Scientific Research Society, the Mac-Arthur Foundation Pre-Doctoral Fellowship Program, the Fulbright-Hays Pre-Doctoral Program Abroad, the National Endowment for the Humanities, the Colby College Social Science Grants Committee, the Colby College Interdisciplinary Studies Grant Program, the Program in Agrarian Studies at Yale University, and the Wenner Gren Foundation for Anthropological Research. I gratefully acknowledge the generous support of all these institutions.

1. Chachapoyas is the capital of the department of Amazonas, the department being located in northern Peru. In the mid-1990s Chachapoyas had a population of about 22,000 people (21,928 in 1991; see INEI 1992). The town (located at an ele-

vation of 2,334 meters) and its extensive agrarian hinterland—which stretches from lowland jungle in the east and north to high mountain sierra in the west and south—is located on the eastern slope of the northern Andes.

2. "Indios," women, and illiterate and non–property-owning men each had a special legal status, with distinct obligations (and limited rights), which distinguished all of these groups from property-owning, literate (and generally white) males (twenty-one years of age or older).

3. While this order helped actualize a new community of individuals, equal before the law, and gave expression to a new form of public culture based on the precepts of popular sovereignty, it also created new marginal groups and re-created existing groups in new forms. See Nugent 1997 for a discussion of these issues.

4. These racial categories were socially and culturally constructed, and had little if anything to do with physical features.

5. "Runa" was a derogatory term applied to "Indian" peasants. "Cholo," also derogatory, was used to refer to individuals of "suspect" racial backgrounds (probably Indian) who had aspirations to be mestizo and middle class.

6. The following quotation is taken from a taped interview with Sr. Carlos Echaiz on August 13, 1990.

7. The most comprehensive overview of the period is provided by Basadre (1968–69, vols. 5–12).

8. These tribute-taking mechanisms consisted of a variety of forms of taxation.

9. APA 1898, "Subprefecto del Cercado al Juez de 1ra Instancia, 21 de Noviembre de 1893."

10. APA 1898, "Subprefecto del Cercado al Juez de 1ra Instancia, 14 de Diciembre de 1893, 8 de Enero de 1894."

11. In the realm of political drama the ruling faction never appeared in its true guise—as an entity that wielded power arbitrarily to advance its own interests, to punish and persecute its enemies, and to allow a small handful of upper-class individuals to live according to the privileged station in life to which all members of the elite aspired. Rather, in the symbolic space elaborated in ritual and discourse, factions were made to disappear entirely. And ruling faction leaders were transformed from dangerous and powerful men into servants of the "general good"—who had sworn to uphold and defend the rights of all "citizens" as a patriotic duty.

12. The most important new regional configuration emerged in relation to the Amazonian rubber trade, and was focused on the jungle city of Iquitos (Brown and Fernandez 1991; Weinstein 1983). Regional configurations that were transformed from within included: the northern coastal plantations involved in the export of cotton and sugarcane—which increasingly resembled "factories-in-the-field" (Gonzales 1985); the Cajamarca highlands, which began to produce and transport foodstuffs and labor for the coastal export economy (ibid.; Taylor 1986); the central highlands, which were transformed because of the increasingly capital-intensive nature of mining and the emergence of a full-time wage-labor force at the Cerro de Pasco mine and the increasingly commercial nature of the regional economy (Mallon 1983b); and the southern highlands, where haciendas grew dramati-

cally in size and number from the late nineteenth century onward (Collins 1988; Spalding 1975).

13. During the 1920s, revolt broke out in Cajamarca (Gitlitz 1979; Taylor 1986; one of Chachapoyas' castas was involved in this movement), Iquitos (Basadre 1968–69, vol. 13: 92; several of Chachapoyas' castas considered joining this movement; Chachapoyas' ruling casta helped the central government stamp it out), briefly in Chachapoyas itself, and in the southern highlands in Puno (Collins 1988) and Cuzco (Rénique 1991). In the 1930s, additional regional movements developed in Trujillo, Cajamarca, Arequipa, and Cuzco, to name only the most important (Genaro Matos 1968; Klaren 1973; Caravedo 1979; Rénique 1979; Taylor 1986; Slater 1989).

14. Because of limitations of space I will discuss only APRA here. For an analysis of the Partido Laboral, as well as a more in-depth discussion of APRA, see Nugent 1997, ch. 6.

15. The "cells" of the APRA that met in secret in Chachapoyas at this time were segregated by gender—there were separate groups of young men and women. The following account is based on interviews with the few surviving members of the original Apristas—all of whom are male.

16. Other Apristas, however, were not so fortunate—a number were killed as they attempted to evade the police, both in Chachapoyas and in the region's smaller towns and villages. Virtually all of my elderly informants who were Apristas in their youth recall the names of those killed, as well as the specific locations and circumstances of their deaths.

17. Standard reference works on the APRA include Bourricaud (1966), Haya de la Torre (1973, 1977), Klaren (1973), and Sanchez (1934); see also Vega-Centeno Bocangel (1991).

18. Informants say they had received the order to establish the Universidad Popular Gonzalez Prada in Chachapoyas from the party headquarters in Lima. For an overview of the university's activities in Lima, see Klaiber (1975).

19. The teachers came predominantly from among the original founders of the party in Chachapoyas.

20. The following is taken from an interview with "Carlos A. Mestanza Chota," carpenter, conducted September 12, 1986 (at the request of "Sr. Mestanza," I have used a pseudonym to conceal his identity).

21. The surviving original Apristas of Chachapoyas were largely silent on issues related to the oppression of women—despite their recognition that rape was one of the most common crimes committed in the region.

22. During an extended period of fieldwork in Chachapoyas (from December of 1982 until November of 1983, and from January of 1985 until December of 1986), and during shorter visits thereafter (during the summers of 1990, 1991, 1992, and 1993), I had the opportunity to speak at length with a number of the founding members of the APRA about their participation in the Popular University—as well as about the organizing activities of the party in general. The following account is based on information provided by these individuals. The following quotation is

taken from a taped interview with Silvestre Rubio Goivin, muleteer, conducted March 20, 1983.

23. The category of el pueblo did not deny the existence of cholos or Indios. It simply side-stepped the thorny issue of the racial character of the groups by uniting them in a broader category that was not explicitly racial.

24. That is, the Apristas seized upon what had been the "public transcript" (Scott 1990) of the regional social order, and used the fact that it had been declared publicly legitimate to undermine the authority of the ruling elite—whose behavior generated a kind of "hidden transcript" that could not be represented in political ritual or discourse.

25. The following is taken from a taped interview with Carlosmagno Guevara, carpenter, conducted September 4, 1986.

26. The following is taken from a taped interview with Sr. Victor Santillan Gutierrez, on June 30, 1990.

27. The following is taken from a taped interview with Sr. Victor Castilla Pizarro conducted on August 3, 1990, in Rimac. Because of his involvement in Aprista activities in Chachapoyas in the early 1930s, Sr. Castilla spent several years as a young man in El Fronton, a prison located on an island off the coast just outside Lima.

28. The following is taken from a taped interview with "Antonio Valdez Vasquez," muleteer, conducted May 16, 1983 (at the request of "Sr Valdez," I have used a pseudonym to conceal his identity).

29. The following is taken from the same interview as the quotation immediately above in the text.

30. The following is taken from a taped interview with Silvestre Rubio Goivin, muleteer, conducted March 22, 1983.

31. Cell leaders in the outlying districts of the department were uniformly "graduates" of the Universidad del Pueblo in Chachapoyas.

32. For background information on the organizational structure of the APRA, see Stein (1980: 159–61).

33. This letter is located in a *legajo* entitled *APRA*, in the Archivo Prefectural de Amazonas.

34. All the members of the cells were men.

35. The 3,200 voters claimed by the APRA in the election of 1931 clearly represent an exaggerated figure. Even so, it is still clear that the APRA had become a major force to contend with by the time the elections of 1931 took place.

36. The Apristas were joined by members of the Partido Laboral Independiente Amazonense (the Independent Labor Party of Amazonas). See Nugent 1997, ch. 6, for a discussion of the Partido Laboral.

37. The details of the uprising of 1930, and the exclusions built into the form of "popular participation" established at the time, are beyond the scope of this paper. See ibid., ch. 8.

38. Prominent exceptions include Centeno (1997), Joseph and Nugent (1994), Lopez-Alves (2000), Smith (1990a, 1990b), and Urban and Sherzer (1991).

References

Aguilar Briceño, Luis A. 1963. "Mi Departamento Amazona." *Estudio Monográfico*. Lima: Imprenta DPPGC.

APA (Archivo Prefectural de Amazonas). 1898. *Subprefectura del Cercado de Chachapoyas: Copiador de Oficios a Diferentes Autoridades, 1893, 1894, 1895, 1896, 1898*.

———. 1924. *Decretos y Resoluciones de la Prefectura del Departamento de Amazonas, 1924*.

Basadre, Jorge. 1968–69. *Historia de la República del Perú, 1822–1933*. 6th ed. 17 vols. Lima: Editorial Universitaria.

Bourricaud, Francois. 1966. *Ideología y Desarrollo: El caso del partido Aprista Peruana*. Mexico: El Colegio de México.

Brown, Michael, and Eduardo Fernandez. 1991. *War of Shadows: The Struggle for Utopia in the Peruvian Amazon*. Berkeley: University of California Press.

Burga, Manuel, and Alberto Flores Galindo. 1979. *Apogeo y Crisis de la República Aristocrática*. Lima: IEP.

Caravedo, Baltazar. 1979. "Poder central y decentralización. Perú, 1931." *Apuntes* 5, no. 9: 111–29.

Centano, Miguel Angel. 1997. "Blood and Debt: War and Taxation in Nineteenth Century Latin America." *American Journal of Sociology* 102, no. 6: 1565–1605.

Collantes Pizarro, Gustavo. 1969. *Datos Historios de Depatamento de Amazonas*. Chiclayo, Peru: Imprente "El Arte."

Collins, Jane L. 1988. *Unseasonal Migrations: Rural Labor Scarcity in Peru*. Princeton: Princeton University Press.

Cotler, Julio. 1978. *Clases, estado y nación en el Peru*. Lima: IEP.

Foucault, Michel. 1980. *Power/Knowledge*. C. Gordon, ed. New York: Pantheon.

Genaro Matos, Teniente Coronel (R.) 1968. *Operaciones Irregulares al Norte de Cajamarca: Chota, Cutervo, Santa Cruz, 1924–25 a 1927*. Lima: Imprenta del Ministerio de Guerra.

Gitlitz, John. 1979. "Conflictos políticos en la sierra norte del Perú: La montonera Benel contra Leguía, 1924." *Estudios Andinos (Lima)* 9: 127–38.

Gonzales, Michael J. 1985. *Plantation Agriculture and Social Control in Northern Peru, 1875–1933*. Austin: University of Texas Press.

Gorman, Stephen. 1979. "The State, Elite and Export in Nineteenth Century Peru." *Journal of Interamerican Studies and World Affairs* 21: 395–418.

Haya de la Torre, Victor Raúl. 1973. *Aprismo: Ideas and Doctrines of Victor Raul Haya de la Torre*. Kent, Ohio: Kent State University Press.

———. 1977. *Obras Completas*. 7 vols. Lima: J. Mejía Baca Editores.

INEI. 1992. *Estrructura de Ingresos y Gastos de los Hogares de la Ciudad de Chachapoyas*. Lima: Instituto Nacional de Estadística e Información.

Joseph, Gilbert M., and Daniel Nugent, eds. 1994. *Everyday Forms of State Formation: Revolution and the Negotiation of Rule in Modern Mexico*. Durham, N.C.: Duke University Press.

Klaiber, Jeffrey L. 1975. "The Popular Universities and the Origins of Aprismo, 1921–24." *Hispanic American Historical Review* 55, no. 4: 693–715.

Klaren, Peter F. 1973. "Modernization, Dislocation and Aprismo." Latin American Monographs no. 32. Institute of Latin American Studies. Austin: University of Texas Press.

Larson, Brooke. 1988. *Colonialism and Agrarian Transformation in Bolivia: Cochabamba, 1550–1900*. Princeton: Princeton University Press.

Lopez-Alves, Fernando. 2000. *State Formation and Democracy in Latin America, 1810–1900*. Durham: Duke University Press.

Mallon, Florencia. 1983a. "Murder in the Andes: Patrons, Clients and the Impact of Foreign Capital, 1860–1922." *Radical History Review* 27: 79–98.

———. 1983b. *The Defense of Community in Peru's Central Highlands*. Princeton: Princeton University Press.

Miller, Rory. 1982. "The Coastal Elite and Peruvian Politics, 1895–1919." *Journal of Latin American Studies* 14: 97–120.

———. 1987. "Introduction." In Rory Miller, ed., *Region and Class in Modern Peruvian History*, 7–20. University of Liverpool, Institute of Latin American Studies Monograph no. 14.

Nugent, David. 1988. "The Mercantile Transformation of Provincial Urban Life: Labor, Value and Time in the Northern Peruvian Sierra." Ph.D. diss., Anthropology Department, Columbia University, New York City.

———. 1994. "Building the State, Making the Nation: The Bases and Limits of State Centralization in 'Modern' Peru." *American Anthropologist* 96, no. 2: 333–69.

———. 1997. *Modernity at the Edge of Empire: State, Individual, and Nation in the Northern Peruvian Andes*. Stanford: Stanford University Press.

Rénique, José Luis. 1979. *El Movimiento Descentralista Arequipeño y La Crisis del '30*. Lima: Taller de Estudios Políticos. Universidad Católica del Perú.

———. 1991. *Los sueños de la sierra: Cusco en el siglo XX*. Lima: CEPES (Centro Peruano de Estudios Sociales).

Sanchez, Luis Alberto. 1934. *Haya de la Torre o el Político*. Santiago de Chile: Biblioteca América.

Scott, James C. 1990. *Domination and the Arts of Resistance: Hidden Transcripts*. New Haven: Yale University Press.

Slater, David. 1989. *Territory and State Power in Latin America*. New York: St. Martin's Press.

Smith, Carol A. 1990a. "Failed Nationalist Movements in 19th-Century Guatemala: A Parable for the Third World." In Richard G. Fox, ed., *Nationalist Ideologies and the Production of National Cultures*, 148–77. American Ethnological Society Monograph Series, no. 2. Washington, D.C.: American Anthropological Association.

———. 1990b. "Introduction: Social Relations in Guatemala over Time and Space." In Carol A. Smith, ed., *Guatemalan Indians and the State: 1540–1988*, 1–30. Austin: University of Texas Press.

Spalding, Karen. 1975. "Hacienda-Village Relations in Andean Society to 1830." *Latin American Perspectives* 2: 107–22.

————. 1984. *Huarochiri: An Andean Society under Inca and Spanish Rule*. Stanford: Stanford University Press.

Stein, Steve. 1980. *Populism in Peru: The Emergence of the Masses and the Politics of Social Control*. Madison: University of Wisconsin Press.

Sulmont, Denis. 1975. *El movimiento obrero en el Perú, 1900–1956*. Lima: Pontificia Universidad Católica del Perú, Fondo Editorial.

Taylor, Lewis. 1986. "Bandits and Politics in Peru: Landlord and Peasant Violence in Hualgayoc 1900–30." Cambridge Latin American Miniatures, no. 2. Centre of Latin American Studies. Cambridge: Cambridge University.

Urban, Greg, and Joel Sherzer. 1991. *Nation-States and Indians in Latin America*. Austin: University of Texas Press.

Vega-Centeno Bocangel, Imelda. 1991. *Aprismo popular: Cultura, religion y política*. Lima: Tarea.

Weinstein, Barbara. 1983. *The Amazon Rubber Boom, 1850–1920*. Stanford: Stanford University Press.

Zubiate Zabarburú, Alejandro. 1979. *Apuntes sobre la fundación de la ciudad de San Juan de la Frontera [Chachapoyas]*. Lima: n.p.

Rites of Purification, Acts of Retribution
Language and Representations of Identity in Northwestern Greece

The September 1, 1959, issue of the Athenian newspaper *Sphera* described what it called a "very peculiar" ceremony held in the village of Atrapos (formerly Krapeshtina) in the Florina prefecture on August 10 of that year.[1] As the article put it, "The simple population of the village, in front of God and people, swore that from now on they will stop using the Slavic idiom in their speech and that they will speak only the Greek language" (Drizo 1959).[2]

According to the above report, the villagers became so encumbered by the influence of repeated Slavic invasions that they borrowed from the language of the outsiders and had made their own language, albeit one with a strong Slavic idiom. The "descent" of the Atrapiotes was explicitly described as clearly Greek. But these so-called simple people now took the heroic decision to rid themselves, and their language, of every Slavic influence. Henceforth, they would speak only the Greek language, "clear," as the account said, "like the ice cold waters of their village."

Even before dawn on the Sunday morning of the ceremony, the village streets were already crowded as all the residents, children included, made their way to the church. This was a historic day in Atrapos. After the Doxology (*Dhoksologhia*), the focus of the ceremony turned to the schoolyard, filled with a capacity crowd. On one side of the yard were the Atrapiotes, across from whom stood one hundred representatives from other area villages, as well as military and political leaders of the region.

Above the congregation, the Greek flag (*ghalanolefki*) flew "proudly." The military band struck up the national anthem. Elderly men who had been partisans in the turn-of-the-century Macedonian Struggle, it was said, could not restrain their tears.[3] The village president made a brief welcoming speech to the official observers, and then asked his fellow villagers to take the great oath. Silence fell as the villagers raised their right hands and repeated after their president:

> I promise in front of God, men, and the formal authorities of our State, that I will stop speaking the Slavic idiom which gives reason for misunderstanding (*pareksighisi*) to the enemies of our country, the Bulgarians, and that I will speak, everywhere and always, the official (*episimi*) language of our country, Greek, in which the Holy Gospel of Jesus Christ is written.

After the oath, the village teacher addressed the congregation. He was described by another observer as a local villager, a "national worker," a descendant of a Macedonian Fighter priest, and a spiritual guide who had inspired his covillagers to take the Greek-language oath.[4] Now he told them:

> We have decided, with pride, all together, to stop speaking the foreign idiom, which has no relation to our Greek descent. . . . In this way, we offer limited honor and gratitude to those . . . Greek copatriots who gave us our freedom with their blood. . . . Long Live the King! Long Live the Greek State! Long Live our Undefeated Army!

Following this, another villager spoke in his own "simple" words about the importance of the oath. A child then recited a poem, and the prefect (*Nomarkhis*) of Florina closed the ceremony with a patriotic speech congratulating the people of Atrapos and their decision. After the ceremony, the hero's monument (*iroo*) of the village was crowned with wreaths, and popular songs and dances were performed.

Reading this account some forty years later, the question that troubled me most was, "Why?" For what reason did the people of Atrapos take this oath? What exactly was this otherness, the cause of their "misunderstandings" with their neighbors? In what way was the oath going to eradicate this otherness? During a brief visit to the now nearly depopulated village of Atrapos in the summer of 1996, visible characteristics of "otherness" were still discernible. The elderly still spoke in public a Slavic vernacular, which is a regional dialect of the standardized Macedonian language. Although a few women I met could not understand Greek, children communicated with one another in Greek while playing in the school's courtyard, where the language oath had been sworn more than thirty-five years earlier. That ceremony was still remembered but rarely discussed. As one man told me: "Yes, we took the oath, but then we went home and continued speaking our language."

This paper will focus not on the question of whether the people of Atrapos were obliged to take this oath or did so voluntarily. That question

I leave for the polemicists on either side to handle. Here I address how language instruction, national education, and the oath ritual functioned as apparatuses for the organization of (national) consent (Bennett 1994: 151). Elsewhere I have dealt with the coercive means employed by the Greek state in its effort to integrate Macedonia into its national body (Karakasidou 2000b).

Genealogical reconstructions, oral histories, and archival research on the prefecture (*Nomos*) of Florina indicate that since the advent of Greek rule in 1913, most of the Slavic-speakers of Greek Macedonia either left the region (voluntarily or not, and most for Bulgaria, Yugoslavia, and beyond) or were absorbed into the emerging Greek national community, slowly losing their native language as well as a sense of their ethnic distinctiveness. Harsh policing measures attempted to remove any recalcitrant Slavs whose foreign-oriented national consciousness defied eradication (Karakasidou 2000b). In addition, a campaign of national enculturation was adopted to extend Greek national consciousness to the area's Macedonian Slavs. Following the prototype set by European nation-states, Greece systematized the learning of a national language. As those national plans had it, the boundaries of the political unit (state) had to coincide with the linguistic borders. Language was, and today still is, considered the single most important defining characteristic of nationality.

It would be rather deterministic, conspiratorial, and naïve to maintain that the identity of the Slav-Macedonians changed because of the ceremonial language oath they undertook. The meaning of the rite was by no means the same as the intention of the organizers. The fact that there still exists an active and vocal minority of Slav Macedonians in the area, who claims Macedonian distinctiveness, testifies to the incompleteness of the Greek national project (Karakasidou 1993a). As I will show here, the language oath took place at a critical time, a point of juncture in the process of the population's amalgamation into the Greek national body. By 1959, the Slavs of Macedonia were at the crossroads of changing their allegiance to the Greek nation-state and their national identity. What was transformed through the ritual, however, was not the identity of the participants per se, but the understanding that people had of who they were within the larger national collectivity.

The ritual will be examined here as a *topos*, a point in time and space that provides powerful images to observe and underlying structures to unravel. The meaningful components of identity changes that took place were crystallized in ritualistic performances of this sort, down to their most basic foundations, as they were acted out for outsider administrators to observe. As Geertz (1973: 127) has put it, rituals "somehow sum up, for those for whom they are resonant, what is known about the way the world is, the quality of the emotional life it supports, and the way one ought to behave while in it."

Nicholas Dirks (1994: 484) has argued that *ritual* is a term that sanctifies and marks off a space and a time of special significance. Some rituals may be part of everyday life; others are fundamentally opposed to the everyday. This quality of being set apart from the everyday (as the oath ceremony clearly was) heightens and intensifies the meaning and symbolism of the ritual beyond the significance of other social interactions. Dirks (ibid.) maintains that while for other anthropologists (such as Geertz) ritual solidifies and strengthens social order, for him "ritual has always been a crucial site of struggle, involving both claims about authority and struggles against (and within) it."

The language oath, in itself was neither a ritual organizing consent nor solely a ceremony laden with "hidden transcripts of resistance" (Scott 1986). One may argue, following Kertzer (1988: 37), that "a political system is rendered sacred through the use of ritual, [while] at the same time the power held by the political leaders is legitimized." Celebrations of national holidays, for example, commemorating historic national events (such as March 25, celebrating the outbreak of the Greek War of Independence in the Peloponnese in 1821) take on an almost mystical power that evoke patriotic sentiments and attachments to the national collectivity (Karakasidou 2000a). Rituals of this sort unite a particular image of the cosmos (for example, the nation) with an emotional attachment to that image (Kertzer 1988: 40). In the Greek context, that attachment is brought about through those symbols of the nation that are omnipresent in everyday life, such as the flag, the colors blue and white, the national anthem and other patriotic songs, or portraits of independence heroes hung on school walls.

The language oath ceremony, however, was a unique event in time and space. It simultaneously embodied the order and essence of a national culture, as well as the resistance against it. It served an important intellectual function, mediating an exchange of values between the poles of externally imposed national norms and introverted personal sentiments (Turner 1974). It was a public ritual that aspired to create "moods and motivations" (Geertz 1973: 112), along with a new sense of allegiance to a society of order and stability—namely, the Greek nation-state. But at the same time, it also re-enforced the attachments that villagers felt to their neighbors and kin undertaking the same journey. While it was a moment of social cohesion (for those who planned it), it was also a moment of challenge for those who participated. It was, in the words of Dirks (1994: 487), "an important arena for the cultural construction of authority and the dramatic display of the social lineaments of power."

Counting and Representing

Since it had been the agents and representatives of the Greek state that had encouraged, organized, and promoted the ritual ceremony described at the outset of this paper, it is important to understand how such agents perceived the relative degree of "otherness" among the area's Slavic-speaking inhabitants. Let us, therefore, pause to examine the diverse composition of the area's population in the first half of the twentieth century, as evidenced in the official archives of the Greek state administrators.

Prior to 1913, the year of the region's incorporation into the Greek nation-state, a diverse ethnic tapestry had characterized Ottoman Macedonia (Karakasidou 1997).[5] The countryside was a patchwork of numerous ethnic groups, many with their own vernaculars, Slavic being among them. The invisible lines or "boundaries" (Barth 1969) that separated ethnic and linguistic groups were primarily religious and occupational, rather than national. By the late Ottoman period (roughly speaking, the nineteenth century), the Greek language was considered an expression of high culture in the Balkans (Gellner 1983). All Orthodox Christian subjects of the Ottoman empire were under the ecclesiastical and administrative jurisdiction of the Ecumenical (Greek) Orthodox Patriarchate in Istanbul. Greek speakers were concentrated primarily in cities and towns, and Greek was the language of administration and commerce, regardless of one's ethnic or national affiliation. Those Christians who aspired to upward mobility within the Ottoman empire were obliged to acquire a facility in Greek (see Stoianovich 1960; Karakasidou 1997).

In 1870, however, a major event altered the dynamics of Balkan politics: the Ottoman Porte granted the re-establishment of an autonomous Bulgarian Orthodox Church, which became known as the Exarchate. Subsequently, Bulgarians took control of ecclesiastical and educational institutions in Slavic-speaking communities throughout Macedonia (Perry 1988: 27). By 1900, Macedonia had become a focus of an increasingly violent territorial and religious-cum-national dispute between two young, expansionist states vying for control over the region: the kingdoms of Greece to the south and Bulgaria to the northeast. This was a period of intensive nation-building activity in Macedonia. Greek and Bulgarian churches and schools spread across the countryside at a rapid pace. National societies were formed both in Athens and in Sofia to sponsor the dispatch of priests, educators, and propagandists into Macedonia. Religious teaching—both in church and in schools—became a conduit through which Greek and Bulgarian national elites attempted to extend their hegemony through the construction of new national identities for the region's Slavic speakers.

When Greece attained sovereignty over the region of Florina (Krapeshtina being one of the prefecture's forty-nine villages), the new administrators collected demographic data on the area's population. Although 39 percent of the region's Christian inhabitants were described as "Greek," none were monolingual in Greek.[6] Put another way, there were no monolingual Greek speakers among the Florina population. Of those multilinguals that declared themselves "Greek" and could speak Greek, 52.8 percent also spoke Bulgarian (as the local Slavic vernacular had been termed), 32.5 percent spoke Koutsovlach (a vernacular akin to Romanian), and 14.7 percent spoke Albanian. On the other hand, the majority of the Christian population (59 percent) was described as "Bulgarians," up to 70 percent of whom were monolingual in "Bulgarian" only.

The specific numbers for the village of Krapeshtina were similar. Of the 400 people living there during 1911, 225 (56 percent) had been labeled by the authorities as "Bulgarians," and 175 (44 percent) as "Greeks." The village itself, however, was described entirely as "Bulgarian-speaking."[7] By 1935, Krapeshtina had 92 families, of which 66 (72 percent) were of Slavic "morale" (*fronima*), while the remaining 26 (28 percent) were "foreign-speakers" of Greek "morale" (Lithoksoou 1992: 41). In a letter dated 1934, First Lieutenant Stefos Grigoriou reported that only one family in the village was Greek, while all the rest were "Bulgarians." The lone family with Greek consciousness was that of the local priest, although even their Greekness was ranked only at "Grade C" (ibid.: 39).

It is important to note that the data on Macedonia collected by Greek state administrative personnel, or at least those documents that still survive today in government archives, do not refer to the ethnicity of the area's inhabitants per se. Rather, the classifications employed and the social divisions made can be more properly termed "national categories," as they refer to perceived ideological inclinations toward particular nation-states in the region (for example, Albania, Bulgaria, Greece, Romania, Turkey). Failure to distinguish between these "national" classifications and the "ethnic" composition of the population has contributed to a conceptual muddle on the part of many scholars dealing with Macedonia (Karakasidou 1993a, 1997).

Government sources indicate that Greek identity did have a presence in Macedonia since at least the turn of the century. But it is equally apparent that Greek national consciousness (or the hegemony of the nation and its implied legitimation) took much longer to develop and achieve deep roots in Western Greek Macedonia. Moreover, my own interviews with elderly *Grkomani* (Slavic speakers who identified with Greece) revealed that few of them had an unchanging or unwavering national Greek consciousness. *Grkoman* was a term used by Slavic speakers in Greek Macedonia to refer to those of their number who came to identify themselves as "Greeks." The term implies one who has a "mania" for Greece. But identity and consciousness changed over time, in response to the material circumstances in people's social, economic, and political milieu.

In light of the above, the motivations behind the policies and practices of Greek government administrators in the Florina region become more clear. The 1920s were a decade marked by out-migration, displacement, and deportation of Slavs, as well as by voluntary exchanges of population between Greece and Bulgaria (Jelavich 1983: 136; Ladas 1932). Many of those who left were replaced in their local communities by more than 500,000 Greek refugees from Thrace and Asia Minor. This influx dramatically transformed the ethnic composition of Greek Macedonia. Moreover, most of these "repatriates," displaced by the Greco-Turkish war in Asia Minor, possessed a Greek national consciousness.

It was during the Metaxas dictatorship (1936–40) that prohibitions against the public or private use of Slavic and other non-Greek dialects and languages were first implemented. In addition, institutionalized forms of national enculturation were also introduced: national holidays, adoration of the Greek flag, and compulsory night schools for the older generations (Karakasidou 2000a). Family names were also changed from Slavic to Greek forms. Admittedly, the Slavic population was hostile to such measures, the memory of which still lingers in the minds of those who lived through them.

When the Germans occupied Greece in 1941, their Bulgarian allies made renewed efforts to proselytize the population to their national ranks. The 1940s were a tumultuous and violent decade that culminated in the Greek Civil War (1947–49). During that conflict, Slav Macedonians entered the ranks of the Greek Communist partisans (Karakasidou 1993b).

Many, however, did not fight for social equality and socialist change as in other parts of Greece, but rather for regional autonomy with the support of Yugoslav partisans on the other side of the border.

By 1959, ten years after the defeat of the Communists and their Slav-Macedonian allies, the Bulgarian threat had disappeared. Yet a new axis of contest had formed between Greece and Yugoslavia, after the establishment of the Yugoslav Socialist Republic of Macedonia in 1944.[8] The 1950s were mostly a period of reconciliation in the Florina area. The most fanatic Slav-Macedonians, so to speak, had left Greece, and those who remained had vivid memories of the retributions and destruction that had been inflicted upon them. Their overt peacefulness reflected both their silenced resistance and their willingness now to integrate themselves into Greek society.[9] But a lingering consciousness—or perhaps subconsciousness—of Slav-Macedonian identity continued to persist among much of the local population. By the time of the language oath, bilingual Greek and Slavic speakers filled positions such as village teacher, priest, president, or other local official. While these *Grkomani*, as they were popularly known, identified expressively with national Hellenism, they also acted as protective patrons for local neighbors, guarding them against the abuses of state power and its local representatives (Karakasidou 2000b).

Importing National Consciousness

Social scientists now widely recognize that identity and consciousness are constructs, the products of human agency. Both are established and defined in opposition to something they are not, to an "Other," as it were. In attempting to understand the construction of national consciousness in the Florina region of Greece, one has to examine the activities of those who might be referred to as the "agents" or "importers" of national consciousness.

Following Greenfeld (1990: 550), the adoption of a national identity or consciousness by a given population is linked to the interests of those influential individuals or groups that import it into a given area and promulgate it among local society. In the process, such agents often change their own identity, consciously or not, because their structural positions within local society become transformed as the locale is linked with a larger economic, social, and political arena. By brokering or mediating the import of a national-level identity and consciousness among an ethnically diverse local population, such agents invest themselves with a powerful form of social and political capital, the values of which are linked to their interstitial positions between (nation) state and locale.

Yet there is an important analytical distinction that needs to be made between "internal" and "external" agents of national identity and consciousness. Throughout Greek Macedonia, the internal agents of national consciousness consisted primarily of schoolteachers, priests, large landowners, and merchants. The prestige that such elite personnel enjoyed in their social milieu was transformed into power when they became official mediators of state and local relations. Recall that it was the teacher (son of the priest, from the only village family with a ["Grade C"] Greek consciousness) who "persuaded" the villagers of Atrapos to take their language oath. He used the power vested in him by the state to transform local notions of identity.

At the same time, there were also "external" agents of national consciousness, including bureaucrats, government officials, tax collectors, policemen, and army personnel (as among the spectators of the 1959 ceremonial oath). Their influence was often profound in densely populated administrative and commercial centers. But in the countryside, it was primarily the interstitial *Grkomani* local elites that played the most critical roles. Education had a vital function in Hellenizing the region's Slavic speakers. The control that the Greek nation-state sought over Macedonia was not only a matter of territorial sovereignty; it also entailed the domination of the cognitive apparatuses of the population. State power and authority are exercised, also through the production of truths (Foucault 1994) and state education both produces and disseminates these national truths. In all the archives I have examined, there is at least one consistent theme: the educational system was intended to serve a national purpose. It was a focal institution of national conversion.[10] Education was, as Mitchell (1988: 69) has pointed out, one of the autonomous state practices that produced the individual citizen.

Educating the Potential Citizens

At the turn of the century, the village of Krapeshtina was located in what Kofos (1980: 48) has called the "central zone" of Macedonia. Still under Ottoman rule, the Orthodox Christians inhabiting this "problematic" area were classified according to their national religious allegiance (or their propensity to show such allegiance). There were *Ellinizondes*, or Orthodox people clearly possessed with Greek national leanings; *Voulgharizondes*, or

Orthodox people who secretly possessed Bulgarian leanings; and *Skhis-matiki*, or those with overt Bulgarian leanings who followed the Bulgarian Exarchate and openly opposed Hellenism (Vouri 1992: 52). The Greek-speakers were mostly concentrated in urban centers, where they participated in a Greek-like (*Ellinophanis*) way of life in their religious, social, and educational sectors. Greek letters, according to Vouri (ibid.: 49) were transmitted through religion, education, and language, and were considered the "true civilization of the Orient."

To the extent that a Greek identity existed at all during the more than four hundred years of Ottoman rule in Macedonia, it was based largely on religion and conditioned by identification with the Orthodox Church (Ecumenical Patriarchate) and its high clergy, rather than on notions of common ethnic or national descent. The centrality of religious authority and liturgical language provided the basis of twentieth-century Greek scholarly definitions of nationality *and* ethnicity.

Vouri has argued that in the 1870s, the promotion of Greek letters as a symbol of high culture in the region was very much a policy of the Greek nation-state to the south. Evidence of this may be found in the establishment of the "Association for the Dissemination of Greek Letters" in Athens in 1869, which focused its activities on the central and more "problematic" zone of Macedonia, where Florina and Krapesthina were located. The Greek nation-state, with its ideology of cultural, linguistic, and religious homogeneity, undertook to integrate Macedonia's ethnically heterogeneous population. Many national activists of the time were well aware of the weak representation of "real" Greeks among the population of Macedonia. The Council for the Reinforcement of Greek Religion and Education (established 1887) replaced the Association for the Dissemination of Greek Letters, and its personnel were appointed by the Ministry of the Exterior (ibid.: 87). The council dubbed educators working in the region as "national enlighteners," particularly those working in high schools, while high school superintendents were referred to as "right revolutionaries" (ibid.: 164–65).

Accordingly, the rhetoric such personnel adopted to promote their policies was disseminated through Greek education and through allegiance with the Orthodox Patriarchate, the two defining characteristics of one's "Greekness" (ibid.: 52). Greek language was a tool of communication that people of Macedonia learned in order to secure positions in the structural division of labor. As Vouri (ibid.: 65) maintained, Vlach- and Slav-speakers of the Monastiri (Bitola) and Florina (Lerin) areas did learn Greek, but mainly for the purpose of providing a means for their livelihood. Moreover, most were indifferent to the prospect of Greek national education. Thus the 1870s efforts of Greek nation-state educators in Macedonia focused on the more developed urban centers of Ottoman Macedonia, where Greek and Greek-speaking elements were more numerous. The common language was instrumental in the creation (and imagining) of the new nation.

By the 1880s, however, there came a realization that Greek schools should be spread throughout the countryside in order to counter the rapidly growing influence of Bulgarian nationalists, who were recruiting many local residents to the cause of the "Schismatics." As the Greek state began financing schools, Greek education took on an overtly nationalist character in competition with Bulgarian propaganda (ibid.: 71–77). The same policies continued through the 1890s, but by the turn of the century it had become apparent that Greek education was achieving successes only in large urban areas. The money earmarked for solely "Slavophone" communities was largely being wasted, as such locales developed "neither Greek letters nor Greek morale" (ibid.: 94).

Over several generations, the acquisition of a Greek education, in conjunction with the political incorporation of the region into Greece in 1913, made those with "Greek letters" the agents of Hellenism and Greek national consciousness. While the idea of Hellenism found roots among many Vlach- and Slavic-speakers in the area before 1913, it was the subsequent creation of national consciousness through education that eventually made the area unquestionably Greek.

One must distinguish here between two distinct yet interrelated national collectivities. The first, dominant during the years preceding incorporation in 1913, relied heavily on the Orthodox (Greek) Church and Greek national educational policies to attract members. The second, which rose to dominance after 1913, used more overt and covert methods of state integration. The Hellenic community at the turn of the century was poorly defined territorially. It was a largely "imaginary" and ideological community that found definition in the alleged superiority of Greek religion, culture, and letters. The community of the Greek nation-state, on the other hand, was territorially more concrete. At the same time, the Greek nation-state not only made allusions to an imaginary community among members of a high culture. Following the region's incorporation, it also provided the bureaucrats, army, police, administrative personnel, and "national" teachers to disseminate the notion of membership in a national collectivity—and the inherent superiority of that collectivity—among the local population. Nationalism was the imposition of a literate "high culture" upon an agrarian illiterate "low culture" (see Gellner 1983).

In both cases, however, education was a focal institution of conversion. As Vouri (1992: 71) put it, there existed a "dialectical relation between the aims of education and national goals." On the level of policy formulation and the subsequent creation of ideology, it was believed that when the aims of education were attained and the population learned the Greek language, letters, and civilization, they would eventually come to conceive of themselves as Greeks.

Vouri has also emphasized the ramifications of the decision to teach the *katharevousa* in Greek schools (1992: 103). When the Greek Kingdom was established in 1829, the absence of linguistic uniformity within the new unit's borders called for the utilization of one language as a diacritic of national homogeneity. *Katharevousa,* an artificially constructed atticized form of classical Greek, served such a purpose. It was a mixture of ancient and spoken Greek. Not only did it provide a linguistic proof for the continuity of Hellenism; it also helped the new kingdom and its inhabitants to present themselves to the outside world as superior, prestigious, and of "high culture." Herzfeld (1982) has explored the linguistic controversy between *katharevousa* and *dhimotiki*, the spoken Greek vernacular. While the former asserts Hellenic identity and reflects the distant, glorious past of classical Greece, the latter asserts familial identity and reflects a more recent past. For Greeks desperately trying to separate themselves from their Ottoman recent past, *katharevousa* provided a tool to "occidentalize" themselves in this early stage of their national awakening. Their membership in a superior European collectivity was more desirable than association with an "oriental," Balkan, and backward community (see Todorova 1997).

After the turn of the century, evidence began to mount that this language was incapable of facilitating the assimilation of foreign-speaking students or of making them more ideologically inclined toward the Greek nation-state. Rather, a communicative gap was being created (Vouri 1992: 124). Although recommendations had been made to replace the teaching of atticized classical Greek with the vernacular, they were not acted upon. The books used in Greek schools were not rewritten to take into consideration the needs or circumstances of the nonnative Greek speakers among the local student population. As I will discuss below, teachers and administrators later made the same recommendations in Greek Macedonia during the 1920s. Vouri maintained that in contrast to this purist ideology that guided Greek educational efforts in Macedonia, Bulgarian agents were providing more focused, simple instruction in the local vernacular. In this manner, students were reportedly "indoctrinated" politically: they learned in the classroom that being a Macedonian meant being a Bulgarian.

Throughout the two decades prior to incorporation, Greek teachers were predominantly of local origin (that is, natives of the area). Specifically designed for the training of teachers, the *Dhidhaskalion* (Educational Academy) opened in Thessaloniki in 1876. Financed by the Greek community of Thessaloniki and by the above-mentioned Athens-based Association for the Dissemination of Greek Letters, the academy enrolled high school graduates from communities throughout Macedonia. Its graduates took up teaching positions in Greek schools in the Macedonian countryside. Later, between 1883 and 1900, emphasis was placed on the establishment of higher educational institutions such as the *Astiki Skholi* (literally, Urban School—equivalent to high school) and *Parthenaghoghion* (Girls' High School) in Florina.

By the 1920s, the place of origin of appointed teachers had become a significant political issue. On the ideological level it was deemed important for such instructors to be natives of the area in order to foster the development of local agents of national activity throughout the countryside. Yet this led to major problems of a practical nature, as we will see below. Greek was not the native language of such teachers, and many in fact taught it poorly. For example, as early as the 1890s, the Monastiri (Bitola) High School was obliged to dismiss a large number of teachers because of their poor education and knowledge (ibid.: 128). In addition, many children lost interest in schooling, and attendance rosters dropped.

Turn-of-the-century educational activities in the region were strongly shaped by nationalist ideologies. The educational and religious institutions of that time took as their mission the creation of national consciousness among the Christians of Macedonia. But this enterprise continued to be most successful only in urban areas, owing mainly to the fact that formal schooling had little practical utility to Slavic-speaking agriculturalists. Apparently, this was particularly true in the central zone, where the region of Florina and the village of Krapeshtina were situated.

Educating the Citizens

Greek government archives indicate that in 1913 only sixteen of forty-nine villages in the Florina district had functioning schools and kindergartens.[11] It is significant that in all sixteen villages with Greek schools, a portion of the population declared themselves to be "Greek." Not one of the villages listed as populated by "Bulgarians" had a Greek school. A total of 34 schools operated in the Florina district, including 16 kindergarten, 11 elementary, and 7 high schools.[12] By February 1930, however, some 27 new schools had been established in the educational district of Florina. Throughout the region of Greek Macedonia, 321 new schools had been built over fifteen years, while another 189 were under construction.[13] Higher educational institutions such as the *Astikes Skholes* (High Schools) existed in only five towns and villages. With the exception of Florina, all of these communities were inhabited solely by Vlachs, the majority of whom declared themselves to be "Greeks," while a few identified themselves as *Roumanizondes,* or those with Romanian national "morale."[14]

The fact remains, however, that by 1925 the achievements of Greek educational institutions in the area were assessed as minimal. As the prefect of Florina reported to the General Directorate of Macedonia, schools did not function properly for a number of reasons, including lack of materials, facilities, and capable teachers.[15] Nor did they make efforts to provide a special linguistic program for "foreign speakers." Instead, children throughout the region were taught with the same textbooks used in Athenian schools. Moreover, local authorities often brought charges against parents who neglected to send their children to school, thus creating an "aversion against the Greek letters . . . [and] impatience and hatred toward the Greek administration."[16] The Greek schools thus functioned only formally, and children learned to read and write Greek only with the greatest of difficulties. In addition, the books used in the schools served only to create "disappointment" (*apoghoitefsi*) and "aversion" (*apostrofi*) toward Greek education.

The prefect maintained that teachers in the area were poorly trained and had no ambitions. Their pedagogy created no "civilizing influence" and failed to construct a Greek national consciousness among the students. He suggested that to solve this problem a new cohort of teachers would have to be recruited from among the best in Southern Greece: those who not only possessed knowledge but also would be capable of fostering the creation of national morale (*fronima*) among their local students. In order to attract such teachers, it was suggested that the government offer financial and moral incentives and arrange for easier promotions. Schools, the prefect cautioned, should be real schools, with an authority that would enable their students to graduate with "consciousness and pride that they could not only speak and write the Greek language but [could] feel and think like Greeks."[17]

For villagers living in communities, where intercourse with the outside world was limited to personal networks of marriage and economic exchange, local schoolteachers represented the principal civil servants with whom they would come into regular contact. But many of these teachers, as noted above, were allegedly of low intellectual caliber. Most were mere graduates of area high schools, although a few had graduated from educational academies (*dhidhaskalia*). Some, in fact, had only a fifth- or sixth-grade education but were appointed to teaching positions under Law 1197, which enabled many inexperienced, ill-trained, or allegedly fraudulent teachers to obtain positions simply by swearing oaths and signing statements that they had lost their diplomas.[18]

For example, of the twenty-one male elementary school teachers in the District of Florina, fourteen (66.7 percent) were high school graduates, while twenty-one of the twenty-six female elementary school teachers (80.8 percent) were high school graduates.[19] As the commander of the Florina gendarmerie, Major K. Lambrakis, put it in a 1925 report, the teachers had no general knowledge, could not fulfill their educational duties, and had no conception of their national mission.[20] They often got involved in township affairs, and they were not preachers of "national grandeur." According to this official, all teachers in the prefecture should be replaced so that new ones could be hired from the ranks of excellent instructors with a developed Greek consciousness. Such teachers would have as their sole mission national progress and the "quickest absorption of the Slavs by infusing in them the Greek idea by any kind of power and means . . . [so that we would] acquire the complete confidence of this agricultural population through proper and well understood propaganda that would successfully attract them to the Greek idea."[21]

In 1925, the Inspector of Elementary Schools in the Educational District of Florina filed a report with the General Directorate of Macedonia in Thessaloniki. The numbers and the opinions he presented echoed those of the prefect and the army major. The entire district, he maintained, was composed of foreign speakers: most were speaking the "Slav-Macedonian" dialect (*Slavomakedhoniki*). Only 23 (18.5 percent) of the district's 124 primary school teachers and 2 (4.2 percent) of the 48 kindergarten teachers had degrees in education, the rest being graduates of high schools or girl's high school (*Parthenaghoghion*).[22]

The inspector noted that while enrollments were up (in 1924, some 6,910 students were enrolled in area schools; the following year the number had risen to 7,072, with the number of male students roughly double that of females), few students attended school regularly. Moreover there were students in the third and fourth grades who were already twelve to fourteen years of age, and who often went on to graduate without gaining any real education. In a now familiar refrain, this inspector also complained that school buildings were in terrible condition, that the books used were inappropriate because they emphasized rote memorization, and that there were no supporting materials available to teachers. Little, he complained, has been accomplished in the realm of "language education." The "Slavophone dialect" had not receded, and students continued to converse in their "mother tongue" while playing at home and in the marketplace. Even teachers, he maintained, speak the "indigenous dialect," while mothers and young children do not speak Greek at all. In addition, the settlement of Pontic Greek refugees in the area had apparently done little to promote the use of Greek.[23] The inspector complained that the Pontics communicated with the "locals" (*endopyi*) in Turkish rather than in Greek.[24] Those students who did graduate remained in a foreign-speaking environment where "the weakest cannot assimilate the powerful."[25] In short, the inhabitants of the region had a "racial hatred" toward the Greeks that prompted many to avoid Greek schools and Greek teachers.

The inspector called for the appointment of ten good teachers from "Old Greece" (that is, Southern Greece) in each school district. He advised that they should be provided with double salaries in order to foster the construction of national character. Only in this manner, he believed, would local children be provided with a nationally oriented education. He admonished the government that it would be to Greece's benefit to make sacrifices until local teachers began graduating from the educational academies in the next decade. Similar reports were also filed by educational inspectors in the districts of Veria, Edessa, and Yiannitsa, noting that the influence of Greek schools in "foreign speaking" areas has been minimal, that people continued to speak "Bulgarian," and that they were generally indifferent to Greek schools.[26]

These archival records indicate that by 1925 the Greek educational system, as established in the newly incorporated areas of Macedonia, was not attaining the goals for which it was intended. The assimilation of the local Slavic-speaking population and the creation of a Greek national consciousness among them was still a long way off. Even those Slav speakers who did send their children to school continued to speak "Bulgarian" in their homes, at their public meetings, in their associations, and at their festivities, weddings, and holidays. They showed no signs of "love" toward their new country, an observation particularly noted of the older generation. Despite the fact that education had been made compulsory through law, many parents were willing to pay fines instead of sending their children to Greek schools. In some cases, they were so opposed to the presence of Greek teachers moving into their communities that they refused to assist in finding them housing. Life for all but a few local teachers was unbearable, and some deserted their postings, thus forcing the schools to close. Only in some villages, claimed the inspector in Edessa, were there people interested in education, and even those could be counted on one hand.[27]

These archives consistently recommend several measures to remedy this discouraging situation: (1) bring in the best qualified teachers from the south and provide them with incentives, bonuses, and special promotions until the local Slavic population produces its own indigenous Greek-trained teachers; (2) emphasize education among the very young (that is, kindergarten) and among women (night schools and schools on Sundays); (3) provide free higher education for those Slav-speaking children who want to go on to the educational academies; (4) establish night schools for the elderly in every village; and (5) make elementary education compulsory.

By the time of the Metaxas dictatorship in 1936, the linguistic situation in the region remained in crisis. In 1938, an Athenian teacher who worked in the Edessa area wrote a confidential report evaluating efforts to Hellenize Western Macedonia, and stressed the important role of the recently enacted language prohibitions.[28] The importance of these prohibitions, he argued, lay in the fact that on the surface they provided for a uniform appearance so that visitors and local inhabitants alike would see and feel that the area was part of Greece. More important, on a deeper level, "the young children will finally understand that they live in Greece, and *that the Greek lessons are not taught in schools as foreign lessons*" (emphasis in original). This teacher also believed that night schools offered the most effective means of achieving substantive results in Hellenization. During the Metaxas dictatorship, both women (between the ages of fifteen and forty) and men (up to the age of fifty) attended night schools. Reading, writing, and history were the primary subjects at these schools, while women were also taught home economics.[29]

This educator's observations grasped the twofold significance of the language prohibitions: on the one hand they contributed to the consolidation of a particular nexus of external characteristics of (national) group identity; on the other, they were efforts geared toward the internalization of national concepts and group characteristics, especially in the hearts and minds of the young and ideologically malleable.

Although reports from the 1920s suggested that schools in the area were falling short in their national mission because of a scarcity of educational materials, disrepair of facilities, poorly qualified teachers, and irregular attendance, after the 1950s education came to assume a more prominent and successful role in influencing the national identity and consciousness of the region's population. The explanation lies in the fact that by then most avenues of economic and social mobility had been restricted to education. Many parents came to realize that their children had little chance of improving their relative socioeconomic position if they continued to learn only the Slavic vernacular. A form of linguistic self-censorship came to be imposed in the home, with many parents discouraging their children from speaking Slavic (Karakasidou 1995). To the extent that the latter continued to learn the language, they did so primarily through their grandparents, who at the same time learned Greek from the grandchildren.

Clearly, it took several generations for Greek language hegemony and Greek national consciousness to take hold among the Slavic-speaking population of Greek Macedonia. By and large, those among the local population who received Greek schooling did tend to redirect their identity, sympathies, and loyalties toward the Greek nation-state. But the fact remains that such individuals were few in number, at least until the 1950s. It was only after World War II—and especially with the advent of free education in the 1960s—that education became both a more widely available and an increasingly important resource through which families and individuals could pursue concrete economic interests. It was only then that the goals of the Greek national educational system came to achieve their intended results. Yet even these accomplishments were predicated on the earlier removal of the most "fanatic Slavs" from the area, leaving few options to those Slavic-speakers that remained. Today, most schoolchildren no longer speak Slavic, and the majority of the Slavic-speaking (and formerly Slavic-speaking) population identify themselves with the Greek national collectivity.

The success of nation-building in Greek Macedonia (especially when evaluated against the experience of other Balkan countries) was due in no small part to the ability of the agents of Hellenism to bring about an internalization of certain normative frames of reference in the minds of a population. Having identified educators as agents or importers of Greek national consciousness in the Florina area, let us pause to consider several arenas in which such new national concepts, values, and notions of collective membership took hold among the local population. Examining the tools and mechanisms through which they internalized such concepts brings us to a discussion of language and rituals.

Conceptualizing the Nation

While language is an external marker of identity, it is also a principal medium through which internal characteristics of identity are framed and expressed. Linguists have recognized that language, as a medium of cultural communication, embodies a structured pattern of concepts that affect or even determine our interpretation of the world around us. It enables us to communicate with those who cohabit our social milieu. Its diversity, its "borrowed idioms" so to speak, are testimony to the fluid character of those social fields. With the shift from a Slav-Macedonian vernacular to a Greek one, a new set of semantic categories was imported into local culture and internalized in the minds of the local population.

At the turn of the century, the Slavic-speakers of Macedonia were caught in a no-man's-land between the converging frontiers of Greek and Bulgarian nationalisms. Their vernacular is considered part of the South Slavic language group.[30] Bulgarian nationalists, however, claimed that the language was a western variant of Bulgarian, despite significant differences in phonology, grammatical forms, and syntax (Friedman 1986). The Greeks, on the other hand, treat the regional Slavic vernacular as a mere "idiom," regarding it as only a spoken vernacular without grammar or syntax. At the turn of the century, religion, education, and a knowledge of Greek (though not necessarily as one's first language or native tongue) were stressed by the Greeks to construct the regional population's link to Greece. The Slavs who migrated to the area during the sixth and seventh centuries were considered to be "peaceful" peasants or shepherds who were Hellenized completely by the time of the Ottoman occupation in the fourteenth century (Vacalopoulos 1970). The Slavic vernacular is still disparaged and stigmatized by Greeks today as a "nonlanguage," a mere "idiom" of Bulgarian, or a so-called gypsy language (*yiftika*). Positions of this sort, however, fail to explain the continuing use of Slavic, along with other overt characteristics of ethnicity, in Greek Macedonia well into the twentieth century.

Beyond the debates that currently rage on the status of the Macedonian language or nonlanguage lie more fundamental issues. Through the political positioning of Greek and Bulgarian nationalists at the turn of the century and of Greek and Macedonian nationalists in the present day, Slavo-Macedonians and their vernacular were relegated to a low cultural status vis-à-vis their elite, nationally based neighbors. Consider a story, proudly related to me by a Florina painter of Arvanitis (Orthodox Albanian) descent, of how one day he heard some laborers outside his house speaking in Slavic.[31] Finding this personally irritating, he went outside and asked them, "Why do you speak this language? Don't you speak Greek?" Or consider the phrase often repeated to me by Slavo-Macedonians during coffee shop conversations: "We give the wrong impression when speaking that language," or "It is not proper to speak that language." As Tambiah (1989: 345) remarked, language not only serves as a mere communicative device but also has "implications for educational advantage, occupation, and historical legitimation of social precedence." Whether through self-censorship or externally imposed prohibitions, the Greek language gradually gained dominance among the Florina region's Slavic-speaking population over the generations.

Yet language, as such, is but one of many tools of communication employed by humankind. We all live within a daily poetics of personhood (Herzfeld 1985). As we strive to present ourselves in everyday life (Goffman 1959), we act in different arenas: concrete settings in which the contests between bearers of competing paradigms are played out (Turner 1974). The power of rituals, as Mary Douglas (1966) noted, lies in the manner in which, as an act of communication, they express, emphasize, and construct agreement upon the level of social structure that is relevant (or, we might say, dominant) to a given social field. In such contexts, actors are made aware of a greater or lesser range of inclusiveness. As highly structured frames of action through which the normative values of moral facts—as defined by the dominant social structure—are given voice, internalized, and reinforced among participants, ritual action is a process of sublimation (Turner 1974: 56).

The Ritual

It may be constructive to return, for a moment, to the language oath ceremony recounted at the outset of this paper. I interpret this ritual—and the narrative accounts of it—as an important moment in Greek nation-building in the Florina area. A closer look at the stage of the ritual, the structure of its action, and the symbols employed in its drama offers poignant insight on the processes through which Greek national consciousness was constructed and internalized among the local population. The Atrapos language oath may be interpreted as a rite of purification held under the legitimizing efficacy of both mystical or supernatural power (that is, God) and secular authority (that is, representatives of the Greek state).

The narrative opens with the villagers swearing an oath before God and state, the dual power of supernatural and secular authority. They pledged to "stop using" the "Slavic idiom" and to "speak" only the "pure Greek language." The juxtaposition here is between a "low culture" idiom that one "uses" and a "high culture" language that one "speaks." The Slavic idiom has been borrowed from invaders, a foreign force that penetrated and threatens the national body and must be expelled. As the Greek language is depicted as "pure," it stands in opposition to a Slavic idiom that is somehow "dirty" or "polluting." The polluting idiom is dangerous (Douglas 1966), as it causes misunderstandings that threaten the national social fabric.

The villagers are depicted as "simple" people, presumably close to nature. Sophistication, on the other hand, lies with the "unpolluted" who speak only the "pure" Greek language of high culture and who had gone through their own purification rites at an earlier time: the teacher, the priest, the village president. The so-called simple villagers, we note, gathered en masse, in the schoolyard, the place where languages are mastered through learning. Situated across from them, representing another semantic pole, were the selected representatives of the Greek state and nation. Metaphorically, these are different people, distinguished from the polluted villagers who are entering a period of liminality before being purified and reintegrated with the national body. Also present were local representatives from scores of other villages in the area. Some, undoubtedly, already possessed a Greek national consciousness and were present as representatives of the successful force of Hellenism. Others, just as likely, were invited to receive warning—or a summons—to join the Greek national fold both as individuals and as representatives of their native villages.

Symbolically mediating between these two social and semantic poles was the Greek flag, flying high above the delegates, its blue field representing the waters of the sea, and its white cross symbolizing the purity (or order) of God and His divine embodiment in the Greek nation-state. While probably few of the village's inhabitants had ever seen the sea, their elixir of life is identified by the narrative as the clear, icy waters of their village. Here the rhetoric of purification emerges again, as these waters—and their life-giving, head-clearing powers—are likened to the Greek language: the language of the church, the language of the state, the language of the nation. The ritual itself begins with the Greek Orthodox Doxology convened in the village church. The invocation of God promotes a spiritual mysticism surrounding the transformative powers of religion. It was through Orthodox Christianity that the Greek nation, it is often argued, was preserved through the millennia (see Martis 1984).

The account maintains that as the military band struck up the national anthem, the emotional strain for many village men became too much. Several wept openly. As Kertzer (1988: 73) has suggested, it is not the content or lyrics of an anthem that carry the greatest emotive significance for participants and observers. Rather it is the "use of marshal music together with graphic symbolism" that creates "a highly charged emotional atmosphere of national solidarity."

It was the village president, an already purified member of the Greek national collectivity and the representative of his fellow "simple" people, who welcomed the visiting dignitaries and administered the oath, an oath that both opens and closes with the invocation of the holy name of the Christian God. The villagers vowed to speak only Greek always and everywhere, in both public and private domains. The Greek language thus becomes a source of secular patriotism and supernatural pride, for it is also the language of the Holy Gospel.

The oath is followed by a commentary or homily, delivered by the local school teacher, himself a purified native villager and son of a former village priest active on the Greek side during the Macedonian Struggle. Described as a "national worker," he is also depicted as a spiritual guide for his fellow villagers and a "heartener" of (national) morale. It was he, as a ritual agent, who had the idea for the language oath and its accompanying ritual in the first place. In his speech, the local vernacular is transformed into a "foreign idiom" bearing no relation to the villagers' "very Greek descent." Here is presented the juxtaposition of foreign: familiar, or Other: Self. The invocation of kinship, descent, and reproduction completes a transformation of

Greekness into a natural, inalienable part of these villagers' lives. Their oath, he declares, "honors" the "co-patriots" from elsewhere in Greece who gave the nation its freedom with their blood, like a mother giving birth. Whereas the oath itself culminated in divine references to God, the teacher's homily concluded with very secular cheers dedicated to the pillars of the Greek nation: the king, the state, and the army.

It is curious—and unfortunate—that the newspaper did not deem it important or appropriate to print the text of the other village man who supposedly spoke in his "own simple" words about what the ritual meant to him, nor the child's poem that followed. We might offer an informed speculation that it was patriotic in content, perhaps not unlike those which countless Greek schoolchildren have had to memorize and recite during national celebrations. Most likely it dealt with heroic themes that reinforced the memory of the struggles of the Greek nation coming into being and protecting its existence.

The pronouncements of the prefect at the end of the ceremony conferred legitimacy upon the proclamation made by the village teacher just moments before: that the once "polluted" villagers, now emerging from a state of liminality into a newly "purified" status, are newly affirmed "Greeks." The once culturally anomalous Slavophones are thus converted into patriotic heroes of the Greek nation-state. At the same time, the ceremony also confirmed the authority of the Greek state over the region and the rights of its appointed representatives and administrators to arbitrate issues of national concern such as this one. As Victor Turner (1974: 56) put it: ritual is akin to a process of "sublimation," establishing a proper relationship between involuntary sentiments and the requirements of the social structure in such a way as to convert that which is socially *obligatory* to something personally *desirable*.

It is important to stress again the central role of religion in this secular ceremony. Nation-building often invokes the supernatural in order to legitimize its secular institutions. In this case, a semantic pole of metaphysical power (symbolized in God) is used to transcend and supplement the limited power represented by secular authority. The agents of the Greek state had had only limited success in Hellenizing the region. Even in 1959 there were still villagers who continued to speak their Slavic vernacular. What the secular authorities of the Greek state had failed to accomplish, God will take care of. The oath itself both opened and closed with the invocation of the holy name of the Christian God. While the oath was explicitly framed in terms of a national mission, the Greek language also became a source of secular patriotism and supernatural pride, for it was portrayed as the language of the Holy Gospel, the Greek Church, the Greek state, and the Greek nation.

State-building, or rather state integration, in Northern Greece was a conquest of fields: both real estate and those "abstract domains where paradigms are formulated, established, and come into conflict" (ibid.: 17). The domain of national consciousness has been one such field of contest. In what the Comaroffs have called the "colonization of consciousness," people are remade "by redefining the taken-for-granted surfaces of their everyday worlds" (Comaroff and Comaroff 1991: 313). Yet the normative paradigms that compete in this field do not only govern behavior or action, they also provide an ideational rhetoric with which action is cloaked in legitimacy. National consciousness is created or established through a process of hegemony, the internalization of the concepts and normative frames of reference of the nation so that they become accepted without question as a "natural" state of things.

Issues of identity and consciousness are intimately tied to definitions of a social collectivity, regardless of its size. In the case of a national collectivity, the internal characteristics of ethnicity (that is, a common descent and culture) are collapsed with those of the nation. Their significance fades as definitions of one's self become overwhelmingly oriented to notions of the national collectivity. Instead, a more grand and more mythical descent is claimed from figures more remote and yet more concrete: those of the nation's ancestors. The process of national enculturation transforms social attachments, which in the Balkans were largely to religion and family, to a secular, national collective identity. This is a process akin to what Anderson (1983) describes as the transformation from the imagined community of Christianity to that of the nation.

Despite the differential positions that individuals occupy along a continuum of national allegiance and ethnic attachment, a homogeneous school-transmitted culture (in Greek) replaced the folk-transmitted culture (in Slavic) of the older generation. The former, Gellner (1983) tells us, refers to the integration of an individual with the larger national collectivity, while the latter was important for the social reproduction of an individual on the level of the kin unit. The forms of legislative power described above suggest one operational vehicle through which national consciousness, by Hobsbawm's theory, moves from an initial phase of liberal ideas of revolutionary spirit associated with state-oriented patriotism, to a second stage of loyalty to the particular ideological construct of nationalism. Gellner

(ibid.: 34) has put it quite succinctly: "The monopoly of legitimate education is now more important than the monopoly of legitimate violence."

The transformation of identity into national consciousness can occur at
various speeds, depending on the particular social and economic conditions of the case at hand. For those individuals tied more closely with the
power structures of the newly dominant state society, such transformations occur quite rapidly. For others, it happens more slowly, or not at all.
Swearing an oath before God and before the authorities of the state—
God's secular parallel in this symbolic imagery—the people of Atrapos
vowed to use a language different from that to which they had been accus-
tomed and enculturated. But in so doing, amid all the elaborate pageantry
or decorum of this ritualistic ceremony, they were accepting—or at least
recognizing—the superiority of the Greek language over the daily vernacular they had learned at home as children and through which they had
communicated all their lives. At the same time, they began to change the
linguistic medium through which they internalized their cultural concepts.
By acquiring a "national" language, they acquired the means to understand
and internalize national concepts.

Notes

Fieldwork and archival research for this paper were supported through generous
grants from the Harry Frank Guggenheim Foundation and the Wenner-Gren
Foundation for Anthropological Research. The present form of this paper grew
from drafts presented at the Modern Greek Studies Association Symposium at
Berkeley in October 1993; Oxford University Workshop on Minorities in Greece,
January 1994; Barnard College, Anthropology Department, March 1994; and
Harvard University, November 1994. A number of colleagues and friends com-
mented on this work. To thank only a few by name, Michael Herzfeld, Loring
Danforth, Nikiforos Diamandouros, Philip Carrabot, Adamantia Pollis, Andonis
Liakos, Laurie Hart, and Gregory Ruf come to the forefront.

   1. As was common throughout the region, the village name (Krapeshtina) was
changed to its present Greek form (Atrapos) in the late 1920s; see Lithoksoou
(1991: 63–64).

   2. For another account of the same ceremony, see Stangos (1959). Similar oath
ceremonies took place in the village of Kria Nera near Kastoria (Y.I.P. 1959) and in
Kardia near Ptolemaida (*Ellinikos Vorras*, July 8, 1959, p. 5). See also Ioannidis
(1960).

   3. The Macedonian Struggle (1903–7) was a bloody guerrilla war waged between Greece and Bulgaria for control over the territory of Macedonia and its predominantly Slavic-speaking inhabitants.

   4. Stangos (1959) provided the account in this paragraph. The term "Macedon-

ian Fighter" (*Makedhonomakhos*) refers to combatants who fought on the Greek side during the bloody Macedonian Struggle.

5. The First Balkan War of 1912 saw an alliance of Bulgaria, Greece, and Serbia against the ailing Ottoman Empire, eventually driving the Turks from the Southern Balkan Peninsula. A year later, the Second Balkan War pitted Greece and Serbia in a victorious alliance against Bulgaria. The European-brokered Treaty of Bucharest in 1913 partitioned the region of Macedonia between Greece (which received 51 percent of the disputed area), Serbia (34 percent), and Bulgaria (15 percent). Each of these young nation-states began to pursue assimilationist policies toward the inhabitants of those parts of Macedonia under their respective political sovereignty.

6. Historical Archives of Macedonia/General Directorate of Macedonia (HAM/GDM) File no. 53 ("Population Statistics of the Educational Districts of Vodena, Karatzova, and Gevgeli, 1911, 1913, 1915"), Table A: "Florina District: Ethnological Census of the Population's Inhabitants."

7. Ibid.

8. The creation of the Yugoslav Socialist Republic of Macedonia in 1944 also entailed a nation-building process. The Slavic vernacular spoken in the southernmost region of Yugoslavia (and in Northern Greece) became the standardized Macedonian language for that republic. Regional authorities also stepped up their own efforts to present themselves as a separate "nation," distinct from neighboring Serbia and Bulgaria. A national Macedonian history found its roots in this period as scholars attempted to link the ancestry of the region's present population to the glorious legacy of Alexander the Great, Cyril and Methodius (the missionaries who spread Christianity to the Slavs in the ninth century), and other illustrious historical personages that would help legitimize the existence of a separate Macedonian nation in the present day.

For some examples of Macedonian nationalist historiography, see Institute of National History, *A History of the Macedonian People* (1979); and Dragan Taskovski (1967).

9. U.S. intelligence reports also drew the same conclusions; see Iatrides (1993: 6).

10. M. McDonald (1989) had examined the French education system in Brittany, which functioned, according to militant Britons, as a tool for the cultural genocide of the non-French population. The ethnographer artfully, however, looked at how education was only one of the symbolic markers used by these militants in order to construct their Briton "traditions."

11. HAM/GDM, File no. 53, Table B "Florina District: Census of Greek Schools."

12. Ibid., File no. 53, "Statistics on Greek Schools."

13. Ibid., File no. 61 ["Educational District of Thessaloniki, 1929–1930–1931"], Tables of Completed and Under-Construction School Buildings in Macedonia and Thrace, February 1930.

14. *Roumanizondes* was a term used in records to refer to those Vlachs who

showed allegiance to Romania and spoke a language akin to Romanian. The Vlachs were a pastoral (and mercantile) people dispersed throughout the Balkans. The Romanians participated in the educational antagonisms that went on in Macedonia, opening Romanian schools where Vlach children were receiving instruction in the Romanian language. According to the records I examined, the Romanian schools in Greece were in existence in the 1920s. The majority of the Vlachs, however, sided with the Greeks and asserted their Greekness. For more on the impact of Greek education on the Vlach communities of Macedonia, see Vouri (1992).

15. HAM/GDM, File no. 90, ("Propagandas: 1924–1925"), Letter from the prefect of Florina to the General Directorate of Macedonia, in Thessaloniki, Confidential Protocol no. 6, Florina, January 13, 1925.

16. Ibid.

17. Ibid.

18. Ibid.

19. HAM/GDM, File no. 53, Table D "Qualifications and salaries of teaching Personnel."

20. Ibid., File no. 90, Letter from Major M. Lambrakis, Commander of the Florina Gendarmerie Command, to the High Gendarmerie Command Macedonia, Confidential, Secret, and Personal, Florina, October 20, 1925, Protocol no. 147/1774 [Confidential Section].

21. Ibid., p. 4.

22. HAM/GDM, File no. 60 ["Public Education in Macedonia: 1922, 1924, 1925"], report entitled "The Condition of the Elementary Schools and Kindergartens of the Educational District of Florina," in response to GDM Command no. 20663 of March 11, 1924.

23. Pontics were refugees from the south coast of the Black Sea who came to Greece after the Asia Minor war and the 1923 Treaty of Lausanne. They spoke their own Pontic Greek vernacular, but they felt Greek in descent and nationality.

24. *Endopyi* means literally "people from the place," or "locals." This term is used to refer to the area's population that the refugees found in situ upon their arrival in Macedonia. In most areas it refers only to Slavic-speakers, but in some locales it encompasses populations of Vlachs (see Karakasidou 1997).

25. Ibid., p. 8.

26. See HAM/GDM, File no. 60.

27. Ibid., Letter from the Inspector of the Edessa Educational District to the General Directorate of Thessaloniki, Protocol no. 1021, Edessa, December 28, 1924.

28. Metaxas Archive, File no. 36, "The Performed Attempt to Hellenize Western Macedonia and the Achieved Results during the Last Two Years (Confidential)," Yiorgos Papadopoulos, Elementary School teacher, July 22, 1938.

29. Ibid., p. 5.

30. Distinctions must be made between the vernacular of the Slavic-speakers of Greek Macedonia and the standardized language spoken and used in the Former

Yugoslav Republic of Macedonia. The latter was standardized in 1944, when that republic was recognized as a distinct ethno-national region and administrative unit of post–World War II Yugoslavia.

31. The term *Arvanites* refers to Christian Albanians who migrated to Greek lands in the fourteenth century and now reside in Greece. Such individuals are distinguished from Albanians, per se, the nationals of the Albanian state.

References

Anderson, Benedict. 1983. *Imagined Communities: Reflections on the Origin and Spread of Nationalism*. London: Verso.

Barth, Frederic, ed. 1969. *Ethnic Groups and Boundaries: The Social Organization of Culture Difference*. Oslo and London: Allen and Unwin.

Bennett, Tony. 1994. "The Exhibitionary Complex." In Nicholas B. Dirks, Geoff Eley, and Sherry B. Ortner, eds., *Culture/Power/History: A Reader in Contemporary Social Theory*, 123–54. Princeton: Princeton University Press.

Comaroff, Jean, and John Comaroff. 1991. *Of Revelation and Revolution: Christianity, Colonialism, and Consciousness in South Africa*. Chicago: University of Chicago Press.

Dirks, Nicholas. 1994. "Ritual and Resistance: Subversion as a Social Fact." In Nicholas B. Dirks, Geoff Eley, and Sherry B. Ortner, eds., *Culture/Power/History: A Reader in Contemporary Social Theory*, 483–503. Princeton: Princeton University Press.

Douglas, Mary. 1966. *Purity and Danger: An Analysis of the Concepts of Pollution and Taboo*. London: Ark Paperbacks.

Drizo. 1959. "Close to Florina: Three Villages Swore . . ." *Sphera* 1 (September) [in Greek].

Ellinikos Vorras. 1959. "They Swore Faith to Greece." Sphera 8 (July): 5 [in Greek].

Foucault, Michel. 1994. "Two Lectures." In Nicholas Dirks, Geof Eley, and Sherry Ortner, eds., *Culture/Power/History: A Reader in Contemporary Social Theory*, 200–235. Princeton: Princeton University Press.

Friedman, Victor A. 1986. "Linguistics, Nationalism, and Literary Languages: A Balkan Perspective." In Victor Raskin and Peter C. Bjarkman, eds., *The Real World Linguist: Linguistic Applications the 1980s*, 287–305. Norwood, N.J.: Ablex.

Geertz, Clifford. 1973. *The Interpretation of Cultures*. New York: Basic Books.

Gellner, Ernest. 1983. *Nations and Nationalism*. Ithaca, N.Y.: Cornell University Press.

Goffman, Erving. 1959. *The Presentation of Self in Everyday Life*. New York: Doubleday, Anchor Books.

Greenfeld, Liah. 1990. "The Formation of the Russian National Identity: The Role of Status Insecurity and Ressentiment." *Comparative Studies in Society and History* 32, no. 3: 549–91.

Herzfeld, Michael. 1982. *Ours Once More: Folklore, Ideology, and the Making of Modern Greece*. Austin: University of Texas Press.

―――. 1985. *The Poetics of Manhood: Contest and Identity in a Cretan Mountain Village*. Princeton: Princeton University Press.

Iatrides, John. 1993. "As Others See It: American Perceptions of Greece's 'Macedonian Problem.'" Paper presented at the Modern Greek Studies Symposium, Berkeley, Calif., October.

Institute of National History. 1979. *A History of the Macedonian People*. Skopje: Institute of National History.

Ioannidis, K. 1960. *About the Assimilation of the Slavophones*. Florina [in Greek].

Jelavich, Barbara. 1983. *History of the Balkans: Twentieth Century*. Cambridge: Cambridge University Press.

Karakasidou, Anastasia. 1993a. "Politicizing Culture: Negating Ethnic Identity in Greek Macedonia." *Journal of Modern Greek Studies* 11, no. 1: 1–27.

―――. 1993b. "Fellow Travelers, Separate Roads: The Greek Communist Party and the Macedonian Question." *East European Quarterly* 27, no. 4: 453–77.

―――. 1995. "Women of the Family, Women of the Nation: National Enculturation among Slavic Speakers in Northwestern Greece." *Women on the Margins: Gender, Ethnicity and Nationalism*, Barbara Einhorn, ed. Special issue of *Women's Studies International Forum* 19, no. 1–2: 99–110.

―――. 1997. *Fields of Wheat, Hills of Blood: Passages to Nationhood in Greek Macedonia, 1870–1990*. Chicago: University of Chicago Press.

―――. 2000a. "Protocol and Pageantry: Celebrating the Nation in Northern Greece." In Mark Mazower, ed., *After the War Was Over: Reconstructing the Family, Nation, and State in Greece, 1943–1960*, 221–46. Princeton: Princeton University Press.

―――. 2000b. "Transforming Identity, Constructing Consciousness: Hegemony and Homogeny in Northwestern Greece." In Victor Roudometof, ed., *The Macedonian Question: Culture, Historiography, Politics*, 55–98. Boulder, Colo.: East European Monographs.

Kertzer, David. 1988. *Ritual, Politics, and Power*. New Haven and London: Yale University Press.

Kofos, Evangelos. 1980. "Dilemmas and Orientations of Greek Policy in Macedonia: 1878–1886." *Balkan Studies* 21: 45–55.

Ladas, S. P. 1932. *The Exchange of Minorities: Bulgaria, Greece, Turkey*. New York: Macmillan.

Lithoksoou, Dimitris. 1991. *Minority Issues and National Consciousness in Greece: Insolence of Greek Historiography*. Athens: Leviathan [in Greek].

―――. 1992. "Two Unpublished Documents about the History and the Consciousness of the Slavo-Macedonian Minority during the Pre-Metaxas Period." *Ektos Orion* 6: 36–47 [in Greek].

Martis, Nikolaos. 1984. *The Falsification of Macedonian History*. Athens: Evroekdhotiki.

McDonald, Maryon. 1989. *"We Are Not French!" Language, Culture and Identity in Brittany*. London: Routledge.

Mitchell, Timothy. 1988. *Colonizing Egypt*. Cambridge: Cambridge University Press.

Perry, Duncan M. 1988. *The Politics of Terror: The Macedonian Liberation Movements, 1893–1903*. Durham, N.C.: Duke University.

Scott, James. 1986. *Weapons of the Weak*. New Haven: Yale University Press.

Stangos, Nikos. 1959. "The Oath of the Inhabitants of Kardia and Kria Nera Was Repeated in Atrapos." *Ellinikos Vorras* 11 (August): 5 [in Greek].

Stoianovich, Trajan. 1960. "The Conquering Balkan Orthodox Merchant." *Journal of Economic History* 20: 269–73.

Tambiah, Stanley J. 1989. "Ethnic Conflict in the World Today," *American Ethnologist* 16, no. 2: 335–49.

Taskovski, Dragan. 1967. *The Genesis of the Macedonian Nation*. Skopje: Institute of National History [in Macedonian].

Todorova, Maria. 1997. *Imagining the Balkans*. New York: Oxford University Press.

Turner, Victor. 1974. *Dramas, Fields, and Metaphors: Symbolic Action in Human Society*. Ithaca, N.Y.: Cornell University Press.

Vacalopoulos, Apostolos. 1970. *The Origins of the Greek Nation: The Byzantine Period, 1204–1461*. New Brunswick, N.J.: Rutgers University Press.

Vouri, Sofia. 1992. *Education and Nationalism in the Balkans: The Case of Northwest Macedonia, 1870–1904*. Athens: Paraskinio [in Greek].

Y.I.P. 1959. "A Praise-Worthy Gesture." *Kastoria* 8 (September): 1 [in Greek].

Livelihood, Citizenship, and the Gender of Politics

In seeking to recover women from the hidden and silent spaces into which androcentric scholarship had relegated them, feminists of different persuasions have urged us to examine the social and cultural arenas where women's practices and voices are important and from where they may challenge local, as well as scholarly, ideas about gender arrangements, ideologies, and politics. Indeed, by focusing on social reproduction, on the private and domestic aspects of social life, on everyday forms of resistance, and on social movements, numerous studies have not only rescued women from oblivion but have also forced us to look at the ethnographic and historical record in new ways. In doing so, feminist scholarship has also questioned many central categories of social research and all forms of power relations. Yet, as often happens with theoretical turns, what was emphasized at first were those aspects that until then had been ignored or downplayed at the expense of other aspects of complex social relations. The focus on women and their spheres of action tended to reduce social reproduction to domestic female tasks rather than analyzing reproduction as a constitutive aspect of production, both of which are necessary processes for the continuity of the household over time. While most feminist anthropologists later rejected this perspective and adopted a more unifying one, other disciplines still maintain a one-sided or dichotomous understanding of gender relations (Stephen 1997). Similarly, in many of these studies, gender has become, as MacEwen Scott points out, "synonymous with women; men are shadowy figures, the invisible oppressors and patriarchs" (1994: 3), in spite of the substitution of gender for women in the titles of most recent publications. And politics is often reduced to questions of identity. Indeed, while most scholars now agree that no transcendental categories exist and recognize that subjects are historically constituted on the basis of class, ethnic, gender, generational, national, regional, and other distinctions, a dominant poststructuralist perspective that seeks to theorize the politics of gender and to formulate research and political strategies to encompass the diversity of subject positions emphasizes more the conjunctural (compare Frankenberg and Mani 1993), discursive, and representational dimensions of politics (compare Butler 1990; Scott 1992) and less the social relations that give rise to historically constituted forms of unequal power relations (di Leonardo 1991). This reductionism, which one encounters in much, but *by no means all*, current feminist scholarship, simplifies the complexity of concepts, whose very meanings encompass dialectical relations rather than oppositions or omissions. By this I mean something quite straightforward: that in order to understand one aspect of these relations, it is necessary to examine both or one in relation to the other: production *and* reproduction; women *and* men (not men in parentheses); the material *and* cultural aspects of power and politics.

The purpose of this paper is to clarify these relationships by examining the ways in which women and men experience and contend with conflicting demands of livelihood in rural Cochabamba, Bolivia.[1] The description and analysis of these experiences is based on a central premise: my contention that, in order to reproduce the conditions of livelihood, peasants and petty commodity producers in Bolivia, as elsewhere, have to carefully balance demands on their labor and time imposed by their productive and reproductive activities within and outside their households and by their need to confront a field of dominant forces and the state that continuously threaten the very viability and relative autonomy of households.

It is precisely because households and villages are embedded within this wider field of force that their welfare depends on their ability to gain or retain a certain degree of control over key resources (land, labor, animals, and money). And this is not an easy task, because few are the households that can maintain or expand themselves on the farm alone. The need to complement or increase household income requires some household members to leave their homes temporarily or permanently, migrating to other regions and countries to work as wage laborers, colonizers, transporters, or traders.[2] Thus the livelihood and opportunities (or lack of them) available to households is dependent on a double process: a relative control over resources and the simultaneous release of some of their working-age members. This process, in which both women and men participate, involves production and reproduction, waged and unwaged economic activities within and outside the household and the village in which it is inserted. When viewed from the perspective of the conflicting demands of livelihood, it is clear then, as many feminist scholars have argued for quite some time, that it is not possible to separate production from reproduction.[3]

In the literature, however, reproduction has many meanings (compare Edholm, Harris, and Young 1977); the word has also been so overused that it is important to clarify what I mean by it. In this paper, it refers to the activities necessary for the continuity of the labor process and the continuity of the household through time. The concept encompasses both work deployed in unwaged and waged production, as well as in those household tasks that are generally carried out by women, and all the other tasks, carried out by both men and women, that are related to the agricultural replacement fund (Wolf 1966). Further, I would argue that reproduction also entails political struggle.

Indeed, as I have demonstrated elsewhere (Lagos 1994), since early colonial times the laboring classes of rural Cochabamba have struggled in everyday and more violent forms of resistance against colonial exactions that depleted villages of their labor force, resources, and land. They also struggled against *hacendados* over the control of land, labor, and rent; and, after the revolution of 1952 and the agrarian reform of 1953, they have struggled against state policies that affect the productive and reproductive capacity of households and villages. Nowadays the demands of the laboring classes center on prices for agricultural products and industrial goods, the availability of credit and chemical inputs, roads and markets, educational and health services, and so on. Since the implementation of neoliberal policies in August 1985 and, more recently, with the passing of legal reforms that seek to restructure Bolivian society, peasants and petty commodity producers, along with other social groups, also struggle against coca eradication programs and the privatization of key resources and sectors of the economy such as water, electricity, the oil industry, and railroads.

Both women and men take an active part in production and reproduction, as well as in political mobilizations. But not surprisingly, the economic and political participation of women is usually devalued or simply not recognized as being important; rather, the tendency is to perceive women's contribution to these activities as merely complementary or supportive to those of men. What is surprising, however, is that women themselves often share this view, even in cases in which they take the initiative and are the main protagonists of specific political actions.

Women are also often critical of the time men spend in union politics. When I was carrying out research in the highlands of Cochabamba, I was often intrigued to hear such complaints, partly because some of these women were themselves involved in regional female rural organizations and because I knew that they were as concerned as men about the continuity of the household over time. As I listened to these complaints, the questions that recurrently came to my mind were: What is it in the politics of men that they actually dislike? Do women criticize men because they are excluded from formal political organizations such as the peasant union? Do women have different perceptions of what is political than men, as some feminist scholars have argued? And if so, what are the reasons for these differences? A central argument of this paper is that instead of attributing these differences to essential distinctions between women and men, to the sexual division of labor, or to the subject position of minority, working-class, or peasant women, it may be more fruitful also to examine the ways in which gendered political perspectives and practices have been influenced by the state.

To make this case, I will first describe the tensions that the conflicting pressures of livelihood generate within households and villages and how women and men deal with them as gendered subjects. The second part of the paper will examine the role of the state, as both a negative and positive force, in defining social categories, in particular the related concepts of gender and citizenship, and in prescribing "appropriate" gendered spheres of public and private practices.[4] As Corrigan and Sayer (1985: 3) indicate, "states state"; these "statements define acceptable forms and images of social activity and individual and collective identity; and regulate social life." States also define "what counts as 'politics,' the 'political nation,'" and public and private arenas. The question is how these state prescriptions interplay with entrenched unequal gender relations and ideologies in shaping the gender of politics.

Conflicting Demands and the Tensions of Livelihood

In the Cochabamba rural highlands, more specifically in the province of Tiraque, where I carried out long-term research, the two processes that I consider necessary aspects of production and social reproduction—multioccupational activities and political struggle—generate diverse and shifting points of contention that divide and unite households and villages in often unexpected ways. These tensions also make manifest diverse understandings about the meaning of *campesino* (peasant) and ethnic representations of self and others, as well as the meaning of social relations such as community, reciprocity, and fictive kinship (Lagos 1994). But a nodal point of contention, and one that to an extent encompasses all others, centers on the very meaning of the domestic and its insertion within a wider public context.

Even though Tiraqueños (as the people from Tiraque call themselves) conceptualize the domestic and the public as being gendered and separate, in practice they are not. Household boundaries are not rigid, because they can expand or reduce in time and space through the establishment of productive alliances with other households in the village, rural towns, or cities,[5] and household members move out of their homes to work in waged labor in order to send back their remittances. Furthermore, as we have seen above, the state and global forces continuously impinge on the domestic sphere as well, affecting interhousehold alliances, out-migration, and many other aspects of social and cultural life. Thus, as several studies have demonstrated, the domestic and the public, household and community, can no longer be conceived as natural units of analysis (compare Harris 1984) but as highly permeable spheres of practice and as arenas of negotiation and struggle (Smith 1990). To understand the issues raised in these debates and negotiations in rural Tiraque, it is first necessary to describe briefly local gender arrangements, gendered spheres of domestic and public practices, and related notions of masculinity and femininity.

Ideally, the principle of complementarity pervades every aspect of gender relations, stressing the interdependence of men and women in production and reproduction, in domestic and public spheres, and in ritual practices in which women and men are responsible for specific activities to be carried out in specific arenas. The concept *qhariwarmi* (Quechua for "man/woman") best symbolizes this ideal in which the couple is perceived as being the basis for the well-being of the household, the family, and the village as a whole.[6] Yet, while labor arrangements and other aspects of social life could be characterized as being complementary, as indeed most Tiraqueños would describe them, in practice gender relations are hierarchical, as evidenced in the control men have over women, in the unequal access to resources, and in violence against women.

According to the notion of complementarity, and even though the entire household participates in every step in the labor process, men are expected to be more directly involved in agriculture, in particular plowing with a team of oxen; they are also supposed to look after draft and traction animals, and to be responsible for the sale of cash crops in the marketplace. As landowning household heads, men represent the household in the village *sindicato campesino* (peasant union). The central responsibilities of women rest on sharing the work of men in the fields in every aspect of sowing and harvesting, but their labor, as well as the labor of adolescents, is valued less than the work of men. Women receive half and adolescents a fourth of the money or produce that men receive for their labor. Women are primarily expected to look after the home and the family; the socialization of children; the appropriate management and organization of household chores such as cooking, washing, spinning wool, taking care of sheep and small animals raised for their consumption value and as readily available sources of cash; and shopping or bartering in the weekly market to provide the household with those goods not produced in the farm. In practice, however, these gendered productive and reproductive labor arrangements, which are applied to generic women and men independently of their marital status (Edholm, Harris, and Young 1977), are not as rigid as they may seem because, when necessary, men or women undertake the tasks ideally assigned to the other. During my first fieldwork experience (1982–85), however, I met only one young woman who plowed, and because of this and the fact that she used to dress in slacks, she was referred as a *qharimacho*, reiterating the concept "male" both in Quechua (*qhari*) and in Spanish (*macho*).

In sum, culturally valued forms of masculinity and femininity rest on idealized, complementary stereotypes, associating men with production, especially cash crops and the use of the ox-driven plow, which is not only conceived as the most important male task but also as a central criterion for men's self-representation as campesinos (male peasants). This and land ownership are what give men access to the village union and, through it, to the public world of formal politics. Women are associated with the domestic: the home and household productive and reproductive activities independently of whether these activities are performed in the home, farm, or marketplace. And these stereotypical images affect how men and women depict one another, what they value for themselves and for the other, and how they deal with social transformations that force them to transgress their expectations and to accommodate to these changes.

The following narrative, based on excerpts from the life of Ambrosio, a former campesino leader, will serve to illustrate the gendered ways in which men and women experience, contend with, and interpret the burdens imposed by the conflicting demands of livelihood.[7] His account begins with the Chaco War, the war between Bolivia and Paraguay (1932–35) that broke out when he was ten years old:

> I was born in Chapapani, the hacienda of the Taborga family. As a child, I saw how the *patrón* [landowner] encouraged my father to go to the Chaco War, promising that none of his three sons would be forced to work without wages and that they would give an education to his children. When he was no longer there [in Chapapani], they made his sons work for free, taking goods on ten mules to Punata, Cochabamba, and Chimoré. And I was crying, complaining. "Mariano [his father], you go," they said, as if guaranteeing their promises to us without fulfilling them.
>
> We left the hacienda because they screwed us. A friend of my father sent a letter from the Chaco—"Mariano has died," it said. My mother almost went crazy with grief. I then went to my mother's mother, taking our little things on our backs and on donkeys to my granny's house in Palca. She was a *piquera* [landowning peasant]. Then came my father's sister, and she took home my two brothers. "I will take care of these children," she said.

Ambrosio's emphasis on the work of men and their sons in the haciendas omits the fact that both women and men, sons and daughters had to provide rent in the form of labor on the estate and on the hacendado's residence in the city. Instead he portrays the significant women in his life—his grandmother, mother, and paternal aunt—as both emotionally vulnerable and as responsible women who were able to take on the role of family caretakers. This gendered vision of the past pervades much of Ambrosio's account.

> In 1941, I went to the army in Cochabamba, where I spent three months. After I left the army, I worked as a peon in Cochabamba for two years. I then returned to Chapapani, where I bought a small plot of land. In 1943, I married Juliana from Puka Wasi and had three children.

During this time, Ambrosio was also active, helping to organize the first Indian Congress (1945) to be held in Bolivia and organizing *colonos* (tenants) in the haciendas. For these activities, he encountered strong opposition and violence on the part of hacendados.

> We have walked with people from the countryside. Some *mayordomos* [hacienda foremen] always wanted to beat us. I was already settled in Chapapani when the authorities from Tiraque wanted to kill me, but when they came, I was in Palca. My wife came to let me know. My granny and my mother cried, saying, "Why do you get involved in those things, *wawa* [child]?" I escaped to Korani to work where they were making the road. I stayed there for four months, after which I returned to Chapapani. I worked peacefully for four years.

Ambrosio does not specify who the "we" are; certainly the pronoun does not refer to him and his wife, but to men, the only ones who, according to this account, seem to have engaged in the political struggle. Women appear as concerned, caring individuals who either offer protection, as with his wife's warning that allowed him to escape, or, like his mother and grandmother, who do not seem to comprehend the reasons for the political engagement of their "child."

> Then came the [agrarian] reform. My compañeros put me in as leader of [the peasant union in] Chapapani, saying, "You are experienced, you know." During the reform, we attacked hacienda houses. Since the patrones used to take away our sheep and oxen, we returned them to their owners. During that time, one could hear the sound of *pututus* [horns] here and there. Because of that, the patrones got scared and left to the cities.

The Agrarian Reform Law was passed in 1953, several months after the National Revolution of 1952 and after the rural poor, organized in rural militias, forcibly took the land of hacendados, mainly in Cochabamba. But the legal implementation of agrarian reform was a drawn-out process, taking from three to eleven years and accompanied by manipulation and violence on the part of hacendados:

> One day, when I was going to Cochabamba, the patrón Lucio hit me with his truck. I was in the hospital for almost three months. When I came back from the hospital, all the leaders of the peasant unions made me secretary general of the subcentral Tiraque. I occupied that position for eight years. We initiated legal procedures for distribution of land in ten haciendas. On one occasion, the patrones, almost thirty of them, caught me in the city of Cochabamba and had me taken to the police station, saying, "This one is abusive." I spent two days at the police station without anyone coming to claim me—not even my compañeros. A few days later, I was in Arani making claims [in the agrarian courts], and there, too, thugs, paid by the patrones, beat me up severely. I spent one week in the hospital in Cochabamba. A year later, the fight between Cliza and Ucureña began [an armed conflict between two campesino factions].[8] That fight lasted, at least, three years. I did not get involved.

Ambrosio did not want to get involved, as he put it, "[in] a war in which they didn't even know what they were fighting for." For this he was persecuted by one of the faction's leaders:

> They sent five men after me. I escaped, but they kicked open the door of my house while my wife and wawas were there. They took my wife to the subcentral, they stole from my fields, and burnt my papers. That is the reason why I went to Cochabamba and Chimoré—for three years to work for the *gringos*

[foreigners], who were looking for oil. Afterward, I worked in the lumberyard located on the road to Santa Cruz. After I returned to Tiraque, they put me in as secretary of justice in the union.

In spite of his unwillingness, Ambrosio and his family were drawn into the peasant conflict, but, while he was able to flee, his wife suffered the brunt of the persecution and revenge. Thus whereas Ambrosio recognizes the suffering of women, he underscores the role of men ("we") in the struggle for land and underplays the participation of women in it, even if, as in this case, they are victims rather than agents. The selectivity of Ambrosio's account is not accidental, but reflects his vision of gendered practices, associating men with the public and the political, and women with their domestic and nurturing roles.

There are two further points worth making about this narrative that illustrate what seem to be the simple facts of life for most peasant and petty commodity producers in Cochabamba and elsewhere since early colonial times to the present. The first is the continuous movement of people. Ambrosio left the hacienda where he was born to move to the village of Palca, where he remained until he was able to buy a small parcel of land in Chapapani. He also left the region several times: to do his military service, a basic male rite of passage into adulthood and a precondition for marriage; and to work as a waged laborer in the city of Cochabamba and in different parts of the countryside, where he worked in diverse kinds of jobs. Before and during the long struggle for land, Ambrosio was also forced to leave his village to avoid persecution and to spend time in jail or in hospitals. What is striking about this, as well as the account of other men in the region, is how he folds both migration and political militancy into his everyday life experiences, as if his absences, and periods of struggle and repression, were not all that different from other times in his life—maybe a little more hectic and dangerous, but not all that much.

The second point refers to the silences in Ambrosio's account regarding the part played by women in production (waged and unwaged) or in the political struggle. This is not surprising to find in a male narrative, not necessarily because Ambrosio downplays the role of women, but rather because his is a culturally specific perspective, one in which men's identity is based on what they perceive to be their central position as producers and public subjects. Women's narratives certainly emphasize other aspects of their daily lives but they tend neither to question the basic premises on which masculinity rests, nor what is expected from them as women. Although I did not ask Ambrosio's wife, Juliana, about her own participation in the political struggle and how she managed the household and the farm by herself during the many, and often prolonged, absences of her husband, the fact is that without her, Ambrosio would not have been able to get as politically involved as he did: she not only provided support but also had to take on many of his productive and reproductive responsibilities in addition to her own. This is, in fact, a major source of conjugal and domestic tensions and negotiations that also tend to exacerbate gender and generational differences.

The need for most households to complement household income by releasing some of their members requires long-term planning because households cannot risk losing all of their working members. And this involves a number of decisions over the distribution of economic resources and cultural capital that end up favoring some household members over others. Among these decisions, in which both husband and wife have to agree, are: determining which child is going to be prepared to succeed outside the household and the village; which one is going to be given the chance for completing elementary school and maybe higher levels of education; which one will inherit more land and other property; which child will leave the household and for what, and which one will stay on the farm. In most of these decisions women are the ones to lose out vis-à-vis their male counterparts. They inherit less land on the understanding that they will marry and move out of the village; their work is valued less than the work of men; they complete fewer years of schooling;[9] and when young women move to the cities, they tend to have fewer opportunities open to them than men and end up working in low-paying jobs, petty trade, and services (Gill 1994).

How the conflicting demands of livelihood impinge upon households will vary, of course, with a number of factors: wealth; number of household members; the household developmental cycle; whether men or women are single, married, or widowed—all of which affect the number of options open to households as well as the outcome of their decisions. I will not elaborate on these differences here, beyond making the point that, as Vincent (1977) suggested more than twenty years ago, we also need to pay attention to the multiple distinctions that exist within such social categories as class, ethnicity, and gender, if we want to understand social processes.[10] But for most households the fact is that the departure of young women and men increases the burden of those left behind, mostly married women, the elderly, and children. Nowadays with increased male migration, married women are carrying out many more male-defined tasks. Some even plow, an activity that, as we saw above, used to be the most important male task. The use of the plow is also one of the most important criteria for men's self-representation as campesinos (male peasants), and when women are forced to plow, they may also subvert local expectations of appropriate male and female practices.

It is within this context of tight resources and time available to carry out productive and reproductive tasks that we can begin to understand how costly it is for campesinos to engage in politics, in terms of both practical costs and personal safety. This is also a major source of complaint among women. They recognize that it is important to oppose the forces that threaten the viability of their households and villages and support men in times of need. But they also resent that, because men attend too many union meetings, occupy positions in them, and are too involved in regional politicking, many productive tasks are left undone or carried out late. Women are particularly critical of their husbands when they engage in time-consuming "male games": the factional disputes to compete for political positions and to control regional political organizations that are detrimental to the household economy. I found the wives of campesino leaders to be the most critical of their husbands, often portraying them as lazy and accusing them of spending an inordinate amount of time and money in union and political activities that took them away from productive tasks, increased women's workloads, and often forced them to seek an income outside their homes. As one woman, for instance, told me: "Because he is lazy and is not always here when we need him, I have to sell goods in the market to earn the money to hire someone else to plow the land." Another one stated: "He spends a lot of money and time traveling to other towns and to the city of Cochabamba to attend union meetings. But no one in the community helps him. And those who stay behind working in their fields are getting rich."

Without dismissing the real and practical concerns of women, I would like to suggest that one of the reasons for the contradictory attitude of women, who both support and resent men's politics, is that in challenging state policies, men simultaneously reproduce the discourse of power as this is embedded in dominant patriarchal, as well as their own, notions and practices of politics, citizenship, and gender.

Gender and Citizenship

In their analysis of the cultural processes leading to the formation of the modern state in England, Corrigan and Sayer (1985) make an important distinction between citizenship and membership in the "political community" or "political nation." Citizenship is an inclusionary concept, incorporating all the members of a nation-state who are subject to the rights and obligations stipulated by the constitution of the state. Political nation instead is an exclusionary concept that, in various ways and through diverse means, limits the rights of some citizens and excludes them from participating in the public affairs of the state, even though these limitations do not exempt them from the obligations of citizenship, such as being subject to state laws and regulations and, in the case of men, the obligation of being drafted into the army. Historically, one of the most common restrictions to the political nation has been the right to vote, which, until quite recently, was denied to women in most modern states. There have been others as well: literacy requirements, grandfather clauses, ownership of property, and so on.

After 1825, when Bolivia became independent from Spain, urban elites were the only ones to become members of the "political nation." The rest of the population, mostly rural mestizos and Indians, was denied this right. Furthermore, Indians continued to pay tribute, which remained the most important source of revenue for the republican government until the consolidation of the state and its reinsertion in the global economy in the 1880s. Only then, several legal reforms were introduced to modernize the state: the abolition of Indian communal lands and Indian tribute, the replacement of church tithes by a head tax paid by landed property owners, and a cadastral tax (compare Klein 1982; Lagos 1994; Sánchez-Albornóz 1978). Yet membership in the political nation was restricted to men who could read and write, thus effectively excluding some 70 percent of the population (Montaño 1993: 57) and all women. The National Revolution of 1952 eliminated the literacy requirement in the franchise, which increased the electorate from 200,000 to one million. At the same time, however, the state also set the conditions that were to lead to the exclusion of women from rural formal political organizations and public spheres of political practice, thus reinforcing already entrenched ideas that politics is a male realm. To understand how this happened, it is necessary to describe two related processes: the distribution of land and the peasant union.

Along with the enactment of the Agrarian Reform Law, the revolutionary government promoted the organization of peasant unions among former hacienda tenants and sharecroppers as a basic precondition for them to make legal land claims and to regulate every aspect of social life within the village. While in other parts of Bolivia the union was superimposed on already existing villages and forms of governance or acted as a parallel form of village organization, in the central valleys and surrounding highlands of Cochabamba the union became the nucleus around which communities were re-created and functioned as the only form of political organization within the village (compare Lagos 1994; Ticona, Rojas, and Albó 1995). Since then both wealthy and poor villagers, and even some townsfolk, identify themselves as campesinos. Because this concept carries diverse meanings and glosses over class distinctions, what it means to be a campesino is contested and negotiated in public, thus pointing to the inherently political and gendered nature of this concept (Lagos 1994).

Whereas land ownership is a basic requirement for union membership, few were the women who were granted parcels of land by the agrarian reform judges. In the province of Tiraque, for instance, there were only one or two cases in which women received land. Thus, by restricting direct access of land to men and privileging the union as the appropriate locus of village politics and the link with the public sphere, the state also defined those who could or could not participate in the public sphere of politics. Partible inheritance and the many years that have elapsed since the implementation of reform have increased the number of women who own land. But still the union is a predominantly male organization, affiliating all the adult male heads of households who own land or crops in a village; only landowning single or widowed women can be full members of the union. But these are few in number. In 1984, for instance, 54 campesino unions in the highlands of Tiraque included 215 women in their rolls, out of a combined total membership of 2,050. Most of these women were widows who took on the place of their deceased husbands in the union and who did not have adult sons living with them. If they did have sons, the eldest son would become the official household head, acting as the household representative in union meetings. The rest, a minority, were single women with children who had been given land by their relatives. The absence of women in union meetings is then conspicuous. The few who attend these meetings tend to sit separately and away from men, who take the center stage. All union members have the right to speak and vote, but the married women who attend the meetings to represent their absent husbands are not allowed to vote. In contrast, this right is accorded to their adolescent sons when they represent their fathers.[11] Although it is difficult to generalize, because the internal dynamics of campesino unions vary from village to village, the tendency in Tiraque is that few full-fledged female union members give their opinions in these public meetings, because their words would usually be received with indifference or contempt. The most common explanations given by men for their resisting the participation of women in union affairs is that, because most women are illiterate and tend to be isolated in their homes, "they do not know what's really happening outside the village," "they don't know the legal system," or "they do not know how to speak in public." In one village, where several married women wanted to participate in union meetings, they met with the resistance of men who told them: "If you start coming to our meetings, we will meet somewhere else without you, women."

Men then seem to consider knowledge of the world and formal speech, along with public visibility and what they perceive to be their central role in production and in the household, as characteristically male attributes, which women should not try to emulate (compare Bourque and Warren 1981, Radcliffe 1993). Above all, and in contrast to women, they consider themselves citizens. This is a claim they validate by their passing the important ritual of manhood, the military service, that also confers on them the right to be included in the national registry of citizens and to receive a *carnet* (national identity card) (Gill 1997). In contrast, some 800,000 women in Bolivia lack a carnet and therefore cannot exercise the rights of citizenship (Montaño 1993). Equally important perhaps, is the control men have over village unions and higher levels of campesino organizations, such as the *centrales*, *subcentrales*, federations, and the national confederation of peasants (Confederación Sindical Unica de Trabajadores Campesinos de Bolivia) through which they formally engage with the state in a tortuous process of accommodation and confrontation.[12] Indeed, when campesinos mobilize to challenge state policies, by staging road blockades, marches, hunger strikes, or market boycotts, they rely on a "modern" official discourse of state and citizenship. In marches and road blockades, for instance, campesinos always carry national flags along with the *wiphalas* (Quechua: large, colorful flags). Every important union event is also accompanied by the national anthem and flag, Spanish-written documents, and by the presence of civic and/or church authorities. These practices and symbols give legitimacy to union practices, but they also reveal the rhetoric of the politics of accommodation and confrontation. In representing themselves as an "imagined class" of male citizens and as integral members of the political nation, in Tiraque, campesinos also reproduce dominant notions of politics, citizenship, and gender by seeking to exclude women from the public sphere and relegating them to subservient roles.

Yet peasant women, like women of other social classes in Bolivia, have often actively participated in political mobilizations. They were present in the Indian rebellions of the eighteenth century, in the wars of independence, and more recently in the road blockades of the 1970s and early 1980s. As a result of this participation, and with the support of some national campesino leaders, a few women organized the national federation of peasant women (Federación Nacional de Mujeres Campesinas de Bolivia "Bartolina Sisa") in the 1980s.[13] But the reach of this organization is limited to departmental and national representation and very little at the village level, mainly because of the reasons described above regarding the unwillingness of most men to allow women into the village union. Still, the women who occupy leadership positions in the federation often find themselves relegated to their domestic roles in peasant congresses. Women resent this as much as they resent the violence that they often suffer at the hands of their politically progressive husbands, a violence that is usually justified because, as the wife of a high-ranking leader told me, "No matter what, in the eyes of men, we, women, are always wrong." Yet, in spite of these complaints and the fact that female leaders of the federation are now seeking to achieve a certain degree of union autonomy from male control, they emphasize that in the political struggle "we have to walk together with men" (Mejía et al. 1985; Rivera 1985; Ticona, Rojas, and Albó 1995).

Unlike members of the Federación Bartolina Sisa, female coca growers in the Trópico de Cochabamba, the steep valleys where coca is produced and much of it processed into cocaine, have recently organized their own village-level unions and provincewide federations, which are both independent from and related to male union organizations. The reasons for the emergence of these unions are basically twofold. The first is related to the social specificity of the Trópico, a colonization area that has attracted men and women from different parts of Bolivia. Having to adjust to a new environment and create new villages often among strangers has certainly relaxed rigid stereotypical gendered ideals and expectations. Furthermore, the terrain does not allow for the use of the plow, and both women and men equally participate in agricultural production.[14] The second and possibly more important reason is the state's ruthless campaign to eradicate coca plantations. Pressured by the United States government and under the continuous threat of being "decertified," which entails a cut in foreign aid, the Bolivian government has passed a controversial law against the marketing of coca and cocaine and militarized the region, thus trampling over the most basic human rights of the population. Because of this, the union organizations of coca producers have become the most militant in Bolivia and have taken the vanguard of the national peasant and labor movement. Six federations of coca producers, encompassing all village unions in the Trópico, are under the leadership of a supralocal organization, the Coordinadora de Productores de Coca del Trópico de Cochabamba.

As part of their struggle against the state, coca growers staged a march in 1994. Most of the marchers were then men. But in December 1995 the *cocaleras* (female coca producers) also caught the attention of the national media and the public in general when they initiated and carried out, against all odds, their own thirty-day march, traversing high mountains and valleys and suffering the effects of cold and hot weather, rain, and snow, along pathways that took them from the tropical lowlands of Cochabamba to the city of La Paz.[15]

Although large crowds of enthusiastic supporters in La Paz welcomed the cocaleras, their eruption in the public sphere of politics was met with a mixture of surprise and admiration, or suspicion. In his welcoming speech, Evo Morales, president of the Coordinadora de Productores de Coca, said:

> I admire the courage of the women cocaleras and, why not say it? of the women of this country. When women make decisions, they do it with responsibility, with seriousness, and with a lot of organization. When women are well informed about a problem, about a topic, they think better than men, better than males. . . . Too late have I come to realize the capacity of women, too late have I come to realize the intelligence of the *compañeras*. And now it is up to the compañeros, the males, to give [women] their place and to give a space of power to our compañeras so that we can continue struggling in defense of national sovereignty (Plaza San Francisco, La Paz, January 18, 1996 [taped by the author]).

Others, especially government officials and their supporters, considered that the cocaleras had been manipulated and used by men or cocaine dealers for their own purposes. These accusations are not only demeaning to women in general but also reflect pervasive patriarchal ideas about women: dependent, nonrational, and easily manipulated, an opinion apparently also held by Evo Morales until the march, when he finally learned that women could think and act "with responsibility and seriousness." During and after the march, however, women not only defied stereotypical gender conceptions but also easy explanations about their motivations to join the struggle. They marched as Quechua and Aymara Bolivian women against U.S. interference and state policies that violate their most basic rights, including their right to plant coca. They also emphasized their traditional roles as mothers, wives, and sisters concerned with the repression their husbands, fathers, brothers, and children suffered in their daily lives. At the same time, they pointed out that as women, they also suffered the daily abuses (including sexual abuse) and violence on the part of the military forces. But they also marched as independent women able to make their own decisions. In fact, when they decided to march, they did it against the advice of male leaders who warned them about the many difficulties they would encounter in their effort: repression, the holiday season, and the rainy season. Acting independently from men, however, does not mean that they struggle separately from them, as one of the marchers told me: "We decided to march because we realized that we could no longer leave the struggle in the hands and responsibility of men alone. We have to fight as one" (Lagos 1997).

The cocaleras' motivations were then simultaneously "practical" and "strategic" (Molyneux 1986),[16] but rather than directly challenging cocalero men, they contested some aspects of the "routines of rule" (Corrigan and Sayer 1985), those everyday forms of state rule that have also been important defining gendered spheres of political practice that, as we have seen above, campesinos in Tiraque seem to accept as being natural. At the same time, the routines of rule reinforce local gender inequalities and stereotypical notions of masculinity and femininity. Although this is not the first time that women have taken an active part in political mobilizations, the fact that they organized their own unions and the march has given them the space to begin to challenge dominant definitions of politics and citizenship, as one woman told the wife of the president of Bolivia in a televised meeting in La Paz: "Para que nos piden carnet a nosotras? Que se lo pidan a los gringos, nosotras nacimos aquí" ("Why do they ask us for a carnet? They should ask that from the gringos, we were born here"). To this woman at least, citizenship is not a right accorded by the state but a birthright.

Conclusion

In a review article on the interrelations of class, race, and gender, Sacks (1989) urges us to shift the focus of analysis of class struggle from the workplace to a broader social context, one that includes the family, the community, and the state. From this perspective, she then concludes that working-class "women of many ethnicities, times, and regions share a broader conception of class struggle than men. In part this results from women's socially assigned responsibility for unwaged domestic labor and their consequent centrality in confrontations with the state over family and welfare issues" (p. 543). This statement reflects a current trend among feminist scholars whose main argument is that, because the subjectivity of men and women is simultaneously shaped by their national, class, ethnic, racial, and gender position, minority, working-class, and peasant women have the potential of becoming the most revolutionary social actors (compare Bookman and Morgen 1988; hooks 1984; Mohanty 1984; Sen and Grown 1987) and the ones who "are more likely to develop the most radical demands for social change" (Sacks 1989: 543). Whereas this perspective is most important in bridging the public/private conceptual dichotomy and in broadening our understanding of politics, the question is whether we can equate subject position with political consciousness. The debate that dominated the literature in the sixties and seventies on the revolutionary potential of the peasantry would lead us to believe that the issue is not so simple. Furthermore, as Haraway (1988) indicates, "There is no way to 'be' simultaneously in all, or wholly in any, of the privileged (i.e. subjugated) positions structured by gender, race, nation, and class. . . . The search for a 'full' and total position is the search for the fetishized perfect subject of oppositional history, sometimes appearing in feminist theory as the essentialized Third World Woman. *Subjugation is not grounds for an ontology; it might be a partial clue*" (p. 586; my emphasis). When, why, and how women and men become aware of their subordinate position and seek to change the social and cultural conditions that give rise to their domination is an empirical question that cannot be elucidated a priori, but it should be examined within a socially and culturally specific historical context.

In this essay I have sought to show that the intimate relationship between multioccupationality and the need to confront a field of dominant forces to satisfy production and reproduction needs engenders tensions and negotiations as well as "a profound ambivalence, a contradictoriness, toward 'the State's' statements and their legitimacy" (Corrigan and Sayer 1985: 179–80). The focus on the conflicting demands and on the tensions of livelihood has served as a window into several aspects of gendered social life: the dynamics of gender configurations and culturally valued notions of masculinity and femininity, as well as the gender of politics. Further, I have argued that in order to understand how men and women experience, contend with, and interpret these pressures and tensions, it is not only necessary to situate households and the villages in which they are inserted within a wider context of social transformations in which both Cochabambinos and the state have played a crucial part, but also to examine the ways in which dominant and subordinate definitions of citizenship and gendered spheres of practice come together and apart.

The description of three historically specific cases to illustrate the gender of politics has shown the extent to which men have used the state's statements regarding citizenship and inclusion in the political nation as ways to justify their reluctance to include women in their unions, which simultaneously reinforces patriarchal relations and their perceptions of appropriate gendered roles and spheres of practice. Although women seem to resent their exclusion from the village union and the fact that men's political engagement increases their workload within and outside the household, they do not seem to question that one of men's principal activities is political participation. But at least some women also seem to be aware that the means men use to challenge state policies also reproduce the patriarchal order of domination within the household, the village, and a wider public context. As we saw above, some cocaleras have alternative ideas about citizenship than those espoused by the state and by campesinos. Simultaneously, however, cocaleras have realized, as men did earlier, that in order to engage with the state, they also have to use its language and symbols, that is, the union, national flags, and so on. As women take on the added "burden" of citizenship (something that the government is also encouraging by seeking to include them in the national registry of citizens) to struggle alongside men, their perceptions regarding the gender of politics are beginning to change. Whether women will also begin to challenge the politics of gender and more forcefully demand equal treatment by their male counterparts and state institutions is, however, an open question. It could only be answered by simultaneously examining the material and cultural aspects of gender relations, identity, and consciousness, and the extent to which and how *both men and women* accept or challenge dominant gender, national, ethnic and other categorical constructions in historically and socially specific moments.

Notes

1. Much of the material for this paper is based on long-term field research carried out in Tiraque province, located sixty kilometers east of Cochabamba, the capital city of the Department of Cochabamba. The province encompasses a town and a number of villages: fifty-eight on the highland area of the province and fifty-five in the steep tropical valleys, or Trópico. The region, which has been connected with the central valleys of Cochabamba since colonial times, saw the early expansion of haciendas and the appropriation of most Indian land. By the eighteenth century, no Indian communities existed in the central valleys and surrounding highlands. Also, by that time, Cochabamba had the highest number of mestizos in Upper Peru (now Bolivia). Nowadays, Quechua is the predominant language in the countryside, even though many, especially men, also speak Spanish (Lagos 1994).

2. There is evidence to suggest that since the implementation of structural adjustment policies in 1985, the multioccupationality of household members has increased, as well as the number of men and women who are forced to migrate out of the countryside into the cities. The population census of 1992 shows both an increase in the urban population and in the so-called informal market.

3. Since early on in the development of women and gender studies, feminist anthropologists in particular have challenged the dualisms that have tended to pervade those early approaches (see the contributors to the following edited volumes: Etienne and Leacock 1980; Nash and Safa 1976; Reiter 1975; and Bourque and Warren 1981).

4. While the literature on the role of the state in defining sociocultural identities, privileging some and marginalizing others, is quite extensive (compare Alvarez 1990; Bourque and Warren 1981; Corrigan and Sayer 1985; Fraser 1989; Moore 1988; Scott 1986; Radcliffe 1993), the authors pay particular attention to the "routines of rule" (Corrigan and Sayer 1985), the legislation and the social, symbolic, and ritual aspects of the state and institutions of civil society that constitute and regulate social identities.

5. Smith (1989) named these alliances "confederation of households," and nicely documented their shifting nature among Huasicanchinos in Peru.

6. This in spite of the fact that 15 percent of the households in Cochabamba are led by women (Caro 1992).

7. The testimony was given in Spanish, which is a second language for this Quechua-speaking man. In translating this account, I have tried to respect his dialectical use of Spanish. I have attempted to replicate his use of Spanish verb forms by using tenses that would not be appropriate in standard English. This and subsequent translations are mine.

8. This conflict—or the Ch'ampa Guerra (1959–64), as it is called in Bolivia—erupted among peasant leaders over the control of the peasant movement, each with his own peasant following and the support of different factions within the government (see Dandler 1984).

9. The 1992 population census shows an overall illiteracy rate of 19.7 percent for

Bolivia. But the total functional illiteracy rate has been calculated at some 37 percent (Montaño 1993: 59–60). In the case of Tiraque province, where most women attend two years of schooling and then forget what they learned, the illiteracy rate for women was 44.5 percent (CIPCA 1994).

10. So concerned are some scholars with the intersection of class, ethnicity, and gender that they tend to disregard these other significant distinctions and to generalize from the experience of a few to all women in a particular subject position. It is then not uncommon to read statements such as: "the femininity of peasant women," "the unionization of peasant women," or the "participation of poor women in urban mobilizations," as if all women in these categories shared a common feminine identity or as if all poor women were active participants in social movements. See Burdick (1992) for an elaboration of this comment.

11. This is not to imply that women's opinions do not count in shaping men's views and how they express them in union meetings.

12. Since the revolution, the state and political parties have sought to influence the course of Bolivian history by attempting to control campesino organizations through various means: prebendalism, efforts to divide the movement and to pit campesinos against other social groups, and by establishing the Pacto Militar-Campesino, an alliance between the military and campesino union organizations, in 1964. In the mid-seventies, some factions within the campesino movement began to challenge state control over their organizations (Iriarte 1980; Rivera 1984; Ticona, Rojas, and Albó 1995).

13. Until then, the only forms of female rural associations were the Club de Madres or Club de Familia (Mothers' Clubs or Family Clubs) that were set up by state, religious, and lay nonprofit organizations to assist women by teaching them tasks related to domestic activities, such as cooking, knitting, sewing, nutrition, child care, and so on.

14. See Spedding (1997) for an argument against "Andean complementarity," based on her research in the tropical regions of the Department of La Paz.

15. Material for this section is based on personal interviews of some of the marchers during the one day I joined their march in January 1996, interviews with other women in the city of La Paz, and news reports.

16. Stephen (1997) argues correctly that Molyneux's distinction between practical and strategic interests does not adequately explain the motivations of women when they join grass-roots mobilizations.

References Cited

Alvarez, Sonia. 1990. *Engendering Democracy in Brazil*. Princeton: Princeton University Press.

Bookman, Ann, and Sandra Morgen, eds. 1988. *Women and the Politics of Empowerment*. Philadelphia: Temple University Press.

Bourque, Susan, and Kay Warren. 1981. *Women of the Andes: Patriarchy and Social Change in Two Peruvian Towns*. Ann Arbor: University of Michigan Press.

Burdick, John. 1992. "Rethinking the Study of Social Movements: The Case of

Christian Base Communities in Urban Brazil." In Arturo Escobar and Sonia E. Alvarez, eds., *The Making of Social Movements in Latin America,* 171–84. Boulder: Westview Press.

Butler, Judith. 1990. *Gender Trouble: Feminism and the Subversion of Identity.* London: Routledge.

Caro, Deborah, et al. 1992. "Encuesta de hogares rurales de Cochabamba: Resultados preliminares." La Paz: Unpublished manuscript.

CIPCA (Centro de Investigación y Promoción del Campesinado). 1994. "Diagnóstico socioeconómico de la micro-región Tiraque." Volume 4: "Educación y medios de comunicación." Cochabamba: Unpublished manuscript.

Corrigan, Philip, and Derek Sayer. 1985. *The Great Arch: English State Formation as Cultural Revolution.* Oxford: Basil Blackwell.

Dandler, Jorge. 1984. "'La Ch'ampa Guerra' de Cochabamba: Un proceso de disgregación política." In Fernando Calderón y Jorge Dandler, eds., *Bolivia: La fuerza histórica del campesinado,* 241–71. La Paz: Centro de Estudios de la Realidad Económica y Social.

di Leonardo, Micaela. 1991. "Gender, Culture and Political Economy: Feminist Anthropology in Historical Perspective." In Micaela di Leonardo, ed., *Gender at the Crossroads of Knowledge: Feminist Anthropology in the Postmodern Era,* 1–48. Berkeley: University of California Press.

Edholm, Felicity, Olivia Harris, and Kate Young. 1977. "Conceptualizing Women." *Critique of Anthropology* 3, no. 9/10: 101–30.

Etienne, Mona, and Eleanor Leacock, eds. 1980. *Women and Colonization: Anthropological Perspectives.* South Hadley, Mass.: J. F. Bergin Publishers.

Frankenberg, Ruth, and Lata Mani. 1993. "Crosscurrents, Crosstalk, Race, 'Postcoloniality' and the Politics of Location." *Cultural Studies* 7, no. 2: 292–310.

Fraser, Nancy. 1989. *Unruly Practices: Power, Discourse and Gender in Contemporary Social Theory.* Cambridge: Polity Press.

Gill, Lesley. 1994. *Precarious Dependencies: Gender, Class, and Domestic Service in Bolivia.* New York: Columbia University Press.

———. 1997. "Creating Citizens, Making Men: The Military and Masculinity in Bolivia." *Cultural Anthropology* 12, no. 4: 527–50.

Haraway, Donna. 1988. "Situated Knowledges: The Science Question in Feminism and the Privilege of Partial Perspective." *Feminist Studies* 14, no. 3: 575–99.

Harris, Olivia. 1984. "Households as Natural Units." In Kate Young, Carol Wolkowitz, and Roslyn McCullagh, eds., *Of Marriage and the Market,* 136–55. London: Routledge and Kegan Paul.

hooks, bell. 1984. *Feminist Theory from Margin to Center.* Boston: South End Press.

Iriarte, Gregorio. 1980. *Sindicalismo campesino: Ayer, hoy y mañana.* La Paz: Centro de Estudios de Investigación y Promoción del Campesinado.

Klein, Herbert S. 1982. *Bolivia. The Evolution of a Multi-Ethnic Society.* Oxford: Oxford University Press.

Lagos, María L. 1994. *Autonomy and Power: The Dynamics of Class and Culture in Rural Bolivia.* Philadelphia: University of Pennsylvania Press.

———. 1997. "'Bolivia la Nueva': Constructing New Citizens." Paper presented at the twentieth International Congress, Latin American Studies Association, Guadalajara, Mexico.

MacEwen Scott, Alison. 1994. *Divisions and Solidarities: Gender, Class, and Employment in Latin America*. London: Routledge.

Mejía de Morales, Lucila, et al. 1985. *Las Hijas de Bartolina Sisa*. La Paz: HISBOL.

Mohanty, Chandra. 1984. "Under Western Eyes." *Boundary* 2, no. 3: 333–58.

Molyneux, Maxine. 1986. "Mobilization without Emancipation? Women's Interests, State and Revolution." In Richard R. Fagen, Carmen Diana Deere, and José Luis Coraggio, eds., *Transition and Development: Problems of Third World Socialism*, 280–302. New York: Monthly Review Press.

Montaño, Sonia. 1993. *Invertir en la equidad: Políticas sociales para la mujer en Bolivia*. La Paz: Ministerio de Planeamiento y Coordinación. Unidad de Análisis de Políticas Sociales.

Moore, Henrietta. 1988. *Feminism and Anthropology*. Cambridge: Polity Press.

Nash, June, and Helen Safa, eds. 1976. *Sex and Class in Latin America*. South Hadley, Mass.: J. F. Bergin Publishers.

Radcliffe, Sarah A. 1993. "'People Have to Rise Up—Like the Great Women Fighters': The State and Peasant Women in Peru." In Sarah A. Radcliffe and Sallie Westwood, eds., *Viva: Women and Popular Protest in Latin America*, 197–218. London: Routledge.

Reiter, Rayna, ed. 1975. *Toward an Anthropology of Women*. New York: Monthly Review Press.

Rivera C., Silvia. 1984. *Oprimidos pero no vencidos: Luchas del campesinado aymara y quechua de Bolivia 1900–1980*, 129–64. La Paz: HISBOL-CSUTCB.

———. 1985. "El movimiento sindical campesino en la coyuntura democrática." In Roberto Laserna, ed., *Crisis, democracia y conflicto social*. Cochabamba: Centro de Estudios de la Realidad Económica y Social.

Sacks, Karen B. 1989. "Toward a Unified Theory of Class, Race, and Gender." *American Ethnologist* 16, no. 3: 534–50.

Sánchez-Albornóz, Nicolás. 1978. *Indios y tributos en el Alto Peru*. Lima: Instituto de Estudios Peruanos.

Scott, Joan W. 1986. "Gender: A Useful Category of Historical Analysis." *American Historical Review* 91: 1053–75.

———. 1992. "Introduction." In Judith Butler and Joan W. Scott, eds., *Feminists Theorize the Political*. London: Routledge.

Sen, Gita, and Caren Grown. 1987. *Development, Crises, and Alternative Visions*. New York: Monthly Review Press.

Smith, Gavin. 1989. *Livelihood and Resistance: Peasants and the Politics of Land in Peru*. Berkeley: University of California Press.

———. 1990. "Negotiating Neighbors: Livelihood and Domestic Politics in Central Peru and the País Valenciano (Spain)." In Jane L. Collins and Martha Gimenez, eds., *Work without Wages*, 50–69. Albany: State University of New York.

Spedding, Alison. 1997. "'Esa mujer no necesita hombre: En contra de la 'dualidad andina.' Imágenes de género en los yungas de La Paz." In Denise Y. Arnold, ed., *Más allá del silencio: Las fronteras de género en los Andes*, 325–43. La Paz: CIASE/ILCA.

Stephen, Lynn. 1997. "Introduction." In L. Stephen, ed., *Women and Social Movements in Latin America: Power from Below*, 1–26. Austin: University of Texas Press.

Ticona, Esteban A., Gonzalo Rojas O., and Xavier Albó C. 1995. *Votos y wiphalas: Campesinos y pueblos originarios en democracia*. La Paz: Fundación Milenio-Centro de Investigación y Promoción del Campesinado.

Vincent, Joan. 1977. "Agrarian Society as Organized Flow: Processes of Development Past and Present." *Peasant Studies* 6, no. 2: 56–65.

Wolf, Eric R. 1966. *Peasants*. Englewood Cliffs, N.J.: Prentice-Hall.

GEORGE C. BOND

Ideology, Dominance, and Inequality
Gender and Control in Muyombe

The Purpose

My purpose in this paper is to examine the manner in which ideologies of inequality related to gender and labor are constructed and operate within the localized social field of Muyombe, a small town in the northern province of Zambia and the capital of Uyombe chiefdom. My position is that the components of these ideologies are fabricated from the meanings and values Yombe attach to organic substances and essences. Yombe customary religion, based on ancestor cults, is deeply implicated in this explication in that it provides for the convergence of nature and culture, that is, the organic and the spiritual, and through their interaction the production of Yombe humanity. Thus the customary religion serves as the initial paradigmatic framework for ideologies of social inequality. Having phrased the exploration thusly, I have tipped my hat in the direction of Feuerbach and Marx; hopefully, without being fully submerged within the constraints of their formulations.

I also intend to argue that Yombe ideology of gender helps to maintain the agnatic-based social hierarchy of male authority in that it is accepted by the very categories of individuals that it subjugates, most women and younger men. From this perspective, this ideology of gender neither applies to nor is a function of social classes and their interaction but is intimately related to the hierarchical structure of society (Ricoeur 1978: 48) based upon more rudimentary properties such as organic substances. Thus the chapter is concerned with intersections of mechanisms of hegemonic and ideological subjugation with momentary expressions of human agency and resistance.

Orienting Perspective:
Organic Ideology and Hegemonic Properties

This brings me to a conundrum that has concerned me for some time: namely, why is it that subjugated peoples accept the structures that subjugate them and only rarely engage in fundamental acts of revolution? Though I am aware of the great complexity of this puzzle and can offer no single encompassing explanation, I do intend to explore a small fragment: those fine webs of local beliefs that relate authority to legitimacy, that order the manner in which individuals apprehend the world and that affect the way in which they act upon it and interpret the actions of others.

Gramsci provides an initial point of departure. In the *Prison Notebooks*, he recognizes the constraining presuppositions of society that channel individual consciousness as well as the transformative nature of individual will. He does so in the distinction he draws between historically organic ideologies and arbitrary, or nonorganic ones (Hoare and Smith 1971: 376–77). The latter are "rationalistic or willed"; "they only create individual 'movements,' polemic and so on." Historically, organic ideologies are deeply embedded in the local cultural terrain. Gramsci characterizes them as having "psychological" validity; "they 'organize' human masses, and create the terrain on which men move, acquire consciousness of their position, struggle, etc." (ibid.: 377). The foundational character of ideology is captured by Paul Ricoeur in his observation that "an ideology is something in which men live and think"; "it operates behind our backs" and "we think from it rather than about it" (Ricoeur 1981: 227). Thus people take organic ideologies as a natural and an essential part of ordinary affairs.

For Gramsci, the essential feature of organic ideologies is that they are "necessary to a given structure" and thus are part of particular historical configurations. They are the products of an era, of an epoch, and a cluster of historical conditions and circumstances. The problem that arises for the individual critic is one of externality; arriving at that point wherein one recognizes the embedded character of ideology and one's relation to it. The movement is from social and ideational encapsulation to individual reflection and potential praxis; that is, the exercise of individual will. It is this very process that I will turn to shortly in exploring the slight but significant changes that have occurred in Yombe ideologies of religion and reproduction.

Within the social context of simple agrarian communities like Gondo, the Uganda Teso small town studied by Vincent, and Muyombe, historical process is important in canonizing ideologies and securing their dominance by anchoring them within the natural order of everyday life. In time they may become embedded in the fabric of fundamental structures such as kinship and religion and gain their power in the use of organic imagery such as blood and semen. They cease to be the ideational constructions of particular social sections and may become part of the thick hegemonic mix from which new ideological text of particular stratum are fabricated or with which they contend. Thus historical context and conditions are important for observing the canonization and also the decanonization of hallowed principles of knowledge and relationships, their subversion and the emergence of new orthodoxies.

Ideology, as distinct from hegemony, carries with it a less pervasive connotation in that it refers to those meanings, values, and beliefs of particular sections. Authority and legitimacy may, however, become conjoined through ideational constructions that preserve the privileges and control of a single section. It is often during the transitional periods of epochal changes, the move from one political or economic order to another, that the essential elements of these constructions are made apparent. In the absence of pronounced and abrupt dramatic changes, as has been the situation in northern Zambia from 1964 until 1991, one is stuck with the careful gleaning of slight shifts in structural patterns, which establish their significance over the long duration.

In the case of many of the postcolonial simple agrarian societies of rural Africa, such as Muyombe, there has developed an uneasy confrontation or continuing intersection between domestic and capitalist principles of production. Neither one nor the other may be said to be fully dominant and to establish the contours of a final synthesis. Instead there are domains of cross-cutting fields of domestic and capitalist activities, meanings, and valuations. As a domestic agrarian community, Muyombe consists of individuals who "(a) practice self-sustaining agriculture; (b) produce and consume together, on common land, access to which is subordinated to membership of the community; and (c) are linked together by unequal ties of personal dependence" (Meillassoux 1981: 3). A final characteristic, at least in the case of Muyombe, is that use-value predominates over exchange-value with money having the situational potential of embodying spirit and spiritual agency (see Bond 1987: 181), a feature also found in the Colombia communities of the Cauca Valley described by Taussig (1980). There is, thus, an ideological and hegemonic component to economic transactions involving money. In the agrarian domestic economy of Muyombe spirit may appropriate money, while in capitalist settings money fragments the total social person and assigns value to that person's labor as a unit of production.

In its most simple and pragmatic form, I take ideology to be a construction of ideas about the world and, in this situation, a system of ideas related to social inequality. As Ricoeur points out, it is intimately related to authority's claim to legitimacy in that it "serves as the code of interpretation which secures integration by justifying the system of authority" (1978: 48). The concept of an ideological field refers to the range of ideologies within a social field, to the domain in which paradigms are formulated, established, and contend, lending some degree of credence to human affairs (see Turner 1974; Barnett 1977; Bond 1987). I take hegemony to refer to that aspect of ideology embedded in structures that lead to a high degree of compliance or conformity to some normative order associated with relations of inequality in power, wealth, and social position. It is a peaceful mechanism of subordinating one section to the interests of another.

There are always counterideologies and hegemonic expressions that bubble up from beneath, from the subjugated and their intellectuals, that attempt to redefine the social field and their position within it. These intellectuals struggle to overcome the cumulative weight of persisting cultural forms. They do not themselves constitute a revolutionary force, though they may be a product of cultural and political transitions. They do, however, have their own agency contending with structure and in their own way contributing to the shape of the emergent social field. Implied in this formulation is that during periods of change social incongruities develop that create new opportunities for innovative thought and action. Hegemonic elements embedded in structures are exposed and confront the realities of changing social circumstances. For the individual there may be more room for maneuver. The intellectuals of the subjugated sections may attempt to assert themselves and their understandings of the world. They are, however, the exception, and most people may seek to preserve the established social order and operate within it.

Muyombe: The Setting of the Scene

The Yombe are a small ethnic population who live in villages dispersed over an area of some 625 square miles in the northern province of Zambia. Although Zambia has been independent for more than thirty years, British colonial rule, between 1924 and 1964, had a most profound effect on Yombe society. Under colonial rule the chiefdom became a series of small rural communities tied, through their capital, the small town of Muyombe, into the administration and judicial apparatus of the colonial central government. The chief was the head of this local administrative and judicial unit and was responsible to a hierarchy of British colonial officers. Together with colonial rule, Christianity and mission and government schools introduced new opportunities and expectations as well as new normative orders and valuative standards for both men and women. Through the taxation of adult males, high rates of male labor migration, and cash cropping, British rule brought the people of Uyombe Chiefdom into the modern world order of capitalist production. During the past thirty-six years of the postcolonial era Zambian central government policies have directly affected the productive activities of rural small maize farmers and indirectly the social position of women. Much of the effect has stemmed from government policies providing subsidies to agriculture, education, health, and transportation and their recent removal under Dr. Frederick Chiluba, the president of Zambia since 1991.

President Chiluba's policies of privatization have the potential of producing fundamental changes in social relationships in that they focus on individuals as economic and political actors. The rights of the individual are emphasized over those of well-established corporate units, such as descent groups. What is, however, unclear is the effect that these policies will have on local structures of power and authority and the extent to which they may allow for the rise of new leadership.

Until these new policies take affect it is possible to argue that, in spite of the effects of colonialism, capitalist intrusions, Christian conversions, involvement in the nationalist struggle against colonial rule, and more than thirty years of independence, Yombe society has preserved many of its basic social and cultural features. Chieftainship and village headmen, exogamous agnatic descent groups, and ancestor cults remain important structures for Yombe living in the rural and urban areas. These structures and social positions are controlled and managed by men. Thus in almost every respect Yombe society is dominated by males with women relegated to subordinate positions.

The Place of Women

Within the visible domain of public interaction in Muyombe an individual's social status is expressed most visibly through manners in the display of gesture, posture, and speech. In formal situations when greeting senior men, women are supposed to kneel, clap their hands, cast their eyes down, and speak in a soft, high manner using the third person plural. Young men are also supposed to behave in this way when greeting elder males. The performance may be singularly disconcerting, especially when one is the recipient. But one learns to decode it and to distinguish the correctness and esthetics of the greeting. In circumstances of marked subjugation a woman may roll on her back with her legs slightly elevated, softly clapping her hands (I observed men follow this behavior only rarely, and that was during a period of major crisis in which the members of the dissident Lumpa Church had to reaffirm their loyalty to the chief). But in the ordinary course of everyday life the performance is markedly abbreviated, rendered in a perfunctory manner. Nonetheless, it is always undertaken in greeting senior men and serves as a preliminary and yet vivid expression of women's subordinate position.

Kate Crehan, however, reminds us in her discussion of gender relations in Mukunashi (during 1984 and 1985), a cluster of small villages in northwestern Zambia, that the subjugation of women begins within the household and extends into the kinship system, which, among the matrilineal Kaonde, is based primarily upon inequalities between social positions and power relations between men. Though the Yombe are agnatic, a similar situation may be said to apply to their households, complex social units of production (see O'Laughlin [1995] for a discussion of the complexities of African households), and to their descent groups, the primary holders of rights in persons, goods, and services.

At a very early age women begin to learn their place and the gendered spaces that are theirs and to which their access is controlled. The training begins within the household. Yombe households are highly structured according to gender, age, and seniority. In every household I have observed for the past three decades, female children are there to serve older females and any male. They perform almost every task, from assisting in domestic chores such as the care of siblings, the fetching of water and wood, and the preparation and cooking of food, to agricultural activities such as hoeing, planting, weeding, and harvesting the crops of maize, millet, peanuts, and the variety of other consumable plants. Though women work very hard in the fields, it is men who control the land and the deployment of labor. In the early morning it is not unusual to see a line of women and children walking to distant fields and some two hours later, observe their husbands on their way to the same destination riding bicycles.

The residential pattern of children reflects their autonomy and yet, their dependency and subordination. Between the ages of five and seven, young girls and boys leave their parents' houses and move in with their grandparents or with other children of the same sex. Since alternate generations are thought to be identical, grandparents are considered to be older siblings. The girls' houses are known as *Ntanganini* and boys' houses as *Mphara*. Though each house has its own social hierarchy and rules, the children remain an intimate part of their parents' household, relying upon its most basic resources.

There is, however, a fundamental difference between *Ntanganini* and *Mphara*, and that difference reflects the dominant position of males within Yombe society. *Ntanganini* are social centers, and though boys and young men often visit them, it is considered improper for an unmarried girl to visit *Mphara*. The social prelude to courtship is supposed to be initiated by males. Thus *Ntanganini* are associated with the domestic sphere of everyday life and do not intrude into the public domain. *Mphara* have a different connotation. They are the initial training grounds for public activities and leadership.

Within the framework of agnatic descent groups, councils consisting of adult men handle all important issues, such as marriage negotiations, bride wealth, and the disbursement of lineage property. Though women are excluded from these councils, they may influence their decisions and at times determine their outcome. They lack authority and yet they have ritual responsibilities involving the preparation of ritual beer, *finga*, whose stages of fermentation may be interpreted by them as representing the sentiments of ancestors. They may also encourage their brothers' children to elope, precipitating a speedy decision.

With marriage and the birth of children, a woman and her husband gain in status, especially if the children are male. Both men and women become eligible for a number of different social positions, but in the case of women, the range is most often limited and restricted to posts that lack authority and power over critical decisions and resources. And even when it is not, at meetings of agricultural, church, and political party associations women are seated separately from men, and, though they are expected to express their views, decisions should be made by men. Within the public domain, central power relationships are supposed to be between men. Any official assemblage of senior men to legislate, arbitrate cases, or to discuss important political issues is known as an *Mphara*. Yombe courts are called *Mphara*, and as jural and legal minors, women involved in disputes and court cases are supposed to be represented by a senior kinsman or male af-fine, a situation that is changing rapidly.

Within Yombe society, though women are expected to work hard, they are also supposed to know their place. And yet, the everyday public dis-plays of subordination mask subtle shifts in the economic and legal stand-ing of women, affecting the ability of men to control them. A major factor contributing to the changing status of women has been their growing par-ticipation in the commercial farming of hybrid maize.

Background to Change

From 1972 until the early 1990s, the Zambian government made a strong push to increase agricultural productivity (Jansen 1988: 71). Hybrid maize, fertilizer, and other farming inputs were made available to small farmers at subsidized prices. The government also bought and sold hybrid maize at subsidized prices and laid on transport to collect it from the rural areas. In Muyombe, the amount of maize increased rapidly. While local maize, cultivated primarily by family labor, remained central to the domes-tic economy of local consumption and regional trade, hybrid maize became the main cash crop linking Yombe farmers into the national economy.

Muyombe farming households responded gradually to cultivating hy-brid maize. In 1972, 12 or 16 percent of the seventy-three Muyombe farm-ing households grew hybrid maize; four were headed by women and eight by men. Three features distinguished these four female household heads. First, they were older women, forty and above, who could readily claim the entitlements or rights bestowed by menopause. Women who have past the childbearing years are often treated as if they were men. Second, they had close male agnates (sons and brothers) who were employed for wages in the towns and sent them money. And finally, they were either the agnates or former spouses of "elite" men or their agnatic groups.

By 1981, the number of households planting hybrid maize had grown to fifty-eight (or 73 percent), with twenty-seven being headed by women and thirty-one by men. The number of hybrid maize bags harvested had increased from 460 in 1972 to 1,874 in 1981. By 1994, almost all of the eighty-three households in Muyombe cultivated hybrid maize, and the twenty-five female heads were actively involved in all aspects of commercial farming from buying hybrid seed and fertilizer to hiring wage laborers. However, as the central government's policies of privatization have taken hold, the commercial farming of hybrid maize has declined drastically, particularly affecting the status of female headed households. In 1997, I surveyed eighty-nine households in Muyombe. The number of households that had planted hybrid maize was twenty-eight (or 31 percent), with only three being headed by women. The number of bags of hybrid maize harvested had declined from 1,446 in 1993, to 737 in 1994, to 142 in 1997.

From one perspective it seems quite remarkable that female heads of households were able to establish and maintain hybrid maize farms in the first place. And yet, from another perspective it appears highly reasonable that they would do so. Their households were much smaller and less well equipped than those of men, having far fewer resources at their disposal. A central issue was access to labor. Male household heads could rely on the customary services of junior agnates for work on their farms, a system of obligations that emphasized the ritual and economic dependence of junior men on their senior agnates. Female heads could not rely on these customary obligations since their husbands were dead, divorced, or otherwise absent. The main disadvantage of being at the periphery of agnatic relationships, their own and that of their husbands, was the lack of ready access to resources. The advantage lay in their independence to pursue their own interests and manage their affairs. Though their independence from male authority was great, so too was their potential for sinking into poverty. Temporary elicit relationships with male benefactors was not uncommon. For female household heads to retain their autonomy and independence and at the same time to improve their standard of living, farming hybrid maize seemed highly appropriate. Moreover, the central government encouraged women to become commercial farmers. As successful commercial farmers they were provided with greater opportunities to regulate their own affairs. Their increased autonomy constituted a wedge in the structure of agnatic control.

In 1994 and 1997, many senior men expressed to me their worry that women were becoming too concerned with the material conditions of life, and had begun to challenge male authority. According to them, women expected too much from their husbands. This view was strongly held by the local court president and members of his staff, who felt that women had become too precipitous in seeking divorces. However, once the cases were brought to court, they had no choice but to consider them and usually find in favor of the women.

In 1994, I was allowed to examine court registers for six-month periods in 1991 and 1992. From January through July of 1991, 99 civil cases were brought to the Muyombe local court. Thirty-nine of these cases involved divorce: 38 were women seeking to divorce their husbands, and only one was a man seeking to divorce his wife. Although ten cases were withdrawn by the female plaintiffs, 18 of the 38 cases were brought by women who claimed that their husbands had abused them and 18 by women who claimed that their husband and his agnates had been negligent in providing for their material well-being. Of the remaining 27 cases heard by the court, 5 were dismissed and 22 (80 percent) were decided in favor of the female plaintiffs. In a six-month period of 1992 I reviewed 67 cases, of which 3 were deferred or dismissed. Of the remaining 64, 14 (or 22 percent) involved women seeking divorces from their husbands. Nine cases were of women who claimed that their husbands had been negligent in providing for their material well-being. The remaining 5 cases involved men abusing or chasing away their wives. In 1997, I reviewed 120 of the 160 civil cases heard by the Uyombe court for the year 1994. Forty (or 33 percent) were cases brought against men by women, and 32 (or 22 percent) involved women seeking divorces from their husbands; only two men brought divorce cases against their wives. In the cases involving divorce, the overwhelming complaints on the part of women were neglect (the husband or his agnates had failed to support them) and cruelty. Six of the 8 remaining cases involved women seeking compensation from men who had failed to pay them for work performed.

The Muyombe local court officers were uncomfortable with what they considered to be the growing assertiveness of women. Though they did not condone wife abuse, they did feel that women needed to be controlled and had become too materialistic. In their view, women had come to expect too much from their husbands. As just mentioned, there were also several other cases in which women were seeking repayments for debts. Court officers took these cases as examples of the growing tendency of women to assert their rights. From the perspective of many senior men, male authority was increasingly losing its claim to female recognition of its full legitimacy. They foresaw an impending crisis, female resistance. Most women did not, however, share their view and accepted the right of men to retain their authority. Women's acceptance of their subjugation may be understood within the context of Yombe concepts of bodily substances, the cultural refractions and interpretations of organic human properties.

The Ancestor Cult:
The Hegemonic Properties of Substance

Hobsbawm observes of subjugated peoples that "there will frequently be not high or low 'classness,' but in the sense of consciousness, no 'classness' at all, beyond the miniature scale" (1972: 10). Consciousness is diffuse and fragmented and thus, it tends not to develop into a moving force in history directly challenging authority and the social order but remains as a diffuse populist expression. If one accepts Ricoeur's view that people think from ideology rather than about it, consciousness may be channeled and constrained by the constituent properties of the embedded dominant ideology. The latter may act to preserve a modicum of cultural continuity, conformity, and legitimacy for the social hierarchy and its patterns of authority. In Muyombe, the principal structures that preserve this continuity are the agnatic descent groups and the ancestor cults and the notions they embody about the substances that are believed to make the individual a social and spiritual being. The very concept of a Yombe "person" then acts as a drag on social consciousness and as a form of social control.

Yombe ancestor cults, based upon the hierarchical structure of agnatic descent groups, are primarily male religious organizations. Their religious ideology and hegemonic conceptualization of reproduction buttress the authority, power, and entitlements of men and their rights in property, labor, persons, and status. The ideology emphasizes the dominant position of men over women, of the old over the young, and the dead over the living. However, this cultural ordering as well as its material investitures and entitlements are not an accurate reflection of practical productive relationships and contributions.

Within the domestic agricultural and wage economies it is those who do the most productive work who are accorded the least authority and benefits. The labor power of women and young men maintain the productive system, not that of old men. The crucial question is why should most Yombe recognize the ancestor cult's order of authority, especially those who are subordinated within it? Why not resist and protest? It is not sufficient to argue that the authority of male elders is due to the fact that they are closer to being full-fledged ancestors than others, or that women, dutiful and industrious workers, accept the cult's designation because they will never be ancestors. The issues are more complex than that; they extend into the hegemonic designations of the ritual field and beyond into the mechanisms of control of the distribution of labor, money, and wealth. Religious beliefs justify the subjugation of women and young men.

Yombe social and ritual domination find their cultural and hegemonic expression in the system of values and meanings that Yombe bring to the natural world. For them the vital forces of biological and social reproduction are contained within their concepts of substances such as blood and semen and essences such as breath and wind. They are the principal properties from which Yombe believe individuals are made as organic, natural creatures. Through rituals, the forces of natural substances are contained and the living creature is transformed into a social person and a spiritual being.

Views of female inferiority and subordination are contained in the ideologies of reproduction and the ancestor cult, both of which designate what constitutes the social person and establish the rights, duties, and entitlements of men and women. There can be little doubt that within the domestic economy women work harder and longer than men. They form the bulk of the agricultural labor and generally manage the domestic economy. And yet they are jural and legal minors with few rights and privileges. Moreover, they are considered by most men to be inferior and incompetent, an opinion also held by some women.

Since my first trip to Muyombe in 1963, I have accumulated data on the relation of senior men to females and young males. During my most recent visits, in 1994 and 1997, I was able to probe further into Yombe views of the organic and social construction of human persons and thus, the ideological basis supporting male authority, providing the justification for controlling the labor of both male and female subordinates. Two views, collected in 1994, as to the process of reproduction will help to point out the basis for the assertion of female inferiority. The first comes from Labe, a well-educated senior man whose more than eighty years of life had included being a labor migrant, schoolteacher, Presbyterian Free Church elder, successful and prosperous trader and shopkeeper, and political activist:

> The human body is made from the blood of man (sperm) and the blood of woman. Together they make the body and the spirit. The body and spirit are one. One can not have a human body without a spirit. But the male sperm is

stronger than the female blood. The woman's blood supports the male's sperm. The blood of women is weaker than and subordinate to the male's sperm.

The second view comes from an eighty-year-old woman, Lwimba, who was a party political activist and an elder of the Presbyterian Free Church: "The male's sperm is stronger than the female egg. The female egg only supports it. The male's sperm dominates. Women do not have spirits (*viwanda*) because they do not have sperm. God told Eve that without a spirit she must suffer."

These two views are almost the same with one major difference. Labe believes that all human beings have a spirit; but Lwinba does not. Her beliefs justify male authority and the subjugation of women. Women are vessels for male sperm; they contribute to the making and nurturing of the biological form but do not provide that essential attribute of spirit that binds people together and to God—either *Leza*, the name used for God in the ancestor cult, or *Chiuta*, the name used to refer to God in the Christian context. They do not establish the conditions for social continuity through descent and the basis for social perpetuity through descent groups. They are essential to the process of biological reproduction but excluded from the posterity of social and historical continuity. They help to construct a future in which they have no authority. As wives, women are a necessary but foreign element in the moral and religious community of the agnatic group. The belief in the absent or the diminished spirit of women makes them a potential source of social disruption.

In *Blood Magic*, Buckley and Gottlieb caution against equating menstrual taboos with the oppression of women. The taboo need not imply female subjugation. They rightly warn that "the social functions of menstrual taboos are culturally variable and specific and should not be generalized" (1988: 14). The Yombe are, however, one of those peoples who do attach social meaning to blood and sperm. From Labe and Lwimba's perspectives, the subordination of women is intimately related to fertility and menstruation. Menstruation is taken as an indication of a woman's fertility and reproductive potential. Menstruating women are regarded as dangerous and polluting and must, therefore, be segregated and constrained. They remain secluded and are relieved of their domestic and agricultural duties. And though the period of seclusion frees them from many of their labors, it does not release them from their situation of subjugation. Their condition of menstruation constrains the behavior of others toward them, and they must strictly avoid material objects that might be used by others. They are thought to be particularly dangerous to the very young and the old, especially elder men who are themselves close to becoming ancestor spirits (*viwanda*). Thus women constitute a potential threat to male authority, the well-being of men, and their social order.

The manner in which many Yombe regard menstruation is not simply and solely a mechanism of female oppression, but also an ideology for maintaining a particular social hierarchy based upon male authority. This particular ideology bridges the gap between authority and its claim for legitimacy. It also reinforces a system of relationships appropriate to domestic agricultural production primarily based upon the use of the unpaid labor of women, children, and young men.

And yet, this hegemonic configuration was not fully accepted by some women. In 1994, these women possessed the same social features as the four women who were the first to cultivate hybrid maize in Muyombe in 1972. They were in their late thirties and early forties, were the heads of their own households, commercial hybrid maize farmers, and active in agricultural associations. The most outspoken was Anna Muko, who, in 1994, also owned a small restaurant and guest house. Their view of reproduction was that the female egg is infused with spirit equal in strength to that of men's sperm. They did not see themselves as inferior to men but as their equals, a position which they were quite willing to argue in public with men of their own generation. (Unfortunately, I was unable to establish whether these debates were carried out in the presence of elder men and women.) In 1994, they constituted the intellectual leaders of a category of subjugated persons. They had taken advantage of the commercial opportunities afforded by growing hybrid maize and yet they could not anticipate two rapidly progressing conditions coming from the urban centers, HIV/AIDS and privatization, compounded by the effects of El Niño.

I am not entirely certain as to the direction in which these women will move, that is, whether they will continue to assert themselves, whether they will be captured within structures, or whether, with privatization and the collapse of commercial farming, they will fall into poverty. In 1994 they were certainly the intellectual leaders of a subjugated section of Yombe society and yet, they, like the rural community in which they lived, appeared to be in a transitional phase.

Since my first visit to Muyombe in 1963 my observations have been that as women moved into menopause and began to reduce their labor activities, they gained in authority. Increasingly they became like men with a wider scope to pursue their own personal and collective interests. With age, authority and power accrued to them and they began to manipulate agnatic relationships to their own advantage and that of their families.

Today, with democratization movements sweeping the rural areas of Zambia and government policies of privatization eliminating agricultural, educational, and health subsidies, both the political and economic landscape are undergoing rapid and unpredictable changes. The domestic economy with its reliance on unpaid domestic labor is assuming greater importance. From the court records cited above, it would seem that to maintain themselves, married women, the mainstay of this local economy, are having to exercise the few rights now available to them. Muyombe court officers are probably correct in observing that women have become increasingly materialistic. But what they fail to add is that so too are men. (This is reflected in the number of bridewealth cases.) The Yombe are experiencing the growing conditions and social affects of rural poverty.

During this period of uncertainty, male authority may gather strength, and these nonorganic, agrarian, women intellectuals may pursue the established path into social and biological menopause. Young men, unable to find jobs in the towns, must increasingly rely upon the land, and with the decline in the authority and powers of the central government, established authorities are reasserting their powers. They too may have to wait their turn to progress into senior positions; even if they become proletarian and religious intellectuals as local political party leaders and prophets, that too is now a well-trodden path. The slogans and entrepreneurial practices of democracy, liberalization, and privatization, rooted in the notion of individual choice and responsibility, may provide the social and ideological space for the reassertion of "traditional" patterns of authority. Agnatic kinship and the ancestor cult may well provide the ideological backdrop for the persistence of a male-dominated social hierarchy. Yet, on the other hand, these same conditions may reduce their importance, placing full weight on the individual.

Conclusion

In this chapter, I have attempted to apply notions of ideology, hegemony, and the resistance of culture to the analysis of the basis of social inequality within a portion of the socioritual field of Yombe society. I have attempted to pursue the unexpressed management of ideologies and their histories in shaping the claims of authority to legitimacy.

The analysis in this paper might appear to bear some resemblance to that of the French Marxists of the 1970s and 1980s (see, for example, Dupres and Rey 1973; Rey 1975; and Terray 1972). Women, young men, and elders might appear as distinct social classes, and the hegemonic properties of the ancestor cult's religious ideology might be treated as militating against class struggle. Though certainly one way of analyzing this material, it is not the one I intend. In my opinion, it was then and is still a mistake to consider these segments of the population social classes. To have dealt with them as such would be to negate the Marxian tradition.

Most French anthropological Marxists' material failed to engage issues of ideological analysis and to probe its hegemonic properties. In any event, for them ideology would have taken on a linear dimension, failing to explore the subtle complexities that relate claims of authority to legitimacy through the cultural organic constructions of humanity and labor. My concern in this chapter has been with extracting ideology from structure and exploring the manner in which its hegemonic properties produced conformity and resistance. It has been an attempt to explore the mechanics of relationships between organic properties and cultural meanings as the basis of ideological and social fabrications.

Any discussion that focuses on ideational constructions embedded in structures and living texts conjures up Foucault's expeditions into subjugated knowledge (1980: 80–91). While Foucault was primarily oriented toward reclamation through genealogical and archeological pursuits, my interests were with the immediate processes of disaggregation, renovation, and the fabrication of ideologies for subjugation. The organic ideologies of agnation and ancestor cults, related to the active persistence of domestic productive activities, are well guarded in their association with Yombe constructions of organic and spiritual reproduction. Yombe reproduction, a social construct, is anchored in the assumed facts of biology, justifying the authority of men over women. The force of the ideology lies in its power to convince the subjugated of the appropriateness of their subjugation. Lwimba served as an example of this entrapment. She accepted her plight and the legitimacy of male authority. Some younger women, who have entered into the commercial markets of hybrid maize farming, having recast the ideology of reproduction have challenged the basic premise of the hegemonic ideas that support the authority of men and their subjugation. Women have asserted their rights through commercial farming and local court cases involving their rights over themselves, property, and goods and services. It remains to be seen, however, whether these women nonorganic intellectuals will succumb to the current uncertainties of the market place and the forces of established Yombe structures.

And yet, the picture is far from complete. Two intrusive elements, that of the HIV/AIDS pandemic and the fluctuations in rainfall due to El Niño, have not been fully taken into account, since the extent of their effects remains unknown. They have already, however, begun to affect patterns of local leadership and organic and social reproduction.

References

Barnett, Steve. 1977. "Identity, Choice and Caste Ideology in Contemporary South India." In J. Dolgin, D. Kemnitz, and D. Schneider, eds., *Symbolic Anthropology*, 270–91. New York: Columbia University Press.

Bond, George C. 1976. *The Politics of Change in a Zambian Community*. Chicago: Chicago University Press.

———. 1987. "Religion, Ideology and Property in Northern Zambia." In I. L. Markovitz, ed., *Studies in Power and Class in Africa*, 170–189. New York: Oxford University Press.

Buckley, Thomas, and Alma Gottlieb. 1988. "A Critical Appraisal of Theories of Menstrual Symbolism." In Thomas Buckley and Alma Gottlieb, eds., *Blood Magic*, 1–53. Berkeley: California University Press.

Crehan, Kate. 1984. "Women and Development in North Western Zambia: From Producer to Housewife." *Review of African Political Economy* 27/28: 51–66.

———. 1985. "Production and Gender in North-Western Zambia." In Johan Pottier, ed., *Food Systems in Central and Southern Africa*, 80–100. London: SOAS.

Dupres, George, and Pierre-Philippe Rey. 1973. "Reflections on the Pertinence of a Theory of the History of Exchange." *Economy and Society* 2: 131–63.

Foucault, Michel. 1980. "Two Lectures." In Colin Gordon, ed., *Power/Knowledge*, 78–100. New York: Pantheon Books.

Hoare, Quitin, and Geoffrey Smith, eds. 1971. *Selections from the Prison Notebooks of Antonio Gramsci*. London: Lawrence and Wishart.

Hobsbawm, Eric. 1972. "Class Consciousness in History." In Istvan Meszaros, ed., *Aspects of History and Class Consciousness*, 5–21. New York: Herder and Herder.

Jansen, Doris. 1988. *Trade, Exchange Rate, and Agricultural Pricing Policies in Zambia*. Washington, D.C.: World Bank.

Meillassoux, Claude. 1981. *Maidens, Meal and Money: Capitalism and the Domestic Community*. Cambridge: Cambridge University Press.

O'Laughlin, Bridget. 1995. "Myth of the African Family." In Deborah Bryceson, ed., *Women Wielding the Hoe*, 63–91. Washington, D.C.: Berg Publishers.

Rey, P. P. 1975. "Class Contradiction in Lineage Societies." *Critique of Anthropology* 2, no. 1: 27–79.

Ricoeur, Paul. 1978. "Can There Be a Scientific Concept of Ideology?" In J. Bien, ed., *Phenomenology and the Social Sciences: A Dialogue*, 44–59. London: Martinus Nijhoff.

———. 1981. "Science and Ideology." In J. B. Thompson, ed., *Hermeneutics and the Human Sciences*, 222–46. Cambridge: Cambridge University Press.

Rude, George. 1980. *Ideology and Popular Protest*. New York: Pantheon Books.

Taussig, Michael. 1980. *The Devil and Commodity Fetishism in South America*. Chapel Hill: University of North Carolina Press.

Terray, Emmanuel. 1972. *Marxism and Primitive Societies*. New York: Monthly Review Press.

Turner, Victor. 1974. *Dramas, Fields and Metaphors*. Ithaca: Cornell University Press.

Vincent, Joan. 1989. "Abiding Women: Sexuality and Control in Modern Teso." In R. R. Randolph, D. M. Schneider, and M. N. Diaz, eds., *Dialectics and Gender*, 211–23. Boulder: Westview Press.

CYNTHIA SALTZMAN

The New Wave of Union Organizing
Shifting Paradigms, Changing Myths

Over the last twenty-five years, Yale University has had one of the stormiest labor histories of any university or institution in the United States (Greenhouse 1995). In 1984, clerical and technical workers staged one of the first strikes in the private sector over the issues of comparable worth in order to obtain a first union contract at Yale. Blue-collar workers also struck in sympathy with their cause in the school's largest work stoppage since its inception in 1701 (Healion 1984). More recently workers struck in 1996. A new dimension of union politics at Yale since the 1984–85 strike has been the ongoing struggle of some of Yale's graduate students to be recognized as a labor union.[1]

This essay is part of a larger project, in which I will be recounting the untold story of the successive "political generations" of women who engaged in clerical and technical workers' union activism at Yale (Segal 1997). Looking at women's strategic priorities and their visions of corporate citizenship, that longer work examines how women's "cultures of activism" struggled to survive in the face of strong management opposition and often weak support from national unions. A major theme in that work, and a central argument in this paper, is that the development of political consciousness neither follows a linear trajectory nor is it automatic. (Bookman and Morgen 1987: 12). A new historically contingent discourse of the clerical worker as activist did emerge at Yale, but early union drives there, opposed by management, often short on resources, and narrowly framed, failed to harmonize the interests of a diverse workforce. Ultimately, the struggle for so-called comparable worth—one particular, much noted theme in the union effort at Yale—helped to sustain clerical and technical workers' "culture of activism" during their first strike. I will show how, appearances to the contrary, that strategic focus on comparable worth did not speak to a fundamental singularity in women's vision but rather provided a galvanizing rhetoric that united women despite their differences.[2]

The Shift in Scholarship on Women and Unions

Views on women and their propensity to join labor unions have shifted radically over the last twenty years, in part as a response to women's increased union activism in the United States. Until about twenty years ago, the scholarly literature focused on why it was so difficult for women to organize collectively into labor unions. Explanations on why so many more men than women were in unions frequently focused on the supposedly inherent difficulty women have in organizing collectively (Strom 1980).

But then something happened. The labor movement in this country has been ailing. But in contrast to the overall national decline in union membership, there has been a gradual increase in the percentage of white-collar workers in unions nationwide, particularly in the public sector and on college campuses. White-collar and technical employees now represent nearly 40 percent of organized labor, up from 12 percent in 1959 (Shostak 1989: 15).

Moreover, the rise in the number of women in unions is particularly significant. In 1959 only 18 percent of rank-and-file union membership were women. Women today are now more than one-third (35 percent) of union membership. By the mid-1990s, two-thirds of all new union members were women (Zieger 1994: 204). Women's organizing has not turned the tide of labor's decline. But to the extent that labor has attracted new members and shown signs of strength, it has often been among women and white-collar workers.

The scholarship on women and unions changed as scholars sought to explain the changing gender demographics of union organizing in this country. Instead of focusing on why women don't organize collectively as frequently as men, scholarship examined women's stepped-up union activity. Under what conditions do women successfully form unions, and when do their efforts fail?

Recent research suggests that clerical workers are just as likely to be prounion as other workers, and trade unionists now acknowledge their capacity for militancy (Hurd 1993: 317; Costello 1987). Some new research has gone so far as to proclaim that women may be more organizable than men. This research also argues that the most successful union strategies focus on gender-related issues. Cobble has written that there is now a gender gap in attitudes toward unionization that parallels an oft-quoted gender gap in political attitudes. She writes, "Countering the conventional wisdom that women are less 'organizable' than men, research in the last decade consistently has shown that women workers are more interested in unions than men and, when given the actual choice, are more likely to vote for unionization" (Cobble 1993: 910). Similarly, legal scholar Marion Crain (1994: 1956-57) writes:

> Recent research in the industrial relations field offers further hope. Two studies conclude that women are more receptive to union organizing than men; that women are more receptive to organizing in gender and race-homogenous female work units (such as those existing in sex-segregated occupations previously perceived as difficult to organize); that minority women are the most organizable of all workers; that women organizers are more effective than male organizers; and that the most successful organizing campaigns are constructed around issues of particular concern to women.

Cobble and Crain are careful scholars, but their work shows that even in the best of scholarship, there is a temptation to idealize the radical possibilities in women's work-based culture. Crain's comments, in particular, can be read as fitting into a larger trend that might be called triumphalist. "Where the old orthodoxy saw in working women an essential passivity, the new one sees an inexhaustible reservoir of female militancy" (Costello 1988: 118; Milkman 1985: xii).

The new triumphalist perspective, which appears both in union discourse and in scholarly writing, overcompensates for an earlier bias that frequently focused on the supposedly inherent difficulty women have in organizing collectively.[3] It exaggerates the degree to which women have a unique and separate union consciousness from men. Crain's emphasis on women's special needs and sensibilities, for example, creates a new dichotomous thinking that reifies essentialist views of gender differences. It also creates new myths about women's new union "consciousness." Potentially, the view of women as more organizable than men, taken as a freestanding truism, will turn deterministic or encourage a dangerous romanticism. It asserts yet another essentialist view of women albeit with a new twist, politically palatable to those who support women's unionization.

The particular view that women's working-class culture makes them more organizable than men creates, in the end, a new cultural artifact, a mythic understanding of women's propensity to join unions that is divorced from context. Moreover, in stressing the effectiveness of gender-specific union strategies, this perspective minimizes union tactics that may be equally effective in organizing both women and men. Most important, an overemphasis on women's culture may neglect how women like men in unions are engaged in a politics of power. At Yale many women were willing to vote for a union only when they were certain that the union could ensure a good contract that would elicit substantial concessions from the Yale administration (Kautzer 1992: 143).

Without minimizing the importance of working women's culture and activism in shaping protest, Costello cautions: "In most work situations, women's work culture combines behaviors and attitudes that both reinforce and challenge managerial prerogatives and control" (Costello 1988: 118). The task of the anthropologist then becomes to understand the processual nature of human interaction in the workplace, how as Giddens and Bourdieu have argued, agency and structure are in dialectic interaction (Giddens 1979: 71; Bourdieu 1977: 78, 94; Lamphere et al. 1993: 18). Many factors—broad historical trends, aspects of the global and local political economy, and specific management tactics—may promote or constrain women's resistance on the job. External demographic change for women and large-scale economic change may create a climate for union organizing. But the politics of protest, and the culture of organizing that "create and sustain" solidarity occur within the locus of a specific organizational context. The dialectic between union and management shapes the form that protest takes in a particular work setting. Workers, in this case largely women, are political actors who both act upon and respond to the interplay between these two forces and help create a dynamic in which collective identities are transformed. Workers, like unions and management, are not divorced from "history and habit," and women bring with them to the job their individual cultural baggage. As Eva Hochswald has noted, however, the workplace is not just a repository of cultural heritage. In the process of organizing—new words, symbols, and organizational forms are created. The social processes that spawn new cultural forms in the workplace create a dynamic that affects cultural practices in the broader society.[4]

An Emerging Discourse of the Clerical Worker as Activist

What are the forms that women's bid for power takes? To begin with, note that some of the dominant discourses that define clerical work have shifted through time, although the different discourses continue to exist in tandem. Rosemary Pringle recognizes three discourses that have defined the secretary: the office-wife, dolly bird, and career woman. Her observations are based on secretaries in Australia, but her categories have cross-cultural resonance and offer a characterization of the clerical worker in the popular social imagination. In the first construction, office relations are cast as a marriage between bosses and secretaries. This model emerged earlier in the century when the most acceptable role for middle-class women was as wife and mother. The office could provide an air of middle-class respectability that mirrored normative middle-class domestic life with the woman playing the wifely role of office housekeeper for her boss.

The second construction, the dolly bird, regularly appeared in the tabloid of the fifties. She was a highly sexualized, voluptuous blonde in miniskirts and high heels. Whereas the office-wife is a paragon of decorum and reserve, the dolly bird is "cheeky and loud," and has a certain amount "of sexual power over the boss" (Pringle 1994: 116–17).

The career woman, the third construction, "resists the familial and sexual definitions, treats secretaries as having serious careers, emphasizes skill and experience, and plays down the special relationship between boss and secretary in favour of viewing both as part of a management team" (ibid.: 117). This discourse focuses on workers' empowerment and lateral decision-making over top-down corporate decision-making. It is an attempt to reframe clerical work as a management team.

In the Yale context, a new discourse emerged. The secretary as activist who is my subject is not just a career woman who tries to equalize relationships on the job. For many women, their identity, sense of purpose, and accomplishment are derived as much from their role as union activist as from their role as clerical worker.[5] This emerging discourse becomes definitive in the local context as workers' protest is shaped by a new vocabulary and an affirming ideology. My ethnographic research revealed how the political process, mediated by both language and relationships of power, creates new cultural meanings for women and men. Seeing union organizing this way as an addendum or correction to Pringle's history, it no longer appears as a self-standing, essentialistically driven, political dynamic, but as a new twist in a continuously evolving story of social construction.

Are women easier to organize than men? It took more than four consecutive years of organizing, fifteen months of negotiating, and a bitter ten-week strike for members of Yale's clerical and technical workers' union to get their first contract in 1984. The national director of organizing for the Hotel and Restaurant Workers Union estimated that the union spent more than $4 million on organizing. The union's success had much to do with the ideological dynamics of women and unions, but it also had to do with economics and the expenditure of energy and resources.

To understand women's successive union organizing efforts at Yale, it is helpful to consider Rick Fantasia's concept of "cultures of solidarity." Fantasia (1988: 19–20) defines "cultures of solidarity" as:

> more or less bounded groupings that may or may not develop a clear organizational identity and structure, but represent the active expression of worker solidarity within an industrial system and a society hostile to it. They are neither ideas of solidarity in the abstract nor bureaucratic trade union activity, but cultural formations that arise in conflict, creating and sustaining solidarity in opposition to the dominant structure.

In Fantasia's definition, "cultures of solidarity" are "not coterminous with unions" (ibid.: 19). Indeed, workers' victories are of secondary importance in Fantasia's analysis, and the emphasis is instead on how class conflict lies in processes of solidarity (ibid.: 21). He points out that workers' militancy is often "fragile, fragmentary, and defensive in character" (ibid.: 23). That is to say, "cultures of solidarity" are celebrations of working-class collective action even when such moments of explosive resistance fizzle.

Nevertheless, central to Fantasia's thesis is the idea that "militant activity creates the context in which class consciousness emerges" (ibid.: 22). For Fantasia, classes have no independent being except as they function in relationship to other classes within the context of collective activity and mobilization in a conflictual setting: "As such class consciousness essentially represents the cultural expression of the lived experience of class, an experience shaped by the process of interaction of these collectivities in opposition to one another" (ibid.: 14). Fantasia views oppositional cultures of solidarity—which may take myriad forms depending on tactical activities and institutional forms—as emerging in opposition to the individualism of American culture.

Although influenced by Fantasia, I want to focus, not so much on cultures of solidarity as on what I will call "cultures of activism." I do not see Yale organizing as an instance in which individuals shed their individualism but as a process in which workers come to see collective representation as the best way to fulfill both their individual and collective aspirations.

For Fantasia, a culture of solidarity creates a group that, in its collective identity, seems to function as a "homogenous political actor." My own theoretical leanings and ethnographic observations, on the other hand, lead me to emphasize the polyvocal diverse expressions of workers' activism (Melucci 1995: 54). Fantasia acknowledges only in passing the internal divisions that have limited workers' mobilization historically. He is less concerned with deciphering the "plurality of levels" in collective action than with showing how oppositional cultures can erupt. But as Melucci notes, "Contemporary movements, in particular, weave together multiple meanings, legacies from the past, the effects of modernization, resistances to change" (ibid.).[6]

Even among the singly defined Yale clerical and technical work unit, there were cultural and later racial divisions that threatened to undermine the activists' quests for solidarity. These differences cannot be overlooked just because they pose a threat to the "common denominator" category of class or feminist unity (Alarcon 1990: 359). Women's fate at Yale was linked by their institutional connections and the unfolding process of unionization.[7] The Yale experience thus affords the opportunity to study a legacy of women's "cultures of activism," and the difficult task that women had in forging union solidarity in light of their diversity, the ineffectual backing of major unions, and strong management opposition.

Comparable Worth as a Political Strategy

At Yale, clerical and technical workers who joined the Hotel and Restaurant Employees International Union (HERE) adopted a specific rhetoric favorable to sustaining a "culture of activism" during a strike to obtain a first contract. Much of that rhetoric focused on the notion of comparable worth. The theme of comparable worth helped to socially construct, foster, and define the emerging discourse of the secretary as activist. It provided the extra incentive some workers needed to walk off their jobs on strike and suffer loss of pay.

On September 26, 1984, 1,600 mostly female clerical and technical employees went on strike against Yale, the largest employer in the city of New Haven, to protest low wages and lack of promotional opportunities. Striking secretaries, typists, research assistants, and laboratory technicians in Local 34 were supported by the 950 blue-collar service and maintenance workers in the brother Local 35. When picket lines appeared, many student and faculty members refused to cross them and moved four hundred classes off campus to churches, private homes, and community centers. During the strike, 625 union members and their supporters were arrested in demonstrations. Reporters flocked to the campus to cover the story, and striking workers made the TV news. The strike at Yale gained national media attention for its innovative tactics and its focus on comparable worth, paying equivalent wages for jobs of comparable economic value.

By declaring its strike as among the first to be a national test case for the principle of comparable worth, the union created an issue with press appeal and persuasive appeal for rallying workers on campus. The idea of comparable worth, or pay equity, posits that because men and women do different jobs in a gender-segregated economy, equal pay for workers performing the same job cannot correct the pay differential between men's and women's wages. Therefore, women should be paid equal pay for work that is comparable to that of men. This idea is premised on the argument, controversial among economists, that workers performing entirely different jobs in unrelated occupations can be compared in terms of the level of their responsibility, education, training, and skill to arrive at just compensation that is free of bias toward either women or men.

Local 34, with a membership of 82 percent women and 17 percent minorities, charged Yale with sex discrimination in its pay structure. At Yale, unionized blue-collar workers, mainly men, who were custodians, dining hall workers, and truck drivers earned more than female clerical and technical workers who often did work that required more responsibility and specialized knowledge.[8]

Activists at Yale contended that the university discriminated against its female employees and that as one of the wealthiest universities in the country, it could well afford to pay clerical and technical staff wages higher than the average of $13,424. (Yale students at the time paid $13,950 annually for tuition, room, and board.) The impact of the comparable worth argument at Yale was powerful even though, for reasons that I will discuss below, Local 34 did not push, as other unions have elsewhere, for a formal "comparable worth" study during its negotiations for a first contract that would attempt to rationalize the pay scales of all white- and blue-collar jobs on campus.

The force of the comparable worth argument seems, on the surface, to confirm the view that women are inherently or distinctively attracted to social justice issues. According to one account, women are allegedly more likely than men to support social justice issues and join unions to pursue those causes. Crain writes, "Women may be more likely to pursue altruistic causes than to pursue matters of economic self-interest. This may occur because women value relational elements of their work lives or because large numbers are employed in the service sector occupations where these issues tend to arise" (Crain 1994: 1950).

But in fact, comparable worth is as much about the differences among women as about their commonalities. It is also an issue that is as much about class as about gender. Moreover, connecting union activities to social justice issues may be equally as effective strategy when organizing men as when organizing women.[9] As one reporter notes, unions that are adopting "tactics that hearken back to the potent activism of the thirties," use campaigns with "in-your-face tactics that range from street theater to civil disobedience," and that "link themselves to broader social aims" have been highly effective in organizing both women and men (Reilly 1995).

Let's unpack the meaning of comparable worth. Comparable worth is not just a "women's issue." It's a politically effective strategy. As the director of employee relations for Yale pointed out, "Yale's employees had relatively few ways to bring pressure to bear on their employer. 'In the private sector, when the union has a problem, they don't go public with it; they shut off your income.' 'Here, you can't shut off the income; endowment, tuition fees, grants, all those things continue. So what they try instead is pressure'" (Coulson 1985: 56). Local 34 chose the comparable worth theme because they foresaw its effectiveness as a political tool for rallying workers and public attention. But they also chose this theme because it resonated with the ways in which Yale clerical and technical workers had already begun to identify their low pay as an issue of gender discrimination.[10]

Part of the power of comparable worth as a conceptual tool was that it exerted two analytically distinct but overlapping claims for recognition and justice on workers' behalf. One was the claim for the recognition of economic injustice and the need to transform basic economic structures through political economic redistribution. The other was an identity-based claim for the recognition of cultural injustice—gender discrimination—and the need for cultural redress (Fraser 1997).

Local 34 effectively used the principle of comparable worth to frame their strike as a battle against wage discrimination. First, the union focused on comparable worth to set the terms of public debate and isolate the Yale administration. Secondly, the union was adept at using the issue not only to rally the support of women, but men as well. Third, the focus on comparable worth was an effective strategy because it provided an overarching rhetoric to link women who were so divided in terms of their class backgrounds, workplace situation, and social horizons.[11] Clerical and technical workers are not a monolithic category of workers who have a unified class position. Women's position in the workplace hierarchy, their educational and social backgrounds, and their marital status determine their social outlook, expectations, and their union consciousness. Union ideology needed to embrace the pluralistic nature of the clerical and technical workforce and had to create mechanisms to unite women and men in their diversity.

As the above outline suggests, and as the following discussion will detail, the strategy of comparable worth, like many other political strategies, had both an external and an internal face. It was, on the one hand, a marketing tool that appealed, instrumentally if not cynically, to currents in public opinion. But it was also a genuine aspect of the self-constitution of workers' ideology, a way that workers convinced themselves that they should unify around the issue of gender and wage discrimination.

One social scientist has noted: "The language of comparable worth may be a great unifying language among women as the abortion debate was the great divisive issue." Comparable worth dramatized the bread and butter issues of the union conflict and translated them into a contemporary issue with broad appeal. Female employees at Yale argued that their low pay and low status was a sign that the university was cooperating in a broad economic pattern of wage discrimination against women. Women began to articulate the relationship between issues of gender and class. Comparable worth appealed to women and men as an issue of economic justice, and its emphasis was particularly effective in drawing together women from disparate backgrounds.

Comparable Worth and the Politics of Community

The comparable worth strategy put the Yale administration on the defensive. The administration publicly stated that comparable worth was a societal issue and not a problem for the university to solve (Healion 1984). This argument alienated and disappointed many clerical workers and Yale students who countered that the university was in a position to assume national leadership on the question. They felt that the administration was merely defending the status quo and supporting conservative politicians and critics who were having a field day attacking the comparable worth idea itself. Clarence Pendleton, head of the United States Civil Rights Commission under President Reagan, called comparable worth the looniest idea since Looney Tunes came on the screen (Hasson 1984). George Will wrote in *Newsweek* magazine: "Yale, a fountain of progressive thoughts, was convulsed by a strike over 'comparable worth' but Mickey Mouse went on strike at Disneyland and why should Yale be different?" (Will 1984).

As others have noted, grass-roots movements and union efforts for comparable worth in the United States have overwhelmingly taken place in the public sector. Yale University's 1984–85 strike is an exception to that pattern, but at Yale comparable worth was less a bargaining tool than a tool for mobilization (Johnston 1994: 115; Kautzer 1992). Johnston (1994: 232) argues that comparable worth has a particular claim on public institutions because in the public sector wage levels are "constrained by 'what makes political sense' rather than by 'what makes economic sense.'" In readjusting salaries, comparable worth plans reduce the influence of the labor market and create an internal bureaucratic mechanism for defining employees' wages (ibid.). The institution adopts its own corrective mechanism for presumed discrimination against women and adjusts its salary scales for women.

At Yale, the comparable worth claim played out in the public arena had weight because the university's character made it vulnerable to community opinion. As a not-for-profit organization with a charitable, tax-exempt status, the university plays both a private and public role. By creating a counterdiscourse and arguing that the university's wage structure conflicted with norms of equality, Local 34 rendered the university sensitive to public opinion and alumni influence, a strategy that threatened Yale's image and ability to raise funds (Gilpin et al. 1988; Kautzer 1992).

The union's use of comparable worth was partially responsible for creating the social movement character of the Yale strike. The issue attracted the backing of intellectuals, liberals (even those who may have been disillusioned with the labor movement), and feminist groups on campus. It also drew the attention and acclaim of public figures beyond the walls of the university, such as AFL-CIO president Lane Kirkland and the National Organization for Women's president Judy Goldsmith and, thus, attracted media attention (Gilpin et al. 1988; Kautzer 1992). Comparable worth helped the union mount a publicity campaign against the university that went from candlelight vigils in front of the president's home to a long roster of women's movement, labor, and civil rights speakers, to employees appearing on the Phil Donahue Show and the MacNeil/Lehrer News Hour. The press declared the Yale strike to be among the first in the private sector over the issues of comparable worth.

Yale employees became articulate public advocates of comparable worth. Lucille Dickess, who worked at Yale for seventeen years and became Local 34's president, explained the rationale for comparable worth on the MacNeil/Lehrer News Hour television program aired on October 19, 1984:

The example that has been cited so often is that of an administrative assistant whose duties include managing, decision making judgments, all kinds of responsible duties, versus that of a truck driver. This is not to minimize a truck driver's job. Make no mistake about that. And the salary that the truck driver is earning now has been fought over long and hard. We understand that. What we are saying is that there should be comparable worth here. An administrative assistant who has a two-page job description which includes running an entire department, managing, handling all sorts of responsibilities surely is worth as much as a truck driver is here.

Clerical and technical workers standing alongside feminist leaders gained public recognition for their cause. Deborah R. Chernoff, an administrative assistant in the Yale College Dean's Office and a leader in Local 34, condemned the university's position on comparable worth. At a Yale rally, she stood alongside Joyce Miller, a board member of the AFL-CIO; Joyce Goldsmith, head of the National Council for Women; and Carol Bellamy, president of the New York City Council, who joined her in their condemnation of Yale (Fitzgerald 1984). Speaking to the *New York Times*, Chernoff said, "If you look at the kinds of women's jobs here, without any disrespect for men's work, there is a much higher degree of job skill, education and job autonomy than for dining hall workers and maintenance workers" (Gargan 1984).

It is one thing for workers to vote for a union in a secret ballot election and quite another for them to publicly identify with the union and walk picket lines in front of professors, students, and passersby. The issue of pay equity gave women a public definition for their struggle and helped to create a collective consciousness of their mutual confinement to low wages. Donna Mitchell, a research assistant at Yale Medical School who made $15,000 a year after six years on the job, stated publicly, "I feel we are economically discriminated against by the university because we are women. We are not paid for what we should be paid for the work we do." Holding a strike placard as she marched in front of Yale's Sterling Library, Janet Wexler, a library employee, said, "This is a fight for equality" (Osterlund 1985: 5).

Comparable worth also honed a potentially controversial political message, a demand for higher wages, and made it palatable to the public. The media often depicts unions as narrow, mercenary, special-interest groups. The message of comparable worth was that women were not power mongers. They could disengage themselves from the "greed" of unions. In transforming their campaign into a moral struggle, "focusing on principles rather than money," the union gave their struggle a national context (Coulson 1985: 56). Women on strike wore eye-catching buttons proclaiming "59 cents," referring to the average *national* ratio of women's pay to men's pay at the time. A spokesperson for Local 34 stated, "It does not help to have guarantees for equal access to so-called better paying jobs (e.g., becoming a doctor vs. a nurse; a lawyer vs. a paralegal). It doesn't correct the $ .59 vs. $1.00 issue."[12]

On campus, the comparable worth issue served a number of purposes. It provided a women's issue that attracted the attention and won the support of female students who more than men on campus gave their endorsement to the Yale strike (ibid.: 62). Janet Gillespie, a junior majoring in literature from Phoenix, Arizona, joined a picket line outside Yale's Sterling Library and expressed a view that other students critical of the university shared: "She said she found Yale's position on comparable worth inconsistent with its teaching. 'I'm going to this university to get a liberal education and am being instilled with various values. I just don't think that behavior coincides with that philosophy,' she said."

The theme of comparable worth also gave the strike intellectual substance that drew the interest of faculty who ran teach-ins and provided classroom forums to discuss and debate the concept. The union's leadership calculated that the issue would have intellectual appeal to the Yale academic community (ibid.: 58).

> Wilhelm, [who spearheaded the Local 34 drive], the star student, knew academics, and he knew what sort of issues would appeal to them. By placing the strike in the context of comparable worth and the changing definitions of discrimination, Wilhelm gave the issue intellectual credibility, transformed it into a focus for scholarship, a topic of debate. The faculty responded, holding debates, sponsoring research efforts, even introducing it in class discussion. Confronted with violent disruption of their lives, the response of the faculty was to set the intellectual apparatus in motion to investigate its cause. (ibid.)

Wilhelm minimized the influence of feminist thought on the Yale drive, but one woman close to the union told me that although (in her view) Wilhelm was no feminist, he was an astute political calculator and knew which strategies would work and were worth pursuing. Once the union drive embraced the issue it took on its own life, whatever the original inclinations of particular individuals.

As Coulson has written, "The Yale strike forged a new link between the labor movement and the women's movement based on the concept of comparable worth. . . . While the support of feminist leaders for Local 34 was more moral than financial, it gave credibility to their cause and fire to their rhetoric" (ibid.: 62). There has been a long-term hostility between unions and the feminist movement, but the Yale strike helped to overcome this tension by providing an issue that spoke to feminists.

Comparable Worth and Rallying Men

Local 34's focus on comparable worth was intentional, and the union made a concerted effort to educate workers about the principle of pay equity. There is some debate though about whether the HERE devoted little more than minimal effort during its first contract negotiation to educate its members about comparable worth and whether its failure to demand contract language about comparable worth indicated that the union was intent on appealing to its traditional male blue-collar base at Yale. But as Kautzer argues, "[W]hile Local 34 may have played down feminist principles, its achievements were also consistent with a number of feminist objectives" (Kautzer 1992: 158).

In one educational conference workshop called "What Is Our Work Really Worth?" the union attempted to raise employees' consciousness about how disproportionately low their salaries were compared with those of the blue-collar workers on campus. In typical union fashion, two Yale employees, Deborah Chernoff, an administrative assistant in the Yale College Dean's Office, and Louisa Cunningham, curatorial assistant at the Art Gallery, led the workshop and asked, "Why shouldn't a private secretary earn as much as a truck driver?" Subsequent union literature publicized the "lively exchange about both salaries and benefits," and accused the university of devaluing its C & T employees (FUE 1983).[13] It reminded employees, "Salary and benefits are not, of course, the only way of determining our worth, but our miserably low pay checks are a bi-monthly reminder that the University does not think very much of what we do" (ibid.).

In providing women with a salary comparison between their wages and those of men in blue-collar jobs at Yale, the union also took care to use language that did not alienate the men who worked in clerical and technical jobs but to incorporate their needs into the discussion. It informed men that working in a job sector that was predominantly female depressed their salaries as well. Moreover, Local 34 did not hold up the unionized men in Local 35 as targets of resentment but as models for white-collar employees to emulate. The following union review of the pay equity workshop shows how Local 34 conceptually crafted the terms of the comparable worth debate to appeal to both women *and men* (ibid.):

> In the workshop we did a brief exercise, ranking different jobs—carpenter, registered nurse, truck driver, private secretary, garbage collector, file clerk, etc.—according to how much they should be paid, from highest to lowest, depending upon the experience, skill, and/or education they require.
>
> The majority of us in the workshop placed registered nurse and private secretary at the top of the list. However, statistically, jobs that are predominantly male and unionized—e.g., carpenter, $12.42 per hour; motor vehicle/car production worker, $11.75 per hour—make, on average, twice as much.
>
> This workshop exercise brought home the fact that clericals and technicals are not recognized for what we do—namely, keep our offices and companies running—because we don't have a unified voice and are primarily women. In a sense, the question of what our work is worth is a women's issue, but one that directly affects the men in this group because men's salaries are held down along with women's.
>
> We need to reassess our own sense of worth, but we also need to understand that employers rarely change their attitudes toward individuals, but do respond to a group, as seen in the case of Unionized workers such as Local 35. People get more notice for what they do when they are visible as a part of a group.

The idea of comparable worth is potentially threatening to men who work in blue-collar, male-dominated jobs, jobs whose status is defined in part by their definition as "manly" work factors (Evans and Nelson 1989: 167). It also threatens to disrupt a culturally prescribed gender hierarchy in which men are paid higher wages than women because they are presumed to be the heads of families and have greater economic need (ibid.). But in presenting Local 34's drive as an essential measure for self-survival, the union stressed that it was in the self-interest of the male blue-collar Local 35 workers to support women's clerical and technical efforts. Consequently, male blue-collar workers in the brother local joined clerical and technical workers who went on strike at Yale.

Comparable worth may be opposed by those who are threatened by the two wage-earner family. But for the majority of married workers at Yale, relying on two wage-earners was already a given. The question became not whether one spouse could support the household but whether their families would have two incomes instead of one and a half, or one and two-thirds (ibid.: 64). Meanwhile, for self-supporting men and women and women supporting a household on their own income, the fight for higher wages was about the fight for economic survival. One divorced women who was forced to seek employment to support herself and children saw herself as battling the forces that have led to the feminization of poverty.

Local 34 saw the potential of building a coalition with blue-collar workers. They recognized that some clerical and technical workers were married to blue-collar workers on campus and that these couples, afraid of losing economic ground, were aware of the need for a strong second income to meet household expenses. Moreover, they saw that a broad coalition between the two unions could exist even where contradictions in rhetoric and outlook existed. Ultimately, the Hotel and Restaurant Employees Local 35 service and maintenance workers at Yale endorsed and covered much of the costs (other than organizers' salaries) for the clerical and technical workers' union drive. Moreover, when Local 34 struck, Local 35 workers also walked off their jobs in sympathy with the clericals and technicals. At [one] union meeting, a Local 35 member spoke with pride about his wife who walked the picket lines and punned, "My mother always said that I would marry a local woman."

Despite the comradeship fostered between the blue- and white-collar unions, the potential for conflict between men and women existed and occasionally did surface at Yale. Secretaries' jobs were compared with men's jobs in comparable categories. Usually, comparable worth battles entail a careful study of internal salary levels. Yale, unlike other public and private employers, had never evaluated jobs to rank them by a point system. Such a study had provided the basis for the biggest comparable worth victory until that time, a federal court decision in September 1984 that ordered the state of Washington to pay up to $1 billion in back wages to fifteen thousand workers in female-dominated jobs (Bittman and Arnold 1984). But at Yale, the union never initiated nor did it endorse such a formal study. Comparable worth was used as a principle, not as a formula for salary adjustments. It existed more as hype or rhetoric for fostering a discourse on clerical workers' activism than as a carefully framed model for salary increases. That the comparable worth debate took this form at Yale is intriguing. Presumably, no detailed comparable worth study was conducted because the union knew that direct comparisons between the two locals might have created antagonisms between the two bargaining units when their alliance was still fragile.[14] Moreover, the strategy avoided precise comparable worth formulas that could have become internally divisive and have led to messy squabbling over how to compare and rank secretaries' versus data entry clerks' jobs.

Comparable Worth and Women's Unity

Comparable worth is a great unifying feature because it masks the differences among women. The rhetoric is effective because justice issues provide a framework for uniting clerical and technical men and women who differ in their cultural and class backgrounds. In truth, the clerical and technical workforce at Yale were divided by their class backgrounds, marriage, level of education, their structural positions in the workplace, and the work they performed. Their world view and their attitudes toward unions were equally varied. It would be wrong to speak about clerical workers as proletarianized and to ascribe to them a homogenous view with regard to their jobs, hopes for the future, and propensity to form unions.

As Pringle writes, "Class is more than a collection of occupational groupings or of individuals with a shared rank in a distribution of specified goodies. If we shift the emphasis from classificatory exercises to look at meaning and experience, then questions about people's social origins, their families, lifestyle, culture and consciousness come into the picture. The meaning of terms like working and middle class changes constantly and they have meant different things for women than for men" (Pringle 1988: 199).

She goes on to say, "For both men and women class identity comes from a variety of sources. No one ever entirely escapes from their class of origin which is constructed not only by 'father's occupation' (or even mother's occupation) but various cultural practices and social institutions. In considering secretaries' experience of class we do need to take into account more than the occupation: their own social backgrounds and that of their spouses are important in the construction of class as well as gender identity" (ibid.: 206).

One of my informants put this issue of class diversity very well. She herself worked briefly at Yale as a clerical worker. She had both a B.A. and master's degree from Bryn Mawr University, taught part-time at a community college, and was writing a novel that was later published. I asked her: "So your impression was that there was some mixture in [employees'] backgrounds?"

> "None of [the women in my office]," she said, "would have met each other if they hadn't been working together because nobody would have traveled in the same circles. Except maybe Rhonda and Elaine. . . . You could tell when people would have conversations about what restaurant they went to and it would always be something the other people had never heard of. Because to each one of

them New Haven is a different city with different possibilities. That was very apparent to me.

"Class has a lot to do with people's experience of restaurants and stuff than it does just with income. Because, for instance, my income is very low now, but I'm middle class. So, you know, how are you going to measure what class people are from? I mean you know how difficult that question is.

"Well, that's how . . . I pick up whether people are from my class or not, how they speak, what experiences they've had."

With so much diversity in the workplace, part of the union's task became to develop a strategy and a language that would bring a unity of purpose to women who were so deeply divided in so many respects. The union needed to find the symbols, words, and imagery that would tap employees' dissatisfaction and fuel a social movement on campus. Comparable worth provided an overarching voice and public forum that could frame the union debate in words that would capture the hearts and minds of Yale employees and the public at large. As this occurred, clerical and technical workers distinctively connected to Yale by virtue of their husbands' positions, young highly educated women, and "townies" from working-class roots began to define their common dilemma and their common prospects at Yale and sought improvement through a union. There was a blurring of boundaries between classes as women's interests and needs achieved a rapprochement.

Classes, as Bourdieu points out, are not rigid, concretized entities but are diverse, socially constructed, and fluctuating.[15] Moreover, class is a broad, complex idea that includes at least two aspects, social and economic. Class status encompasses among other things both economic capital and cultural capital intangible items like one's tastes, knowledge, and "lifestyle" that are acquired through education and may, in cases, secure access to economic capital. Some employees at Yale were, to use Bourdieu's terms, high on cultural capital but low on economic capital. Others had neither.

At first, women's social differentiation through their level of education and social backgrounds divided women into different status groupings at Yale. But during the course of organizing, women's recognition of their low pay and their growing sense that they were exploited because they worked in pink-collar jobs served to unite them. In other words, women's burgeoning union consciousness resulted in women developing a sense of their exploitation in real economic terms. Their status-focused sense of class gave way during the course of organizing to a definition of class based on women's low economic capital.

Women's identity began to take the form of a gender solidarity that cut across employees' diverse social and class backgrounds and became based instead on a mutual identification of women's shared discrimination in the workplace. At Yale, women's conceptions of class began to be transformed during the course of organizing, and women began to place more emphasis on their class position in terms of their low pay on their jobs. I am not arguing that women's growing solidarity meant that they came to recognize their "true" or "natural" class interests. Indeed, Yale women's new economic understanding of their class identity was just as socially constructed as their old status-based understanding. Rather, my point is just that the union, through the rhetoric of comparable worth, was able to effect that new socially constructed understanding.

Women from across the spectrum began to see their personal battle for higher wages as a larger battle for gender equality and pay equity. Those who were living close to the poverty level felt emboldened to strike because their economic struggle now had a name, a public meaning, and a broader purpose in common with other women. In an event that the union named "59-cent day," marked by a day-long walkout and demonstration on May 23, 1984, prior to the actual strike, women wore placards saying, "Pay Us What We're Worth." A circulation assistant in the Beinecke Rare Books and Manuscript Library who carried a placard that day said that she had trouble supporting herself on $9,000 annual salary. "I think we don't get enough money," said Efland, forty-eight, who had worked at the library for five years. "We've got to tell people what we're worth." A cataloger in Sterling Memorial Library who also walked off her job to dramatize the claim that Yale discriminated against women said, "In today's economy, you just can't live on these salaries" (Stevens 1984; N.H. Register, 5/23/84).

Yale employees who were relatively better off saw the strike as a way to have a job that made sense in terms of meeting their family's financial needs and in maintaining a middle-class standard of living. Thus, even many of those women whose marital status gave them an economic cushion began to identify how their personal income, that is, their low salary at Yale, threatened their family's middle-class economic standing. They perceived the discriminatory nature of their low pay as unfair and as unjust reward for their skill and job performance. Women who were pursuing middle-class life goals such as sending children to college were particularly struck by the discrepancies between their low pay and tangible economic realities—that is, the high cost of tuition. Mary Skurat, an art library assistant with a college degree working at a $12,000 per year job, complained that she and others were underpaid. She and her husband were paying tuition at various schools for their three children. She pointed out the irony of earning less than the cost of sending her son, a college junior, to Yale: "'I don't make what I pay to send him here for one year,' she said. Yale tuition, room, and board is $13,950 annually" (Healion 1984).

The idea of comparable worth gave those few workers who were relatively well off and spoke about their wages as supplementary income a rationale to fight discrimination on behalf of their coworkers. A secretary at the Yale Art Gallery said, "I returned to the work force for the same reasons many women from middle class families return. I wanted to help with a large tuition bill and contribute toward a few extras that make our lives more comfortable and enjoyable. . . . I will vote Union for several reasons. The main reason will be because I personally feel an obligation to those striving to be self-sufficient." In the same way, it provided employees who didn't want to admit to themselves or others their own economic need an incentive to stand behind the union and support others in the cause of achieving pay equity. Furthermore, the comparable worth concept shifted the emphasis away from a sheer focus on wages to the issue of gender exploitation and the fight for justice. Pay equity was an issue that the comparatively affluent and those who didn't admit their own need could nonetheless freely support.

Converging understandings among clerical and technical workers became possible in part through the language of comparable worth that led to women's and men's emerging sense of how class and gender issues were intertwined. By unpacking the meaning of comparable worth, we see how a politics of class and gender are constructed and how a linking ideology can be an important strategy in uniting workers.

What ultimately proved most effective in attracting white-collar workers to the union at Yale was what philosopher Nancy Fraser has called a "bivalent approach," one that framed issues around both the theme of economic justice and a "politics of recognition"—cultural recognition for marginalized groups. As many theorists have noted, any discussion of office work that is so heavily dominated by female employment must also necessarily entail an analysis of the complex interplay of conceptions of gender and class. Gender, Fraser has noted, is a "bivalent" axis of collectivity in that it is a compound defined by class and status inequities, marked by economic disadvantage and cultural disrespect. As an aspect of the political economy, gender structures the division between "productive" labor and unpaid "reproductive" female typed domestic labor. It also structures the division between lower-paid, female-dominated "pink-collar" and domestic service occupations from higher-paid, mostly male manufacturing and professional occupations (Fraser 1997: 19). Gender as a political-economic differentiation is "endowed with certain classlike characteristics" that needs redistributive redress (ibid.: 20). But gender is not only a political-economic differentiation but a "cultural-valuational differentiation as well. As such, it also encompasses elements that are more like sexuality than class and bring it squarely within the problematic of recognition." Fraser argues that to achieve social justice in a society marked more by identity politics than concerns with economic justice, a bivalent approach is needed, one that combines a critical theory of recognition that identifies a cultural politics of difference and combines it with a social politics of equality. A social justice paradigm must integrate a "politics of redistribution," a focus on the more equitable distribution of economic resources in society, with a "politics of recognition."

In a move toward what we may call "transformational" politics, borrowing the term from Fraser, the union did not just reify categories of gender difference and identity politics but blurred them. It highlighted issues of gender, not by separating women from men but by drawing parallels between the largely female white-collar workforce's interests with that of the mostly male blue-collar workers to forge a coalition between the two groups. Using transformational politics, an attempt to redress gender inequities while forging a coalition with male workers, Local 34 inadvertently destabilized gender boundaries as it also acknowledged women's struggles. This seemingly contradictory strategy provided a paradoxical vision that sustained workers' culture of activism, helped to galvanize workers despite their differences, and underscored their ability to sustain a strike. New cultural meanings for women and men were created as part of political process, but this says more about history and politics than about the concretization of female norms.

Notes

1. As I note in Saltzman (n.d.), most recently Yale employees (including both the clerical and technical workers as well as the service and maintenance staff)

struck in 1996. One of the hotly debated issues of that strike was Yale's right to hire subcontractors.

A new dimension of union politics at Yale since the 1984–85 strike has been the organization of Yale's graduate students. In 1990, a small group of students organized into the Graduate Employees and Students Organization, GESO, to help them lobby for better fellowships, medical and dental benefits, and a stronger voice in university policies. In April 1994, graduate students in humanities and social sciences voted for GESO to become their collective bargaining agent. Yale has consistently opposed the unionization of graduate students, whereas Locals 34 and 35 have expressed their ongoing support for the graduate students. Between April 2 and 7, 1995, graduate student teaching assistants staged a brief walkout resulting in several canceled classes. Their withholding of student grades became the subject of a court hearing.

For a more recent discussion of how the Hotel and Restaurant Employees International Union has bridged the worlds of workplace, local New Haven community, and civil rights organizations, see Warren and Cohen (2000).

2. See Saltzman (n.d.) for a brief discussion on the theme of comparable worth in the Yale 1984–85 strike.

3. Crain relies on an AFL-CIO report to support the position that women may now be easier to organize than men. But there is a problem with scholars' borrowing categories and conceptions from the people whom they presume to critique and accepting these categories as new doctrine.

The new union ideology inverts the old view that women's socialization or culture prevents them from forming unions, and sees women's culture as uniquely suited to labor organizing. It calls attention to the recurring tension between essentialist and social constructionist theories of women's political consciousness. At a conference on women and work at Rutgers University held on May 21, 1996, a woman who had been a union organizer with the United Electrical Workers said, "Women are more likely to vote for a union than white men." She went on to say, "The more active women are women of color." Another woman who was an organizer with the Office and Professional Employees International Union (OPEIU) told me, "Women are going to be at the forefront of the union revolution. Women are easier to organize because they are easier to talk to. They have better communication skills." The binary approach of this current view is more puzzling and ironic because of the evidence of a more imaginative and comprehensive approach to the topic of women's organizing. After all, it is not for scholars' or even unions' lack of imagination that one-sided perspectives on women's propensity to organize keep surfacing.

In subsequent articles, Dorothy Sue Cobble offers an amended account of labor's focus on women, shifting her emphasis from the "organizability" of women and their likeliness to vote for unions to the strategic choices of unions. She notes that labor could do much to reverse its decline if it were willing to feminize even more and to recognize that its structures, organizing strategies, and institutional forms were created to meet the needs of a male, factory work force. See, for example, Cobble 1996.

4. Note that there are an underlying set of historical conditions that are promoting women's unionization nationwide, conditions that themselves are responsible for shaping women's culture. These include global economic trends, the changing demographics of women in the workforce, the introduction of feminist values as a supportive ideology, and the changing organization of work itself.

The globalization of the economy hit American workers and unions hard. By 1975, the composition of the labor force had clearly shifted from jobs dominated by male blue-collar workers in areas like automobile manufacturing and mining to jobs in the clerical and service sector, long considered "women's work." Faced with the exportation of jobs abroad and the loss of its traditional male blue-collar base, unions began to target women in the growing service-information economy. In many, though by no means all of these service occupations, workers had the additional security of knowing that an employer could not just leave the community. They knew that the formation of a union or the occurrence of a strike was not going to induce the firm to close up shop and vacate the premises. Yale was obviously one such setting.

Several factors have also led women in particular to look more favorably toward unions. As women work for an increasing number of their adult years, they become increasingly concerned with higher wages and a greater voice in their job situation. A feminist sensibility, or what Milkman (1985) calls "trade union feminism," has begun to pervade clerical workers' orientation toward work and lead to changed attitudes about unionization. Moreover, a paternalistic management grown out of step with the times as well as the effects of the changing nature of work itself, which has tended to become more mechanized and impersonal, have led to employees' prounion sentiment.

5. This fourth discourse, so clearly emerging in the U.S. context, may differ from Pringle's observations of secretarial work in Australia.

6. "Cultures of activism," as I define them elsewhere, are collective expressions of oppositional behavior, thought, symbols, and action that arise as groups of individuals seek societal or institutional change in specific settings. These political groupings may be marked by internal pluralism and incorporate people from broad social backgrounds even as individuals unite against the status quo or engage in confrontational tactics. "Cultures of activism" may be linked to larger social movements (that is, the labor movement) and may entail a "class consciousness" (an awareness of being in an economically inegalitarian relation), but they are often characterized by views and goals that remain particular to a local domain. Thus cultures of activism may be connected to larger social struggles but are not synonymous with them (see Saltzman n.d.).

7. Although women were commonly united in that they worked at Yale, they were differently located subjects from varying social backgrounds. Both Lamphere et al. (1993) and Gregg (1993) explore how women's differential social location affected their views about work and unions.

8. Blue-collar workers were themselves a racially and ethnically diverse workforce representing skilled and unskilled employees. Women, many of whom

worked in the dining halls, were a more visible portion of Local 35 than their numbers represented.

9. Crain also notes that there is evidence that labor organizing drives are most effective and appeal most to workers as well as the general public when they appeal to workers' altruistic motives and the welfare of all workers (Crain 1994: 1952–53).

10. Local 34 also charged Yale with racial discrimination, of assigning black women to the lowest paid jobs (see Saltzman n.d.).

11. The analysis of comparable worth in this paper overlaps to some extent with some of the arguments that Coulson (1985) and Kautzer (1992) have made about the use of comparable worth as an organizing tool during the Yale strike of 1984–85. My approach differs from theirs, however, in that I emphasize how comparable worth was in one respect a rhetorical strategy, but it also served as a galvanizing force to unite a clerical and technical workforce divided in many respects. The strategy, as I will show, represented a move toward "transformational politics," an attempt to redress gender inequities while also forging a coalition with male workers to redress economic injustice.

12. Deanna Jacobs, *New Haven County Woman*, November 1984.

13. Yale Local 34 Hotel and Restaurant Employees International Union literature.

14. Molly Ladd-Taylor says that Local 34 did not use comparable worth terminology in its first contract because it would have been based on technical studies that were both confusing and reinforcing of hierarchical assumptions about salaries and job classifications (Ladd-Taylor 1985). Kathleen Kautzer (1992: 149) points out, "While the union did not achieve any contract language referring to comparable worth in its first contract, it did lay the groundwork for revising Yale's job-classification system by obtaining a clause establishing a Joint Committee on Job Descriptions and Classifications, composed of four union representatives, four university managers, and a neutral faculty chairperson. This Joint Committee later played a critical role in Local 34's drive to win a new job-classification system in its second contract." The union did conduct a sophisticated study of comparable worth issues for its second round of contract negotiations in 1987. The study upheld that there were strong gender and racial disparities in employees' pay and assignment to salary grades (ibid.: 151–52).

15. In an incisive discussion of the sociological literature on class analysis, Rosemary Crompton, who supports many of Bourdieu's arguments, writes, "In the late twentieth century, a criticism that is increasingly made of both authors [Weber and Marx] (particularly Marx), and indeed, of 'class analysis' in general is that such arguments place too much emphasis on the significance of economically determined classes at the expense of other, competing sources of social identity such as nationality, gender, locality, or ethnic group. In short, it is argued, nineteenth-century sociology cannot adequately grasp the complexities of late twentieth-century society" (Crompton 1993: 45).

References

Alarcon, Norma. 1990. "The Theoretical Subject(s) of This Bridge Called My Back and Anglo-American Feminism." In Gloria Anzaldua, ed., *Making Face, Making Soul: Haciendo Caras*, 356–69. San Francisco: Aunt Lute Foundations Books.

Bell, Deborah E. 1985. "Unionized Women in State and Local Government." In Ruth Milkman, ed., *Women, Work and Protest: A Century of U.S. Women's Labor History*, 280–300. Boston: Routledge and Kegan Paul.

Bittman, Mark, and Bob Arnold. 1984. "Comparable Worth Is Put to the Test at Yale: A Bitter Strike May Determine Whether the Concept Gets a Foothold in the Private Sector." *Business Week* (November 26): 92.

Bookman, Ann, and Sandra Morgen, eds. 1987. *Women and the Politics of Empowerment: Perspectives from the Workplace and the Community*. Philadelphia: Temple University Press.

Bourdieu, Pierre. 1977. *Outline of a Theory of Practice*. Cambridge: Cambridge University Press.

Cobble, Dorothy Sue. 1993. "Introduction: Remaking Unions for the New Majority." In Dorothy Sue Cobble, ed., *Women and Unions: Forging a Partnership*, 3–23. Ithaca, N.Y.: Cornell University ILR Press.

Costello, Cynthia. 1987. "Working Women's Consciousness: Traditional or Oppositional?" In C. Groneman and M. B. Norton, eds., *To Toil the Live Long Day*, 284–302. Ithaca: Cornell University Press.

———. 1988. "Women Workers and Collective Action: A Case Study from the Insurance Industry." In A. Bookman and S. Morgen, eds., *Women and the Politics of Empowerment: Perspectives from the Workplace and the Community*, 116–36. Philadelphia: Temple University.

Crompton, Rosemary. 1993. *Class and Stratification: An Introduction to Current Debates*. Cambridge, U.K.: Polity Press.

Coulson, Crocker. 1985. "Labor Unrest in the Ivy League." *Arbitration Journal* 40, no. 3: 53–62.

Crain, Marion. 1994. "Between Feminism and Unionism: Working Class Women, Sex Equality, and Labor Speech." *Georgetown Law Journal* 82: 1903–2001.

Educational Broadcasting and GWETA. 1984. *The MacNeil/Lehrer NewsHour*. "Political Flap: Comparable Pay." Transcript no. 2365, November 19.

Evans, Sara M., and Barbara J. Nelson. 1989. *Wage Justice: Comparable Worth and the Paradox of Technocratic Reform*. Chicago: University of Chicago Press.

Fantasia, Rick. 1988. *Cultures of Solidarity: Consciousness, Action, and Contemporary American Workers*. Berkeley: University of California Press.

Feldberg, Roslyn L. 1988. "'Union Fever': Organizing among Clerical Workers, 1900–1930." *Radical America* 14 (May/June 1980): 53–67.

Fitzgerald, William. U.P.I., December 3, 1984.

Fraser, Nancy. 1997. *Justice Interruptus: Critical Reflections on the 'Postsocialist' Condition*. New York: Routledge.

FUE (Federation of University Employees). 1983. *Common Sense*, no. 1, March 28,

2. New Haven, Conn.: Local 34, Federation of University Employees, AFL-CIO.

Gargan, Edward A. "For Some Employees, Yale Is a College of Hard Knocks." *New York Times*. Sunday, December, 9, 1984, Late City Final Edition, sect. 4, p. 22, col. 1, Week in Review Desk.

Giddens, Anthony. 1979. *Central Problems in Social Theory: Action, Structure, and Contradiction in Social Analysis*. Berkeley: University of California Press.

Gilpin, Tony, Gary Isaac, Dan Letwin, and Jack McKivigan. 1988. *On Strike for Respect: The Yale Strike of 1984–5*. Chicago: Charles H. Kerr.

Greenhouse, Steven. 1995. "New Fire for Labor: John Joseph Sweeney." *New York Times*, October 26, 1995, pp. 1, D25.

Gregg, Nina. 1993. "Politics of Identity/Politics of Location: Women Workers Organizing in a Postmodern World." *Women's Studies in Communication* 16, no. 1: 1–33.

Hasson, Judi. U.P.I., November 30, 1984.

Healion, James V. U.P.I., September 27, 1984, "Yale Students Cope with Strike."

Hurd, Richard W. 1993. "Organizing and Representing Clerical Workers: The Harvard Model." In Dorothy Sue Cobble, ed., *Women and Unions: Forging a Partnership*, 136–336. Ithaca, N.Y.: Cornell University ILR Press.

Johnston, Paul. 1994. *Success while Others Fail: Social Movement Unionism and the Public Workplace*. Ithaca, N.Y.: Cornell University ILR Press.

Kautzer, Kathleen. 1992. "'We Can't Eat Prestige': The Yale University Workers' Campaign for Comparable Worth." In Peggy Kahn and Elizabeth Meehan, eds., *Equal Value/Comparable Worth in the UK and the USA*, 137–65. New York: St. Martin's Press.

Ladd-Taylor, Molly. 1985. "Women Workers and the Yale Strike." *Feminist Studies* 11, no. 3: 465–90.

Lamphere, Louise, Patricia Zavella, Felipe Gonzales, and Peter B. Evans. 1993. *Sunbelt Working Mothers: Reconciling Family and Factory*. Ithaca, N.Y.: Cornell University Press.

Melucci, Alberto. 1995. "The Process of Collective Identity." In Hank Johnston and Bert Klandermans, eds., *Social Movements and Culture* (Social Movements, Protest, and Contention, Vol. 4,), 41–64. Minneapolis: University of Minnesota Press.

Meyerson, Harold. 1995. "Labor Pains: Toward Less Imperfect Unions." *New Yorker* 71, no. 34 (October 30): 78.

Milkman, Ruth. 1985. "Women Workers, Feminism and the Labor Movement since the 1960's." In Ruth Milkman, ed., *Women, Work and Protest: A Century of U.S. Women's Labor History*, 300–322. Boston: Routledge and Kegan Paul.

Osterlund, Peter. 1985. "'Wage Struggle' or 'Fight for Equality,' Yale Union Bout Goes On." *Christian Science Monitor*, January 17, p. 5.

Pringle, Rosemary. 1988. *Secretaries Talk: Sexuality, Power, and Work*. London: Verso.

———. 1994. "Office Affairs." In Susan Wright, ed., *Anthropology of Organizations*, 115–23. London: Routledge.

Reilly, Sean. 1995. "The Case for Unions." *Washington Monthly* 27, no. 7/8: 26–32.

Saltzman, Cynthia. 1988. "You Can't Eat Prestige: Women and Unions at Yale." Ph.D. dissertation, Columbia University.

———. 1990. "Unseen Women at the Academy." In Faye Ginsberg and Anna Tsing, eds., *The Negotiation of Gender in American Culture*, 152–68. Boston: Beacon Press.

———. 1999. "Candlelight Vigils and Comparable Worth." In *Power Practice and Agency—Working Papers in the Women in the Public Sphere Conference, 1997–1998*. Institute for Research on Women, Rutgers University.

———. n.d. "The Many Faces of Activism." In Marianne Dekoven, ed., *Feminist Locations: Global/Local/Theory/Practice in the Twenty-First Century*. New Brunswick, N.J.: Rutgers University Press (forthcoming).

Segal, Lynne. 1997. "Generations of Feminism." *Radical Philosophy* 83: 6–17.

Shostak, Arthur B. 1989. "Organized Labor: Hopeful Signs, Too." *Chicago Tribune*, September 4, p. 15.

Stevens, Barbara. 1984. "Yale Talks Collapse: Strike Begins Today." In *New Haven Journal Courier*, Sept. 26, 1984.

Strom, Sharon, Ellen Cantarow, and Susan Gushee O' Malley. 1980. *Moving the Mountain: Women Working for Social Change*. New York: Feminist Press.

Vincent, Joan. 1990. *Anthropology and Politics: Visions, Traditions, and Trends*. Tucson: University of Arizona Press.

Warren, Dorian T., and Cathy J. Cohen. 2000. "Organizing at the Intersection of Labor and Civil Rights Movements." *University of Pennsylvania Journal of Labor and Employment Law* 2, no. 4: 629–55.

Will, George. 1984. "God Help Us Everyone." *Newsweek*, December 31.

Wright, Susan. 1994. "Culture in Anthropology and Organizational Studies." In Susan Wright, ed., *Anthropology of Organizations*, 135. London: Routledge.

Zieger, Robert. 1994. *American Workers, American Unions*. 2d ed. Baltimore: Johns Hopkins University Press.

Losing Ground / Finding Space

The Changing Experience of
Working-Class People in New York City

This paper focuses on the experiences of poor people in New York City whose lives have been structured by the transition to the "informational" city. I examine in particular changing patterns of work, social stratification, and public assistance, as well as shifts in community organization and social movements that have emerged in association with this transition. These materials are brought to bear on contemporary debates about how to best serve the needs of the country's urban poor. Is it true, as many would argue, that "a rising tide lifts all boats"?[1] Or is there a more complex and contingent relationship between general economic well-being, on the one hand, and the well-being of the most vulnerable segments of the population on the other? In order to address this question I first examine how NYC's working-class communities were affected by the demise of Fordism and the rise of flexible accumulation (Harvey 1989). I then reconstruct the living conditions of the people who were displaced by this transformation—people who were forced to contend with the loss of work, home, neighborhood, and government assistance. I finish the paper with a consideration of the (mild) economic recovery of the late 1990s, assess its impact on the city's poor, and discuss the new forms of organization and resistance that have emerged in the new economic environment. In each era I describe the decisions made by city government officials that transformed working-class communities, the social movements that members of these communities organized to question city government priorities, and the ways in which the working poor perceived their lives. I suggest that the formation of working-class movements concerned with social reproduction (such as the block associations and neighborhood preservation movements of the 1970s) were undermined by a variety of dislocating processes associated with the transition to flexible accumulation. At the same time, however, these movements had been based in neighborhoods whose rental, housing, and school policies had reinforced racial and ethnic stereotypes and discrimination. As a response to increasing poverty and homelessness, new movements briefly emerged that were not based in racially or ethnically defined neighborhoods but drew on poor people from around the city.[2] Most recently, in the late 1990s, immigrant service workers and other low-paid workers in the city have begun to reinvigorate unions, and to mount neighborhood and community-based protests to economic hardship and state intrusion into their lives (Nash 2001).

Working-Class Neighborhoods at the End of Fordism

As late as the 1970s, a number of working-class neighborhoods in NYC remained intact and stable. Between 1969 and 1974, the city lost thousands of jobs in small manufacturing (Alcaly and Mermelstein 1977), the economic underpinning of these communities since the 1890s, and thus working-class families had to struggle in order to survive. Nonetheless, through 1980, the combination of factory employment, work in city government, controls on the cost of real estate (which made rental housing affordable), and the availability of government services (health care, education, sanitation, and public assistance) had allowed these communities to reproduce themselves.

Greenpoint-Williamsburg was one such neighborhood. The structure of community life in the early 1970s reflected the efforts of community residents to maintain themselves in a context of growing hardship and instability (Susser 1982, 1986). In general during this period, community reproduction was a function of the strong connections that were built among neighbors, friends, and kin. The precarious nature of livelihood for all families encouraged extensive patterns of interfamily mutual assistance, patterns widely documented among poor and working-class communities (Stack 1974, Sharff 1998). For example, families commonly shared electricity, laundry, telephones, and food. They also pooled expenses in general. When households could not pay their rent, families doubled up in small tenement apartments. Neighbors shared child-watching, washing machines, and meals. In the summer, children played together in the street and mothers watched from the sidewalk. The summer evenings had an air of warmth, peacefulness, and relaxed conversation. People sat out on their stoops, watching the street and talking until late into the night.

Other features of neighborhood life, however, reflected the growing deterioration of the NYC economy, especially for poor youth (see also Sharff 1998). Not only had drug dealing become a familiar part of community life, but the drug dealers lived on the streets of the neighborhood itself. At the same time, however, the dealers were recognized by older adults on the block, who had known them as children. These adults still had the authority necessary to keep gangs from fighting around children, and to keep the young drug users and dealers from controlling the street. The people who lived in Greenpoint-Williamsburg were therefore not afraid to walk the streets at night. Nor did they hesitate to allow their children to play on the block. Instead, the fact that community controls over public space remained strong allowed residents to view their few blocks as "my neighborhood," "my community." Indeed, most neighborhood residents had strong ties to schools, churches, and several generations of kin and friends (Susser 1982, 1986, 1988).

The structure of public violence in working-class communities during this period reveals much about the organization of community life. Greenpoint-Williamsburg, as one of the poorer neighborhoods of Brooklyn, had one of the higher homicide rates. Murders in public space occurred predominantly in bars and on the streets. Local explanations for the violence and newspaper reports alike tended to associate conflict with territorial battles among contending minority groups, such as white versus Latino youth. One Latino man was killed, for example, when he walked into a white working-class bar. Similarly, a young black man was attacked by his white girlfriend's male kin when they were walking home together one night, and a building was burned down when the landlord rented to black tenants. While such violence represented powerful symbolic community divisions, it was not an accurate portrayal of interpersonal violence, which was much more frequent within each population group than across them. In fact, a woman was more likely to be murdered by her own partner than by a stranger from another ethnic group.[3]

Working-class Neighborhoods and the Fiscal Crisis of 1975

In 1975, the New York City fiscal crisis was announced. Initially, both the federal government and the state of New York refused to fund any city services. After extensive negotiations, a fiscal control board was created, made up of businessmen and public officials. This board implemented extensive cuts in public spending, through a policy known as "planned shrinkage."

The board's decisions represented a dramatic reversal of the public policies and spending of the 1960s and resulted in a multipronged attack on the ability of the working class to maintain viable communities. Indeed, the 1975 fiscal crisis marks an historical watershed in the dislocation of working-class communities in New York City. One crucial way that crisis-generated changes in public policy undermined the viability of working-class communities concerned the availability of jobs. Until 1975, municipal employment was the only area in which jobs had been expanding. In 1975 alone, however, New York City lost sixty-one thousand public sector jobs, more than one-sixth of all municipal employees. In the years that followed, the layoffs continued (Alcaly and Mermelstein 1977). Working-class neighborhoods were deeply affected by these massive layoffs, as the public sector had become a particularly important source of employment for these communities, especially for African American households. With the manufacturing sector no longer a source of jobs for the working class, the reduction of employment opportunities with the city meant that many working-class families, disproportionately minorities, lost their last remaining source of steady income (Waldinger 1996).

Another way that the changes in public policy generated by the fiscal crisis undermined working-class communities concerned the availability of basic social services. Not only did many working-class people lose their jobs as a result of the layoffs, but the remaining teachers, nurses, street cleaners, and fire fighters were forced to work many hours of overtime; the quality of the services they were able to provide to city residents declined in proportion to the degree they were overworked. Beyond this, however, "planned shrinkage" also meant more extensive reductions in social spending. Municipal hospitals built in the 1960s were closed down and staff was laid off. Well-baby clinics and community health centers were dismantled. Firehouses built in the 1960s were closed after 1975, library hours were shortened, and sanitation services reduced. The City University of New York, which had expanded extensively in the 1960s, began to lay off faculty and to impose tuition charges. In short, municipal services were suddenly reduced at the same time that industrial and municipal jobs were disappearing from the city. As working-class people lost their jobs they became more dependent on government services, but found that these services had been dramatically reduced (Jones et al. 1992).[4]

Despite this wave of cutbacks and reductions in public services, however, people still had homes. Homelessness was not yet commonplace; indeed, the word "homeless" was not yet in common usage. Additional changes in public policy, however, were to have devastating effects on the ability of working people to provide adequate shelter for themselves. These changes resulted from the efforts of New York City's economic and political elite to remake the city's economy—to transform New York from a center of manufacturing into a global node of corporate finance, insurance, and real estate (Castells 1989, 1996; Sassen 1991).

As part of their effort to attract global finance capital into New York, city officials instituted a series of changes in tax laws that were intended to foster the construction, renovation, and gentrification of commercial and residential property. These changes in public policy made investment in real estate highly advantageous. As the new laws began to take effect, capital poured into tax-exempt office buildings located on highly valued land, and into commercial real estate in general (Fitch 1990; Henwood 1998). At the same time, the city's new financial elite began to look for housing that was appropriate to their station in life, resulting in gentrification and re-valuation (upward) of residential property not only in Manhattan but also in the surrounding boroughs (Smith 1996).

This real estate boom was to prove extremely harmful to working-class communities, where the vast majority of apartments had been rent-regulated since World War II as a result of the continuing housing shortage. Owners of rent-regulated buildings were quick to see the potential profits represented by the new conditions of the post-Fordist era and responded by trying to force their tenants to leave (so that landlords could raise the rents to "market rate"). Landlords had recourse to a number of strategies in order to accomplish that goal. Tenants in working-class neighborhoods, for example, were frequently left without heat or hot water for long periods of time. It was also common for landlords to eliminate building maintenance, or reduce it to a bare minimum. The most extreme strategy employed in order to remove tenants from rent-regulated apartments, however, was arson. Between 1975 and 1980, large sections of poor neighborhoods in Harlem, the Lower East Side of Manhattan, the South Bronx, and the Bushwick and Bedford Stuyvesant sections of Brooklyn burned down. Often these fires were deliberately set. Landlords could collect insurance on burned-out buildings and still retain rights to land. They therefore had no incentive to protect buildings or residents from fires. Rather, it was more profitable to allow buildings to deteriorate and then to rebuild more profitable high-rent apartments or luxury cooperatives that catered to New York City's new economic elite.

The 1975 fiscal crisis also marks an historical watershed in the emergence of new forms of social movements in New York City. In the context of the citywide crisis, local organizations emerged that sought to preserve working-class neighborhoods. The protest movements that arose in Greenpoint-Williamsburg in Brooklyn between 1975 and 1978 typify processes of organization and protest that occurred in many working-class neighborhoods. Several forms of protest occurred in Greenpoint during this period, all of them focused on the deterioration of neighborhood services ensuing from the fiscal crisis. A committee was formed to keep the local hospital open, a parents' slate competed in school board elections, and a committee was formed to support subsidized housing for senior citizens. However, the most remarkable and extended struggle converged on a condemned firehouse (Susser 1982). For three years, residents of Greenpoint organized local protest actions to persuade the city government to reopen a firehouse that had been closed in response to the 1975 fiscal crisis.[5]

Local protest movements fought for the preservation of neighborhoods and social services because these were the areas where working-class people experienced changes in fiscal priorities most acutely. The latter changes in turn reflected the political and economic transformation of the city after 1975, and serve as an indicator of the processes through which the corporate changes toward a gentrified informational city were wrought, as well as the social costs they engendered.

Homelessness, the Shelter System, and "Dispersed Community" in the 1980s

As a result of these processes, by the early 1980s homelessness had become a problem of major proportions. Literally tens of thousands of individuals who had formerly had secure housing in stable neighborhood communities found themselves without a place to live. Their efforts to adapt to this state of affairs compelled them to utilize the woefully inadequate services made available by the city of New York to assist such people. These services included homeless shelters, homeless hotels (deteriorated buildings adapted by the city to provide single rooms for homeless families), family residences run by volunteer organizations, and church facilities.[6] In the course of using these services, homeless individuals were forced to construct "institutional communities" in conditions that made virtually all social relationships fleeting and ephemeral. Families in homeless hotels and other transitional residences created social networks that included kin, coresidents, and staff. Such "communities," however, were geographically constrained by the building regulations that defined specific buildings as transitional residences, by the "outcast" nature of these buildings within the commercial, central-city business districts in which the buildings tended to be located, and even by the whims of guards assigned to monitor activities in the buildings. The ephemeral nature of these institutional communities was virtually guaranteed by the fact that new people arrived daily, others found housing and left the residences, and many people simply wandered through the buildings unofficially for a variety of purposes. Accentuating the ephemeral nature of these communities was the fact that staff turnovers were constant, being subject to budget cuts, policy shifts, and changes in funding sources. In short, institutional communities were temporary, unstable, and artificial "community" environments.

The goal of the shelter system, however, was not to retain families so as to establish stable new communities, but rather to relocate displaced families to new accommodations and new neighborhoods. As families were relocated into new and unfamiliar surroundings they were forced to adapt to difficult new circumstances. Indeed, the process of relocation generated new forms of community that were geographically dispersed rather than bounded. One of the novel features of these dispersed communities was that residents had a very difficult time asserting control over public space.

When people left the shelter system they seldom moved to apartments in their old neighborhoods. As a result, they were forced to build new connections, establish new social bonds, and familiarize themselves with a new geographic territory, new transportation facilities, social services, and local institutions. Unfortunately, individuals who had been through the shelter system were most often relocated to neglected buildings in the very kinds of run-down neighborhoods they had been forced to leave when they became homeless. Efforts to establish stable and safe forms of community in these settings were confounded by a variety of forces. Prominent among them were high rates of homicide and drug-related crime, and the neglected state of the buildings themselves. Relocated families commonly found themselves placed in deteriorated buildings where the front doors did not lock, where windows were broken, and where hallways smelled of urine and rotting food. On surrounding blocks, abandoned buildings alternated with empty lots that were strewn with bricks and garbage. Drug dealers commonly worked out of apartments in the same buildings as those in which families had been relocated. In these conditions, users and dealers were constantly entering the building, and the violence that the illegal trade precipitates spilled over to threaten other residents. These hazardous conditions compelled people to move from apartment to apartment, ever in search of a safe haven.

One major consequence of this unstable state of affairs was that new and old residents alike developed a pervasive and well-grounded sense of fear of their surroundings. People who were relocated into new neighborhoods feared both the neighborhoods into which they were resettled as well as the people who lived there. Similarly, those already resident in these neighborhoods not only feared their surroundings but also tended to be suspicious of and to stigmatize the families from the shelters. High rates of homicide, drug-related crime, and mutual suspicion militated strongly against the development of any sense of local "community."

In these circumstances, a perception of community life emerged that was in marked contrast to that of the 1970s, prior to the destruction of working-class neighborhoods. In place of the control, attachment to place, and sense of security that had characterized the previous decade, by the 1980s people were fearful of neighbors, fearful of the street, distrustful of schools and other local institutions, and alienated from the public space in which they were forced to live. So fearful of their environment were many residents that they refused to allow their children out of their apartments and into public space. So removed from their surroundings were they that many did not know who was responsible for the maintenance of their buildings, or where to go to find someone to remove garbage from the hallways. So suspicious of the local schools were many residents that they refused to place their children there, preferring instead to transport them long distances to their old, familiar neighborhoods.[7]

During the 1980s geographically dispersed forms of community based on dispersed family networks came to replace the stable, geographically bounded communities of the 1970s that had been strongly rooted to place. Rather than rely on suspect individuals or institutions in their immediate vicinity, relocated families tended to fall back on safe if distant connections—generally, a small circle of relatives (parents, in-laws, adult children, sisters, and cousins) and fictive kin. These individuals commonly traveled long distances (from Brooklyn to the Bronx, from New Jersey to Central Harlem, from the East Village to Harlem, and from Brooklyn to Harlem) in order to help with chores, baby-sitting, cooking, or simply for company. They also came in times of emergency involving domestic violence or hospitalization. Those involved in these dispersed family networks were often forced to commute for as much as two hours each way on public transportation, but nonetheless did so several times a week or even daily. While the difficult conditions in which these family networks were activated meant that members were often in conflict with each other, the networks continued to be maintained despite the difficulties posed by distance and cost.[8]

The 1980s thus helped produce a dislocated and transient population of poor people with few ties to "place." Although the real estate boom that followed the fiscal crisis of 1975 resulted in the increasing accumulation of wealth among the professional and high-income residents of New York City, the lives of the poor deteriorated (Castells and Mollenkopf 1991). In addition to rising homelessness and joblessness, the reduction in public services combined with the decreasing availability of affordable housing to produce major negative health consequences. Infant mortality rates rose in the 1980s in a number of poor neighborhoods, as did the incidence of infectious disease and the number of children living in poverty (see McCord and Freeman 1988; Mullings and Susser 1992; Susser 1991). The appearance of tuberculosis, long related to overcrowding and poor housing conditions, also marked the 1980s.

Another consequence of the post–fiscal crisis era, however, was the development of a broader set of connections among working-class people and a more generalized recognition of the common problems faced by all. As people were burned out of their homes, priced out of the neighborhoods where they grew up, forced into homelessness, and finally relocated to new accommodations, they met many others in similar situations. This common experience made it possible to challenge the stereotypes and forms of parochialism, racism, and discrimination generated in the more segregated, stable neighborhoods of the precrisis era.

In the 1980s and early 1990s, new social movements and new organizations emerged among the homeless population. Groups such as the Coalition for the Homeless and Parents on the Move (Mathieu 1991) articulated new concerns for poor people, and fought for new kinds of rights. And although organizations such as these did much to advance the cause of the homeless and the poor, there were multiple pressures conspiring against working-class people.

Coalition for the Homeless, which formed in 1980, was composed of lawyers, political activists, and homeless people. This group adopted a legislative approach to advancing the cause of the city's poor population, and in a series of landmark court cases was able to establish for all people in New York State the fundamental right to shelter. The court cases associated with this victory have been crucial in shaping the shelter system as well as in framing the political issues of homelessness in New York City. Indeed, since 1980 each new mayor has had to confront the issue of homelessness and the obligation to provide shelter for individuals and families in New York City (Hopper 1989; Hopper and Cox 1982; Dehavenon 1997). However, legislative battles have not been able to force the city or the state to provide adequate access to low-income housing, although programs for community housing of the mentally ill homeless were implemented as a result of the struggles. As real estate investment has become a crucial factor in the era of the "informational city," policies that stimulate gentrification rather than low-income housing have increasingly become municipal priorities (Castells 1989).

Parents on the Move, which also formed in the 1980s, was made up of women living in "homeless hotels" (Mathieu 1990). This organization was different from the Coalition for the Homeless in that it was established by poor women themselves. Parents on the Move was headed by two women from one large hotel who mobilized other women living in similar settings. These two women were very effective representatives for their cause, able to articulate the needs of poor and homeless parents for a variety of services and facilities. They printed a newsletter and spoke extensively at conferences concerned with the homeless, attempting to give voice to the perspectives of homeless women.[9] Although they were successful in many ways, the limits of their success reflect the material conditions that gave birth to Parents. When the organization's leading women were relocated out of the homeless hotels and into apartments, the group lost momentum.

The most dramatic series of events concerning homelessness and housing protests during the 1980s and early 1990s, however, took place on the Lower East Side. Perhaps the most significant aspect of these events was that they were not organized by the homeless alone but rather represented a coalition of homeless people, squatters, and some local residents. All of these groups came together to make two related demands: for the right of homeless people to stay in public spaces and the need for low-income housing.

As occurred in many other poor neighborhoods, during the 1970s large sections of the Lower East Side burned down. People were forced to move from tenement to tenement as entire blocks were destroyed (Sharff 1998). Many lost their homes. Pressures on housing during the 1980s were complicated by the fact that there was also an influx of artists and other lower-income professionals who were looking for affordable places to live (Smith 1996). As a result of these forces, by the late 1980s the Lower East Side had a sizable population of homeless and struggling, low-income individuals.

As a result of these developments, by the late 1980s Tompkins Square Park, the central open space on the Lower East Side, had become a shanty-town where homeless people would nightly erect cardboard shacks and lay out their bedding. The park was also a meeting place for a variety of political groups that sought to establish low-income housing in surrounding buildings, and to set up community centers and other neighborhood organizations. The area also began to attract corporate investment, however, and in the face of rising rents and an influx of higher income residents, conflict ensued. Some residents complained about the night-long noise and the loud music coming from the park. Other people complained about their fears of using the park. The New York City administration responded by attempting to enforce a curfew, which would have prevented homeless people from spending the night in the park. As conflict escalated, Mayor David Dinkins ordered the police to remove the homeless people from their shacks. A violent riot ensued (blamed by many on police overreaction and brutality), and in its aftermath the homeless were removed from the park. This historic park, famous for union demonstrations from the nineteenth century and for free rock concerts from the 1960s, was then closed for several years, completely renovated, and reorganized. Sections were allotted to toddlers, basketball, and dog walkers. Today, in the new park, as in parks all over the city, a curfew is enforced and police systematically arrest those found in the area an hour after midnight.

The use of police force to resolve the conflict in Tompkins Square Park was indicative of more general social processes and tensions. The increasing social stratification that characterized the post-1975 era, combined with the disintegration of poor neighborhoods, the decreasing ability of working-class families to control public space, escalating levels of homelessness, and rising levels of homicide and violent crime led to increasing interference in public life by the New York City police. From the tragedies of police shooting young men in the streets to the removal of homeless people from the subways and the railroad stations, to the apparently less serious police interference with street vendors, street artists, and taxi drivers, the administration of New York City began to intervene in the livelihood of the new immigrant population, the working poor, and the general public who walk the streets of Manhattan (ibid.).

In the 1980s and early 1990s poor people organized not to preserve their neighborhoods (as they had in the 1970s) but simply for the right to shelter or even for the right to sleep in public space. In these collective protests we find a critique of social conditions and inequality that has much in common with those of earlier poor people's movements (Gonzalez et al., n.d.). However, the dispersed character of community and the transient nature of the homeless meant that the protests of the 1980s and early 1990s were scattered and discontinuous, and were conducted on rapidly shifting ground. The poor won important skirmishes over the provision of shelters for their families, but they were losing the larger battle for adequate food and affordable rent.

Shifts of the Late 1990s

From the mid-1970s until the mid-1990s the "new poverty" of U.S. cities, associated with the end of Fordism, the rise of flexible accumulation, and the transition to the informational city, continued to grow. The result was significant increases in inequality combined with few successful community-based protest movements (Susser 1996). Since the mid-1990s, however, two major historical shifts have taken place. The first of these is the dismantlement of public assistance as it was implemented by the government for more than fifty years. The second is an upturn in the U.S. economy, which, for the first time since the 1970s, has actually led to real gains in working-class wages and a decrease in unemployment figures, even for African Americans in the inner cities.

In the past few years more people are working, but, ironically, in New York City, the population falling below the poverty line are the working poor, not the unemployed. In other words, although there has been a reduction in unemployment, there has been an increase in the number of people living in poverty. Nevertheless, at the same time the leadership of U.S. unions, faced with dramatically declining membership and declining influence, has finally reversed their ban on organizing new immigrant workers. Now that the poor are in fact working, they are also more able to organize for higher living standards.

All over New York City interesting developments in union organizing are taking place, among groups who were formerly excluded from union membership. This includes restaurant and garment workers in Chinatown, some of the groups most likely to be earning below minimum wage. It includes as well Latino/a workers from Latin America and the Caribbean, many of whom work in delicatessens, restaurants, and other service-sector jobs. It also includes African immigrant workers, who are often employed as delivery people and grocery packers. All these groups are beginning to demand better working conditions, and to join union organizations that can help them defend their interests. Even the nonunionized homeless have won court cases, against the Grand Central Partnership and the 34th Street Partnership, which hired workers at a dollar an hour as security guards to harass homeless people or to clean up streets and shelters. Back wages were paid to 196 workers to bring them up to the legal minimum wage, at a cost of $816,000.[10]

Another important form of collective protest to the conditions of the present concerns a widespread movement against police brutality. This broad-based movement has emerged since 1998 and brings together city residents of diverse backgrounds, interests, and orientations. Many professionals and city officials, including the former mayor David Dinkins, have been arrested on the steps of City Hall in protests against the shooting of young black men by members of the New York City Police Department. An alliance of students from across the city's public high schools has also emerged in order to protest the harassment of youth by the police.

These two forms of organization—one that has grown in opposition to police harassment, the other that seeks to organize important sectors of the "new poor"—suggest that the working-class population of New York City may finally be developing some important responses to the changes of recent decades.

New York City is changing once again, not only with respect to the largely immigrant service economy but also among other workers in the city, who include large numbers of minority workers, specifically Latino/a and African American workers. These changes can perhaps be seen as a historical consequence of the global shifts in the economy of the city, combined with the low rates of unemployment nationwide. The general shift in the policies and power of U.S. labor—in direct correspondence with the protests around world trade that began in Europe and have become part of the current U.S. political context—have had a significant impact on the experience of New York City workers.

It appears that New York City, as a central "node" in the global economy, came to be characterized by extreme rates of inequality, which were exacerbated by the lack of many welfare state provisions and the strong labor history more characteristic of Europe. Now, in some small way, the immigrants and poor residents of New York City are beginning to develop a working-class response to their difficulties, as reflected in struggles over nonunionized, low-paid labor and in protests against police harassment.

Notes

1. See the critical commentary on this position by William Julius Wilson (2000), who stresses the importance of racism and inequality in limiting the generalized, positive effects of economic growth.

2. However, such movements were partial and somewhat ephemeral. They were fighting something of a rear-guard action for rights such as shelter and low-income housing—rights that the older working class had taken for granted since the formation of the strong industrial unions and the struggles of the Great Depression (which led to the formulation of policies of the now-embattled welfare state).

3. In my ethnographic research in New York City in the 1970s, I defined the neighborhood of Greenpoint-Williamsburg according to the community district boundaries, which were decreed by the Planning Board for New York City in 1969. Within that context, it became clear that local perceptions of "community" varied dramatically and that even the municipality had multiple methods for defining this section of the city (Susser 1982). Neither health area districts nor the census statistics nor the numerous forms of electoral districts corresponded directly to the community district divisions. These divisions, in turn, limited and constrained the portrayal and perceptions of the "community" by local residents. In addition, images of racial and ethnic divisions concretized by housing discrimination and income cut across the municipal divisions of community.

4. It was not until the 1990s that the city would recoup these losses, only to be faced by new budget deficits and cutbacks.

5. The protest movement was partially successful but required a tremendous output of time and resources by people with few resources to spare.

6. For a review of the places to which homeless people were assigned, see Susser (1999a).

7. For a similar description of changes on Manhattan's Lower East Side, see Sharff (1998).

8. These dispersed family networks were in marked contrast to conditions in the 1970s, when there were few instances of family connections or reciprocity reaching beyond the neighborhood level (Susser 1982, 1986, 1988).

9. The concerns of these women contradict popular stereotypes and perspectives of social service providers, which suggest that homeless and poor women are not able to take responsibility for their children.

10. See Nina Bernstein, *New York Times*, October 25, 2000, p. B1.

References

Alcaly, R., and D. Mermelstein. 1977. *The Fiscal Crisis of American Cities*. New York: Random House.

Bookman, A., and S. Morgen. 1988. *Women and the Politics of Empowerment*. Philadelphia: Temple University Press.

Castells. M. 1989. *The Informational City*. Oxford: Blackwell.

———. 1996. *The Informational Age*. Oxford: Blackwell.

Castells, M., and J. Mollenkopf. 1991. "Conclusion: Is New York a Dual City?" In J. Mollenkopf and M. Castells, eds., *The Dual City*, 399–418. New York: Russell Sage Foundation.

Dehavenon, A. 1993. "Where Did All the Men Go? An Etic Model for the Cross-Cultural Study of the Causes of Matrifocality." In J. Mencher and A. Okongwu, eds., *Where Did All the Men Go? Female-Headed Households Cross-Culturally*. Boulder, Colo.: Westview Press.

Dehavenon, A., ed. 1997. *There's No Place Like Home*. Westport, Conn.: Bergin and Garvey.

Gonzalez, A., A. Marcus, and W. Ewing. n.d. "The Battle for Tompkins Square Park." Unpublished manuscript, City University of New York.

Harvey, D. 1989. *The Condition of Postmodernity*. Oxford: Blackwell.

Henwood, D. 1998. *Wall Street*. New York: Verso.

Hopper, K. 1989. "The Ordeal of Shelter: Continuities and Discontinuities in the Public Response to Homelessness." *Notre Dame Journal of Law, Ethics and Public Policy* 4, no. 2: 301–23.

Hopper, K., and L. Cox. 1982. "Litigation in Advocacy for the Homeless: The Case of New York City." *Developing Seeds of Change,* no. 2: 57–62.

Jones, D., and I. Susser, eds. 1993. "The Widening Gap between Rich and Poor." *Critique of Anthropology* (special issue) 13, no. 3: 211–15.

Jones, D., J. Turner, and J. Montbach. 1992. "Declining Social Services and the Threat to Social Reproduction: An Urban Dilemma." *City & Society* 6, no. 2: 99–114.

Mathieu, A. 1991. "Parents on the Move." Ph.D. dissertation, New School for Social Research, New York.

McCord, C., and H. Freeman. 1989. "Excess Mortality in Harlem." *New England Journal of Medicine* 320, no. 3: 173–77.

Mullings, I., and I. Susser, eds. 1992. *Harlem Redevelopment Proposal*. Ms.: Files of the authors.

Nash, J. 2001. "Labor Struggles: Gender, Ethnicity and the New Migration." In I. Susser and T. Patterson, eds., *Cultural Diversity in the U.S.: A Critical Reader*, 206–29. Malden, Mass.: Blackwell.

Sassen, S. 1991. *The Global City*. Princeton: Princeton University Press.

Sharff, J. 1997. *King Kong on 4th Street*. Boulder, Colo.: Westview Press.

Smith, N. 1996. *The New Urban Frontier*. London: Routledge.

Stack, C. 1974. *All Our Kin*. New York: Harper and Row.

Susser, I. 1982. *Norman Street: Poverty and Politics in an Urban Neighborhood*. New York: Oxford University Press.

———. 1986. "Political Activity among Working Class Women in a U.S. City." *American Ethnologist* 13, no. 1: 108–17.

———. 1988. "Working Class Women, Social Protest and Changing Ideologies." In A. Bookman and S. Morgen, eds., *Women and the Politics of Empowerment*, 252–72. Philadelphia: Temple University Press.

———. 1991. "The Separation of Mothers and Children." In J. Mollenkopf and M. Castells, eds., *The Dual City*. New York: Russell Sage Foundation.

———. 1996. "The Construction of Poverty and Homelessness in US Cities." *Annual Review of Anthropology* 25: 411–35.

———. 1997. "The Flexible Woman: Regendering Labour in the Informational Society." *Critique of Anthropology* 17, no. 4: 389–402.

———. 1999a. "Creating Family Forms: The Exclusion of Men and Teenage Boys from Families in the New York City Shelter System, 1987–91." In S. Low, ed., *Theorizing the City*, 67–83. New Brunswick: Rutgers University Press.

———. 1999b. "Inequality, Violence and Gender Relations in a Global City: New York, 1986–96." *Identities* 5, no. 2: 219–48.

Susser, I., and M. Gonzalez. 1992. "Sex, Drugs and Videotape: The Prevention of AIDS in a New York City Shelter for Homeless Men." *Medical Anthropology* 14: 307–22.

Susser, I., and J. Kreniske. 1987. "The Welfare Trap: A Public Policy for Deprivation." In L. Mullings, ed., *Cities of the United States*, 51–68. New York: Columbia University Press.

Waldinger, R. 1996. *Still the Promised City: African-Americans and New Immigrants in Postindustrial New York*. Cambridge: Harvard University Press.

Wilson, William Julius. 2000. "All Boats Rise. Now What?" *New York Times*, April 12, Section A: 31.

Transition without Transformation

Russia's Involutionary Road to Capitalism

The messianic reformers of the Soviet transition, whether Western or Russian, considered the socialist economy so moribund, so inefficient, and so obsolete that it was an article of faith that only markets could bring economic improvement. But conditions have only gotten worse, much worse. Over the last ten years Russia's gross domestic product has fallen by more than half; living standards for most have plummeted along with increased material insecurity; and the population continues to shrink with falling life expectancy. A decade of market reform has been a decade of unprecedented economic decline.

The advocates of shock therapy have their pet explanations for the degeneration—Jeffrey Sachs (1994) writes of the betrayal of the IMF; Anders Aslund (1995) of the sabotage of former Stalinist managers; Clifford Gaddy and Barry Ickes (1998) of a collective collusion to support hidden subsidies for loss-making enterprises. In their views this was an incomplete application of shock therapy—the political will, whether domestic or foreign, for economic restructuring was missing. Evolutionary economists (Murrell 1991, 1992; Poznanski 1996; Stiglitz 1999), on the other hand, were critical of shock therapy from the beginning. They argued that a dynamic capitalist economy required institutions that cannot be created overnight. Markets do not spontaneously generate a banking system, rule of law, stock exchange, and so forth. These have to be nurtured. Tearing down the old without erecting the new was a recipe for disaster. While neoliberals and evolutionary economists argue why Russia has failed to travel the road to a modern capitalist economy, or why Russia has lagged behind Poland, Hungary, and the Czech republics, these commentators have limited grasp of what has actually happened in Russia. Theirs are deficit models of failure to realize a particular Western goal—either bad prescription or bad execution—rather than accounts and explanations of where Russia is heading.

Instead of the anticipated neoliberal *revolutionary* break with the past or the neoinstitutional aspiration to *evolutionary* ascent to a future capitalism, Russia has experienced what I call an *involutionary* degeneration, brought about by the expansion of the sphere of exchange at the expense of production (Burawoy 1996; Burawoy, Krotov, and Lytkina 2000).[1] Economic and political reform has spawned a retreat to old forms of production, an inward turn of society, and the recomposition of the party state into a neofeudal polity. There has indeed been a market transition but without the anticipated economic, social, and political transformation—that is, without the accumulation of capital, the expansion of society, or the rise of a developmental state. This "transition without transformation" is the terrain to be excavated, the puzzle to be explored.

Bringing Polanyi to Russia

Like others, I turn to Karl Polanyi's *The Great Transformation* to elucidate the character and the causes of this peculiar market transition, Russia's "Great Involution." Many, especially the evolutionary economists referred to above, have adopted Polanyi's framework to understand what has gone wrong in Russia: his critique of market utopianism, and his insistence on the centrality of the state in any transition to a market economy. They have pointed to the institutional framework necessary for markets to work efficiently and dynamically. Critics have also drawn on Polanyi's depiction of multiple historical trajectories, thereby replacing a teleological notion of transition with the more agnostic concept of postsocialist transformation (Stark and Bruszt 1998; Bryant and Mokrzycki 1994). In other words, they argue that there is no market road to a market economy, just as there is no singular and inevitable end point to economic reform.

These are important lessons to draw from Polanyi, but I propose to adopt his broader historical vision, which encompasses one and a half centuries, from the end of the eighteenth century to the middle of the twentieth century—a history of the dynamic processes that lead first to the expansion of and then to the reaction against the market. This double movement I argue has been telescoped into ten years in Russia, although its form and effects have been profoundly different because it has occurred at such a different tempo and in such a different context. To make the case that Polanyi's account of England is relevant to Russia today, I divide the historical account of England's *Great Transformation* into phases that parallel Russia's *Great Involution*.

First, Polanyi devotes almost a third of his book to the genesis of the market and the breakdown of the Speenhamland welfare system, in which livelihood of the indigent was supplemented with cash payments according to the price of bread. As an obstacle to a national labor market, Speenhamland was, in Polanyi's view, a form of "reactionary paternalism" that demoralized and degraded laborers while stifling the entrepreneurial energies of employers. As Maurice Glasman (1994, 1996) has argued, Polanyi's hostility to the "totalitarian" Speenhamland conjures up the liberal wrath against communism—its despotism, its paternalism, its stifling of freedom. There are limits to the analogy—Speenhamland was not a comprehensive "planned economy" but the last bulwark against the market society. Nonetheless, the invective Polanyi deploys against Speenhamland's stifling administrative order makes the parallel with communism worth pursuing.

The second phase began when Speenhamland was finally rescinded with the New Poor Law Act of 1834, which abolished outdoor poor relief. The last obstacle to the self-regulating market was vanquished, and the working class was left to fend for itself against the ravishes of the market society. The equivalent breakthrough to the market is played out in Russia with the "great liberal reforms" of 1992: freeing of prices, opening the economy to market forces, and voucher privatization of state enterprises—all of which threw the population into turmoil and back onto its private resources. As in England, in the face of economic devastation, Russia's neoliberal utopians trumpeted the supernatural, redemptive powers of the market, what Polanyi calls the "liberal creed."

Polanyi's third phase is the reaction to the self-regulating market. Here lies his most original contribution: society's movement against the commodification of land, labor, and money that took place in the second half of the nineteenth century. Russia presents its own distinctive response to the commodification of these three pillars of social and economic life, which, as we shall see, was less an active regulation and more a self-protective retreat.

Finally, in Polanyi's fourth phase the reaction against the self-regulating market assumed international proportions in the 1930s, when countries abandoned the gold standard, undermined the international balance of power, and adopted statist solutions to economic problems—communism's collectivization and planning, fascism, social democracy, and the

TABLE I

The Market Transition in England and Russia

	Polanyi's England TRANSFORMATION	Post-Soviet Russia INVOLUTION
Antecedents: Authoritarian Paternalism	Speenhamland	Communism
Ideology: Market Utopianism	Liberal Creed	Neoliberalism
Reaction to the Market: Decommodification	Regulation of the Market	Retreat from the Market
Global Effects on State-Society Relations	Statism: State-Society Interaction	Neo-Feudalism: State-Society Repulsion

New Deal. We will have to consider whether Russia today might be moving toward a similar protectionism and restoration of statism, or alternatively, as I will propose, we are witnessing the appearance of a form of neofeudalism. Table 1 summarizes the two accounts of market transition.

Taking Polanyi's account of England as our analytical template compels us to recognize discrete phases and dynamic processes in the postcommunist market transition. It also gives us a template with which to make comparisons among countries facing the transition from socialism. In order to avoid yet another deficit reading of Russia, however, we need to uncover the unstated assumptions of *The Great Transformation*, assumptions that make England's transition historically specific, and thereby provide the grounds for alternative assumptions that fit the Russian case.

Problematizing the Great Transformation

To what historical event or complex of events does the "Great Transformation" refer? In the conventional reading, "The Great Transformation" refers to the *rise of the self-regulating market,* or what Polanyi also calls "market society" in nineteenth-century Europe. Yet this singular *market transition* is accompanied by three equally important transformations that Polanyi assumes but does not explain: namely, first, an *economic transformation* of the means of production; second, a *social transformation* that involves the expansion of society to counter the commodification of labor; and third, a *political transformation* required for the national consolidation of a money economy. The Russian transition to a market economy highlights just how problematic are each of these unremarked, taken-for-granted transformations.

First, Polanyi deliberately pushes aside how the market promotes the accumulation of capital through the transformation of production. Whereas both Marx and Weber placed accumulation at the center of their analysis of modern capitalism, Polanyi deliberately relegates this to the peripheral vision. He takes for granted the enormous economic expansion of the nineteenth century. To focus on it, he argues, is to create the basis of a dangerous justificatory ideology for overlooking the enormous human suffering, and the devastation of community. Yet that economic expansion also provided resources for the phenomena he highlights: for containing the market, for compelling capital to restrain its exploitative tendencies, for building up the regulatory apparatuses of the state, and for ameliorating the conditions of existence for large sections of the working class. Without economic expansion, protection and regulation would not have been possible. From the standpoint of Russia, and of course many other countries, the expansion of production is precisely what is absent, what seems beyond their grasp. That is the first distinguishing feature: *transition without economic transformation*—a transition to a market without the transformation of production.[2]

The second assumption Polanyi makes concerns the transformation of society. As we have seen, Polanyi focuses on exchange—the way the commodification of labor brings about cultural degradation and human demoralization. This leads to a spontaneous reaction against the market that in England took the form of the rise of trade unions, the factory movement for the restriction of working hours, the Chartist movement for the expansion of working-class political rights, and new economic forms such as the self-regulating cooperatives. Polanyi describes but does not explain the rise of civil society in the second half of the nineteenth century.[3] For Polanyi, survival dictated the necessity of aggressive social regulation, but he does not ask under what circumstances that might take place. The Russian transition to the market suggests that the nineteenth-century English societal reaction is by no means universal but that it presupposes already existing resources and capacities. In Russia the communist society of institutions gave way to a world of social networks, deployed around the strategic manipulation of resources. Thus the second distinguishing mark is a *transition without social transformation*, a transition to the market without the rise of a vibrant society.[4]

The third transformation that Polanyi assumes without explanation is the rise of a sovereign state. David Woodruff (1999) makes this argument explicitly in his explanation of barter relations. Monetary consolidation cannot be secured through a package of liberal economic reforms if there is no prior consolidation of the state. Polanyi takes for granted the subordination of regions to the English state when market reforms are introduced in the nineteenth century. In Russia, on the other hand, the breakup of the Soviet Union gave autonomy to the regions that, so far, have not been effectively subjugated to the nation-state. The result was strategies of regional self-protection in which local states helped to promote their own forms of money and encouraged enterprises to avoid bankruptcy by constituting systems of barter exchange and avoiding the punitive national monetary system. Thus the third distinguishing mark of the Russian market transition is the *absence of political transformation*, a transition to the market without an effective nation-state to orchestrate monetary consolidation.

In other words, contemporary Russia is remarkable not for the rise and fall of the market but for the absence of these three alternative significations of the nineteenth-century great transformation—the transformation of production, of society, and of the state. The economy undergoes neither a neoliberal revolution nor an institutional evolution but rather an economic involution, a market that sucks resources out of production, sending it into a spiraling contraction. Instead of a vibrant synergy between civil society and the state, we find their mutual repulsion, in which society turns in on itself—societal involution—and the federal state turns outward to the global economy, unable to contain the tendency toward regional autonomy—political involution. We need to ask, therefore: Why a "great involution" rather than a second great transformation?

Economic Involution: The Expansion of the Market

Although Polanyi intends his work to be a radical critique of the liberal creed, of market dogmatism, in one respect he recapitulates that account, namely in divorcing the *genesis of the market*, the breakdown of barriers to the free exchange of the factors of production, from the subsequent *dynamics of the market economy*. Once the corrosive welfare system of Speenhamland, the last dam holding back the onrushing market society, is defeated, its traces cannot be discovered in the new order. Once the self-regulating economy is established, its logic pre-empts any legacies from the past, obliterates vestiges of its genesis. According to Polanyi, therefore, the magic and indeed devastation of the market will work itself out irrespective of origins, irrespective of the particular path to the market economy. This too was the anticipation of Russia's neoliberal reformers (and their Western advisors). They assumed that the market logic would sweep the calumniated communism into the dustbin of history. A thick line could be drawn between the past and the present, opening up a future with all of capitalism's blessings. Instead it turned out that Russia's market economy was infused with, one might say even dominated by, its past.

When Speenhamland was struck down, and the New Poor Law introduced in 1834, bringing about a national market in labor, England had been developing a market economy for centuries. In Russia's case the programmatic introduction of the market economy took place overnight, and in the rush features of the old order were consolidated rather than obliterated.

In order to understand the way the past has taken revenge on the new order, we need to first characterize the old order. It was an administered economy in which goods and services were centrally appropriated and then redistributed. This established a bargaining relation between the administrative center and enterprise production, conducted on the terrain of planning targets and indices. For our purposes, three features of this order are important:

1. The system of planning gave the economy a *monopolistic character,* as targets were assigned to specific enterprises and duplication was regarded as wasteful. Within each region industries were organized into conglomerates that organized each sector. Enterprises for their part sought to increase their power with their supervisory centers through expansion and further monopolization of the production of goods and services.

2. In the absence of hard budget constraints, the compulsion to expand led to an insatiable appetite for expansion at all costs, which deepened monopolistic tendencies but also generated a *shortage economy.* Enterprises faced constraints from the side of supply, which led them to incorporate the production of inputs into their organization or circumvent the command economy by entering into informal relations with their suppliers. The semilegal system of lateral barter relations was organized by regional party officials and by a class of intermediaries or pushers known as *tolkachi.*

3. The administered economy enhanced *worker control over production* for two reasons. First, full employment gave workers leverage because they, like everything else, were in short supply. It was difficult and coun-

terproductive for managers to get rid of workers. This gave workers the power to resist managerial encroachments on their autonomy. But second, that autonomy was also necessary because the shortage economy required flexible adaptation to unreliable machinery and unpredictable material flows. The result was a compromise in which workers sought to realize the plan so long as managers provided the conditions for its fulfillment and a minimal standard of living.

When the party state disintegrated in the period of late perestroika and the center no longer commanded, the pre-existing monopolies were not weakened but strengthened. No longer subject to control either from party or ministries, their monopolistic tendencies were unfettered. Local conglomerates begin to act like enormous trading companies with a monopoly over specific resources and products. At the same time the breakdown of the redistributive economy led to an increase in lateral exchanges which, in the absence of cash flows and an effective banking system, initially took the form of barter. Finally, with the collapse of the party, workers assumed even greater control over production, especially as managers were absorbed in organizing barter transactions—for themselves as well as the enterprise.

One can regard the new order as the deepening of distinctive features of the old one or, alternatively, as the emergence of a new order of merchant capital. With the disintegration of the administered economy, each unit seeks to maximize profit—but not through investing in or regulating production but through exploiting its monopoly position within a system of trade. Directors use their inherited ties to government organs to protect their subsidies, credits, and export licenses, and at the same time stifle independent capital accumulation. Workers control production, and so managers seek compromises with workers that give them a cut in the proceeds of barter operations; surplus, however, is not used to reinvest in or transform production. Indeed, productive activity is parallel to a putting-out system in which managers organize the supply of materials and the exchange of products while workers are paid for what they deliver. Pre-existing monopolies and effective worker control of production combine to lead Russia down the road to merchant capitalism and economic involution.

The disintegration of the party state was the terrain onto which reforms were introduced. Price liberalization comes first at the beginning of 1992, fueling inflation and further lubricating the appetite for profits from trade. Instead of begging for resources, enterprises now pleaded for financial credits. The old system of plan bargaining was made easier, and soft budget constraints were merely monetized. Independent banks mushroomed and flourished as the conduit of government credits on the one side and as the conversion of enterprise assets into managerial profiteering on the other. Interenterprise arrears and nonpayment of wages spiraled out of control as bills were left outstanding. Voucher privatization in the summer of 1992 turned enterprise assets over to de facto managerial control while workers were left hanging onto the leaky bag of production.

In other words, every reform took Russia further down the path of merchant capital, making more difficult the transition to a "bourgeois capitalism" based on accumulation and self-transformation. This was a dynamic economy, but dynamic in the sphere of exchange—a dynamics that came at the cost of production. The market opened up trade, barter, and banking, and at the same time gave new meaning and place to a "mafia"—a shadow state that enforced transactions in the absence of an effective state. Productive activity shrank, interenterprise arrears expanded even further, and wages were not paid or paid only in kind. This was a "prebourgeois" pursuit of profit, what Weber called speculative, adventure, booty capitalism, a form of mercantilism, and not his "rational capitalistic organization of (formally) free labor" that motored dynamic accumulation. Instead it impelled economic involution in which exchange leaches production without offering means of resuscitation.

The Russian "Great Transformation" never happened. The neoliberal reformers waited every year for signs of market revivalism, for the start of the market revolution. The reforms were radical but skin deep. From the beginning they were plagued with unanticipated consequences because they peeled off only the outer layer of the Soviet order, revealing a resilient substratum that resisted the reorganization of the economy and its institutions. The evolutionary economists diagnosed the errors of shock therapy, but they did not have the conceptual tools to understand Russia's actual abortive trajectory: economic involution followed by societal involution.

Societal and Political Involution: The Retreat from the Market

The advance of the market into the Russian hinterland along the tributaries of the Soviet economy set in its train a reaction to the market. Economic involution gave rise to *societal and political involution*. To explore the contrast with Polanyi's societal and political transformation we draw on his most original insight, namely the analysis of fictitious commodities. When labor, land, and money are subject to open purchase and sale, Polanyi argues, they lose their essential nature. When it is hired and fired at will, labor is dehumanized; when land is commodified the environment is destroyed, and agriculture becomes precarious; when money is the object of speculation, the survival of business is threatened.

The self-regulating market, therefore, destroys the social order upon which it rests. Polanyi shows how in England the commodification of land, labor, and money comes to be hedged with restriction and protection. Labor organizes itself into trade unions, cooperatives, the factory movement for the restriction of the length of the working day and the abolition of child labor, the Chartist Movement for the extension of political rights to the working people. Society emerges to protect labor from the extremes of immiseration, degradation, and subjugation. The commercialization of land threatened to shatter the agrarian community, but it was the landed gentry, in their position as ruling class, who tamed the market with land laws and tariffs. Finally, a national monetary system, with its central bank guaranteed stability in the value of money, controlling inflation, as well as exchange rates, created that certainty in the environment without which businesses flounder. In Polanyi's scheme the state protects the fictitious commodities by negotiating the compromise between market and society.

Facing the commodification of labor, land, and money, Russia in the 1990s arrives at a fundamentally different solution. Whereas in England the market spawned, in reaction, a vibrant society that was aided and abetted by a regulatory state, in Russia society took a headlong retreat from the market to more primitive economic forms. By the same token the central state, rather than forging a synergic alliance with society, hooked itself into the global economy and became enmeshed in the organization of transnational flows of natural resources, finance, and information. At the same time it became detached from the local economy, raiding it for immediate riches without concern for its reproduction, let alone expansion. What does involution mean in the case of each of our fictitious commodities? We will deal in turn with labor, land, and money.

THE DECOMMODIFICATION OF LABOR AND THE TURN TO
SUBSISTENCE AND PETTY COMMODITY PRODUCTION

Labor has been decommodified by not being paid a cash wage. Workers still go to work because there they find all sorts of nonmonetary resources. They can use enterprise equipment and materials to work for themselves or directly for others on a contract basis. Work is a place where information about economic opportunities circulates, where workers can pick up unofficial "work on the side" or "second jobs." Just as managers began to strip enterprises of their assets, so workers intensified their own petty stealing. Finally, without a job workers are denied benefits from the state—supplementary benefits for low-income families, child allowances, and in the future unemployment compensation and various pensions.

While the enterprise acts as an informal welfare order, working-class families increasingly produce the means of their livelihood outside work. Most notoriously there are the dachas with adjoining plots of land where some half of Russian families spend their weekends and holidays, looking after children and cultivating crops. Even without dachas, families grow basic food, especially potatoes, on allotments that are usually not too far from their homes. Self-maintenance extends beyond subsistence agriculture to include making clothes or furniture, home repair, and much sharing of scarce commodities such as books and toys. In short, decommodifying labor does not take the form of hedging the labor market with protection but retreating from the labor market into more primitive self-maintaining communities.

THE DECOMMODIFICATION OF LAND AND THE
REPEASANTIZATION OF AGRICULTURE

In the area of agriculture we observe similar processes (Kitching 1998a, 1998b). Despite pressure from the World Bank and IMF, the Duma has so far refused to privatize land. Members of collective farms can sell their share of the land but only to other members of the same collective and not to outsiders. The collective farm itself has not disappeared, but like the industrial enterprise its function has changed. It too acts like a welfare order of last resort, but its economic function has turned from a center of agricultural production increasingly to a service center for the independent agriculture of its members. As the collective farm has little money for wages, so members spend more time on their own plots of land. The collective farm becomes a service center that loans out machinery, distributes fertilizer, offers limited credit, provides transportation to markets, and so forth. More and more agricultural produce is consumed by its producers as cheap foreign food floods the urban markets, as urbanites themselves reduce their levels of consumption or grow their own food. Along with the rest of society there is a move toward subsistence. Effectively, agriculture is being re-peasantized.

THE DECOMMODIFICATION OF MONEY
AND THE RISE OF BARTER

Finally, we come to the third fictitious commodity, money. The argument here is that enterprises cannot survive when the value of money fluctuates. The medium of exchange has to have a certain stability, which is secured by the creation of a national monetary system regulated by a central bank. Russia has its Central Bank but has not managed to sustain the regulation of the ruble exchange rate. In the first two years of the reforms the bank fueled inflation by extending liberal credits to enterprises to keep them afloat. Then in 1994 we entered the period of stabilization, when the ruble-dollar exchange rate was held firm and inflation slowed down. But in August 1998 the value of the ruble again plummeted, from six to twenty-five rubles to the dollar.

The availability of cheap credit, the expansion of an independent banking system, and the possibility of increasing prices to counter inflation led to the expansion of cash transactions in the first two years of the transition. With tightening credit, central regulation of banking, and the freezing of accounts in the red, enterprises began to circumvent the money economy by engaging in barter relations. This had the advantage of making revenues more invisible and the enforcement of taxation more difficult. According to most estimates, around 70 percent of economic transactions between enterprises are conducted through barter.[5] Market prices provide the baseline for the terms of exchange, with a supplement depending on the fungibility of the commodity being exchanged. Thus if oil is bartered for apartments, the exchange rate will favor oil, just as bricks will be favored over timber.[6]

Economic transactions take place through extensive "barter chains" in which an initiating enterprise has to organize a series of material exchanges that bring needed goods in exchange for its own products. A factory manufacturing concrete blocks for housing construction requires steel. The director or his agent goes to the steel plant to see what it needs. If it needs coal, the director now goes to the coal managers to see what they need. They are interested in apartments in which to relocate their employees. Now, the director can see light at the end of the tunnel, since he knows that the construction company needs concrete panels. The chain is closed: concrete blocks go to the construction company, apartments go to the coal industry, coal goes to the metallurgical plant, and steel goes to the concrete factory. Such barter chains might be organized by the originating manager or by intermediaries who specialize in organizing the connections. To facilitate these chains all sorts of pseudo currencies emerge. Thus large enterprises that produce basic commodities, such as oil or steel companies, or the regional Ministry of Finance issue their own "IOU's," known as *vekselia*, which are traded at discounted prices. Often the originating company will not recognize the nominal value of their own *vekselia*. Regional taxes are often paid in kind so that the government re-creates its own clearinghouse, a center for the redistribution of resources, what one might call a return to a rudimentary and hidden planning system.

Barter is not an enduring legacy of Soviet planning since the latter was dissolved, and in 1992–93 the economy was monetized. It was only later with stabilization and the effective bankruptcy of most enterprises that barter returned as a means of survival outside the monetary sphere. As David Woodruff (1999) has shown, barter relations are a reaction against the anarchy of the market, insulating regional economies from the destructive fluctuations in the value of money, provoked by international speculators and by a state absorbed in transnational circuits of finance. If the chains of barter re-create the network of relations that were established under the Soviet economy, they are impelled by and represent a creative response to the exigencies of a weak national regulation of the commodification of money.

Thus instead of a great transformation we have a great involution; instead of a self-expanding market society hedged in and propelled by a vibrant society working together with a regulatory state, we have a society in headlong retreat from the market, a state dancing to the tune of global financial markets, and an economy conjoined by networks of barter. Where in England and Europe the market provoked a resilient civil society connected to the state, in Russia there is little associational life outside the emptying shell of the multifunctional enterprise on the one side and the local state on the other. Instead of a civil society we have a *network society*, the thin strands of reciprocity connecting households of subsistence but without the institutional knots that characterize advanced capitalism.

The Class Basis of Involution

We come now to the question of the relation between economic involution on the one hand and societal and political involution on the other. Does economic involution necessarily lead to societal and political involution? Does societal and political involution deepen economic involution? What are the causal mechanisms that link the two?

Certainly, when there is economic transformation, then there is also the material basis of an expansive state and a vibrant society that can re-embed labor, land, and money. Without economic transformation, however, there cannot be enduring state-society synergy. But Polanyi is more concerned with the reverse causality from state-society synergy to economic transformation.[7] Why do some states become effective regulators whereas other states fail abysmally? Polanyi himself seems to have two types of argument. On the one hand he claims that states spontaneously manifest that regulatory intervention necessary to balance market and society. On the other hand he argues that classes are the vehicle of the general interest and are able to transmit it to the state. In explaining the divergence between England's and Russia's transition to the market—the one leading to transformation and the other to involution—I too propose to focus on the class character of the two transitions: in the one case a manufacturing bourgeoisie, emerging as a hegemonic force both nationally and globally, and in the other case a merchant-financial bourgeoisie, dependent on its close ties to the state and an appendage of international capital.

For Polanyi, ideology plays an important role in shaping the development of England in the nineteenth century. The liberal creed of the political economists not only galvanized the bourgeoisie but also seeped into the lived experience of subordinate classes, most importantly the working class. Market utopianism captured the popular imagination because the manufacturing class could indeed begin to present their interests as the interests of all, because it was possible to coordinate the material advance of capital and labor, and also because workers' power was real. Capital depended on labor. The development of working-class organizations through the nineteenth century together with state restrictions on the deployment of labor drove manufacturing capital toward new strategies of accumulation, moving from simply sweating labor to newfangled techniques of production.

In Russia the transition is in the opposite direction. Under the Soviet order the working class was a central player in the political economy not just in ideology but also in practice. As I have already outlined, under the shortage economy of state socialism, workers were especially powerful because of the control they necessarily exercised over production. It was essential, therefore, for the party state not only to justify and maintain its domination but also to elicit the active consent of its working class, thereby giving the latter considerable leverage. The proletariat's prominence in ideology, therefore, was not merely a cynical ploy but had a material basis. With the disintegration of the administered economy and the transition from a nomenclatura to a financial-merchant bourgeoisie, centered on banks, trading, mafia, and exploitation of natural resources, industry collapsed and the working class became a superfluous residue of the past.

The "liberal creed" of the New Russians, on the other hand, far from being a "hegemonic" ideology that wins the active consent of the mass of the population, became a thin veil of justification and legitimation for pursuing narrow economic interests. Perhaps in the beginning consumerism had a mass appeal, but as expectations were dashed and labor grew poorer, it generated hostility, opposition, or cynicism combined with a nostalgia for the radiant past. The emptying out of production and the retreat of the state destroyed the ground from underneath the working class, so that it no longer possessed the collective will to organize effective opposition. Apart from occasional local outbreaks, only the coal miners were able to mount nationwide strikes, demanding that the state pay off its wage arrears. But even the miners found their position hopeless as mines closed down, one after the other, following the government-backed deindustrialization program of the World Bank.

Just as with ideology so with the state: it became the transparent arm of the new merchant-finance capital. In Polanyi's analysis of England, the state represents the "collective interest," negotiating a balance between market and society. It does this not because it spontaneously rises above society but because it acts at the behest of the landed aristocracy—the ruling class that constitutes hegemony on behalf of the dominant capitalist class. In Russia, on the other hand, the state has been hijacked by the emergent financial/natural-resource/media oligarchy that bankrolled the crucial 1996 Yeltsin election campaign in return for shares (at discounted rates) in the most profitable Russian enterprises. They orchestrated—or a fraction of them orchestrated—Yeltsin's cabinet reshuffles, and more or less dictated the policy of the executive branch of government. In line with the financial oligarchy's speculative interests, the executive of the Russian state has pursued short-term borrowing from Western banks and collaborated with the World Bank and IMF conditions for loans. Although the Duma is more firmly rooted in the national economy, it is too weak to counter the collusion between the relatively powerful executive and financial oligarchy.

Finally, the class basis of involution explains the different modes of incorporation into the world economy. England in the nineteenth century and Russia at the end of the twentieth century occupy opposite positions in the global economy of their times. In the one, foreign explorations offered new markets and cheap resources that drove domestic accumulation, while in the other foreign connections propel domestic disaccumulation, draining off its human and natural resources. The two nations may not only occupy different places, but the global order has itself changed. Transnational processes are of greater importance now than they were, driving a wedge between Russia's global city, Moscow, and its retarding hinterland. Russia is polarized between two worlds: the hypermodern world of currency exchange and international commodity flows, and the premodern world of barter, trade, petty commodity production, and peasant subsistence (Castells and Kiselyova 1998).

As the center is integrating into the most advanced circuits of the global information society, the hinterland is hurtling in the other direction toward a neofeudalism. The parcelized sovereignty of feudalism is recapitulated in Russia's regional suzerainties. Their local economies are organized through extraeconomic force, the racketeering mafias, connected to the local patrimonial state. On the ground, the working classes turn increasingly to subsistence production, small-scale trade, and familial exchange, while relying on a cash economy for basic goods that they cannot produce. Their unpaid "wage-labor" becomes a rent for minimal social protection, health care, child care, disability and old-age pensions, unemployment compensation, wage supplements, housing subsidies, and child support. Society is primordial and gelatinous, increasingly cut off from the Sturm und Drang of Moscow politics.

Russia in Comparative Perspective

In trying to make sense of Russia's experience since 1991, I have taken the broadest comparative canvas. I have drawn on Karl Polanyi's account of the fall of reactionary paternalism in nineteenth-century England, its replacement by a market society, followed by statist reaction that countered the unregulated market. In broad sweep we can say that this century-long transition and reaction was telescoped into a decade of Russian history. But what Polanyi took for granted, namely economic, social, and political transformation, has proved to be an elusive outcome for those entering the world market today.

In Russia, the consequences of the market transition have been especially destructive. Did the Russian transition have to be the way it was? Was Russia destined to take its own road to economic and societal involution? It is all too easy to say that it was inevitable because Russia's history shows it to be inimical to capitalist development. Here comparative analysis suggests alternative explanations. Comparing the trajectories of Russia with Central European countries—Poland, Hungary and the Czech Republic—suggests that both antecedent conditions and alternative strategies of transition are important.

First, let us consider antecedent conditions. The market economy had advanced much further in these countries, especially Hungary and Poland, than in Russia. Indeed, the physical planning that dominated the Soviet economy had been left behind in the 1970s with the rise of fiscal planning, the marketization of trade and retail, and greater autonomy for agriculture. When the party state disintegrated in Hungary and Poland, it revealed a flourishing entrepreneurial economy, whereas in Russia it augmented the power of the large monopolistic conglomerates that continued to dominate the economy.

Second, we observe alternative strategies of transition. Precisely because Russia was so backward with respect to the development of a market economy, it tried to catch up overnight with radical and dramatic plans, beginning with Shatalin's famous five-hundred-day transition to capitalism. But the very speed of the attempted transition had the effect of breaking up the administrative system and reconcentrating power in the hands of the conglomerates. While the Czech government talked up the virtues of the market and the importance of radical transformation, in practice it took a slow and evolutionary road, with protective trade policies, controlled liberalization of prices, and a gradual privatization scheme.

Hungary had always taken an evolutionary road. In Poland the Solidarity government's attempt at shock therapy had mixed results until the Social Democrats were returned to office and introduced more state-centered, evolutionary policies.

The contrast with China is perhaps the most remarkable. Since 1990 the Chinese economy has expanded at the same rate that the Russian economy has collapsed. The state has nurtured the development of an expanding private sector while seeking to enforce harder budget constraints on its state monopolies (Oi 1998; Walder 1994; Naughton 1995; Rawski 1994). State and party bureaucracy continues to direct the economy, coordinating public and private sectors, combining administered and market enterprises. Its entry into the global economy has been on the terms of a developmental state bureaucracy rather than a financial-merchant oligarchy. We might say that in contrast to Russia's involutionary *transition without transformation*, China has accomplished a developmental *transformation but without a transition* to a market society.

Like the neoliberals who inspired Russia's exit from communism, Polanyi assumed that transition meant transformation. Today the experience of many Third World countries, as well as of Russia, testifies that transition not only does not lead to transformation but actually stimulates its opposite: in the case of Russia, what I have called involution. The Chinese case suggests, however, that state socialism can supply the foundations of a thriving market economy, by incubating the state-society synergy that Polanyi took for granted. Russia lost this opportunity because it fell victim to a programmatic destruction of the state-administered economy, as if destruction itself were sufficient for genesis. China took the reformist road to transition and created a transformation, while Russia took the revolutionary road and produced involution.

Notes

For reading and commenting on earlier versions of this paper, I would like to thank Kazimierz Poznanski, Linus Huang, Bill Hayes, Rachel Sherman, and Michelle Williams, members of the Berkeley seminar on "Challenges to Sovereignty from Above and Below," and participants in the Chicago miniconference entitled "Socializing Knowledge: Revolution, Transformation and Continuity in the Cultural Forms of Post-socialist Europe."

1. I have borrowed the concept of involution from Clifford Geertz's (1963) description of the Javanese peasant's response to the expansion of the Dutch sugar, agro-export industry. Involution is economic change without transformation, or,

as Geertz (p. 63) puts it, "the overdriving of an established form in such a way that it becomes rigid through over elaboration of detail." I have tried to give "involution" a more dynamic meaning by connecting the degeneration of production, society, and state to the expansion of the sphere of exchange.

2. Thane Gustafson's (1999) account of Russian capitalism juxtaposes market transition on the one side, and collapse, legacy, and takeover by oligarchy on the other as competing forces whose relative strengths will determine Russia's fate. He talks of Russia's as-yet-indeterminate revolution. An involutionary framework argues that Russia's market transition has *produced* economic, social, and political degeneration.

3. In Polanyi's account, the working class spontaneously rises up against the degrading effects of the market as soon as Speenhamland is dissolved. The Poor Law Reform Act marked the birth of the working class. The historical record shows, however, that the working class appeared in the north of England, where there was no legacy of Speenhamland; in the south, where Speenhamland did exist, there was no working class (Block and Somers 1999; Somers 1993). Polanyi's explanation—that the rise of society was a spontaneous reaction to the market—is patently inadequate.

4. Maurice Glasman (1994, 1996) makes a similar point for Eastern Europe, asking why the postsocialist transition, especially the unrealized potential of the Polish Solidarity movement, did not result in a vibrant, self-regulating society. He lays the blame at the doorstep of the market utopian reaction to communism: the market experiment corroded society.

5. In 1999 things began to change again as money became more important and replaced many of the barter transactions. This does not signify any permanent change, any more than it did in 1992–93. Nor does it mean that the power of intermediaries has declined, since they now exploit monopolistic pricing structures.

6. By far the best and most detailed account of the double movement in the sphere of exchange is to be found in Woodruff (1999). In the first reform phase, the monetization takes off, while in the second phase bankruptcy is avoided through exiting the national ruble economy by engaging in barter and creating surrogate monies, promoted by the local state. In a third phase, the central authorities are also drawn in to supporting regional barter economies.

7. The political and social conditions of economic transformation have been the focus of much recent work. See, for example, Evans (1995, 1997) and Poznanski (1999).

References

Aslund, Anders. 1995. *How Russia Became a Market Economy*. Washington, D.C.: Brookings Institution.

Block, Fred, and Margaret Somers. 1999. "Speenhamland, Perversity, and Naturalism: Ideational Embeddedness in Welfare Reform." Unpublished ms. Department of Sociology, University of California, Davis.

Bryant, Christopher, and Edmund Mokrzycki. 1994. "Introduction: Theorizing the Changes in East-Central Europe." In Christopher Bryant and Edmund Mokrzycki, eds., *The New Great Transformation*, 1–14. London: Routledge.

Burawoy, Michael. 1996. "The State and Economic Involution: Russia through a Chinese Lens." *World Development* 24: 1105–17.

Burawoy, Michael, Pavel Krotov, and Tatyana Lytkina. 2000. "Involution and Destitution in Capitalist Russia." *Ethnography* 1, no. 1: 43–65.

Castells, Manuel, and Emma Kiselyova. 1998. "Russia and the Network Society: An Analytical Exploration." Paper prepared for the conference entitled "Russia at the End of the 20th Century." School of Humanities, Stanford University, November 5–7.

Evans, Peter. 1995. *Embedded Autonomy*. Princeton: Princeton University Press.

Evans, Peter, ed. 1997. *State-Society Synergy: Government and Social Capital in Development*. Berkeley: International and Area Studies, University of California at Berkeley.

Gaddy, Clifford, and Barry Ickes. 1998. "Russia's Virtual Economy." *Foreign Affairs* 77 (September–October): 53–67.

Geertz, Clifford. 1963. *Agrarian Involution*. Berkeley: University of California Press.

Glasman, Maurice. 1994. "The Great Deformation: Polanyi, Poland and the Terrors of Planned Spontaneity." In Christopher Bryant and Edmund Mokrzycki, eds., *The New Great Transformation*, 191–217. London: Routledge.

———. 1996. *Unnecessary Suffering*. London: Verso.

Gustafson, Thane. 1999. *Capitalism Russian-Style*. Cambridge: Cambridge University Press.

Kitching, Gavin. 1998a. "The Development of Agrarian Capitalism in Russia 1991–97: Some Observations from Fieldwork." *Journal of Peasant Studies* 25, no. 3: 1–30.

———. 1998b. "The Revenge of the Peasant: The Collapse of Large-scale Russian Agriculture and the Role of the Peasant 'Private Plot' in that Collapse." *Journal of Peasant Studies* 26, no. 1: 43–81.

Murrell, Peter. 1991. "Can Neoclassical Economics Underpin the Reform of Centrally Planned Economies?" *Journal of Economic Perspectives* 5, no. 4: 59–78.

———. 1992. "Evolution in Economics and in the Economic Reform of the Centrally Planned Economies." In Christopher Clague and Gorden C. Rausser, eds., *The Emergence of Market Economies in Eastern Europe*, 35–54. Oxford: Basil Blackwell.

Naughton, Barry. 1995. *Growing out of the Plan: Chinese Economic Reform, 1978–1993*. New York: Cambridge University Press.

Oi, Jean C. 1999. *Rural China Takes Off: Institutional Foundations of Economic Reform*. Berkeley: University of California Press.

Polanyi, Karl. 1957 [1944]. *The Great Transformation: The Political and Economic Origins of Our Time*. Boston: Beacon Press.

Poznanski, Kazimierz Z. 1996. *Poland's Protracted Transition: Institutional Change and Economic Growth, 1970–1994*. Cambridge: Cambridge University Press.

———. 1999. "The Postcommunist Transition as an Institutional Disintegration:

Explaining the Regional Economic Recession." Unpublished ms. Seattle: University of Washington.

Rawski, Thomas. 1994. "Progress without Privatization." In Vedat Milor, ed., *Changing Political Economies*, 27–52. Boulder, Colo.: Lynne Rienner.

Sachs, Jeffrey. 1994. "Toward Glasnost in the IMF." *Challenge* 47, no. 3: 4–11.

Somers, Margaret. 1993. "Citizenship and the Place of the Public Sphere: Law, Community and Political Culture in the Transition to Democracy." *American Sociological Review* 58, no. 5: 587–620.

Stark, David, and Lazslo Bruszt. 1998. *Postsocialist Pathways: Transforming Politics and Property in East Central Europe*. Cambridge: Cambridge University Press.

Stiglitz, Joseph. 1999. "Whither Reform? Ten Years of the Transition." Keynote address at the World Bank Annual Conference on Development Economics, Washington, D.C., April 28–30.

Walder, Andrew. 1994. "Corporate Organization and Local Government Property Rights in China." In Vedat Milor, ed., *Changing Political Economies*, 53–66. Boulder, Colo.: Lynne Rienner.

Woodruff, David. 1999. *Money Unmade: Barter and the Fate of Russian Capitalism*. Ithaca: Cornell University Press.

The Family Romance of Mandarin Capital

In this chapter I draw on and recast the ideas of Joan Vincent about the strategic importance of "men in motion" (1971)[1] in the "moving frontier" of colonial capitalism (1971, 1982),[2] as well as the question of class consciousness (1982) in late-twentieth-century capitalisms.[3] In her study of British rule in colonial Uganda, Vincent wondered what factors in colonial capitalism accounted for the lack of class consciousness among subaltern groups.[4] Influenced, perhaps, by Marx's comparison of French peasants to "a sack of potatoes"—"[T]hey cannot represent themselves, they must be represented"[5]—Vincent suggested that the mobility of capitalist agents disguised the class character of imperial capital, leaving local groups unconnected to each other even as they were objectively exploited by the same system. By arguing that the mobility of capital and its agents was dialectically linked to the fixity of subaltern groups, in both geographical and ideological senses, Vincent identified the critical process whereby transnational capital reinforces the mobility of some at the expense of many, a power mechanism that is especially significant in the era of late capitalism.[6]

The ideological murkiness of traveling agents of capitalism, and the "class unawareness" of subaltern groups, are complex ethnographic questions that challenge us to move beyond a class-centered analysis. While other scholars of colonial and postcolonial societies have dealt with issues of class consciousness in relatively stable situations of class exploitation,[7] Vincent's focus on the moving frontiers of capitalism vividly problematizes analytical linkages between capitalist mobility and the political (un)conscious of subaltern groups. Indirectly, her work on Teso poses the question, How does one account for political consciousness when the material links to capital are so attenuated as to seem invisible to the dominated?[8] This question suggests the obverse, that is, What happens when the material relations of exploitation are keenly felt and yet are not symbolically linked to a politics of class identity? This is an especially important theme in the contemporary world, where so much of what we take to be reality is complexly mediated by the dynamic flows of images that make all systems of referents highly fragmented, destabilized, and not directly connected to the structure of production.[9] While it is fashionable among orthodox Marxists to reject such observations as "postmodernist," I maintain that the days are over for calmly plotting a structural relationship between the "objective" and the "subjective" aspects of (class) consciousness. Capital remains fundamental to our understanding of contemporary social life, and it is sensible to think of capital as highly sped-up, constantly mutating sets of material, technological, and discursive relations, of production and consumption, in which everything is reduced to an exchange value. Donald Lowe refers to this phenomenon in the United States, where accelerated production/consumption has annihilated use values, as "the hegemony of exchangist practices."[10] Even when we move away from the centers of global capitalism, subaltern groups in the new transnational publics shaped by capital, travel, and mass media cannot develop political consciousness in a way that escapes the mediations of ethnic identifications, mass culture, and national ideologies. Indeed, transnational capitalism in Asia has been linked not so much to the rise of class hostility but to other forms of cultural struggle that privilege gender, family, ethnicity, and nationality.[11]

The problem of subaltern consciousness, then, is not merely one of the "invisibility" of dominant relations to subalterns or the impossibility of the "authentic" representation of subalterns by nonsubalterns;[12] rather, it is also one of linking "subaltern" imagination not to the structure of production but to what Foucault calls "knowledge power." In the contemporary world, where so much of everyday consciousness is mediated by "print (and electronic) capitalism," discursive knowledges constitute a field of power that defines entities such as the family, gender, ethnicity, race, and nationality and thus constitutes the political consciousness of class-differentiated subjects.[13] How are social identities rooted in objective class differences shaped not by an ideology of class exploitation but by the corporatist hegemony of exchangist values? I find Fredric Jameson's notion of "the political unconscious" especially useful for unmasking ideological messages embedded in cultural narratives about the traveling subject of contemporary Asian capitalism.[14] Although Jameson is interested in uncovering the political unconscious—a structure of psyche that is historical—in literary works, I wish here to uncover the political unconscious in commercialized cultural and political forms linked to mobile Chinese families that have recently dominated public cultures in Southeast Asia. What are the ideological messages in the figuration of traveling masculine subjects and entrepreneurial families? What do they tell us about the popular imagination of power, authority, and desires in the brave new Asian world of authoritarian states and free-flowing capitalism?

The Governmentality of Family Romances

This rise of Chinese corporate forms in the Southeast Asian public landscape has been sudden and quite startling. I remember visiting Malaysia in 1992 on Chinese New Year and being amazed by the huge commercial displays of Chinese words, figures, and banners on major hotels and stores. Despite Malaysia's large Chinese minority, the public display of Chinese symbols had been muted throughout the 1970s and 1980s, when Malaysianization policies established Malay language, personalities, and cultural icons as the appropriate vehicles for public prestige and pageantry. The new prominence of Chinese iconography outside "Chinatown," I was told, was a sign of welcome for Taiwanese businessmen, who have become the main investors in Malaysia, overtaking the Japanese. Ironically, while blatant displays of Chinese artifacts in public culture have been suppressed for fear of inciting local ethnic-Chinese chauvinism, commercial images of Chineseness as symbols are permitted and even encouraged for their links to transnational capital and entrepreneurs, in effect casting them as "'thoroughly modern' Asians."[15]

This flamboyant display of Chinese corporatism indexes a new accommodation between translocal capital and the developmental state, an alliance that enables cosmopolitan Chinese iconography to dominate public culture. These, however, are not apolitical images of culture and consumption but are imbued with messages about the stereotypical "Asian" family order, gender hierarchy, and subscription to a particular state vision of communitarian capitalism. Indeed, just as the world of Walt Disney disseminates capitalist ideology,[16] the new Asian public culture creates a realm in which cosmopolitan images promote a kind of ideological conformity that is especially powerful because it is cast in the language of family romance and modern adventure.[17]

Embedded in these public cultural forms are political messages about power, masculinity, and a mobile economic liberalism. As Foucault has reminded us, economic liberalism is not simply a theory of political and economic behavior but "a style of thinking quintessentially concerned with the art of governing."[18] The objective of political economy resituates "governmental reason within a newly complicated, open and unstable politico-epistemic configuration."[19] One can say that a kind of laissez-faire governmentality infuses the market behavior of overseas Chinese, among whom a premium is placed on norms that allow the free play of market forces, flexible activities, and the self-discipline of the profit maximizer. In Adam Smithian thinking, the state is ideally a solicitous institution that makes corrective adjustments to open channels to free trade, but its interventions should be limited so as not to hamper the workings of market rationality. Indeed, while nation-states such as Singapore, Malaysia, and Indonesia may be politically repressive now and again, the state ensures the freedom of economic activities across the region. Prime Minister Mahathir Mohamad of Malaysia calls such a combination of "not-so-liberal democracy" and government intervention into the economy "communitarian capitalism."[20] These ideas about the inseparable links between economic liberalism and authoritarian rule are disseminated through public cultures that recast capitalist strategies and state control as family romances.

The new Asian publics are increasingly contexts through which, in Lynn Hunt's words, "private sentiments and public politics"[21] are interwoven and struggled over by different class, ethnic, and nationality groups." Following Hunt, I use the construct of family romance(s) to mean the collective and unconscious images of family order that underlie public politics.[22] Narratives of affluent Chinese families provide a kind of structure to political imaginaries, which (like nationalism) can cross-cut and neutralize the interpellations of class, gender, and ethnicity.[23] Family romances do not operate in an apolitical manner but inform the way people imagine the operations of power between individuals and the state, between different ethnic groups, and of course between men and women. Below, I suggest that family romances—as articulated in public displays, images, and narratives—are vehicles that variously encode political messages about (1) a fraternal tribal capitalism; (2) Chinese-native elite alliances; (3) the moral economy of the state; and (4) working-class women's dreams. These are different facets of "the family model of politics,"[24] and they speak to the differing notions of authority and legitimacy among transnational capitalists, their bureaucratic partners, and the new middle classes; they also shape the notions of authority and legitimacy of subaltern subjects in Asian modernity.

The Romance of Family Empires

Over the past two decades, Southeast Asia has seen the emergence of about a dozen major Chinese business families whose multinational holdings place them among the world's richest people. Chinese-owned companies that enjoy the patronage of politicians have become "larger than all but the biggest local branches of the global MNCs [multinational corporations] which proliferated throughout the region" in the 1980s.[25] Their owners include Robert Kuok and the Kwek brothers of Malaysia and Hong Kong, Liern Sioe Liong and William Soeryadjaya of Indonesia, and the late Chin Sophronphanich and the Lamsarn family of Thailand.[26] Taken together, overseas-Chinese corporate families and professionals are the new economic elite in Asia (outside Japan); their activities, mobility, and stories are the stuff of a regional thinking about "communitarian capitalism."

The symbolic qualities of Chinese corporate families—interpersonal relations based on fraternity and mandarin ideals—are key elements in a political imaginary of regional development and interethnic dependence between rulers and capitalists. This Chinese capitalist triumphalism arose in the context of a sustained economic boom that began in the 1970s, when Singapore and Hong Kong joined South Korea as the new "dragons" in Asia. In the next decade, as Malaysia, Thailand, and Indonesia won the label "minidragons," ethnic Chinese business groups began to exercise their critical role in forming economic linkages that supplemented and went beyond the strategies of the developmental states. In 1991, the Singapore Chinese Chamber of Commerce held the first global meeting of Chinese chambers of commerce from all over the world, inviting participants from seventy-five countries. This meeting of business interests was represented as a model of postcolonial fraternal bonds that overcame regional and political differences. A leader of the Singapore Chamber of Commerce told me that there was no language barrier at the gathering because the Chinese entrepreneurs were all bound by kinship, in the double sense of having both blood and fictive fraternal bonds.[27] This rediscovered brotherhood in the context of transnational capitalism has been dubbed a "momentary glow of fraternity"; it asserts a transnational autonomy vis-à-vis the less flexible patriarchal authority of the state.[28]

Emboldened by their successes in forming transnational networks, overseas entrepreneurs boast of using fraternal links to bypass or do without political and legal regulations. In an interview, a member of the Singapore Chamber of Commerce recalled for me: "Overseas Chinese grew more confident and more concerned about their identity. Globalization requires going beyond just national identity in enlarging our scope and permutations of what we're trying to do. Although investments are directed by our government regionalization policy, most important linkages are made through company levels, and again at the local level through human relations."[29]

Ethnic Chinese solidarity based on male bonding and networks has created what Joel Kotkin calls "the most economically important of the Asian global tribes" and has made the "old government ideology of nation-states . . . outmoded."[30] This use of the term *tribe* to refer to traveling ethnic business men constructs an essentialist concept of cultural difference and brings to mind the band of brothers who ritually sacrificed the original father figure in Freud's *Totem and Taboo*.[31] Fraternal networks are represented as the modern Asian way of doing business man to man, usurping the paternalistic role of the government in economic activities. The familial morality of Chinese capitalism, then, is not that of the autocratic father but rather the fraternal flexibility that forms alliances across ideological, political, and ethnic borders.

The oxymoron *Confucian merchant* is a sign of the extravagance of Chinese capitalism.[32] That Confucian philosophy puts traders at the bottom of the occupational hierarchy and regards their singular pursuit of wealth as the very antithesis of Confucian values has not been an obstacle to business-news images of capitalists as reborn Confucians. In narratives of East Asian triumphalism, Chinese merchants are likened to mandarins whose high status stems not only from their fortunes but also from their representation of a reworked Confucianism of the "all-men-are-brothers" sort.

The merchant mandarin par excellence is Robert Kuok, a Malaysian-born tycoon who has been called "the embodiment of a Confucian gentleman" in the region's authoritative business magazine, the *Far Eastern Economic Review*.[33] The cover of the issue in which this assessment appears displays Kuok dressed in an emperor's yellow dragon robes in the regal pose of an ancestor figure. His spectacular economic success has been attributed not only to his masterful cultivation of relationships with capitalists and politicians but also to his loyalty to business subordinates and to his sense of business discretion. The family romance behind this merchant prince celebrates the values of discipline, pragmatism, and economic success; it opposes political idealism and the impractical goals of the anticolonial revolutionary. The trader and the revolutionary are key figures in overseas Chinese history.[34] The story of Robert Kuok and his younger brother, Willie, is presented as a morality tale of overseas Chinese who are torn between a foolish anti-imperialist struggle (Willie) and practical adjustments to imperial rule and global capitalism (Robert). The sensible influence is represented by Kuok's mother, a "very austere, very religious" and "old-fashioned" woman—that is, an authentic Chinese parental figure of piety and moral uprightness.[35] It is instructive that maternal, rather than paternal, influence is constructed as the key influence on sons in this diasporan Chinese family. Emigration from China breaks with the traditional patriarchal power associated with the lineages and the ancestral temples of the home culture.

The Kuok brothers were educated in elite colonial British schools (where Robert's classmates included future politicians such as Lee Kuan Yew). The Second World War, which precipitated the process of decolonization, set the brothers off on radically different paths. While Robert worked with the occupying Japanese forces and learned from their rice trade, his younger brother, Willie, entered the jungle to join the anti-imperialist Communist Party of Malaysia as a propagandist. By the end of the war, both brothers had gained fame. Willie's death at the hands of British troops was announced in the British House of Commons. A few years later, Robert Kuok established a major sugar mill and, through rapid expansion, soon became the "sugar king" of Southeast Asia. Expanding his strategic ties to overseas Chinese trades and indigenous politicians, Robert Kuok has built an empire based on commodities, shipping, banking, and property development, with offices in Hong Kong, Beijing, Paris, and Santiago.

This story, which has been reported in the international press and circulates among overseas Chinese, contrasts "good" and "bad" overseas Chinese male subjects. Robert Kuok is the reassuring image of a new diasporan masculine ideal—open to all kinds of advantageous alliances, tempered by an astute judgment of human relations, and always nurturing social relations with associates. This mandarin image was further promoted by *Forbes*, the world's leading business magazine. "Nearly all the first-generation tycoons, such as Indonesia's Liem [Sioe Liong], Malaysia's Kuok, and Hong Kong's Li Kashing, have the same image: trustworthy, loyal, humble, gentlemanly, skilled at networking and willing to leave something on the table for partners."[36]

In his study of the intertwining of nationalism and sexuality in Nazi Germany and Great Britain, George Mosse notes that bourgeois manhood was often represented by values of restraint and self-control. "Manliness was not just a matter of courage, it was a pattern of manners and morals" that appealed to the middle classes as virtue and respectability, or the control of passion.[37] In Chinese dynastic romances, the manly virtues of the new bourgeoisie are a mix of restrained flamboyance and benevolence toward those who are less well endowed. This vision of a gentrified tycoon culture—a world away from the hubbub of Chinese commercial streets—appeals to the new middle classes, who have been keeping up with global "middling" norms of the good life.[38]

Such images of family morality—restraint, fraternity, princeliness—both represent and resonate with the fantasies of Chinese families with their nostalgia for a remembered glorious culture, and with the ways they understand economic and political experiences. There is growing evidence that the middle classes in Southeast Asia now look to (Chinese) business families rather than to the families of sultans or kings as models for appropriate, modern, Asian masculine conduct, practices, and values. Chinese communities in Malaysia take great pride in the Kuoks, who are viewed as homegrown sons who have become global empire builders. They closely follow the business decisions and property acquisitions of the Kuoks (that is, of Robert, the surviving brother, and both brothers' children), seeking clues as to how to conduct themselves and attain economic success. Furthermore, the media prominence of the Kuoks, together with that of the Lis of Hong Kong, the Liems of Indonesia, and so on, has given ethnic Chinese minorities in Southeast Asia a new respectability; spurred by the new political tolerance toward Chinese business, even the assimilated are "coming out of the closet" as "Chinese." For instance, with the end of military rule, more and more Sino-Thais are asserting their Chinese origins, and culture in Bangkok has become "more openly Chinese."[39] In visits to Singapore or Hong Kong, ethnic Chinese from ASEAN countries can discard their batik or Thai-silk shirts, drop their indigenous names, and speak Chinese dialects and perform kinship rituals, especially around business banquets.[40] More and more, in cities such as Kuala Lumpur and Bangkok, and in trips back to the mainland, corporate power is stamped with Chinese business practices and rituals.[41]

Even indigenous ASEAN leaders, long suspicious of ethnic Chinese business, now strategically position themselves as closer to Chinese corporate practices. Malaysian and Singaporean leaders use the category "East Asian" to refer to their own countries, seeking to link their "minidragon" status to the economic boom in China. Malay businessmen are taking up Mandarin to do business and learn from ethnic Chinese entrepreneurs. Recently, the Malaysian deputy prime minister invoked the Chinese sage Lao Tse to urge "the youth of East Asia" to combine spiritual with material success. He said that they should struggle for both free trade (against Western protectionist policies) and ethical values (against the complacency that comes with affluence).[42] This yoking of free trade with reified Chinese values is one example of attempts by Malaysian leaders to proclaim that theirs is "a noncapitalist market economy" that is founded on the communitarian but flexible relations of the "bamboo network."

Cross-Ethnic and Cross-National Fraternities

What do these images of fraternal capitalism and economic dynasties tell us about the ways elite power sharing is imagined? In postcolonial Southeast Asian nation-states, whether monarchist or republican, discussion of dynastic rule is often tightly controlled, if not banned outright. In Thailand, subjects are forbidden to discuss the power and authority of the monarchy, while in Indonesia and Singapore, the state does not tolerate any commentary about the political and economic privileges of ruling families. In recent years, Lee Kuan Yew has sued foreign scholars and newspapers for writing about alleged nepotism in Singapore's political system.[43] While any discussion of patriarchal political rule is suppressed, there has been an explosion of stories about business dynasties.

Economic dynasties and alliances, not dynastic politics, are the narratives of elite power. Even as stories celebrate the restraint of the merchant princes, they also valorize the extravagance of their corporate networks. As is clear from the above, this fascination with Asian business empires is often fed by Western publications such as the *Far Eastern Economic Review*, which is owned by Dow Jones and Company, the Wall Street firm. In many ways, the family model of Asian capitalism is also a creation of Western media barons and reflects a mix of orientalist fantasy, business instrumentalism, and an American spin on economic opportunities and contacts in Asia. The *Review* has a new series called "Family Ties," devoted to "Asia's family-held business groups." One such story, about a Hong Kong beverage entrepreneur, is subtitled "Grandson of Indentured Servant in

Malaysia Epitomizes the Overseas Chinese Success Story."[44] This rags-to-riches story is repeated many times because "probably at no point in history have so many families accumulated so much wealth in a single generation."[45] These stories are an endorsement and a celebration of the transnational expansion of business families beyond their host countries and beyond even the region. More fundamentally, they constitute a regime of truth about the ascent of a new kind of transnational fraternal alliance in the new Southeast Asia. They also note the role of strategic links to officials and the importance of cross-ethnic relations—business partnerships, marriages, kinship relations—in the rise of the new Asian tycoons.

The image of merchant princes has helped legitimize the new moral order of capitalist-state alliances. Although Islamic leaders in Indonesia have for years criticized the links between Chinese bosses (*cukong*) and the Soeharto family, the fortunes of the Indonesian ruling class are intertwined with and dependent on their contacts with Chinese businessmen.[46] Under the cukong system, Chinese bosses bankroll and otherwise support Indonesian politicians in exchange for patronage and protection from excessive attacks on the Chinese. The biggest cukong is Liem Sioe Liong, whose great fortune has been tied to that of President Soeharto's family. Their partnership began during the Second World War, when Soeharto was an army man in the provinces and Liem was a commodities trader and suspected gunrunner.[47] The rise of Soeharto as president and the growth of Liem's Salim Group of companies are intertwined events that have led to many suspicions among the indigenous (*pribumi*) business community. The economic fortunes of the Soeharto family have also expanded as a result of the cukong connection, which won the late Madam Hartinah Tien Soeharto the nickname "Mrs. Ten Percent" in reference to commissions she gathered through wielding nepotistic influence. The Soeharto children are partners in many of the Salim Group ventures. The Soeharto government has suppressed Western press reports about the rise of many Chinese firms that, with their ability to attract foreign investments, have led Indonesia's economic resurgence.[48]

Across the water, Malay-Chinese business alliances, called Ali-Baba partnerships,[49] have also been a key to the rise of powerful companies. For instance, one top Malay stockbroker not only has his de rigueur Chinese business partner but also a Chinese wife (Robert Kuok's daughter); in addition, he has access to top Malay government officials.[50] Someone else who participates in an Ali-Baba partnership is Francis Yeoh. Despite being an ethnic Chinese Christian in a predominantly Muslim, Malay-chauvinist state, he has been called "the master builder of Malaysia [who] thrives with a little help from his friends."[51] Indeed, like virtually every successful corporate heavyweight here, he is a familiar presence in the halls of political power and is an intimate of Prime Minister Mahathir. That symbiosis of political power and entrepreneurial energy is a phenomenon that has spread throughout much of Southeast Asia and helps explain the region's economic dynamic. These stories suggest that fraternal alliances between (Chinese) businessmen and (indigenous) bureaucrats are partnerships that thrive because fraternal business links are meshed with authoritarian structures.

But in a globalized economy, such business-government fraternizing is not limited to Southeast Asian countries. The overseas Chinese corporate practice of providing credit and payoffs in exchange for political favors and protection has spread to the United States. Liern's banking partner, Mocthar Riady, was caught up in a recent uproar over giving "soft money" to the Democratic Party (see Ong 1999, ch. 6). But precisely because the alliances between Chinese financiers and politicians in Southeast Asia have their limits in attracting capital from overseas, and because Chinese firms have become modern transnational corporations, they are moving beyond their own governments to seek relations with politicians in a number of countries. In transnational business fraternities, governments are resources that can be made to share power through capitalism.

Although indigenous communities in Southeast Asia continue to be suspicious of Chinese traders, their gentrification as merchant princes casts a glow of respectability and modernity onto generals and politicians often suspected of economic incompetence and corruption. The wider acceptance of Chinese business by political elites is reflected in the number of Beijing-bound trade delegations from ASEAN countries that are composed of ethnic Chinese businessmen. Government-business partnerships are touted in the Malaysian press as the new vehicles for strengthening the national economy through the expansion of transnational contacts that build on Chinese networks. Ethnic Chinese in partnership with state enterprises are viewed as less disloyal, especially if, like Liem, they are careful to invest in their home country while exploring other opportunities abroad.

Another feather in the cap of the Chinese tycoon is his new image as a multicultural leader who is an effective mediator for governments, and not only between, say, Kuala Lumpur or Jakarta and Beijing. As their operations expand overseas, the press celebrates their ideologically indiscriminate flexibility in doing business: "Robert Kuok appears to blend just as easily with Cuban leader Fidel Castro and Chinese premier Li Peng as he does with Malaysian prime minister Datuk Seri Mahathir Mohamad and Indonesian president Soeharto. . . . 'Robert Kuok has funded the entire world,' a Malaysian broker points out. 'He is everyone's friend.'"[52] Overseas Chinese entrepreneurs are the new heroes, glad-handing world leaders while spreading fraternal friendship and business to any spots that remain resistant to global capitalism.

The Family Romance of the State

The romance of Chinese families is also deployed by academics and government officials to organize popular understanding of political morality. Since the 1980s, states such as Taiwan and Singapore have undertaken Confucianizing campaigns as a way to shape the cultural imagination of citizenship. These discourses allow the state to produce disciplinary knowledges and ideologically align family and state interests along a single moral continuum. In Singapore, an educational campaign was launched to promote religious knowledge and moral education through the systematic introduction of Confucian studies into the school curriculum. This strategy reached beyond the school gates through the promotion of research to support these Confucianizing claims.

In Singapore in 1994, a book on Chinese pioneers in capitalism was published to great fanfare: "They are selling like hotcakes," a scholar told me. Drawing on the life stories of forty-seven Chinese businessmen, *Stepping Out: The Making of Chinese Entrepreneurs* was presented as a collective morality tale of Singapore's success. The authors claimed that these businessmen's Confucian morality had been essential to their capitalist success, which in turn had contributed to national strength. These rags-to-riches Singaporeans were constructed as paragons of Confucian virtue—self-sacrificing, honest, trustworthy, respectful—who were impelled by a moral ethos of "doing life. . . . with others, for others, because of others." These capitalist pioneers were defined as examples of a Singapore Everyman, benevolent patriarchs who treated their business partners and workers "like brothers." The authors claimed that the "Confucian merchant" of contemporary Singapore was formed in a moral order that emphasized trust, confidentiality, and the social control of subordinates.[53] This relentlessly male vision of society—one that traces family genealogies from fathers to sons, who are construed as male-to-male partners—excludes women from the public sphere; women are constructed, almost by omission, as exclusively creatures of the private sphere, who never step out. Sociologist Claire Chiang, one of the authors of *Stepping Out*, seems quite content with this romantic picture she has helped produce. In an interview, she confided that in the course of her research among the business families, "there is no mention of the daughters holding the [reins]. But daughters are often on the cashier's side, holding the purse."[54] This rigid public/private division along gender lines, with female power being relegated to the realm of the domestic budget, conjures up a fantasy about "traditional" Chinese gender roles, in which women remain fixed within the household. The book received the imprimatur of Gob Keng Swee, the architect of Singapore's modern economy, who maintained in a foreword that Singapore's economic affluence is proof that the moral basis of entrepreneurial success in Singapore was "founded on the Confucian ethic" of these male pioneers.[55]

Such a scenario makes public masculinity and private femininity the foundation of state. Indeed, there is a clear attempt to coordinate what I have called "the moral economy of the family" with the moral economy of the state (see Ong 1999, ch. 2). For besides constructing the Confucianized family as the backbone of economic development, the state reiterates its policies of strengthening the family by providing guarantees of social security and order.[56] A Singapore official describes Singapore as a capitalist society built upon "socialist" families: "For many East Asian societies, it is not only the family that is socialist, it is the extended family and sometimes the extended clan."[57] The fact that women are an important part of the workforce, that divorce rates are rising, and that government campaigns promoting marriage among the professional elite fail to make a big dent in the number of unmarried women does not deter such profamily claims. On the contrary, it is the very anxiety engendered by such trends that accounts for the twinned ideologies of feminine domesticity and masculine public life.

The romance of the invented Confucian family is an ideological expression of the state's promotion of extended family formation through its housing, educational, and savings schemes.[58] These themes, which integrate the family romance with state policy, are further developed in profamily campaigns that encourage marriage and reproduction among professional women; these women are urged to return home, almost as a patriotic duty, to make babies who are deemed to be of a higher "quality" than those of lower-class women. By providing ideological and institutional supports to families threatened with individualism and fragmentation, the state restores faith that the moral power of Confucian ideology can forge a successful alliance with capitalism so that fraternal power can flourish in the public sphere without the threat of bad mothers undoing gender difference and hierarchy in the home. Geraldine Heng and Janadas Devan have coined the term "state fatherhood" to describe the state engineering of racial demographics, family, gender, and class relations in Singapore.[59]

Working Women's Dreams of Traveling Romance

Thus far, I have discussed how different romances of the Chinese family express messages about fraternal power, interethnic alliances, and the gendered public-private division that betray unifying themes of an emerging political imagination in Southeast Asia, which is grappling with the forces of late capitalism. In what ways do these masculinist imaginaries resonate with the consciousness of working-class women, who, after all, form the bulk of the labor force in Asia? In his study of petit bourgeois and working-class Malaysian Chinese, Don Nonini identifies a dialectic of mobility and location that is highly gendered. He observes that their familial strategies send men overseas for education and work, while women are required to stay at home and care for the remaining family members.[60] How, one may ask, does the family romance resonate with working-class women who also migrate but whose experiences are different from those of traveling men? Do men in charge of mobility represent a kind of symbolic capital working women may identify with? I turn to the experiences of working-class women in south China, a region undergoing major transformations as a result of economic activities by ethnic Chinese from Southeast Asia.

In the fall of 1993, I visited China's most successful special economic zones, which are based in coastal cities such as Shenzhen, Xiamen, Guangzhou (Canton), and Shantou, where tens of thousands of young women from the inland provinces have descended to work in factories that are mainly financed and operated by overseas Chinese capital. For instance, in Shenzhen, the roaring metropolis of China's future, right across the water from Hong Kong, 80 percent of the investors are Chinese from Hong Kong and the Asia Pacific region. These "Chinese from overseas," who are so vaunted in the mass media, are viewed in an intensely ambivalent way by local women (see Ong 1999, ch. 1). In their workaday world, female workers in Shenzhen want to maintain distance from Hong Kong and overseas Chinese managers, visitors, and businessmen. According to Ching Lee, young migrant women from the impoverished interior consider overseas Chinese to be outsiders who do not share their culture or appreciate their own very different backgrounds.[61] Furthermore, as Lee's research has shown, overseas managers enjoy enormous discretionary power over the treatment of workers on the shop floor, as well as over their chances of remaining in the cities. Many female workers prefer to be supervised by their own kinsmen or townsfolk who work in the same factory. Indeed, regimes of control based on kinship and localistic ties are pervasive throughout the manufacturing industry, for personalistic relations increase workers' compliance and also lift the burden of direct confrontation from overseas Chinese bosses. The cultural divide is deepened because female workers feel that their foreign bosses are unable to empathize with their problems and their very limited options in the labor force. There is also the image of overseas Chinese men as uncontrollable agents of sexual exploitation, now made more flexible and invasive by the flows of capital.

In the Women's Federation (Funu Lianhehui) office of Shenzhen, the director told me that Hong Kong and overseas Chinese men were perceived as good catches by local women, although "their cultural standards are not so high." This was her way of saying that for young women, these men are chiefly attractive because of their money and mobility. "Hong Kong visitors are bad for public morality. There are about ten thousand truck drivers coming into Shenzhen each day, and they contribute to prostitution."[62] The booming mistress trade is sparked by the Hong Kong men's "railroad policy" of keeping a mistress at each stop on their circuit, and there is a "concubine village" near a container-truck border crossing where many Hong Kong men have set up a home away from home, sometimes with children.[63] Some of these women may take second jobs as agents for their patrons' businesses in China. Such practices recall the early days of Chinese sojourning in Southeast Asia, when families were left in different sites in the diaspora. It is one of the many ironies of late capitalism that premodern family forms and female exploitation, which the communist state had largely erased in the cities, are being resurrected.

In the Deng era, the mass-entertainment industry has redefined the passive and self-sacrificing young woman, an icon of the precommunist era, as a cultural ideal. After having viewed *Yearnings*, a phenomenally popular TV series about family upheavals in post-Tiananmen China, Lisa Rofel notes that the family and female self-sacrifice have become new symbols of national unity. She argues that an underlying theme in the melodrama is the emergence of a strong and controlled masculinity that may lead the battered nation into the future.[64] We must note, however, that the urban population in coastal China seems to favor foreign programs beamed from the Star TV satellite network, which has created a whole new trans-Asian public through its bewildering variety of Asian and Western offerings, including MTV, talk shows, movies, and so forth. In Shenzhen, working women watch Hong Kong soap operas for cultural scripts on how to be independent modern women. I visited a beauty parlor set up by three enterprising female migrants in one of the hastily built workers' apartment complexes to serve the increasing demand for personal grooming. While attending to the customers, the hairdressers watched Hong Kong soaps on television and made a running commentary on what they imagined to be women's greater choices and strategies in overseas Chinese communities. For these young women, who had left their rural villages for the bright city lights and begun the difficult climb toward middle-class status, the lure of capitalism lay in the possibility for self-reliance, not self-sacrifice. They were preoccupied with figuring out strategies and networks for crossing into this brave new world. While young women routinely rely on family, neighbors, and friends to leave their villages and survive in the industrial cities, many are now seeking new relations that are not based on already constituted kinship or social bonds. Among Shenzhen's female working class, most kinship and hometown networks lead straight back to the village; at best, they prove to be only a weak source of coercion and support in the workplace.[65] Women who desire wealth and travel to rich places outside China answer to a different family romance.

For these women, overseas Chinese men represent a vision of capitalist autonomy and a source of new "network capital."[66] In an interesting reformulation of Pierre Bourdieu's concept of symbolic capital,[67] Siu-lun Wong and Janet Salaff use network capital to mean acquired personal networks based on friendship, school ties, and professional contacts (rather than networks formed from links based on family, family name, and hometown).[68] They argue that the accumulation of network capital has been a critical practice of well-to-do Hong Kongers in their emigration strategies. Working-class women in coastal China are less well positioned to build on professional contacts, but many depend on personal charms to create new personal connections. So even a road-trip Romeo from Hong Kong can be an irresistible catch because he literally and figuratively embodies the guanxi (ideally through marriage) that will lead to the dazzling world of overseas Chinese capitalism. Marriage to a traveling man enables one to expand one's accumulation of network capital and can also benefit the members of one's family, who eventually may also immigrate to the capitalist world, where their desires for wealth and personal freedom can be met.

So mobility, wealth, and an imagined metropolitan future, rather than love or class solidarity, account for the lure of family romances. Feelings of regional, cultural, and class differences from overseas Chinese men may remain, but not sufficiently to deter working women from marrying them to "develop a bridge to leave China," a common expression used by the women I met. One of the three hairdressers I visited was corresponding with a Chinese Canadian and a white American she had met in a bar. I later learned that she had begun a courtship with a male cousin who had immigrated to California, and she eventually flew to San Francisco to marry him.[69] Hers was a particularly creative weaving of acquired and created networks in a successful migration strategy. Another young woman I met, who is considered a classic north China beauty, has a faithful, perfectly respectable Chinese boyfriend who works in the government. This beauty, however, frequents bars; she hopes to meet an overseas Chinese man who can help her leave China.

That karaoke bars are the sites of mobility and new wealth is apparent from their video equipment and their clientele of foreign businessmen, hustlers, and upwardly mobile women. Indeed, the bar has taken over from the workplace, where worker politics have become too contaminated by Communist Party and capitalist interests to protect the collective interests of workers. Instead, many working women prefer the "state-free" arena of bars and discos to work out individual strategies of eluding economic exploitation, at least of the factory kind. The romance of mobile capitalism, then, conjures up a felicitous brew of imagined personal freedom and wealth, a heady mix that young women imagine traveling men can provide the passports to. This particular conjunction of working women's middle-class dreams and mobile men has reinforced conditions ripe for the masculinist thrust and scope of sexual and class exploitation throughout Asia.

Conclusion

I have traced the different family romances between corporate brothers, state and capital, and men and women that have proliferated in the public cultures of the new Asia. These unifying themes indicate that the family imaginary both expresses and normalizes the tensions between fluidity and rigidity, the public and the private, economic power and political power, exploitation and romance, and domination and subordination. David Harvey notes that the flexible operation of late capitalism is exceptionally creative in its destruction of rigidities. But he has not considered how cultural messages that romanticize mobile capital can also reinforce, ramify, and reinstall various relations of inequality and thus promote a new kind of conformity to flexible accumulation and state authority. Cultural forms labeled Chinese or Confucian in modern state regimes, corporate networks, and individual practices express and shape a political uncon- scious that construes male corporate power as benevolent, enlightened, and progressive for individuals and for the state. While capitalism has in- creased female employment at most levels of the labor market, its institu- tions and family metaphors have also made more mobile, more extensive, and more complex the sexual and class exploitation of women and the working population. The romance of merchant mandarins and the Confu- cian family defines men to be in charge of both wealth and mobility, while women are localized in domestic situations or workplaces commanded by men. These visions of social and family order resonate with aspirations of different classes and underlie the sense of a distinctive transnational Asian publicness that obscures the divisions of class and gender. Such family ro- mances reinforce the dark secrets of family, nation-state, and global capi- talism that promise wealth, security, and escape but deliver exploitation, despair, and entrapment. By stripping off the veil of romance, we reveal that the mobile forces of capitalism, as Joan Vincent has documented and theorized in her life's work, are alternately destructive and creative of the class, ethnic, and gender relations that constitute the very transnational networks that have developed within and alongside global capitalism.

Notes

1. Joan Vincent, *African Elite: The Big Man of a Small Town* (New York: Co- lumbia University Press, 1971).

2. Joan Vincent, *Teso in Transformation: The Political Economy of Peasant and Class in Eastern Africa* (Berkeley: University of California Press, 1982).

3. In her first book, *African Elite*, Vincent drew critical attention to the strategic importance of "men in motion" circulating through small towns in East Africa as agents in the expansion of British capital; the movements of these indigenous men became inseparable from the "moving frontier" of imperial capitalism. See Vincent (1982: 9–11).

4. Ibid., 259–62.

5. Marx (1869/1963: 124). Marx described the nineteenth-century French peas- antry as atomized household units that did not enter into social relations with each other. Unaware of the wider relations that exploited them as a collectivity, they were incapable of enforcing class interests in their own name.

6. This insight was later echoed in Massey (1993).

7. There is a huge literature on this topic, but among the more innovative works are Wolf (1966); Scott (1989); and Guha and Spivak (1988).

8. To Marx, the "stupefied seclusion" of the French peasantry under the Bonaparte dynasty was compounded by the priest—"the anointed bloodhound of the earthly police"—as the ideological instrument of the government (Marx 1869/1963: 125, 129–30). Marxist approaches to the problems of cultural consciousness among third-world peasants are dominated by notions of ideological mystification, as, for example, in Wolf (1966), and a variant of ideological mystification that incorporates the concept of a resistant peasant subculture, as, for example, in Scott (1976).

9. For cultural approaches to relations of production and consumption in our highly technologized, late-capitalist world, see Harvey (1989), Jameson (1991), and Lowe (1995).

10. Lowe (1995: 15). See also Jameson (1991).

11. Ong (1991).

12. See Spivak (1988), who maintains that subalterns can neither be depicted by nor spoken for by elites, whose relations of domination prevent them from portraying the "real" interests of subalterns.

13. Lowe (1995: 8). Like Donald Lowe, I do not see a problem in combining both Marxist and Foucauldian approaches as a way to better grasp the constitution of contemporary social consciousness. See, for example, Ong (1987).

14. Jameson (1981).

15. Blanc (1997).

16. Dorfman and Mattelart (1975).

17. Of course, American popular culture continues to be widespread throughout the region, and Japanese mass culture is growing in appeal among young Taiwan and Hong Kong Chinese. Nevertheless, I maintain that whatever cultural forms are used and borrowed from the United States or Japan, they are often deployed and woven within cultural scripts about Chinese ethnicity or national identity, depending on the particular programs.

18. Gordon (1992: 14).

19. Ibid., 16.

20. Mahathir and Ishihara (1995). For a fuller discussion of this idea, see Ong (1997).

21. Hunt (1992: 4).

22. Ibid., viii.

23. Hall (1988).

24. Hunt (1992: 1).

25. Mackie (1992: 161). Most of the international financing for this elite Chinese minority came from the wider network of overseas Chinese investments, and the increased mobility of capital has served to decrease Chinese leeway vis-à-vis local governments.

26. Ibid.; see other chapters in McVey (1992).

27. Interview by author, Singapore, August 1994.

28. *Business Week*, November 29, 1993.

29. Interview by author, Singapore, August 1994.

30. Kotkin (1993: 21–22).

31. Freud (1958). See Hunt (1992: 1–16) for a fascinating analysis of Freud's "primal scene" and its subthemes.

32. "Confucian capitalist" has also been used to describe the South Korean founder of Hyundai, one of Asia's wealthiest industrialists, but it has been used more to refer to his "stern domination" and even "autocratic predilections" than to the positive fraternal values that have been attributed to Chinese capitalists (*Far Eastern Economic Review*, June 22, 1995, 60).

33. Friedland (1991a: 46).

34. In Southeast Asia, whereas contemporary scholarly and media discussions about the rise of entrepreneurs are becoming ever more common, there is a deafening silence on the history of anti-imperialist struggles and the patriots who fought and died for national independence.

35. Friedland (1991b: 48–49).

36. *Forbes*, July 18, 1994, 12.

37. Mosse (1985: 10–13).

38. I borrow the term "middling" from Rabinow (1989), who talks about the "middling modernity" of middlebrow expertise in shaping social knowledges, norms, and sensibilities in modern society.

39. Barnes (1994: 4).

40. ASEAN is the Association of Southeast Asian Nations, a security zone formed during the Vietnam War that has now become a trading bloc seeking greater regional integration to offset China's rising economic power. ASEAN has nine members: the original member states of Malaysia, Singapore, Indonesia, Brunei, Thailand, and the Philippines, and the new member states of Vietnam, Laos, and Burma.

41. See Ong and Nonini (1997, chs. 5, 9).

42. "Anwar: Be Committed to Ethical Values," *New Straits Times*, August 7, 1994, A1.

43. See "Singapore Charges Scholar, Herald Tribune," *San Francisco Chronicle*, November 19, 1994, 8.

44. Clifford (1994a: 78).

45. Clifford (1994b: 78).

46. See Robison (1986) for a discussion of the state-private capital alliances in Indonesia.

47. See Schwarz (1994: 109–14) for an account of Liem's vast family business and long-term links with Soeharto.

48. Ibid., 108.

49. Ali is a common Malay name, and Baba refers to the Straits Chinese men who under colonialism often played the role of comprador to British concerns.

50. Jayasankaran (1995: 76–77).

51. Edward A. Gargan, "The Master Builder," *New York Times,* March 27, 1996, C1, C6.

52. *Far Eastern Economic Review*, February 8, 1991, 47.

53. Chan and Chiang (1994: 15, 98, 354).

54. Claire Chang, interview, *Asian Wall Street Journal*, November 25, 1993, 5.

55. Swee (1994: viii–ix).

56. Scott (1976) maintains that in Southeast Asian peasant societies, the unequal exchanges between peasants and their clients are morally justified in terms of the patrons' guarantees of their social and economic security.

57. *International Herald Tribune*, June 22, 1994, 4.

58. See Chua (1995).

59. See Heng and Devan (1995).

60. Nonini (1997).

61. Lee (1997).

62. Interview by author, Shenzhen, P.R.C., November 1993.

63. See Lee (1995: 64–65).

64. See Rofel (1994).

65. See Lee (1997).

66. This term was first used in Yang (1989), where the author comments on the practice of accumulating network capital in contemporary China as a way to bypass and subvert state regulations. See also Yang (1994).

67. See Bourdieu (1977: 171–83).

68. See Wong and Salaff (1994).

69. I am grateful to Connie Clark, a graduate student in anthropology at the University of California, Berkeley, for keeping me abreast of developments in these women's lives. Clark, who was conducting dissertation research in Shenzhen, introduced me to these women and, together with Chin Kwan Lee, showed me various aspects of working women's lives during my field trip.

References

Barnes, William. 1994. "Chinese out of Thais' Closet." *South China Morning Post*, February 26.

Blanc, Cristina S. 1997. "The 'Thoroughly Modern Asian': Capital, Culture, and Nation in Thailand and the Philippines." In Ong and Nonini, 261–86.

Bourdieu, Pierre. 1977. *Outline of a Theory of Practice*. Translated by Richard Nice. Cambridge: Cambridge University Press.

Chan, Kowk Bun, and Claire Chiang. 1994. *Stepping Out: The Making of Chinese Entrepreneurs*. Singapore: Simon and Schuster.

Chua, Beng-huat. 1995. *Communitarian Ideology and Democracy in Singapore*. London: Routledge.

Clifford, Mark. 1994a. "Profile K. S. Lo: Milk for the Millions." *Far Eastern Economic Review*, June 9.

———. 1994b. "Heir Force." *Far Eastern Economic Review*, November 17.

Dorfman, Ariel, and Armand Mattelart. 1975. *How to Read Donald Duck: Imperialist Ideology in the Disney Comic*. Translated by David Kunzie. New York: I. G. Editions.

Friedland, Jonathan. 1991a. "Kuok the Kingpin." *Far Eastern Economic Review*, February 7.

———. 1991b. "Friends of the Family." *Far Eastern Economic Review*, February 7.

Freud, Sigmund. 1958. "Totem and Taboo: Some Points of Agreement between the Mental Lives of Savages and Neurotics." In *The Standard Edition of the Complete Psychological Works*, vol. 13, trans. James Strachey. London: Hogarth Press.

Gordon, Colin. 1991. "Governmental Rationality: An Introduction." In G. Burchell, C. Gordon, and P. Miller, eds. *The Foucault Effect: Studies in Governmentality*, 1–52. Chicago: University of Chicago Press.

Guha, Ranajit, and Gayatri Chakravorty Spivak, eds. 1988. *Selected Subaltern Studies*. New York: Oxford University Press.

Hall, Stuart. 1988. "The Toad in the Garden: Theorists among the Thatcherites." In C. Nelson and L. Grossberg, eds. *Marxism and the Interpretation of Culture*, 35–57. Urbana: University of Illinois Press.

Harvey, David. 1989. *The Condition of Postmodernity*. Oxford: Basil Blackwell.

Heng, Geraldine, and Janadas Devan. 1995. "State Fatherhood: The Politics of Nationalism, Sexuality and Race in Singapore." In A. Ong and M. Peletz, eds. *Bewitching Women, Pious Men: Gender and Body Politics in Southeast Asia*, 195–215. Berkeley: University of California Press.

Hunt, Lynn. 1992. *The Family Romance of the French Revolution*. Berkeley: University of California Press.

Jameson, Fredric. 1981. *The Political Unconscious: Narrative as a Socially Symbolic Act*. Ithaca, N.Y.: Cornell University Press.

———. 1991. *Postmodernism, Or the Cultural Logic of Late Capitalism*. Durham: Duke University Press.

Jayasankaran, S. 1995. "Taking Stock: Malaysia's Rashid Hussain: At the Crossroads." *Far Eastern Economic Review*, April 20.

Kotkin, Joel. 1993. "Family Ties in the New Global Economy." *Los Angeles Times Magazine*, January 17.

Lee, Ching Kwan. 1997. "Factory Regimes of Chinese Capitalism: Different Cultural Logics in Labor Control." In Ong and Nonini 1997, 115–42.

Lee, Nora. 1995. "Duplicitous Liaisons." *Far Eastern Economic Review*, April 20.

Lowe, Donald M. 1995. *The Body in Late-Capitalist USA*. Durham, N.C.: Duke University Press.

Mackie, James. 1992. "Changing Patterns of Chinese Big Business in Southeast Asia." In Ruth McVey, ed. *Southeast Asian Capitalists*, 160–90. Ithaca, N.Y.: South East Asia Program, Cornell University.

Mahathir, Mohamad, and Shintaro Ishihara. 1995. "Will East Beat West?" *World Press Review*, December 6–11.

Marx, Karl. 1869/1963. *The Eighteenth Brumaire of Louis Bonaparte*. New York: International Publishers.

Massey, Doreen. 1993. "Power-Geometry and Progressive Sense of Place." In J. Bird et al., eds. *Mapping the Futures: Local Cultures, Global Change*, 59–69. New York: Routledge.

McVey, Ruth, ed. 1992. *Southeast Asian Capitalists*. Ithaca: South East Asia Program, Cornell University.

Mosse, George L. 1985. *Nationalism and Sexuality: Middle-Class Morality and Sexual Norms in Modern Europe*. Madison: University of Wisconsin Press.

Nonini, Donald M. 1997. "Shifting Identities, Positioned Imaginaries: Transnational Traversals and Reversals by Malaysian Chinese." In Ong and Nonini, 1997, 203–27.

Ong, Aihwa. 1987. *Spirits of Resistance and Capitalist Discipline: Factory Women in Malaysia*. Albany: State University of New York Press.

———. 1991. "The Gender and Labor Politics of Postmodernity." *Annual Review of Anthropology* 20: 279–309.

———. 1999. *Flexible Citizenship: The Cultural Logics of Transnationality*. Durham: Duke University Press.

Ong, Aihwa, and Donald M. Nonini, eds. 1997. *Ungrounded Empires: The Cultural Politics of Modern Chinese Transnationalism*. New York: Routledge.

———. 1989. *Weapons of the Weak: Everyday Forms of Peasant Resistance*. New Haven: Yale University Press.

Rabinow, Paul. 1989. *French Modern*. Cambridge: MIT Press.

Robison, Richard. 1986. *Indonesia: The Rise of Capital*. Sydney: Allen and Unwin.

Rofel, Lisa. 1994. "'Yearnings': Televisual Love and Melodramatic Politics in Contemporary China." *American Ethnologist* 21, no. 4: 700–722.

Schwarz, Adam. 1994. *A Nation in Waiting: Indonesia in the 1990s*. Sydney: Allen and Unwin.

Scott, James C. 1976. *The Moral Economy of the Peasant*. New Haven: Yale University Press.

———. 1989. *Weapons of the Weak: Everyday Forms of Peasant Resistance*. New Haven: Yale University Press.

Spivak, Gayatri C. 1988. "Can the Subaltern Speak?" In C. Nelson and L. Grossberg, eds. *Marxism and the Interpretation of Culture*, 271–313. Urbana: University of Illinois Press.

Swee, Joh Keng. 1994. "Foreword." In Chan and Chiang.

Vincent, Joan. 1971. *African Elite: The Big Men of a Small Town*. New York: Columbia University Press.

———. 1982. *Teso in Transformation: The Political Economy of Peasant and Class in Eastern Africa*. Berkeley: University of California Press.

Wolf, Eric R. 1966. *Peasants*. Englewood Cliffs, N.J.: Prentice Hall.

Wong, Siu-lun, and Janet W. Salaff. 1994. "Network Capital: Emigration from Hong Kong." Paper presented at the conference, "The Transnationalization of Chinese Capitalism." National University of Singapore, August 8, 1994.

Yang, Mayfair. 1989. "The Gift Economy and State Power in China." *Comparative Studies in Society and History* 31: 25–54.

———. 1994. *Gifts, Favors, and Banquets: The Art of Social Relationships in China*. Ithaca: Cornell University Press.

INDEX

Index

In this index an "f" after a number indicates a separate reference on the next page, and an "ff" indicates separate references on the next two pages. A continuous discussion over two or more pages is indicated by a span of page numbers, e.g., "57–59." *Passim* is used for a cluster of references in close but not consecutive sequence.